Criminal Justice

A Brief Introduction

Frank Schmalleger, Ph.D.
Pembroke State University, Pembroke, North Carolina

REGENTS / PRENTICE HALL, Englewood Cliffs, New Jersey 07632

Library of Congress Cataloging-in-Publication Data

SCHMALLEGER, FRANK.
    Criminal justice: a brief introduction / Frank Schmalleger.
        p. cm.
    Includes bibliographical references and index.
    ISBN: 0-13-014649-8
    1. Criminal justice.   2. Crime—United States.
    3. Law enforcement—United States.   I. Title.
    KF9223.S29   1993
    364.973—dc20   93-17153
                                                   CIP

Editorial/production supervision: *Barbara Marttine*
Cover illustration: *Rob Day*
Cover design: *Bryant Design*
Acquisitions editor: *Robin Baliszewski*
Prepress buyer: *Ilene Sanford*
Manufacturing buyer: *Ed O'Dougherty*

©1994 by REGENTS/PRENTICE HALL
A Division of Simon & Schuster
Englewood Cliffs, New Jersey 07632

Printed in the United States of America

10 9 8 7 6 5 4 3 2 1

ISBN   0-13-014649-8

Prentice-Hall International (UK) Limited, *London*
Prentice-Hall of Australia Pty. Limited, *Sydney*
Prentice-Hall Canada Inc., *Toronto*
Prentice-Hall Hispanoamericana, S.A., *Mexico*
Prentice-Hall of India Private Limited, *New Delhi*
Prentice-Hall of Japan, Inc., *Tokyo*
Simon & Schuster Asia Pte. Ltd., *Singapore*
Editora Prentice-Hall do Brasil, Ltda., *Rio de Janeiro*

For my daughter:

Nicole (Ariel) Schmalleger

Contents

Chapter 3: Criminal Law　　55

Chapter 7: The Criminal Trial   197

Chapter 8: Sentencing   219

Acknowledgments

Many thanks go to all who assisted in so many different ways in the development of this textbook. The manuscript reviewers, Joan Luxenburg at the University of Central Oklahoma, Gary J. Prawel at Monroe Community College, Carl E. Russell at Scottsdale Community College, and Kevin M. Thompson at North Dakota State University, should know how grateful I am to them for their helpful comments and valuable insights. The efforts of production editor Barbara Marttine, copy editor Sally Ann Bailey, and editorial assistant Rose Mary Florio, are all recognized and appreciated. Special thanks go to Robin Baliszewski, who is that perfect combination of editor and friend, and to my wife, Harmonie Star-Schmalleger, for the personal support she has so lovingly and consistently offered. Thank you, also, to my beautiful daughter, Nicole, to whom this book is dedicated, for her support and encouragement as writing progressed.

About the Author

Frank Schmalleger is Chairman of the Department of Sociology, Social Work, and Criminal Justice at Pembroke State University in Pembroke, North Carolina. Since receiving his Ph.D. from the Ohio State University in 1974, Schmalleger has taught criminal justice and security administration classes on both the graduate and undergraduate level for over 20 years. The winner of numerous teaching and writing awards, Schmalleger is the author of nine books and dozens of articles. His philosophy toward teaching and writing can be summed up in these words:

"What we teach and what we write must be the most current, up-to-date, relevant, and informative material we can offer our students. Anything less would be unfair to them. At the same time, instructional materials today must be packaged in a format which appeals to students and holds their attention. A good teacher is fascinating in his or her delivery; a good book can't be put down."

Instructions to the Student for Using the Disk Which Accompanies *Criminal Justice: A Brief Introduction*

A number of student-oriented disk-based simulations are available for IBM-compatible computers for use with *Criminal Justice: A Brief Introduction*. If your instructor has elected to assign the disk provided by Regents/Prentice Hall, you should be especially attentive to this symbol:

The symbol, commonly called a "disk icon," is placed throughout the text at points where scenarios may be assigned which are relevant to the text material that appears on those pages. Your instructor may require you to complete the assignments keyed to text material identified by the icon, and may also ask that you turn in your disk at specified intervals or at the completion of the course for grading. The disk also contains a self-administered survey which allows for an assessment of your attitudes along a continuum of social order versus individual rights advocacy. Take care of your disk, for it maintains an internal record of your progress through whatever scenarios may be assigned!

The ABC News/Regents/Prentice Hall Video Library

Available to adopters of *Criminal Justice: A Brief Introduction*, the ABC News/Regents/Prentice Hall Video Library brings real-life criminal justice scenarios into the classroom with all the impact of professional journalistic television. The library offers high-quality feature and documentary-style videos from Nightline, 20/20, This Week with David Brinkley, Prime Time Live and World News Tonight. The videos are keyed to specific sections within *Criminal Justice: A Brief Introduction* as indicated by the following icon, which appears throughout the text:

Introduction

Criminal justice is a dynamic and fluid field of study. Ever-changing crime statistics, newsworthy events involving American law enforcement, precedent-setting U.S. Supreme Court decisions, and rapidly breaking changes in correctional practice all challenge professors and students alike to keep pace with the field as it undergoes constant modification.

Criminal Justice: A Brief Introduction results from the realization that today's justice professionals need to have the latest information available to them in a concise and affordable source. The paperback format of this book has made it possible to translate quickly the latest happenings in the justice field into a pragmatic textbook which is both inexpensive and easily read. *Criminal Justice: A Brief Introduction* focuses directly upon the crime picture in America and the three traditional elements of the criminal justice system: police, courts, and corrections. The text is enhanced by the addition of career boxes that can assist today's pragmatically minded students make appropriate career choices. Cartoons, charts and graphs, and other visual aids help keep student attention and add variety to the text itself.

As the world approaches the twenty-first century, it is appropriate that a streamlined and up-to-date book such as this should be in the hands of students. The "information age" is truly upon us, and the quick dissemination of information has become a vital part of contemporary life. No doubt new technologies will facilitate even faster information transfer in the near future. Many of them — including on-line data retrieval, electronic updates, and computer publishing — are already at work behind the scenes in the molding of *Criminal Justice: A Brief Introduction*.

As the author of numerous texts on the criminal justice system, I have often been amazed at how the end result of the justice process is sometimes barely recognizable to anyone involved in the process as "justice" in any practical sense of the word. It is my sincere hope that the technological and publishing revolutions now upon us will combine with a growing social awareness to facilitate needed changes in our system—supplanting what have at times appeared as self-serving system-perpetuated injustices with new standards of equity, compassion, understanding, fairness, and heartfelt justice for all.

Frank Schmalleger, Ph.D.
Pembroke, NC
August 1993

Justice in American Context:
"The Rodney King" Trials

As we approach the twenty-first century the American system of criminal justice stands poised at a crossroads unlike any it has known before. Until the summer of 1992 most Americans would probably have agreed that the justice system, though flawed in numerous individual instances, was the most equitable mechanism available for the apprehension of wrongdoers, for determinations of guilt or innocence, and for the imposition of punishment upon criminal offenders in an otherwise imperfect world. At the same time, most probably felt, at least intuitively, that the exercise of criminal justice occurred within a framework that was basically fair and impartial, and which embodied our highest cultural ideals of social justice. In short, the symbolism of "blind justice" as equitable justice was, for many Americans, an article of faith.

This is not to say that the system was without its detractors. On the contrary, the voices of the poor, the disenfranchised, the unempowered — in particular ethnic minorities, and what sociologists have come to call "underrepresented groups" — have long appealed to the conscience of the American people, chanting a litany of claimed injustices for over 200 years. The system, they said, understood only one type of justice: justice for the rich and for the powerful, justice for those who make the laws and for those who stand to benefit from them. From time to time, academicians and liberal politicians joined the fray on the side of the disenfranchised, claiming that law enforcement is fundamentally a tool of power, exercised exclusively in the service of the wealthy and the well-connected. They, along with a variety of social commentators, portrayed criminal justice as one more aspect of a much broader issue — social *in*justice.

Then came an event which grabbed our nation's attention. In 1991 the videotaped police beating of a black Los Angeles motorist, Rodney King, burst upon the national scene and transfixed the American national conscience via television. And the images wouldn't fade. In 1992 a Simi Valley, California, jury, with but one minority member, found the police officers who had been arrested for assaulting King innocent of the charges brought against them. The nation was aghast — unable to reconcile what it had perceived clearly in the media with the workings of American criminal justice. In an instant Rodney King became, to many, the symbol of justice denied. Within hours Los Angeles was embroiled in social protests, rioting, and looting. Racial tensions increased dramatically. In the spring of 1993 two of the officers, Sergeant Stacey Koon and Officer Laurence Powell, were found guilty by a jury in federal court of depriving King of his constitutional right "not to be deprived of liberty without due process of law, including the right to be . . . free from the intentional use of unreasonable force."[1] Officers Theodore Briseno and Timothy Wind were found not guilty of the same charge. Commenting on the differences between the two trials *Newsweek* magazine said "A . . . cynical explanation for the convictions this time is that the 12 jurors knew all too well what a full acquittal could mean. 'The difference between this case and last year's were the riots,' says Harland Braun, Briseno's lawyer. The Simi Valley trial surely taught the perils of a criminal justice system that's perceived to be racist. But a system that's perceived as political — one that responds to public pressure as much as evidence — isn't much better."[2]   As controversy over the case continued, the American Civil Liberties Union, in heated debate, voted to protest the convictions, claiming that "repeat prosecution by different jurisdictions for the same act amounted to double jeopardy."[3]

The Rodney King "incident" was a transfiguring event in the history of American criminal justice. It brought us to realize that the strokes which paint the canvas of inter-group relations in the United States are broader than the particulars of any one case. There is little denying that minorities are over represented at all stages of criminal justice processing.   Similarly, there is little denying that minority youth violate laws with considerably greater frequency than other youths, and that the violations they commit are often found to be especially socially reprehensible — typified by crimes of violence, drug dealing, and the like. And yet whose laws are these people violating? By whose standards are they being held accountable? Because crime is a social construct arising out of a nexus of legislative action, social conditions, and individual choice, it becomes possible to ask: "*whose crime is it, after all?*" From the perspective of those involved in it, drug dealing may seem like a reasonable way out from poverty, and violence a day-to-day necessity rooted in the will to survive. From the perspective of official agents of justice these same behaviors confer criminal responsibility, and those who engage in them are condemned — arrested and sentenced to be removed from society until such time as they are adjudged fit to return. And therein lies the rub. Return to what? To the social order understood by the lawmakers? Or to a society inherently different, and populated by less forgiving foes than criminal justice policymakers and enforcers of official law?

Ultimately we have to ask: is there one form of justice for the poor and another for the rich? Is there a separate system of justice which embodies the values of the powerful, while condemning the strivings of the underclass? Are the felt needs of certain people being denied by the contemporary American criminal justice system? Can the scales of justice be balanced? In a more fundamental sense, can justice be truly equitable in a society built upon the free pursuit of individual wealth and the often unbridled drive toward personal power?

Some have suggested creating two systems of criminal justice: one for the rich and one for the poor; one for the socially downtrodden and another for the well-connected. After all, they say, isn't it necessary for enforcement agents, judges, juries, and probation/parole officers to understand the backgrounds and values of the criminal justice clients with whom they must deal? Shouldn't the system recognize the harsh realities of life in the inner city, and the desperation of the indigent and the disenfranchised? But, if we lose faith in our existing system's ability to deliver justice, what is left? How do we remake a system which for over 200 years has formed the bedrock of a tenuous social order, and which has held in check the excesses of the criminally compelled? That, it seems to me, is the challenge held by the next decade of American criminal justice — no, by the next century.

---

1. "Cries of Relief," *Time*, April 26, 1993, p. 18.
2. "King II: What Made the Difference?" *Newsweek*, April 26, 1993, p. 26.
3. "A.C.L.U. — Not all That Civil," *Time*, April 26, 1993, p. 31.

Criminal Justice

A Brief Introduction

INDIVIDUAL RIGHTS VERSUS SOCIAL CONCERNS
✪ Goals of the Criminal Justice System ✪

Common law, constitutional, statutory, and humanitarian rights
of the accused:

Justice for the Individual
Personal Liberty
Dignity as a Human Being
The Right to Due Process

The individual rights listed must be effectively balanced against
these community concerns:

Social Justice
Equality Before the Law
The Protection of Society
Freedom from Fear

How does our system of justice work toward balance?

PART 1
Crime and Justice in America

Whenever a separation is made between liberty and justice,
neither, in my opinion, is safe.
— *Edmund Burke* (1729–1797)

Justice is the great interest of man on earth. It is
the ligament which holds civilized beings and civilized
nations together.
— *Daniel Webster* (1782–1852)

Justice is my being allowed to do whatever I like.
Injustice is whatever prevents my doing so.
— *Samuel Johnson* (1709–1784)

CHAPTER 1

WHAT IS CRIMINAL JUSTICE?

Crime does more than expose the weaknesses in social relationships; it undermines the social order itself, by destroying the assumptions on which it is based.[1]

— Charles E. Silberman
Criminal Violence, Criminal Justice

I know not whether Laws be right,
*   Or whether Laws be wrong;*
All that we know who lie in jail
*   Is that the wall is strong;*
And that each day is like a year,
*   A year whose days are long.*

— Oscar Wilde (1856–1900)

KEY CONCEPTS

consensus model   due process   crime control model

conflict model   individual rights

◻ JUSTICE AND CRIMINAL JUSTICE

A little over a decade ago Ken Rex McElroy was shot to death on the main street of Skidmore, Missouri. Twenty people witnessed the midday shooting. Not one of them would talk to authorities, and after an extensive investigation, the Federal Bureau of Investigation closed the case without an arrest. State and local police were similarly unable to mount a successful inquiry.[2] Ken McElroy, it turned out, was the town bully. Convicted a few years earlier of shooting the town's grocer, he had been released on parole. McElroy was also accused by local residents of taking "pot shots" at them and of rustling cattle. Twice arrested for raping a minor, McElroy beat the charges. His favorite pastime was terrorizing citizens. He often swaggered through a local bar with a rifle and bayonet, threatening to kill the men he didn't like.

Do-it-Yourself
Justice

    As McElroy drove his pickup truck into town on July 10, 1981, a single blast from a shotgun took his head off. His wife, also in the truck, was uninjured. She identified a killer, but no one who witnessed the shooting would support her accusation. The story of Ken McElroy is an example of social control through informal means. His death was the result of agreement among the citizens of his small town that he had gone too far. Frustrated by the inability of the formal system of justice to restrain McElroy, residents took the law "into their own hands." One contemporary account described McElroy as a "man who needed killing." "Justice was done!" declared another.[3]

◻ THE FOCUS OF THIS BOOK

This book has an orientation which we think is especially valuable for studying criminal justice today. The materials presented in the text are built around the following theme: *there is a growing realization in contemporary society of the need to balance the respect accorded the rights of the individual with the interests of society. While the personal freedoms guaranteed by the Constitution must be closely guarded, so too must the urgent social needs of local communities for controlling unacceptable behavior and protecting law-abiding citizens from harm be recognized.* Many people today who intelligently consider the criminal justice system assume either one or the other of these two perspectives. We shall refer to those who seek to protect personal freedom as individual rights advocates. Those who suggest that, under certain circumstances involving criminal threats to public safety, the interests of society should take precedence over individual rights will be called public order advocates. Both perspectives have their roots in the values which formed our nation. However, the past 30 years have been especially important in clarifying the differences between the two points of view. The past few decades have seen a burgeoning concern with the rights of ethnic minorities, women, the physically and mentally handicapped, and many other groups. The civil rights movement of the 1960s and 1970s emphasized equality of opportunity and respect for individuals regardless of race, color, creed, or personal attributes. As new laws were passed and suits filed, court involvement in the movement grew. Soon a plethora of hard-won individual rights and prerogatives, based upon the U.S. Constitution and the Bill of Rights, were recognized and guaranteed. By the early 1980s the rights movement had profoundly affected all areas of social life — from education, through employment, to the activities of the criminal justice system.

This emphasis on individual rights was accompanied by a dramatic increase in criminal activity. "Traditional" crimes such as murder, rape, and assault, as reported by the FBI, increased astronomically during the 1970s. Some analysts of American culture suggested that increased criminality was the result of new-found freedoms which combined with the long pent-up hostilities of the socially and economically deprived to produce social disorganization. Others doubted the accuracy of "official" accounts, claiming that any actual rise in crime was much less than that portrayed in the reports.

By the mid-1980s, however, popular perceptions identified one particularly insidious form of criminal activity — the dramatic increase in the sale and use of illicit drugs — as a threat to the very fabric of American society. Cocaine in particular, and later laboratory-processed "crack," had spread to every corner of America. The country's borders were inundated with smugglers intent on reaping quick fortunes. Large cities became havens for drug gangs, and many inner-city areas were all but abandoned to highly armed and well-financed racketeers. Some famous personalities succumbed to the allure of drugs, and athletic teams and sporting events became focal points for drug busts. Like wildfire, drugs soon spread to even younger users. Even small-town elementary schools found themselves facing the specter of campus drug dealing and associated violence. Worse still were the seemingly ineffective government measures to stem the drug tide. Drug peddlers, because of the huge reserves of money available to them, were often able to escape prosecution or wrangle plea bargains and avoid imprisonment. Media coverage of such "miscarriages of justice" became epidemic and public anger grew.

Drug
Legalization

By the close of the 1980s neighborhoods and towns felt themselves fighting for their communal lives. City businesses faced dramatic declines in property values, and residents wrestled with the eroding quality of life. Huge rents had been torn in the national social fabric. The American way of life, long taken for granted, was under the gun. Traditional values appeared in danger of going up in smoke along with the "crack" now being smoked openly in some parks and resorts. Looking for a way to stem the tide, many took up the call for "law and order." In response, then-President Reagan initiated a "War on Drugs" and created a "drug czar" cabinet-level post to coordinate the war. Careful thought was given at the highest levels to using the military to patrol the sea lanes and air corridors through which many of the illegal drugs entered the country. President Bush, who followed President Reagan into office, quickly embraced and expanded the government's antidrug efforts.

In 1992, the videotaped beating of Rodney King, a black motorist, at the hands of Los Angeles–area police officers, splashed across TV screens throughout the country, and reintroduced the nation to the concerns of what sociologists now call "underrepresented groups." As the King incident seemed to show, when members of such groups come face to face with agents of the American criminal justice system, something less than justice may be the result. Although initially acquitted by a California jury which contained no black members, two of the officers who beat King were convicted in a 1993 federal courtroom of violating his civil rights.

The year 1993 saw an especially violent encounter in Waco, Texas, between agents of the Bureau of Alcohol, Tobacco, and Firearms, the FBI, and members of cult leader David Koresh's Branch Davidian. The fray, which began when ATF agents assaulted

Koresh's fortress-like compound, leaving four agents and six cultists dead, ended 51 days later with the firery deaths of Koresh and 71 of his followers. Many of them were children. The assault on Koresh's compound led to a congressional investigation and charges that the ATF and FBI had been ill-prepared to deal successfully with large-scale domestic resistance and had reacted more out of alarm and frustration than with wisdom.

The situation surrounding the criminal justice system today is a result of all these elements. Calls for public order still echo through government chambers and newspaper columns. Now, however, they are often tempered with cries for social justice from those who have come to mistrust the official agents of criminal justice. Some contemporary social commentators charge that in America today there is one sort of justice for whites, the rich, and the powerful and quite another form of justice for blacks, native Americans, Hispanics, the poor, and the disenfranchised. They suggest that suburban-dwelling white-collar criminals, such as embezzlers and rich investors who violate regulatory laws while often costing society millions of dollars, are treated deferentially by a system which holds out harsh punishments for those who are typically inner-city drug traffickers — even though both types of offenders commit predominately economic forms of crime.

Copyright 1989 by USA Today. Reprinted with permission.

Many people fear that a growing concern with social order may endanger hard won individual rights and liberties.

Rights advocates, on the one hand, continue to fight for an expansion of civil and criminal rights, seeing both as necessary to an equitable and just social order. The treatment of the accused, they argue, should ideally mirror sound cultural values. The purpose of any civilized society, they claim, should be to secure rights and freedoms for each of its citizens. They fear unnecessarily restrictive government action and view it as an assault upon basic human dignity. In the defense of general principles, criminal rights activists tend to recognize that it is sometimes necessary to sacrifice some degree of public safety and predictability in order to guarantee basic freedoms. Rights advocates are content with a justice system which limits police powers and holds justice agencies accountable to the highest evidentiary standards. A national news story,[4] which showed undercover agents of the Broward County, Florida, Sheriff's Department selling crack cocaine manufactured in a police crime lab as a lure to capture drug users, is the kind of activity civil libertarians strongly question. Another example comes from the case of James Richardson, who served 21 years in a Florida prison for a crime he did not commit.[5] Following perjured testimony Richardson was convicted in 1968 of the poi[s] deaths of his seven children. He was released in 1989 after a baby-sitter confessed to poisoning the children's last meal because of personal jealousies. The criminal rights perspective allows that it is necessary to see some guilty people go free in order to reduce the likelihood of convicting the innocent.

Social order advocates, on the other hand, seeking to reduce crime and to increase the level of personal safety for all of us, continue to issue demands to unfetter the criminal justice system, to make arrests easier and punishments swifter and harsher. These advocates of law and order, wanting ever-greater police powers, have mounted a drive to abandon some of the gains made in the rights of criminal defendants during the civil rights era. Citing high rates of recidivism, uncertain punishments, and an inefficient courtroom maze, they claim that the present system coddles the offender and encourages law violation. Society, they say, if it is to survive, can no longer afford to accord too many rights to the individual, to special interest groups, nor can it place the interests of any one person over that of society as a whole.

This text has two basic purposes: (1) describing in detail the criminal justice system, while (2) helping students develop an appreciation for the delicacy of the balancing act now facing it. The question for the future will be how to manage a justice system which is as fair to the individual, and as sensitive to the concerns of the historically disenfranchised, as it is supportive of the needs of society. Is justice for all a reasonable expectation of today's system of criminal justice? As the book will show, this question is complicated by the fact that individual needs and social interests sometimes diverge, while at other times they parallel one other.

□ THE JUSTICE IDEAL

Early settlers who came to America were often in flight from governments which had little regard for individual freedoms and rights. By the late 1700s, however, democratic processes were in place which allowed for shared understandings of justice to be forged into the principles we find today in our Constitution and Bill of Rights. Formed to achieve social equity and to protect the innocent, our type of government has been valued and imitated throughout the world.

> **Criminal Justice:** The criminal law, the law of criminal procedure, and that array of procedures and activities having to do with the enforcement of this body of law. [6]

Social justice is a concept which embraces all aspects of civilized life. Social justice extends to relationships between parties, between the rich and the poor, between the sexes, between ethnic groups and minorities, and to social linkages of all sorts. In the abstract, the concept of justice embodies the highest cultural ideals. Reality, however, typically falls short of the ideal and is severely complicated by the fact that justice seems to wear different guises when viewed from diverse social vantage points.

Criminal justice, in its broadest sense, refers to those aspects of social justice which concern violations of the criminal law. Community interests demand apprehension and punishment of the guilty. At the same time, criminal justice ideals extend to the protection of the innocent, the fair treatment of offenders, and fair play by the agencies of law enforcement, including the courts and correctional institutions.

Once again, reality generally falls short of the ideal. To many people, the criminal justice system and criminal justice agencies often seem biased in favor of the powerful. The laws they enforce seem to emanate more from well-financed, organized, and vocal interest groups than they do from an idealized sense of social justice. Disenfranchised groups, those who do not feel as though they share in the political and economic power of society, are often wary of the agencies of justice, seeing them more as enemies than as benefactors.

On the other hand, justice practitioners, including police officers, prosecutors, judges, and correctional officials, frequently complain of unfair criticism of their efforts to uphold the law. The "realities" of law enforcement, they say, and of justice itself, are often overlooked by critics of the system who have little experience in dealing with offenders and victims.

> **Social Control:** The use of sanctions and rewards available through a group to influence and shape the behavior of individual members of that group.

Whichever side we choose in the ongoing debate over the nature and quality of justice in America we should recognize that the process of criminal justice is especially important in achieving and maintaining social order. From the perspective of social order, law is an instrument of control. Laws set limits on behavior and define particular forms of social interaction as unacceptable. Laws, including whatever inequities they may embody, are a primary device for order creation in any society.

JUSTICE IS A PRODUCT

Once a law is created, people who are suspected of violations are apprehended and face handling by the criminal justice system. The system is generally described as composed of the agencies of police, courts, and corrections. There are many actors within the justice system, from the police officer walking a beat, to a Supreme Court justice sitting on the bench in Washington, D.C.

Defendants processed by the system come into contact with numerous justice professionals whose duty it is to enforce the law, but who also have a stake in the agencies which employ them, and who hold their own personal interests and values. As they wend their way through the system, defendants may be held accountable to the law, but in the process they will also be buffeted by personal whims as well as by the practical needs of the system. Hence, a complete view of American criminal justice needs to recognize that the final outcome of any encounter with the criminal justice system will be a consequence of decisions made not just at the legislative level, but in the day-to-day activities undertaken by everyone involved in the system.

The Justice Ideal: A Modern Conflict

Most of us agree that laws against murder, rape, assault, and other serious crimes are necessary. Certain other laws, such as those against marijuana use, prostitution, gambling, and some "victimless crimes" rest upon a less certain consensus.

Where a near-consensus exists as to the legitimacy of a specific statute, questions may still be raised as to how specific behavior fits the law under consideration. Even more fundamental questions can center on the process by which justice is achieved. Two cases which received much media attention during the late 1980s illustrate these points. One involved the "subway gunman" Bernhard Goetz.[7] Goetz, a 39-year-old electronics specialist, admitted shooting four young men who, he said, approached him in a threatening manner. Goetz had been mugged previously and carried a concealed weapon. Goetz was white; the young men were black.

Few would disagree that mugging is wrong, and most would grant that some form of self-defense is justifiable under certain circumstances, including robbery. The Goetz situation, however, was complicated by many things, among them the fact that Goetz fled after the shootings; he shot one of the men twice — after telling him, "You don't look too bad. Here's another"; and it was later shown that some of the young men had committed crimes both previous to, and after the subway incident. Although no one died, one of the people shot was permanently paralyzed.

Bernhard Goetz finally was convicted of a firearms violation and received a sentence of six months in prison. He was also ordered to undergo psychiatric treatment, placed on five years probation, fined $5,000, and made to perform 280 hours of community service.

The "Howard Beach incident" had some characteristics in common with the "subway gunman" case.[8] Howard Beach is a densely populated white section of New York City. On a night in 1987 three black men were riding through Howard Beach when their car broke down. A gang of white youths, some armed with baseball bats, attacked the men. One man was injured in the attack, while another fled onto a busy highway where he was struck by a car and killed. Eventually manslaughter convictions were

Copyright 1990 by USA Today. Reprinted with permission.
Recently, some police departments have proposed a direct approach to crime reduction.

returned against three of the youths involved in the incident, and they were sentenced to prison terms which may run for 15 years. A fourth was found innocent of all charges.

To most people, the law was clear in both cases. Goetz should not have been carrying a concealed weapon. He should not have shot the young men who surrounded him unless there was an immediate and serious threat to his safety. The white youths in Howard Beach violated the law in assaulting two men. Yet while a considerable consensus existed as to the law and as to the facts of each case, actors in the criminal justice system found themselves embroiled in a raging debate about what an appropriate outcome should be. One famous legal scholar, analyzing the Goetz case relative to the social context of the times, referred to Goetz's actions as "a crime of self-defense."[9]

Basic to both cases was the belief, held by some, including many members of the black community in New York, that minorities historically have not been fairly represented in the justice process. The fact that black men approached a white in New York's subways was said to be automatically interpreted much differently than if the races involved had been reversed. Other critics said that the Howard Beach incident reflected the system's devaluation of the life of a black man.

Both the Howard Beach and subway gunman cases are illustrative of the fact that any formal resolution of law violations occurs through an elaborate process. Justice, while it can be fine-tuned in order to take into consideration the interests of ever wider numbers of people, rarely pleases everyone. Justice is a social product, and, like any product which is the result of group effort, it is a patchwork quilt of human emotions and concerns. One of the major challenges faced by the justice system today comes in the form of disenfranchised groups who are not convinced that they receive "justice" under current arrangements. Was justice done in the Howard Beach or the Goetz case? While the question will be debated for years, it is doubtful that an answer acceptable to everyone will ever be found.

◻ AMERICAN CRIMINAL JUSTICE: SYSTEM OR NONSYSTEM?

To this point we have described the agencies of law enforcement, the courts, and corrections as a system of criminal justice.[10] The systems model of criminal justice, however, is more an analytical tool than a reality. Any analytical model, whether it be in the so-called "hard" sciences or in the social sciences, is simply a convention chosen for its explanatory power. By explaining the actions of criminal justice officials (such as arrest, prosecution, sentencing, etc.) as though they are systematically related, we are able to envision a fairly smooth and predictable process. The advantage we gain from this convention is a reduction in complexity which allows us to describe the totality of criminal justice at a conceptually manageable level.

> **The Criminal Justice System:** The aggregate of all operating and administrative or technical support agencies which perform criminal justice functions. The basic divisions of the operational aspect of criminal justice are law enforcement, courts, and corrections.

Those who speak of a system of criminal justice usually define it as consisting of the agencies of police, courts, and corrections. Each of these agencies can, in turn, be described in terms of their subsystems. Corrections, for example, includes jails, prisons, community based treatment programs such as "halfway houses," and programs for probation and parole. Students of corrections also study the process of sentencing, through which an offender's fate is decided by the justice system.

The systems model has been criticized for implying a greater level of organization and cooperation among the various agencies of justice than actually exists. The word "system" calls to mind a near-perfect form of social organization. The modern mind associates the idea of a system with machinelike precision in which wasted effort, redundancy, and conflicting actions are quickly abandoned and their causes repaired. The justice system has nowhere near this level of perfection. Conflicts among and within agencies are rife, immediate goals are often not shared by individual actors in the system, and the system may move in different directions depending upon political currents, informal arrangements, and personal discretionary decisions.

A CAREER WITH THE FBI

Typical Positions. Special agent, crime laboratory technician, ballistics technician, computer operator, fingerprint specialist, explosives examiner, document expert, and other nonagent technical positions.

Employment Requirements. General employment requirements include (1) an age of between 23 and 37; (2) excellent physical health; (3) uncorrected vision of not less than 20/200, correctable to 20/20 in one eye, and at least 20/40 in the other eye; (4) good hearing; (5) U.S. citizenship; (6) a valid driver's license; (7) successful completion of a background investigation; (8) a law degree or a Bachelor's degree from an accredited college or university; (9) successful completion of an initial written examination; (10) an intensive formal interview; and (11) urinalysis. A polygraph examination may also be required.

Other Requirements. Five special agent entry programs exist in the areas of law, accounting, languages, engineering/science, and a general "diversified" area that requires a minimum of three years of full-time work experience, preferably with a law enforcement agency. The FBI emphasizes education, and especially values degrees in law, graduate studies, and business and accounting. Most nonagent technical career paths also require Bachelor's or advanced degrees and U.S. citizenship.

Salary. Special agents enter the Bureau in Government Service (GS) grade 10 and can advance to grade GS-13 in field assignments and GS-15 or higher in supervisory and management positions. Entry-level salary in 1993 was $30,603, with an additional $7,377.75 typically paid for overtime work after completion of the required 15-week training period.

Benefits. Benefits include (1) 13 days of sick leave annually, (2) 2½ to 5 weeks of annual paid vacation and 10 paid federal holidays each year, (3) federal health and life insurance, and (4) a comprehensive retirement program.

Direct inquiries to: Federal Bureau of Investigation, U.S. Department of Justice, 9th Street and Pennsylvania Ave., N.W., Washington, D.C. 20535.

The systems model of criminal justice is part of a larger point of view called the consensus model of justice. The consensus model of the justice system assumes that all parts of the system work together toward a common goal and that the movement of cases and people through the system is smooth due to cooperation between components of the system. The conflict model provides another approach to the study of American criminal justice. The conflict model says that agency interests tend to make actors within the system self-serving. Pressures for success, promotion, pay increases, and general accountability, according to this model, fragment the efforts of the system as a whole, leading to a criminal justice non-system.[11] Both models have something to tell us. Agencies of justice are linked closely enough for the term "system" to be meaningfully applied to them. On the other hand, the very size of the criminal justice undertaking makes effective cooperation between component agencies difficult. The police, for example, may have an interest in seeing offenders put behind bars. Prison officials, on the other hand, may be working with extremely overcrowded facilities. They may desire to see early release programs for certain categories of offenders such as those who are judged to be nonviolent. Who wins out in the long run could be just a matter of internal politics. Everyone should be concerned, however, when the goal of justice is impacted, and sometimes even sacrificed, because of conflicts within the system.

THE JUSTICE NONSYSTEM: A CLASSIC CASE

Jerome Skolnick's classic study of clearance rates provides support for the idea of a criminal justice nonsystem.[12] Clearance rates are a measure of crimes solved by the police. The more crimes the police can show they have solved, the happier is the public they serve.

Skolnick discovered an instance in which an individual burglar was caught red-handed during the commission of a burglary. After his arrest, the police suggested that he should confess to many unsolved burglaries which they knew he had not committed. In effect they said, "Help us out, and we will try to help you out!" The burglar did confess — to over 400 other burglaries. Following the confession, the police were satisfied because they could say they had "solved" many burglaries, and the suspect was pleased as well because the police had agreed to speak on his behalf before the judge.

❏ THE DUE PROCESS MODEL

Both the systems and nonsystems models of criminal justice provide a view of agency relationships. Another way to view American criminal justice is in terms of its goals. Two primary goals were identified at the start of this chapter: (1) the need to enforce the law and maintain social order and (2) the need to protect individuals from injustice. The first of these principles values the efficient arrest and conviction of criminal offenders. It is often referred to as the crime control model of justice. The crime control model was first brought to the attention of the academic community in Herbert Packer's cogent analysis of the state of criminal justice in the late 1960s.[13] For that reason it is sometimes referred to as Packer's crime control model.

The second principle is called the due process model for its emphasis on individual rights. Due process is a central and necessary part of American criminal justice. It requires a careful and informed consideration of the facts of each individual case. Under the model, police are required to recognize the rights of suspects during arrest, questioning, and handling. Prosecutors and judges must recognize constitutional and other guarantees during trial and the presentation of evidence. Due process is intended to ensure that innocent people are not convicted of crimes. The due process model became reality following a number of far-reaching Supreme Court decisions affecting criminal procedure which were made during the 1960s. The 1960s were the era of the Warren court, a Supreme Court that is remembered for its concern with protecting the innocent against the massive power of the state in criminal proceedings.[14]

> **Due Process of Law:** A right guaranteed by the Fifth, Sixth, and Fourteenth Amendments of the U.S. Constitution, and generally understood, in legal contexts, to mean the due course of legal proceedings according to the rules and forms which have been established for the protection of private rights.

The guarantee of due process is found throughout the Bill of Rights. Of special importance is the Fourteenth Amendment which makes due process binding upon the states — that is, it requires individual states in the union to respect the rights of individuals who come under their jurisdiction. The Fourteenth Amendment reads as follows:

> *nor shall any State deprive any person of life, liberty, or property, without due process of law; nor deny to any person within its jurisdiction the equal protection of the laws.*

As a result of the tireless efforts of the Warren court to institutionalize the Bill of Rights, the daily practice of modern American criminal justice is set squarely upon the due process standard. Under the due process model rights, violations may become the basis for the dismissal of evidence or criminal charges, especially at the appellate level.

❑ INDIVIDUAL RIGHTS

The due process clause of the U.S. Constitution mandates the recognition of individual rights, especially when criminal defendants are faced with prosecution by the states or the federal government. The first ten amendments to the Constitution are known as the "Bill of Rights" and specify the basic rights of all persons within the United States. These rights have been interpreted and clarified by courts (especially the U.S. Supreme Court) over time. Due process requires that agencies of justice recognize these rights in their enforcement of the law. Table 1-1 outlines the basic rights to which defendants in criminal proceedings are generally entitled.

INDIVIDUAL RIGHTS AND THE COURTS

Although the Constitution deals with many issues, what we have been calling "rights" are often open to interpretation. Many modern rights, although written into the Constitution, would not exist in practice were it not for the fact that the U.S. Supreme Court decided, at some point in history, to recognize them in cases brought before it. The well-known Supreme Court case of *Gideon* v. *Wainwright*[15] (1963), for example (which is discussed in detail in Chapter 6, The Courts), found the Court embracing the Sixth Amendment guarantee of a right to a lawyer for all criminal defendants. Prior to *Gideon*, court-appointed attorneys for defendants unable to afford their own counsel were practically unknown, except in capital cases and some federal courts. After the *Gideon* decision court-appointed counsel became commonplace, and measures were instituted in jurisdictions across the nation to select attorneys fairly for indigent defendants.

Unlike the high courts of many nations, the U.S. Supreme Court is very powerful, and its decisions often have far-reaching consequences. The decisions rendered by the justices in cases like *Gideon* become, in effect, the law of the land. For all practical purposes such decisions often carry as much weight as legislative action. For this reason some writers speak of judge-made law in describing judicial precedents which impact the process of justice.

TABLE 1-1
Individual Rights Guaranteed
by the "Bill of Rights"

A Right to Be Assumed Innocent Until Proven Guilty
A Right Against Unreasonable Searches of Person and Place of Residence
A Right Against Arrest Without Probable Cause
A Right Against Unreasonable Seizures of Personal Property
A Right Against Self-incrimination
A Right to Fair Questioning by the Police
A Right to Protection from Physical Harm Throughout the Justice Process
A Right to an Attorney
A Right to Trial by Jury
A Right to Know the Charges
A Right to Cross-examine Prosecution Witnesses
A Right to Speak and Present Witnesses
A Right Not to Be Tried Twice for the Same Crime
A Right Against Cruel or Unusual Punishments
A Right to Due Process
A Right to a Speedy Trial
A Right Against Excessive Bail
A Right Against Excessive Fines
A Right to Be Treated the Same as Others, Regardless of Race, Sex, Religious
Preference, and Other Personal Attributes

Rights which have been recognized by court decision are often subject to continual refinement. New interpretations may broaden or narrow the scope of applicability accorded to constitutional guarantees. Although the process of change is usually very slow, we should recognize that any right is subject to continual interpretation by the courts — and especially by the U.S. Supreme Court. Any potential whittling away of procedural rights is of considerable concern to a great many people. It was in recognition of just such a possibility that the U.S. Senate held lengthy hearings over Supreme Court candidates nominated by

President Reagan during the late 1980s. Senators were concerned that some nominees might have personal agendas which included wanting to eliminate precedents set by the Court in earlier times.

CRIME CONTROL THROUGH DUE PROCESS

We have suggested that the dual goals of crime control and due process are in constant and unavoidable opposition to one another. Some critics of American criminal justice have argued that the practice of justice is too often concerned with crime control at the expense of due process. Other conservative analysts of the American scene maintain that our type of justice coddles offenders and does too little to protect the innocent.

While it is impossible to avoid ideological conflicts such as these, it is also realistic to think of the American system of justice as representative of crime control through due process. It is this model, of law enforcement infused with the recognition of individual rights, which provides a conceptual framework for the chapters that follow.

☐ SUMMARY

In this chapter the process of American criminal justice and the agencies which contribute to it have been described as a system. As we have warned, however, such a viewpoint is useful primarily for the reduction in complexity it provides. A more realistic approach to understanding criminal justice may be the nonsystem approach. As a nonsystem, criminal justice is depicted as a fragmented activity in which individuals and agencies within the process have interests and goals which at times coincide, but often conflict. An alternative way of viewing the practice of criminal justice is in terms of its two goals: crime control and due process. The crime control perspective urges rapid and effective law enforcement, and calls for the stiff punishment of law breakers. Due process, on the other hand, requires a recognition of the defendant's rights and holds the agents of justice accountable for any actions which might contravene those rights. The goals of due process and crime control are often in conflict. Popular opinion may even see them as mutually exclusive. As we describe the agencies of justice in the various chapters which follow, the goals of crime control and due process will appear again and again. As we shall see, the challenge of criminal justice in America is one of achieving efficient enforcement of the laws while recognizing the rights of individuals. The mandate of crime control through due process ensures that criminal justice will remain an exciting and ever-evolving undertaking.

DISCUSSION QUESTIONS

1. What are the two models of the criminal justice process described in this chapter? Which model do you think is more useful? Which is more accurate?

2. What does this chapter suggest are the two primary goals of the criminal justice system?

Do you think one goal is more important than the other? If so, which one? Why?

3. What do we mean when we say that the "primary purpose of law is the maintenance of order"? Why is social order necessary?

4. What might a large, complex society such as our own be like without laws? Without a system of criminal justice? Would you want to live in such a society? Why or why not?

NOTES

1. Charles E. Silberman, *Criminal Violence, Criminal Justice* (New York: Random House, 1978), p. 12.

2. "FBI Ends Mo. 'Bully' Slaying Probe," in *Facts on File, 1982* (New York: Facts on File, 1982), p. 692.

3. Ibid.

4. "Some Worry Police 'Out of Control'," *USA Today,* November 15, 1989, pp. 1A—2A.

5. "A Free Man," *USA Today,* April 27, 1989, p. 13A.

6. Most of the definitions contained in *Criminal Justice: A Brief Introduction* are adapted from the *Dictionary of Criminal Justice Data Terminology* 2nd ed. (Washington, D.C.: Bureau of Justice Statistics, 1981).

7. *Facts on File, 1987* (New York: Facts on File, 1987), p. 792.

8. Ibid., p. 88.

9. George P. Fletcher, *A Crime of Self-defense: Bernhard Goetz and Law on Trial* (New York: The Free Press, 1988).

10. The systems model of criminal justice is often attributed to the frequent use of the term "system" by the 1967 Presidential Commission in its report, *The Challenge of Crime in a Free Society* (Washington, D.C.: U.S. Government Printing Office, 1967).

11. One of the first published works to utilize the nonsystems approach to criminal justice was the American Bar Association's *New Perspective on Urban Crime* (Washington, D.C.: ABA Special Committee on Crime Prevention and Control, 1972).

12. Jerome H. Skolnick, *Justice Without Trial* (New York: John Wiley and Sons, 1966), p. 179.

13. Herbert Packer, *The Limits of the Criminal Sanction* (Stanford, CA: Stanford University Press, 1968).

14. For a complete analysis of the impact of decisions made by the Warren Court, see Fred P. Graham, *The Due Process Revolution: The Warren Court's Impact on Criminal Law* (New York: Hayden Press, 1970).

15. *Gideon* v. *Wainwright,* 372 U.S. 353 (1963).

CHAPTER 2

THE CRIME PICTURE

No one way of describing crime describes it well enough.
— The President's Commission on Law
Enforcement and Administration of
Justice.[1]

KEY CONCEPTS

Bureau of Justice Statistics	Uniform Crime Reports	Part I offenses
victimization surveys	major crimes	Part II offenses
National Crime Victimization Survey	crime index	property crime
violent crime	clearance rates	date rape

☐ INTRODUCTION: SOURCES OF DATA

On June 16, 1991, a well-dressed, silver-haired mustached white man in his forties walked into the 52-story United Bank of Denver wearing sunglasses and a brown derby hat. When he walked out, four bank guards, who had been counting money in the bank's high-security area, were dead and $100,000 of the depositors' money was missing. The guards had been killed execution style — each shot repeatedly. The dead were William McCullom, 33, of Aurora; Philip Mankoff, 41, also of Aurora; Scott McCarthy, 21 of Littleton; and Todd Wilson, 21, of Englewood. McCarthy had wanted to be a police officer and had been married just months before the shooting. Wilson was best man at the wedding. While each of these men led intricate lives and had families, dreams and desires, their deaths were reported — like so many other murders that year — as a statistical count in the 1991 FBI's Uniform Crime Reports (UCR), released in August 1992. UCR statistics do not contain details on the personal lives of crime victims but represent an objective statistical compilation of law violations — ranging from murder to petty theft and beyond. Unfortunately, social events — including crime — are not as easy to quantify as are commodity transactions. The choice of which crimes should be included in statistical reports is itself a judgment which reflects the interests and biases of policymakers. The FBI, for example, classifies certain crimes as "Part I offenses" — often called "major crimes." Part I offenses include:

- Murder
- Forcible rape
- Robbery
- Aggravated assault
- Burglary
- Larceny
- Motor vehicle theft
- Arson

Part I offenses do not encompass most large-scale white-collar crimes, such as insider trading in securities, price fixing by corporate executives, and unfair business practices. Nor are statistics on "victimless" crimes included. Such crimes, however, probably result in far more monetary damage than most of the traditionally classified "major offenses."

Crime statistics are also difficult to interpret because of the way in which they are collected. Most widely quoted numbers come from the FBI's Uniform Crime Reports and depend upon *reports to the police* by victims of crime. One problem with such summaries is that citizens may not always make official reports, sometimes because they are afraid to report, or perhaps because they don't think the police can do anything about the offense. Even when reports are made, they are filtered through a number of bureaucratic levels. As Frank Hagan points out, quoting an earlier source: "The government is very keen on amassing statistics. They collect them, add to them, raise them to the nth power, take the cube root and prepare wonderful diagrams. But what you must never forget is that every one of these figures comes in the first instance from the *chowty dar* (village watchman), who puts down what he damn pleases."[2]

Another problem is the fact that certain kinds of crimes are rarely reported and are especially difficult to detect. These include "victimless crimes," or crimes which, by their nature, involve willing participants. Victimless crimes include such things as drug use, prostitution, and gambling. Similarly, white collar and high-technology offenses such as embezzlement, computer crime, and corporate misdeeds, probably enter the official statistics only rarely. Hence, a large amount of criminal activity goes undetected in the United States, while those types of crimes which are detected may paint a misleading picture of criminal activity by virtue of the publicity accorded to them.

A second data collection format is typified by the Bureau of Justice Statistics' (BJS) National Crime Victimization Survey (NCVS). It relies upon *personal interpretations* of what may (or may not) have been criminal events, and upon quasi-confidential surveys which may selectively include data from those most willing to answer interviewer's questions, and excludes information from less gregarious respondents. Some victims are afraid to report crimes even to nonpolice interviewers. Others may inaccurately interpret their own experiences, or may be tempted to invent victimizations for the sake of interviewers. As the first page of the NCVS admits, "Details about the crimes come directly from the victims, and no attempt is made to validate the information against police records or any other source."[3]

Although the FBI's Uniform Crime Reports and the BJS's National Crime Victimization Survey are the major sources of crime data, other regular publications contribute to our knowledge of crime patterns. Available yearly is the *Sourcebook of Criminal Justice Statistics*, a compilation of national information on crime and on the criminal justice system. The *Sourcebook* is published by the Bureau of Justice Statistics through monies provided by the Justice System Improvement Act of 1979. A less frequent, but more concise, document is the *Report to the Nation on Crime and Justice,* issued in updated editions every few years. The National Institute of Justice, the primary research arm of the U.S. Department of Justice, along with the Office of Juvenile Justice and Delinquency Prevention, the Federal Justice Research Program, and the National Victim's Resource Center, provide still more information on crime patterns.

This chapter describes crime in America through a summation of available data drawn from many of these sources. The fact that such data may be flawed in ways already mentioned, however, is important to remember in making decisions based on it.

❑ THE UNIFORM CRIME REPORTS

DEVELOPMENT OF THE UCR PROGRAM

In 1930 Congress authorized the Attorney General of the United States to survey crime in America, and the FBI was designated to implement the program. The Bureau quickly built upon early efforts by the International Association of Chiefs of Police (IACP) to create a national system of uniform crime statistics. As a practical measure IACP recommendations had utilized readily available information, and so it was that citizens' reports of crimes to the police became the basis of the plan.[4]

During its first year of operation the UCR Program received reports from 400 cities in 43 states. Twenty million people were covered by that first comprehensive survey. Today almost 16,000 law enforcement agencies provide crime information for the program, with data coming from city, state, and county departments. To assure uniformity in reporting, the FBI has developed standardized definitions of offenses and terminologies used in the program. A number of publications, including the *Uniform Crime Reporting Handbook* and the *Manual of Law Enforcement Records*, are supplied to participating agencies, and training for effective reporting is made available through FBI sponsored seminars and instructional literature.

Following IACP recommendations, the original UCR Program was designed to permit comparisons over time through construction of a Crime Index. The Index summed the total of seven major offenses — murder, forcible rape, robbery, aggravated assault, burglary, larceny-theft, and motor vehicle theft — and expressed the result as a crime *rate* based on population. In 1979, by Congressional mandate, an eighth offense — arson — was added to the Index. Although Uniform Crime Reporting categories today parallel statutory definitions of criminal behavior, they are not legal classifications but only conveniences created for statistical reporting purposes.

Beginning in 1987 the UCR Program discontinued the practice of collecting data on ethnic origin for persons arrested. The last year such data were reported was in 1986.

HISTORICAL TRENDS

Since the UCR Program began there have been two major shifts in crime rates. One occurred during the early 1940s, when crime decreased due to the large number of young men who entered military service during World War II. Young males comprise the most "crime-prone" segment of the population, and their removal to the European and Pacific theaters of war did much to lower crime rates.

The other noteworthy shift in offense statistics — a dramatic increase in most forms of crime beginning in the 1960s — also had a link to World War II. With the end of the war, and the return of millions of young men to civilian life, birth rates skyrocketed during the period 1945–1955, creating a postwar "baby boom." By 1960, "baby boomers" were entering their teenage years. A disproportionate number of young people produced a dramatic increase in most major crimes.

Other factors contributed to the increase in reported crime during the same period. Modified reporting requirements, which reduced the stress associated with filing police reports, and the publicity associated with the rise in crime, sensitized victims to the importance of reporting. Crimes which may have gone undetected in the past began to figure more prominently in official statistics. Similarly, the growing professionalization of some police departments resulted in more accurate and increased data collection, causing some of the most progressive departments to be associated with the largest crime increases.[5]

UCR TERMINOLOGY

In its annual report on crime, the FBI distinguishes between two general categories of crime: violent (or personal) and property crime. Violent crimes include murder, forcible rape, robbery and aggravated assault. Property crimes are burglary, larceny, and motor vehicle theft. FBI statistics (shown in Table 2-1) are based upon crimes reported to (or discovered by) the police.

TABLE 2-1
Major Crimes
Known to the Police, 1991
(Part I Offenses from the UCR)

Offense	Number	Rate per 100,000	Clearance Rate
Personal/Violent Crimes			
Murder	24,703	9.8	67%
Forcible rape	106,593	42.3	52
Robbery	687,732	272.7	24
Aggravated assault	1,092,739	433.3	57
Property Crimes			
Burglary	3,157,150	1,252.1	13
Larceny	8,142,228	3,228.8	20
Motor vehicle theft	1,661,738	659.0	14
Arson[1]	99,784	48.3	18
U.S. TOTAL	14,872,883	5,897.8	20.7

[1]Arson can be classified as either a property crime or a violent crime, depending upon whether or not personal injury or loss of life results from its commission. It is generally classified as a property crime, however. Arson statistics are incomplete for 1991 and do not enter in the "total" tabulations.

Source: Adapted from Federal Bureau of Investigation, *Crime in the United States, 1991* (Washington, D.C: U.S. Government Printing Office, 1992).

For a few offenses the numbers reported are probably close to the numbers which actually occur. Murder, for example, is a crime which is difficult to conceal because of its seriousness. Even where the crime is not immediately discovered, the victim is often quickly missed by friends and associates, and a "missing persons" report is filed with the police.

Auto theft is another crime which is reported with a frequency similar to its actual rate of occurrence, probably because insurance companies require that a police report be filed before any claims can be collected. Unfortunately, most crimes other than murder and auto theft appear to be seriously underreported. Victims may not report for various reasons, including (1) the belief that the police can't do anything; (2) a fear of reprisal; (3) embarrassment about the crime itself, or a fear of being embarrassed during the reporting process; and (4) an acceptance of criminal victimization as a normal part of life.

Copyright 1991 by USA Today. Reprinted with permission.
Many people believe that the ready availability of handguns in the United States is a major contributor to violent crime.

UCR data tend to underestimate the amount of crime which actually occurs for another reason: built into the reporting system is the hierarchy rule — a way of "counting" crime reports such that only the most serious out of a series of events is scored. If a man and woman go on a picnic, for example, and their party is set upon by a criminal who kills the man, rapes the woman, steals the couple's car, and later burns the vehicle, the hierarchy rule dictates that only one crime will be reported in official statistics — that of murder. The offender, if apprehended, may later be charged with each of the offenses listed, but only one report of murder will appear in UCR data.

Most UCR information is reported as a *rate* of crime. Rates are computed as the number of crimes *per* some unit of population. National reports generally make use of large units of population, such as *100,000 persons*. Hence, the rate of rape reported by the UCR for 1991 was 42.3 forcible rapes per every 100,000 inhabitants of the United States.[6]   Rates allow for a meaningful comparison over areas, and across time. The rate of reported rape for 1975, for example, was about 26 per 100,000.[7]   We expect the number of crimes to increase as population grows, but rate increases are cause for concern because they indicate that crimes are increasing faster than the population is growing. Rates, however, require interpretation. Since the FBI definition of rape includes only female victims, for example, the rate of victimization might be more meaningfully expressed in terms of every 100,000 *female* inhabitants. Similarly, although there is a tendency to judge an individual's risk of victimization based upon rates, such judgments tend to be inaccurate since they are based purely on averages and do not take into consideration individual life circumstances. While rates may tell us about aggregate conditions and trends, we must be very careful in applying them to individual cases.

A commonly used term in today's UCRs is clearance rate. The clearance rate of any crime refers to the proportion of reported crimes which have been "solved." Clearances are judged primarily on the basis of arrests, and do not involve judicial disposition. Once an arrest has been made, a crime is regarded as "cleared" for purposes of reporting in the UCR program. Exceptional clearances (sometimes called clearances by exceptional means) can result when law enforcement authorities believe they know who the perpetrator of a crime is, but cannot make an arrest. The perpetrator may, for example, flee the country, commit suicide, or die. Figure 2-1 shows clearance rates for major crimes.

For data gathering and reporting purposes, the UCR Program divides the country into four geographic regions — the Northeast, West, South, and Midwest. Unfortunately, no real attempt has been made to create divisions with nearly equal populations or similar demographic characteristics, and it is difficult to meaningfully compare one region of the country with another.

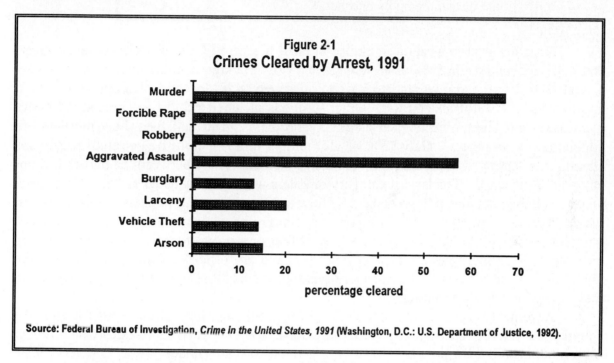

Figure 2-1
Crimes Cleared by Arrest, 1991

percentage cleared

Source: Federal Bureau of Investigation, *Crime in the United States, 1991* (Washington, D.C.: U.S. Department of Justice, 1992).

PART I OFFENSES

Murder

UCR statistics on murder include nonnegligent manslaughter or any willful homicide. Not included in the count are suicides, justifiable homicides, deaths caused by negligence or accident, and attempts to murder. The year 1991 saw 24,703 murders come to the attention of police departments across the United States.[8] Murder is the smallest numerical category in the Part I offenses. The 1991 murder rate was 9.8 homicides for every 100,000 persons in the country — an increase of 4.3% over the previous year.

Murder rates tend to peak annually in the warmest months. In many years, July and August show the highest number of homicides. Typically, in 1991 the month of August showed the highest number of murders.

Geographically, murder is most common in the southern states. However, because the southern states are the most populous, a meaningful comparison with other regions of the country is difficult. The largest increases in homicide between 1991 and 1992 were recorded in small cities.   Rural areas of the country showed a small (1%) decline.

Age is no barrier to murder.   Statistics for 1991 reveal that 304 infants (under the age of 1) were victims of homicide, as were 424 persons aged 75 and over.[9] Persons aged 20–24 were the most likely to be murdered. Murder perpetrators, on the other hand, were most common in the 15–19-year-old age group.

> **Murder:** The willful (nonnegligent) and unlawful killing of one human being by another.[10]

Firearms are the weapon of choice in most murders. Ours is a well-armed society, and guns accounted for 55% of all killings in 1991. Handguns outnumbered shotguns by almost 10 to 1 in the murder statistics, while rifles were a distant third. Knives were used in approximately 16% of all murders. Other weapons included explosives; poison; narcotics overdoses; and blunt objects such as clubs, and hands, feet, and fists. Few murders are committed by strangers. Only 15% of all murders in 1991 were perpetrated by persons classified as "strangers." In 38.3% of all killings the relationship between the parties had not yet been determined. The largest category of killers was officially listed as "acquaintances," which probably includes a large number of former "friends." Murders may occur in sprees, which "involve killings at two or more locations with almost no time break between murders."[11] Mass murders entail "the killing of four or more victims at one location, within one event."[12] Serial murders happen over time and are officially defined to "involve the killing of several victims in three or more separate events."[13] Days, months, or even years may elapse between the murders.

Arguments cause most murders (32%), but murders also occur during the commission of other crimes, such as robbery, rape, and burglary. Homicides which follow from other crimes are more likely to be impulsive rather than planned.

Murder is a serious crime and, when it occurs, consumes a substantial number of police resources. Consequently, over the years the offense has shown the highest clearance rate of any index crime. Sixty-seven percent of all homicides were cleared in 1991.

Forcible Rape

Forcible rape is the least reported of all violent crimes. Estimates are that only one out of every four forcible rapes which actually occur are reported to the police.   The victim's fear of embarrassment has been cited as the reason most often given for non-reports.   In the past, reports of rape were usually taken by seemingly hardened desk sergeants or male detectives who may not have been sensitive to the needs of the victim. In addition, the physical examination which victims had to endure was often a traumatizing experience in itself. Finally, many states routinely permitted the woman's past sexual history to be revealed in detail in the courtroom if a trial ensued.   All these practices contributed to a considerable hesitancy on the part of rape victims to report their victimization.

The last decade has seen many changes designed to facilitate accurate reporting of rape and other sex offenses.   Sexual histories are no longer regarded as relevant in most trials, trained female detectives often act as victim interviewers, and physicians have been better educated in handling the psychological needs of victims.

UCR statistics show 106,593 reported rapes for 1991, a slight increase over the number of offenses reported for the previous year. Rape is a crime which has shown a consistent increase in reporting even in years when other personal crimes have been on the decline (see Figure 2-2). By definition rapes reported under the UCR program are always of females. Homosexual rape is excluded from the count, but attempts to commit rape by force or the threat of force are included. Statutory rape, where no force is involved, but the female is below the age of consent, is not included in rape statistics.

> **Forcible Rape:** Unlawful sexual intercourse or attempted sexual intercourse with a female against her will, by force or threat of force.

Rape: 3
parts

The offense of rape follows homicide in its seasonal variation. Most rapes in 1991 were reported in the hot summer months, while January, February, and December recorded the lowest number of reports. Most rapes are committed by acquaintances of the victims and often betray a trust or friendship. Date rape, which falls into this category, appears to be far more common than previously believed.

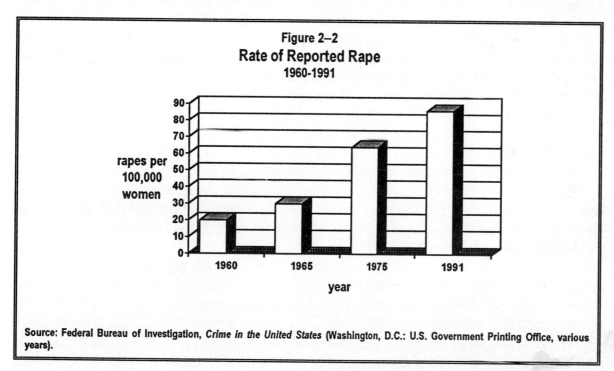

Figure 2–2
Rate of Reported Rape
1960-1991

Source: Federal Bureau of Investigation, *Crime in the United States* (Washington, D.C.: U.S. Government Printing Office, various years).

Rape is a complex crime involving strong emotions and injuries to the victim which often go beyond the physical. As a consequence, it is not a well-understood offense. Ronald Barri Flowers[14] has identified many cultural myths which surround the crime of rape. They include:

Fallacy **❶**: Rape Cannot Occur If the Woman Resists.

Fallacy ❷: All Women Secretly Desire to Be Raped.
Fallacy ❸: The Majority of Rapes Are Triggered by Women Being
        Out Alone at Night.
Fallacy ❹: Rape Is a Victim-Precipitated Crime.
Fallacy ❺: Only Young Attractive Women Are Raped.
Fallacy ❻: It Cannot Happen to Me.
Fallacy ❼: Rape Is Motivated by the Need for Sexual Gratification.
Fallacy ❽: Most Rapes Are Perpetrated by Strangers.
Fallacy ❾: The Rapist Looks the Part.
Fallacy ❿: Rape Is an Impulsive Act.

Rape is often a planned violent crime which serves the offender's need for power rather than sexual gratification.[15] It is frequently committed by a man known to the victim — as in the case of date or acquaintance rape. Victims may be held captive and subjected to repeated assaults.[16] In the crime of heterosexual rape, any female — regardless of age, appearance, or occupation — is a potential victim. Through personal violation, humiliation, and physical battering, rapists seek a sense of personal aggrandizement and feelings of dominance. Victims of rape, on the other hand, often experience a lessened sense of personal worth; increased feelings of despair, helplessness, and vulnerability; a misplaced sense of guilt, and a lack of control over their personal lives.[17]

Rape within marriage is a growing area of concern in American criminal justice, and new laws are being written to recognize it. Some states have redefined their rape statutes to include homosexual rape and marriage rape, although the latter is sometimes classified as sexual battery (indicating that force has been used), a lesser offense than the crime of rape.

Robbery

Robbery is sometimes confused with burglary. Robbery is a personal crime and involves a face-to-face confrontation between victim and perpetrator. Weapons may be used, or strong-armed robbery may occur through intimidation, especially where gangs threaten victims by sheer numbers. Purse snatching is not classified as robbery by the UCR Program, but is included under the category "larceny-theft."

In 1991 individuals (versus business and banks) were typical targets of robbers. Banks, gas stations, convenience stores, and other businesses were the second most common target of robbers, with residential robberies accounting for only 9.8% of the total. In 1991, 687,732 robberies were reported to the police and 56.2% of them were highway robberies, or muggings (meaning that they occurred outdoors, probably as the victim was walking). Strong-armed robberies were the most common, accounting for 40% of total robberies reported. Guns were used in 40% of all robberies, and knives in 11%.

Armed robbers are dangerous. Guns are actually discharged in 20% of all robberies.[18] Whenever a robbery occurs, the UCR Program scores the event as one robbery, even though there may be a number of victims robbed during the occurrence. With the move toward incident-driven reporting (discussed later in this chapter), however, UCR reports now make data available on the number of individuals robbed in each instance of robbery. Because statistics on crime show only the most serious offense which occurred during a particular episode, robberies are often hidden when they occur in conjunction with other, more serious, crimes. For example, in a recent year 3% of robbery victims were also raped, and a large number of homicide victims were robbed.[19]

> **Robbery**: The unlawful taking or attempting to take anything of value from the care, custody, or control of a person, or persons by force or threat of force or violence and/or by putting the victim in fear.

Robbery is primarily an urban offense, and most arrestees are young males who are members of minority groups. The robbery rate in large cities in 1991 was 341 (per every 100,000 inhabitants), while it was only 17 in rural areas. Ninety-two percent of those arrested for robbery in 1991 were male, 24% were under the age of 18, and 63.3% were minorities.[20]

Aggravated Assault

Assaults are of two types: aggravated and simple. Simple assaults may involve pushing and shoving or even fistfights. Aggravated assaults are distinguished from simple assaults by the fact that they involve the use of a weapon or the individual assaulted requires medical assistance. When deadly weapons are employed, even though no injury may result, aggravated assaults may be chargeable as attempted murder.[21] Hence, because of their potentially serious consequences, the UCR Program scores some cases of attempted assault as aggravated assaults.

In 1991, 1,092,739 cases of aggravated assault were reported to law enforcement agencies in the United States. The summer months evidenced the greatest frequency of assault, while February was once again the month with the lowest number of reports. Most aggravated assaults were committed with blunt objects, or objects near at hand (31%), while hands, feet, and fists were also commonly used (27%). Less frequent were knives and firearms (18% and 24%, respectively).

> **Aggravated Assault:** The unlawful attack by one person upon another for the purpose of inflicting severe or aggravated bodily injury.

Burglary

Although it may involve personal and even violent confrontations, burglary is primarily a property crime. Burglars are interested in financial gain, and usually fence stolen items in order to recover a fraction of their cash value. More than 3 million burglaries were reported to the police in 1991. Dollar losses to burglary victims totaled over $3.9 billion, with an average loss per offense of $1,246.

Many people fear nighttime burglary of their residence. They imagine themselves asleep in bed as a stranger breaks into their home, and then conjure up visions of a violent confrontation. While such scenarios do occur, daytime burglary is also common. Many families now have two or more bread-winners, and since children are in school during the day, some homes — and even entire neighborhoods — are virtually unoccupied during daylight hours. This shift in patterns of social activity has led to a growing burglary threat against residences during daytime.

The UCR Program employs three classifications of burglary: (1) forcible entry, (2) unlawful entry where no force is used, and (3) attempted forcible entry. In most jurisdictions force need not be employed for a crime to be classified as burglary. Unlocked doors and open windows are invitations to burglars, and the crime of burglary consists not so much in a forcible entry as it does in the intent of the offender to trespass and steal. In a ten-year period analyzed by the Bureau of Justice Statistics, 45% of all burglaries were unlawful entries, 33% were forcible entries, and 22% were attempted forcible entries.[22] The most dangerous burglaries were those in which a household member was home (about 10% of all burglaries[23]). Residents who were home during a burglary suffered a greater than 30% chance of becoming the victim of a violent crime.[24]

> **Burglary:** An unlawful entry or attempted entry of a structure to commit a felony or theft.

Property crimes generally involve low rates of clearance. Burglary is no exception. The clearance rate for burglary in 1991 was only 13%. Burglars are usually unknown to their victims, and even if known conceal their identity by committing their crime when the victim is not present.

Larceny

Larceny is another name for theft. Some states distinguish between simple larceny and grand larceny. Grand larceny is usually defined as theft of valuables in excess of a certain set dollar amount, such as $200. Categorizing the crime by dollar amount can present unique problems, as during the high fiscal inflation periods of the 1970s, when legislatures found themselves unable to enact statutory revisions fast enough to keep pace with inflation.

Larceny, as defined by the UCR Program, includes thefts of any amount. The Reports specifically list the following offenses as types of larceny:

- Shoplifting
- Pocket picking
- Purse snatching
- Thefts from motor vehicles
- Thefts of motor vehicle parts and accessories
- Bicycle thefts
- Thefts from coin-operated machines

Thefts of farm animals, or rustling, and thefts of most types of farm machinery also fall into the larceny category.   In fact, larceny is such a broad category that it serves as a kind of "catchall" in the UCR Reports.   Technically, reported thefts can involve amounts that range anywhere from pocket change to the stealing of a $100 million aircraft. Specifically excluded from the count of larceny for reporting purposes, however, are crimes of embezzlement, "con" games, forgery, and worthless checks.   Larceny is thought of as a crime which requires physical possession of the item appropriated.   Hence, most high-technology crimes, including thefts engineered through the use of computers or thefts of technology itself, are not scored as larcenies — unless electronic circuitry or machines themselves are actually stolen.

> **Larceny-Theft:** The unlawful taking, carrying, leading, or riding away of property from the possession or constructive possession of another.

Reports to the police in 1991 showed 8,142,228 larcenies nationwide, with the total value of property stolen placed at almost $4 billion.   The most common form of larceny in most recent years has been the theft of motor vehicle parts, accessories, and contents.   The theft of tires, wheels, stereos, hubcaps, radar detectors, CB radios, cassette tapes, compact disks, and assorted packages account for many of the items reported stolen.

Larceny is the most frequent major crime according to the UCRs.   It may also be the UCR's most underreported crime category, because small thefts rarely come to the attention of the police.   The average value of items reported stolen in 1991 was about $478.

Motor Vehicle Theft

The UCR Program defines motor vehicles as self-propelled vehicles which run on the ground and not on rails.   Included in the definition are automobiles, motorcycles, trucks, buses, and some farm machinery.   Excluded are trains, airplanes, ships, boats, and spacecraft — whose theft would be scored as larceny.   Vehicles which are temporarily taken by individuals who have lawful access to them are not scored as thefts.   Hence, spouses who jointly own most property may drive the family car, even though one spouse may think of the vehicle as their exclusive personal property.

As mentioned earlier, motor vehicle theft is a crime in which most occurrences are reported to law enforcement agencies.   Insurance companies require police reports before they will reimburse car owners for their losses.   Some reports of motor vehicle thefts, however, may be false.   People who have damaged their own vehicles in solitary crashes, or who have been unable to sell them, may try to force insurance companies to "buy" them through reports of theft.

In 1991 more than 1.6 million motor vehicles were reported stolen.   The average value per vehicle was $4,983, making motor vehicle theft an $8.3 billion crime.   The clearance rate for motor vehicle theft was only 14% in 1991.   City agencies reported the lowest rates of clearance (13%), while rural counties had the highest rate (33%).   Many stolen vehicles are routinely and quickly disassembled, with parts being resold through chop shops.

In late 1992 "carjacking," the stealing of a motor vehicle, often at gunpoint, while it is still occupied, made headlines across the country. On September 8 of that year, 34-year-old Pamela Basu of Savage, Maryland, was accosted by two men who climbed into her brown BMW and drove off, dragging her along for about 2 miles. Ms. Basu's arm had become entangled in the car's safety belt, and the thieves had to sideswipe a chain-link fence in order to finally dislodge her. Her 2-year-old daughter, still strapped into her carseat was apparently tossed from the vehicle. The child survived.

Carjackers are after auto parts, which are, of course, much more difficult to identify and trace than intact vehicles. In some parts of the country, chop shops operate like big business, and one shop may strip a dozen or more cars per day.

> **Motor Vehicle Theft:** The theft or attempted theft of a motor vehicle.

Arrest reports for motor vehicle theft show that the typical offender is a young male. Sixty-two percent of all arrestees in 1991 were under the age of 21, and 90% were male.

Arson

The crime of arson exists in a kind of statistical limbo. In 1979 Congress ordered that it be added as an eighth Index offense. To date, however, the UCR Program has been unable to integrate statistics successfully on arson into the yearly Crime Index.   The problem is twofold: (1) many law enforcement agencies have not yet begun making regular reports to the FBI on arson offenses which come under their jurisdiction, and (2) any change in the number of index offenses produces a Crime Index which will not permit meaningful comparisons to earlier crime data. The Crime Index is a composite offense rate which provides for useful comparisons over time and between jurisdictions, so long as it retains definitional consistency. Adding a new offense to the Index, or substantially changing the definition of any of its categories, still provides a measure of "crime," but it changes the meaning of term.

> **Arson:** Any willful or malicious burning or attempt to burn, with or without intent to defraud, a dwelling house, public building, motor vehicle or aircraft, personal property of another, etc.

The UCR Program received crime reports from nearly 16,000 law enforcement agencies in 1991.[25] Of these, only 8,963 submitted arson reports for all 12 months of the year. Few agencies provided complete data as to the type of arson (nature of the item burned), the estimated monetary value of the property damaged, ownership of the property, and so on.

Some of these difficulties may soon be resolved through the Special Arson Program, authorized by Congress in 1982. The FBI, in conjunction with the National Fire Data

Center, now operates a Special Arson Reporting System which focuses upon fire departments across the nation. The Arson Reporting System is designed to provide data which will supplement the yearly UCRs.[26]

Current arson data include only those fires which, through investigation, are determined to have been willfully or maliciously set. Fires of unknown or suspicious origin are excluded from arson statistics.[27]

The intentional burning of structures (houses, storage buildings, manufacturing facilities, etc.) was the type of arson most often reported in 1991 (46,478 instances). The arson of vehicles was the second most common category, with 21,917 such burnings reported. The average dollar loss per instance of arson in 1991 was $11,980, and total property damage was placed at over $1 billion.[28]   As with most property crimes, the clearance rate for arson was low — only 16% nationally.

PART II OFFENSES

TABLE 2-2
UCR Part II Offenses, 1991

Offense Category	Number of Arrests
Simple assault	789,144
Forgery and counterfeiting	77,066
Fraud	292,597
Embezzlement	10,602
Stolen property (receiving, etc.)	130,579
Vandalism	252,469
Weapons (carrying, etc.)	178,955
Prostitution and related offenses	81,536
Sex offenses (statutory rape, etc.)	82,228
Drug law violations	781,250
Gambling	12,913
Offenses against the family (nonsupport, etc.)	72,527
Driving under the influence	1,288,876
Liquor law violations	453,807
Public drunkenness	657,119
Disorderly conduct	569,314
Vagrancy	31,262
Curfew/loitering	73,125
Runaways	135,471

Source: Federal Bureau of Investigation, *Crime in the United States, 1991* (Washington, D.C.: U.S. Government Printing Office, 1992), p. 216.

The Uniform Crime Reports also include information on what the FBI calls Part II offenses. Part II offenses are generally less serious than those which make up the Crime Index, and include a number of victimless crimes. The statistics on Part II offenses are for recorded arrests — not crimes reported to the police. The logic inherent in this form of scoring is that most Part II offenses would never come to the attention of the police were it not for arrests. Included in the Part II category are the crimes shown in Table 2-2 with the number of arrests reported in each category for 1991.

Part II arrests are counted each time a person is taken into custody. As a result, the statistics in Table 2-2 do not measure the number of persons arrested, but rather the number of arrests made. Some persons were arrested more than once.

PROPOSED CHANGES IN THE UCR

Changes are coming in the Uniform Crime Reports. From 1982 to 1985 the UCR Program was comprehensively evaluated under federal contract by Abt Associates, Inc., of Cambridge, Massachusetts. The final report of the UCR study group, entitled a *Blueprint for the Future of the Uniform Crime Reporting System*, recommended a number of sweeping changes. Among them are:

❶ Each category of offense should clearly distinguish statistics on attempts versus actual commissions.

❷ The rape category should be broadened to include all forcible sex offenses. Sexual battery, sodomy, and oral copulation — accomplished through the use of force — should be counted.

❸ The "Hierarchy Rule" should be modified so as to count the most serious offense for each individual victim during an incident.[29]

❹ Crimes against individuals, households, and businesses should be more clearly distinguished in most categories.

❺ Aggravated assault should be more clearly defined in terms of the weapons used and the degree of injury suffered.

❻ A code of professional standards should be developed for reporting agencies, and for the system as a whole.

❼ The UCR should be modified so as to permit easier and more meaningful comparisons with the National Crime Victimization Survey and with Offender-Based Transaction Statistics (OBTS).

A pilot study to test some of these recommendations, and to integrate computerized scoring and reporting more fully into the UCR Program, was initiated in 1987 by the South Carolina Law Enforcement Division (SLED). Following the SLED pilot program, law enforcement experts from around the country met to discuss the results. They recommended[30] (1) establishment of a new incident-driven national crime reporting system,

(2) FBI management of the new program, and (3) the creation of an Advisory Policy Board composed of law enforcement executives to assist in implementation of the new program.

Whereas the original UCR system was "summary based," the new "enhanced" Uniform Crime Reports, to be called the National Incident-Based Reporting Program — or NIBRS, will be incident driven. The old system depended upon statistical tabulations of crime data which were often little more than frequency counts. Under the new system many details will be gathered about each criminal incident. Included among them will be information on place of occurrence, weapon used, type and value of property damaged or stolen, the personal characteristics of the offender and the victim, the nature of any relationship between the two, nature of the disposition of the complaint, and so on. The new reporting system will replace the old Part I and Part II offenses with 22 general offenses, to include arson, assault, bribery, burglary, counterfeiting, vandalism, narcotic offenses, embezzlement, extortion, fraud, gambling, homicide, kidnapping, larceny, motor vehicle theft, pornography, prostitution, robbery, forcible sex offenses, nonforcible sex offenses, receiving stolen property, and weapons violations. Other offenses on which data will be gathered are bad checks, vagrancy, disorderly conduct, driving under the influence, drunkenness, nonviolent family offenses, liquor law violations, "peeping Tom"–type activity, runaway, trespass, and a general category of all "other" criminal law violations. The FBI began accepting crime data in the NIBRS format in January 1989, although it is doubtful that all agencies participating in the crime reporting program will be able to make the switch in reporting formats until 1994 or later.

The 1990 Crime Awareness and Campus Security Act, which required college campuses to commence publishing annual "security reports" beginning in September of 1992, has the potential to additionally affect crime rates reported through the UCR Program. Although campuses are not required by the law to share crime data with the FBI, it is expected that many will — increasing the reported incidence of a variety of offenses.

A final change in reporting practices will no doubt follow from the Hate Crime Statistics Act, signed into law by then-President Bush in April 1990. The act mandates a statistical tally of "hate crimes," and data collection under the law began in January 1991.

❑ THE NATIONAL CRIME VICTIMIZATION SURVEY

A second major source of statistical data about crime in the United States is the National Crime Victimization Survey (NCVS), which uses victim self-reports in place of crime reported to the police. The NCVS began operation in 1972 and built upon earlier attempts by both the National Opinion Research Center and the President's Commission on Law Enforcement and the Administration of Justice in the late 1960s.

Early data from the NCVS changed the way criminologists thought about crime in the United States. The use of victim self-reports led to the discovery that crime of all types was more prevalent than the UCR statistics indicated. Many cities were shown to have victimization rates more than twice the rate of reported offenses. Others, such as St. Louis, Missouri, and Newark, New Jersey, were found to have rates of victimization which very nearly approximated reported crime. New York, often thought of as a "high crime" city, was discovered to have one of the lowest rates of self-reported victimization.

National Crime Victimization Survey data are gathered by the Bureau of Justice Statistics through a cooperative arrangement with the U.S. Census Bureau.[31] NCVS interviewers work with a national sample of about 49,000 households which are interviewed twice each year.   Household lists are completely revised at the end of every three-year period.   BJS statistics are published as "research briefs" called *Households Touched by Crime*, and *Criminal Victimization*, and annual reports entitled *Criminal Victimization in the United States*.

Crimes covered by the NCVS include rape, robbery, assault, burglary, personal and household larceny, and motor vehicle theft.   Not included are murder, kidnapping, and victimless crimes.   Commercial robbery and the burglary of businesses were dropped from NCVS reports in 1977.   Definitions of crime categories are generally similar to those used by the UCR Program.   The NCVS employs a hierarchical counting system similar to that of the UCR: it counts only the most "serious" incident in any series of criminal events perpetrated against the same individual.   Both completed and attempted offenses are counted, although only persons 12 years of age and older are included in household surveys.   Highlights of recent NCVS statistics reveal that:[32]

- Approximately 23 million American households per year are touched by crime — or 25% of all households.

- Nearly 35 million victimizations are reported to the NCVS per year.

- City residents are about twice as likely as rural residents to be victims of crime.

- About half of all violent crimes, two-fifths of all household crimes, and slightly more than one-fourth of all crimes of personal theft are reported to police.[33]

- The total "personal cost" of crime to victims is about $12.5 billion per year for the United States as a whole.

- Victims of crime are more often men than women.

- Younger people are more likely than the elderly to be victims of crime.

- Blacks are more likely than whites or members of other racial groups to be victims of violent crimes.[34]

- Violent victimization rates are higher among people in lower income families.

- Young males have the highest violent victimization rates; elderly females have the lowest.

♦ The chance of violent criminal victimization is much higher for young black males than for any other segment of the population. (The life chances of murder run from a high of 1 in 21 for a black male to a low of 1 in 369 for a white female.)[35]

PROBLEMS WITH THE NCVS

The tendency among researchers today seems to be to accept NCVS data in preference to that of the UCR. The National Crime Victimization Survey, however, is not without its problems. Primary among them is the potential for false or exaggerated reports. False reports may be generated by overzealous interviewers or self-aggrandizing respondents and are difficult to filter out. There are no reliable estimates as to the proportion of such responses which make up NCVS totals. Unintentional inaccuracies create other problems. Respondents may suffer from faulty memories, they may misinterpret events, and they may ascribe criminal intent to accidents and mistakes. Likewise, the lapse of time between the event itself and the conduct of the interview may cause some crime to be forgotten and others to be inaccurately reported.

COMING CHANGES IN THE NCVS

Just as the Uniform Crime Reports are undergoing change, so too is the National Crime Victimization Survey. In 1986 the Bureau of Justice Statistics implemented the first phase in a massive overhaul of the NCVS.[36] With that implementation, the NCVS began to gather information in three new areas:[37]

♦ Victims perceptions of drug and alcohol use by violent offenders

♦ Protective actions taken by victims and bystanders

♦ The response of the police and other criminal justice agencies to reported crimes

Initial findings indicate that 36% of victims of violent crimes believed their assailants to be under the influence of drugs or alcohol. In cases of rape, the proportion of assailants believed under the influence jumped to 46% — the highest reported by the survey.

Seventy-three percent of violent crime victims reported taking some self-protective measure. Self-protective measures included struggling or fighting with the assailant, threats, running away, efforts at appeasement, or pleading. Sixty percent of victims who took self-protective measures reported that their actions reduced the severity of their victimization.

Justice agency response, as measured by the survey, shows that the police came to see the victim in 76% of violent crimes, 71% of household crimes (such as burglary and motor vehicle theft), and 54% of all larcenies. Police response was fastest in violent crimes, averaging under 10 minutes, and slowest where household crimes were involved. Plans for additional changes in the NCVS are in the works. A new survey form, which will require the gradual retraining of interviewers is beginning to be used.[38] The new form (1) utilizes questions designed to prod victim's memories; (2) reduces complexity in terminology; and (3) includes questions dealing with ecological factors, victim characteristics, lifestyle, and protective or preventive measures undertaken by all victims. Victimizations will be classified according to various life "domains," such as work or leisure, in which they occurred.

COMPARISONS OF THE UCR AND NCVS

Table 2-3 summarizes differences between the UCR and the NCVS. Both provide estimates of crime in America. Both are limited by the types of crimes they choose to measure, by those they exclude from measurement, and by the methods they use to gather crime data.

Crime statistics from the UCR and NCVS are often used in building explanations of crime. Unfortunately, however, researchers too often forget that descriptive statistics can be weak in explanatory power. For example, NCVS data shows that "household crime rates" are highest for households (1) headed by blacks, (2) headed by younger people, (3) with six or more members, (4) headed by renters, and (5) in central cities.[39] Such findings, combined with statistics that show that most crime occurs among members of the same race, have led some researchers to conclude that values among black subcultural group members propel them into crime and make them targets of criminal victimization. The truth may be, however, that crime in this case is more a function of geography (inner-city location) than of culture.

☐ EMERGING PATTERNS

Planned revisions in both the National Crime Victimization Survey and the Uniform Crime Reports reflect the fact that patterns of criminal activity in the United States are changing. Georgette Bennett has termed the shift in crime patterns crimewarps.[40] Crimewarps, says Bennett, represent major changes in both what society considers criminal, and in who future criminal offenders will be. Some areas of coming change that she predicts are:[41]

- ◆ The decline of street crime.
- ◆ The growth of white-collar crime.
- ◆ Increasing female involvement in crime.
- ◆ Increased crime commission among the elderly.
- ◆ A shift in high crime rates from the "Frost Belt" to the "Sun Belt."
- ◆ Safer cities, with increasing criminal activity in rural areas.
- ◆ The growth of high-technology crimes.

TABLE 2-3
How Do the UCR and NCVS Compare?

	Uniform Crime Reports	National Crime Victimization Survey
Offenses measured	Homicide Rape Robbery (personal) Assault (aggravated and simple) Burglary (commercial and household) Larceny (commercial and household) Motor vehicle theft Arson	Rape Robbery (personal & commercial) Assault (aggravated) Household burglary Larceny (personal & household) Motor vehicle theft
Scope	Crimes reported to the police in most jurisdictions; considerable flexibility in developing small-area data	Crimes both reported and not reported to police; all data are available for a few large geographic areas
Collection method	Police department reports to FBI or to centralized state agencies that then report to FBI	Survey interviews; periodically measures the total number of crimes committed by asking a national sample of 49,000 households encompassing 101,000 persons age 12 and over about their experiences as victims of crime during a specified period
Kinds of information	In addition to offense counts, provides information on crime clearances, persons arrested, persons charged, law enforcement officers killed and assaulted, and characteristics of homicide victims	Provides details about victims (such as age, race, sex, education, income, and whether the victim and offender were related to each other and about crimes (such as time and place of occurrence, whether or not reported to police, use of weapons, occurrence of injury, and economic consequences)
Sponsor	Department of Justice, Federal Bureau of Investigation	Department of Justice, Bureau of Justice Statistics

Source: Bureau of Justice Statistics, *Report to the Nation on Crime and Justice,* 2nd ed. (Washington, D.C.: U.S. Department of Justice, 1988).

TABLE 2-4
Life Chances of Serious Events[1]
How do crime rates compare with the rates of other life events?

Events	Rate per 1,000 Adults per Year[2]
Accidental injury, all circumstances	242
Accidental injury at home	79
Personal theft	72
Accidental injury at work	58
Violent victimization	31
Assault (aggravated and simple)	24
Injury in motor vehicle accident	17
Death, all causes	11
Victimization with injury	10
Serious (aggravated) assault	9
Robbery	6
Heart disease death	4
Cancer death	2
Rape (women only)	2
Accidental death, all circumstances	0.5
Pneumonia/influenza death	0.3
Motor vehicle accident death	0.2
Suicide	0.2
Injury from fire	0.1
Homicide/legal intervention death	0.1
Death from fire	0.03

[1]These rates approximate your chances of becoming a victim of these events. More precise estimates can be derived by taking account of such factors as your age, sex, race, place of residence, and life-style. Findings are based on 1982–1984 data, but there is little variation in rates from year to year.

[2]These rates exclude children from the calculations (those under ages 12–17, depending on the series). Fire injury/death data are based on the total population, because no age-specific data are available in this series.

Current estimates are from the National Center for Health Statistics, *National Health Interview Survey: United States, 1982;* National Center for Health Statistics, *Advance Report Of Final Mortality Statistics, 1983: Monthly Vital Statistics Report;* U.S. Bureau of the Census, *Estimates of the Population of the United States, by Age, Sex, and Race: 1980 to 1984;* National Fire Protection Association, *The 1984 Fire Almanac;* and "Criminal Victimization 1984," *BJS Bulletin,* October 1985.

Source: Bureau of Justice Statistics, *Report to the Nation on Crime and Justice,* 2nd ed. (Washington, D.C.: U.S. Department of Justice, 1988), p. 24.

THE FEAR OF CRIME

The decline in traditional violent street crimes predicted by Bennett will not automatically lead to a reduction in the fear of crime felt by many. As Bennett recognizes[42] the fear of crime is often out of proportion to the likelihood of criminal victimization. Table 2-4 shows the chance of violent victimization compared to life chances of other serious events. For most people, the chance of accidental injury at work or at home is far greater than the chance of being criminally attacked.

The Bureau of Justice Statistics points out that "the fear of crime affects many people, including some who have never been victims of crime."[43] Sources of fear are diverse. Some flow from personal experience with victimization, but most people fear crime because of dramatizations on television and in movies, and because of frequent newspaper and media reports on crime. Feelings of vulnerability may result from learning that a friend has been victimized or from hearing that a neighbor's home has been burglarized.[44]

Interestingly, the groups at highest risk of becoming crime victims are not the ones who experience the greatest fear of crime. The elderly and women report the greatest fear of victimization, even though they are

Copyright 1990 by USA Today. Reprinted with permission
The fear of crime is pervasive in America.

among the lowest risk groups for violent crime. Young males, on the other hand, who stand the greatest statistical risk of victimization, often report feeling the least fear.[45] Similarly, although most people most fear violent victimization by a stranger, many such crimes are committed by nonstrangers or by people known to victims by sight.[46]

WOMEN AND CRIME

Women Victims

Women are victimized far less frequently than are men in every major crime category other than rape.[47] When women are victimized, however, they are more likely than men to be injured.[48] Even though experiencing lower rates of victimization, it is realistic to acknowledge that a larger proportion of women than men make modifications in the way they live because of the threat of crime.[49] Women, especially those living in cities, are increasingly careful about where they travel, and the time of day they leave their homes — particularly if unaccompanied — and are wary of unfamiliar males in a diversity of settings.

The popular media, special interest groups, and even the government have contributed to a certain degree of confusion about women's victimization. Very real concerns reflected in movies, television programs, and newspaper editorial pages, have properly identified date rape, familial incest, spouse abuse, and the exploitation of women through social order offenses such as prostitution and pornography, as major issues facing American society today. Testimony before Congress[50] has tagged domestic violence as the largest cause of injury to American women, and former Surgeon General Everett Koop identified violence against women by their partners as the number one health problem facing women in America today.

A CAREER WITH THE U.S. SECRET SERVICE

Typical Positions. Special agent, uniformed division police officer, and special officer. Clerical and administrative positions are also available.

Employment Requirements. Requirements for appointment at GS-5 level include (1) successful completion of the Treasury Enforcement Agent examination; (2) a Bachelor's degree from an accredited college or university; (3) excellent physical condition, including at least 20/40 vision in each eye, correctable to 20/20; and (4) successful completion of a thorough background investigation. Appointment at the GS-7 level also requires (1) one additional year of specialized experience, (2) a Bachelor's degree with Superior Academic Achievement, or (3) one year of graduate study in a related field (police science, police administration, criminology, law, law enforcement, business administration, accounting, economics, finance, or other directly related fields). Superior academic achievement is defined as meeting one or more of the following criteria: (1) a "B" average (2.9 on a 4.0 scale) for all courses completed at time of application or for all courses during the last two years of the undergraduate curriculum, (2) a "B+" average (3.5 on a 4.0 scale) for all courses in the major field of study or all courses in the major during the last two years of the undergraduate curriculum, (3) rank in the upper third of the undergraduate class or major subdivision (i.e., school of liberal arts), and (4) membership in an honorary scholastic society which meets the requirements of the Association of College Honor Societies. Specialized experience is defined as responsible criminal investigative or comparable experience which required (1) the exercise of tact, resourcefulness and judgment in collecting, assembling and developing facts, evidence and other pertinent data through investigative techniques which include personal interviews; (2) the ability to make oral and written reports and presentations of personally conducted or personally directed investigations; and (3) the ability to analyze and evaluate evidence and arrive at sound conclusions.

Other Requirements. Valid driver's license, urinalysis test for the presence of illegal drugs prior to appointment, and the ability to qualify for top secret security clearance.

Salary. GS-5 of $18,340 to GS-7 of $22,717 as of 1993, with special higher salary rates for selected metropolitan areas. Uniformed Division officers start at $26,375.

Benefits. Benefits include (1) 13 days of sick leave annually, (2) 2½ to 5 weeks of annual paid vacation and 10 paid federal holidays each year, (3) federal health and life insurance, and (4) a comprehensive retirement program.

Direct inquiries to: Chief of Staffing, U.S. Secret Service, 1800 G Street, N.W., Room 912, Washington, D.C. 20223. Phone: (202) 535-5800. Applications are not accepted earlier than nine months prior to graduation.

When the data on women's victimization is examined closely, however, a slightly different pattern emerges. The Bureau of Justice Statistics,[51] in a detailed analysis of female victims of violent crime, found that about twice as many women who are victims of violent crimes are likely to be victimized by strangers than by people whom they know. However, when women do fall victim to violent crime they are far more likely to be victimized by individuals with whom they are (or have been) in intimate relationships than are men. Where the perpetrators are known to them, women are most likely to be violently victimized by ex-spouses, boyfriends, and spouses, respectively. The BJS study also found that separated or divorced women are 6 times more likely to be victims of violent crime than widows, 4 and 1/2 times more likely than married women, and 3 times more likely than widowers and married men. Other findings indicated that (1) women living in central city areas are considerably more likely to be victimized than are women residing in the suburbs; (2) suburban women, in turn, are more likely to be victimized than are women living in rural areas; (3) women from low-income families experience the highest amount of violent crime; (4) the victimization of women falls as family income rises; (5) unemployed women, female students, and those in the armed forces are the most likely of all women to experience violent victimization; (6) black women are victims of violent crimes more frequently than are women of any other race; (7) Hispanic women find themselves victimized more frequently than white women; and (8) women in the age range of 20–24 are most at risk for violent victimization, while those aged 16–19 constitute the second most likely group of victims.

These findings show that greater emphasis needs to be placed on alleviating the social conditions that victimize women. Suggestions already under consideration call for expansion in the number of federal and state laws designed to control domestic violence, a broadening of the federal Family Violence Prevention and Services Act, federal help in setting up state advocacy offices for battered women, increased funding for battered-women's shelters, and additional monies for prosecutors and courts to develop spouse-abuse units. In an insightful article built around issues in criminal justice education, Nanci Koser Wilson[52] suggests a multifaceted role for women who are interested in improving the position of like-gender individuals in the criminal justice system.

Aspects of the role include:

❶ "Women lobbying for change in the criminal justice system." Wilson points to the success which has met women who have worked to change rape laws, police procedure in domestic violence cases, and the recognition of the plight of battered women in cases of spousal homicide.

❷ "Women creating help for women outside the system." The creation of rape crisis centers, centers for battered women, and the like all point to the possibility of women helping individuals of like gender through non-criminal justice channels.

❸ "Women working in movements outside traditional crime areas." Ecofeminism, peace work, and other social movements have done much to enhance the status of women in general, and may work in the long run to reduce some of the factors which result in the criminal victimization of women.

❹ "Women producing research from a woman's perspective."

Wilson points out that the tendency to dismiss the criminality of women because it is less frequent than that of males misses the opportunity to learn about crime in general via the model provided by women's criminality.   Dismissing the criminality of women implies that the criminality of men is somehow "normal" and that other behavior patterns are less worthy of study. A gender-balanced approach to the study of crime should have something to teach us all.

❺ "Women working within the traditional criminal justice system in woman-defined ways."   Women who choose police work, or who work within correctional environments, have something to contribute to both professions by virtue of the unique perspective they bring to their jobs.   Because of potential benefits to the system and to themselves, women should not be expected to accept automatically traditional masculinized understandings of criminal justice roles.

Women Offenders

On January 8, 1991, Aileen Carol Wuornos was arrested in Ocala, Florida, and charged with the murder of a man who had apparently offered her a ride as she hitchhiked through Florida.[53]   The would-be Samaritan was shot, stripped of his clothing, and dumped on a roadside, while Aileen and a female companion allegedly drove off in his car. Prosecutors indicated that she would soon be indicted in as many as six other similar killings.   Property belonging to the seven victims — most of whom were robbed, killed, and left naked — was found in a storage unit rented by Ms. Wuornos.   One victim was a former police chief, another a security guard.   All were white, middle-aged men with blue-collar jobs who were traveling alone.   Each was killed with a small-caliber handgun.[54]   In 1992 Ms. Wuornos was convicted of first-degree murder and sentenced to death.   By mid-1993, however, new information had arisen concerning one of her victims, leading many to conclude that Mrs. Wuornos's original conviction might be reversed on the grounds of self-defense.

Aileen Wuornos's alleged crimes, gruesome as they may be, fall outside what we know of as the pattern for female criminality.   Although the popular media has sometimes portrayed female criminals as similar to their male counterparts in motivation and behavior — as in the movie *Thelma and Louise,* starring Susan Sarandon and Geena Davis — that image is misleading.   Similarly, the academic study of women's criminality has been fraught with misconceptions.

One of the first writers to attempt a definitive explanation of the criminality of women was Otto Pollak.   Pollak's book, *The Criminality of Women,*[55] written in 1950, suggested that women commit the same number of offenses as men — but that most of their criminality is hidden.   Pollak claimed that women's roles (at the time, primarily those of homemaker and mother) served to disguise the criminal undertakings of women.   He also proposed that chivalrous treatment by a male-dominated justice system acted to bias every stage of criminal justice processing in favor of women. Hence, according to Pollak, although women are just as criminal as men, they are rarely arrested, tried, or imprisoned. In fact, while the criminality of women may approach or exceed that of men in selected offense categories, it is safe to say today that Pollak was incorrect in his assessment of the degree of female criminality.

TABLE 2-5
Male/Female Involvement in Crime Commission

UCR Index Crimes	Percentage of All Arrests Males	Females	Likelihood of Commission
Murder and nonnegligent/ manslaughter	89.7%	10.3%	Men are more likely than women to be arrested for more serious crimes, such as murder, rape, robbery, or burglary
Rape	98.7	1.3	
Robbery	91.4	8.6	
Aggravated assault	86.3	13.7	
Burglary	91.1	8.9	Arrest, jail, and prison data all suggest that a higher proportion of women than of men who commit crimes are involved in property crimes, such as larceny, forgery, fraud, and embezzlement, and in drug offenses.
Larceny-theft	68.0	32.0	
Motor vehicle theft	90.0	10.0	
Arson	86.9	13.1	

Source: Federal Bureau of Investigation, *Crime in the United States, 1991* (Washington, D.C.: U.S. Government Printing Office, 1992).

Contemporary statistics tell us that, although females comprise 51% of the population of the United States, they are arrested for only 11.6% of all violent crime and 25.4% of property crimes. The relatively small amount of reported female involvement in the FBI's eight major crimes can be seen in Table 2-5. The number of women committing crime appears to be increasing faster than the number of male offenders, however. Between 1978 and 1991 crimes committed by men grew 36.2%, while crimes reported to have been committed by women increased 53.2%. Violent crimes by males increased 53.4%; by women, 61.8%. Property crimes perpetrated by men grew by 20.9%; by women, 37.5%.[56] Nonetheless, as the table shows, female offenders still account for only a small proportion of all reported crimes.

Such statistics are difficult to interpret, however, since reports of female involvement in crime may reflect more the growing equality accorded women in contemporary society than they do actual increases in criminal activity. In the past, when women committed crimes, they may have been dealt with less officiously than is likely to be the case today. In only two officially reported crime categories — prostitution and runaways — do women outnumber men in the actual volume of offenses committed.[57] Other crimes in which significant numbers of women (relative to men) are involved include larceny-theft (where 31% of reported crimes are committed by women), forgery and counterfeiting (34%), fraud (45%), and embezzlement (38%).

These statistics dispel the myth that the female criminal has taken her place alongside male offenders — at least in terms of the absolute number of crimes committed. During the 1970s a number of writers had, in fact, suggested that as women achieve social equality, female criminality would emulate what had previously been male crime patterns. Two influential thinkers of the period were Rita Simon, who wrote *Women and Crime*,[58] and Freda Adler, author of *Sisters in Crime*.[59] Both books were published in 1975. Adler's work, subtitled *The Rise of the New Female Criminal,* suggested that, as women entered "nontraditional occupations," there "would be a movement toward parity with men in the commission of crime in terms of both incidence and type."[60] However, Darrell Steffensmeir[61] who studied changes in women's criminality over a 12-year period following the publication of Simon's and Adler's works, found almost no evidence to support the belief that gender differences in criminality are disappearing. Hence, although the criminality of women is changing, as evidenced by growing female involvement in a variety of offenses, "there is little to support the theory of a new female criminal."[62]

One reason why the changes foreseen by Adler and Simon have not occurred may be that the majority of women involved in the commission of crimes have not benefited substantially from women's movements which have tended to increase opportunities primarily for middle class women. Most incarcerated women, and many women who are charged with male-dominated violent and property crimes may come from the lower social classes. If equal rates of crime commission are to occur, based upon the predictive formula of Simon and Adler, they would most likely be seen first among women who stand most to benefit immediately from the women's movement of recent years — those of the upper middle class.

THE ECONOMIC COST OF CRIME

The Bureau of Justice Statistics estimates the personal cost of crime (direct dollar losses to individuals) at around $13 billion per year.[63] Robberies, burglaries, and larceny-thefts account for approximately $6 billion in losses per year. Not included in the Bureau's figures are the costs to crime victims of lost work, needed medical care, and the expense of new security measures they may implement. Lost work time is reported in 11% of aggravated assaults and 15% of rapes. A significant shortcoming of the BJS estimates is that they involve only dollar amounts and give no real picture of personal trauma, psychological disabilities resulting from victimization, and individual suffering caused by crime.

The economic impact of crime is different for different groups. In a recent year, for example, households with annual incomes above $15,000 averaged burglary losses of approximately $200 per incident, twice the value of property stolen in burglaries from lower income households.   Similarly, wealthier households suffered damages to stolen vehicles averaging $2000, in contrast with $700 losses suffered by households with lower incomes.[64]

The commercial costs of crime are substantial as well. Losses from commercial robberies (including bank robberies) and business burglaries have been put at $1.2 billion per year.[65]   Credit card fraud losses have been estimated at $500 million, and approximately $100 million worth of counterfeit notes and currency are printed yearly.[66]   The cost to businesses of white collar crime are not known, but are thought to be substantial. To guard against crimes by employees and members of the public, private businesses spend in excess of $21 billion per year for alarms, surveillance, and private security operations.[67]

Costs to the government for the apprehension, prosecution, and disposition of offenders, including crime prevention efforts by the police, far outstrip the known dollar losses to all criminal enterprises other than drugs. Federal criminal justice expenditures in 1990 were estimated to be in excess of $8 billion,[68] while federal, state, and local expenditures totaled over $64 billion.[69]   Nonetheless, government spending on criminal justice services amounts to only about 5% of all governmental expenditures. State and local governments absorb most of the costs of criminal justice–related activity.

DRUGS AND CRIME

Drugs and crime are often found together. Drug law violations are themselves criminal, but more and more studies are linking drug abuse to other serious crimes. A study by The RAND Corporation found that most of the "violent predators" among prisoners had extensive histories of heroin abuse, often in combination with alcohol and other drugs.[70] Some cities report that a large percentage of their homicides are drug related.[71] Many property crimes are committed to sustain "habits," and the numbers of both violent and property crimes committed by drug users have been shown to be directly related to the level at which they use drugs.[72]   Substance abuse may well be the most expensive of all crimes. The social cost of drug abuse has been estimated at nearly $60 billion per year, with half of that amount being in lost job productivity.[73] Drunk driving alone is thought to cost over $13 billion in property losses and medical expenses yearly.[74]

THE ELDERLY AND CRIME

UCR statistics define "older offenders" as those over 55 years of age. Relative to other age groups, older offenders rarely appear in the crime statistics. Criminality seems to decline with age, suggesting that a burnout factor applies to criminal behavior as it does to many other areas of life.   In 1991 persons aged 65 and over accounted for less than 1% of all arrests.[75]

The type and number of crimes committed by older people, however, appear to be changing. According to the UCR, arrests of the elderly for serious crimes doubled between 1970 and 1980, while arrests in the same age category for minor crimes dropped by half since 1964.[76] Arrests of persons 65 and older increased by 172% between 1965 and 1985, and fraud arrests for the same group rose by 163%.[77] When elderly people are sent to prison it is usually for violent crimes, while violent crimes account for far less than 50% of prison admissions among younger people.[78]

Some authors have interpreted these statistics to presage the growth of a "geriatric delinquent" population, freed by age and retirement from jobs and responsibilities. Such people, say these authors, may turn to crime as one way of averting boredom and adding a little spice to life.[79] Statistics on geriatric offenders, however, probably require a more cautious interpretation. They are based upon relatively small numbers, and to say that "serious crimes among the elderly doubled" does not mean that a geriatric crime wave is upon us. The apparent increase in criminal activity among the elderly may be due to the fact that the older population in this country is growing substantially, with even greater increases expected over the next three decades. Advances in health care have increased life expectancy and have made the added years more productive than ever before. World War II "baby boomers" will be reaching their late middle years by the year 2000 and present trends in criminal involvement among the elderly can be expected to continue. Hence, it may not be that elderly individuals in this country are committing crimes more frequently than before, but rather that the greater number of elderly in the population make for a greater prevalence of crimes committed by the elderly in the official statistics.

The elderly are also victims of crime. Although persons aged 65 and older generally experience the lowest rate of victimization of any age group,[80] some aspects of serious crime against older people are worth noting. Elderly violent crime victims are more likely than younger victims to face offenders armed with guns. They are more likely to be victimized by total strangers. They are more likely than younger victims to be victimized in or near their homes. The older the victim, the greater the likelihood of physical injury.[81] When victimized by violent crime, elderly people are less likely to attempt to protect themselves and more apt to report their victimization to the police than are younger people.[82]

Elderly people are most likely to be victimized if they fall into certain categories. Relative to their numbers in the elderly population, black men are overrepresented as victims. Similarly, separated or divorced persons and urban residents have higher rates of victimization than do other elderly persons.[83] As observed earlier, older people live in greater fear of crime than do younger people, even though their risk of victimization is considerably less. Elderly people, however, are the least likely to take crime preventive measures than are any other age group.[84] Only 6% of households headed by persons over the age of 65 have a burglar alarm, and only 16% engrave their valuables (versus a 25% national average).[85]

EMERGING CRIMINAL ACTIVITIES

Later chapters will examine the role of technology in both the prevention and commission of crime. It is important to note in any discussion of the crime picture today, however, that the number of "high-tech" crimes, while still a small proportion of all crimes, is rapidly increasing. Because high-technology crimes are committed by well-educated individuals utilizing a special knowledge base, they are especially difficult to uncover and may often go undiscovered. As a consequence, statistics on high-tech crimes tend to underestimate the pervasiveness of such crimes in modern society.

Many other high-technology crimes are hidden in existing data for another reason: few special reporting categories are in use today which allow for an accurate appraisal of the extent of such crime. Most computer crimes, the theft and use of high-technology, and the misappropriation of funds and services through technological manipulations are simply reported — if at all — as crimes of theft or embezzlement.

One type of high-technology crime on which fledgling statistics do exist is that involving thefts from automatic teller machines (ATMs). Although thefts from ATMs are classified as "high-technology" crimes, many of them are committed with only a rudimentary technical knowledge. In one year for which data are available, $262 billion were transferred through 2.7 billion separate automatic teller machine transactions. An estimated $70–100 million was lost through ATM fraud in this workload.[86] The largest category of known ATM fraud was perpetrated through the unauthorized use of lost or stolen bank cards. Two-thirds of such illegal use resulted from theft of a wallet or from purse snatching. The average loss to account holders from ATM fraud in 1983 was $255, while banks lost an average of $365 per incident.[87]

New procedures are being developed to thwart high-tech criminals. Today most banks require use of a secret code which is magnetically imprinted on bank cards to prevent unauthorized use. (According to victims of credit card theft, 72% of such personal identification numbers were kept near the card in a purse or wallet and stolen along with it; 6% admitted they had written the number on the card!)[88] The increase in availability of home computers, combined with an increasing computer expertise among the general population, is soon expected to combine with increased public access (via modems) to personal bank accounts, to create yet another widespread opportunity for high-technology crime.

☐ SUMMARY

Crime statistics provide a useful but conceptually limited approach to the social reality of crime. Statistics delineate the extent of crime according to the categories they are designed to measure, and they give a picture of victim characteristics through both self-reports and reports to the police. Today's comprehensive program of data gathering allows for a tabulation of the dollar costs of crime and permits a degree of predictability as to trends in crime.

Lacking in most crime statistics, however, are any realistic appraisals of the human costs of crime. The trauma suffered by victims and survivors, the lowered sense of security experienced after victimization, and the loss of human productivity and quality of life caused by crime are difficult to gauge.

On the other side of the balance sheet, statistics fail to identify social costs suffered by offenders and their families. The social deprivation which may lead to crime, the fragmentation of private lives following conviction, and the loss of individuality which comes with confinement are all costs to society, just as they are the culturally imposed consequences of crime and failure. Except for numbers on crimes committed, arrests, and figures on persons incarcerated, today's data gathering strategies fall far short of gauging the human suffering and wasted human potential which both causes and follows from crime.

Even where reports do provide quantitative measures, they may still fail to assess some of the objective costs of crime, including lowered property values in high-crime areas and inflated prices for consumer goods caused by the underground economy in stolen goods. White-collar crimes in particular are often well hidden and difficult to measure, yet may produce the largest direct dollar losses of any type of criminal activity.

Modern crime statistics are useful, but they do not provide the whole picture. Students of criminal justice need to be continually aware of aspects of the crime picture which fall outside of official data.

DISCUSSION QUESTIONS

1. What are the two major sources of crime statistics for the United States? How do they differ?

2. What can crime statistics tell us about the crime "picture" in America? How has that "picture" changed over time?

3. What are the potential sources of error in the major reports on crime? Can you imagine some popular usage of those statistics that might be especially misleading?

4. Why are many crime statistics expressed as a *rate*? How does the use of crime rates improve the reporting of crime data (over a simple numerical tabulation)?

5. What is the crime index? Why is it difficult to add offenses to (or remove them from) the index and still have it retain its value as a comparative tool?

6. What are the two major offense categories in Part I crimes? Are there some property crimes which might have a violent aspect? Are there any personal crimes which could be non-violent?

7. What is the hierarchy rule in crime reporting programs? What purpose does it serve? What do you think of the proposed modifications in the hierarchy rule?

8. What does it mean to say that a crime has been "cleared"? Can you imagine a better way of reporting clearances?

NOTES

1. President's Commission on Law Enforcement and Administration of Justice, *The Challenge of Crime in a Free Society* (Washington, D.C.: U.S. Government Printing Office, 1967), p. 18.

2. Eugene Webb et al., *Nonreactive Measures in the Social Sciences,* 2nd ed. (Boston: Houghton Mifflin, 1981), as quoted in Frank Hagan, *Research Methods in Criminal Justice* (New York: Macmillan, 1982), p. 89.

3. U.S. Bureau of Justice Statistics (BJS). *Criminal Victimization in the United States, 1985* (Washington,

D.C.: U.S. Government Printing Office, 1987), p. 1.

4. Federal Bureau of Investigation (FBI), *Uniform Crime Reports for the United States, 1987* (Washington, D.C.: U.S. Government Printing Office, 1988), p. 1.

5. Hagan, *Research Methods in Criminal Justice and Criminology.*

6. Federal Bureau of Investigation (FBI), *Crime in the United States, 1991* (Washington, D.C.: U.S. Government Printing Office, 1992).

7. Federal Bureau of Investigation (FBI), *Uniform Crime Reports for the United States, 1975* (Washington: U.S. Government Printing Office, 1976), p. 22.

8. FBI, *Crime in the United States, 1991.*

9. These and other statistics in this chapter are derived primarily from FBI, *Crime in the United States, 1991.*

10. All offense definitions in this chapter are derived from those used by the UCR reporting program and are taken from the FBI, *Uniform Crime Reports for the United States, 1990,* or from BJS, *Criminal Justice Data Terminology,* 2nd ed. (Washington, D.C: Bureau of Justice Statistics, 1981).

11. U.S. Department of Justice (DOJ), *Report to the Nation on Crime and Justice,* 2nd ed. (Washington, D.C.: Bureau of Justice Statistics, 1988). p. 4.

12. Ibid.

13. Ibid.

14. Ronald Barri Flowers, *Women and Criminality: The Woman as Victim, Offender and Practitioner* (Westport, CT: Greenwood Press, 1987), pp. 33–36.

15. A. Nicholas Groth, *Men Who Rape: The Psychology of the Offender* (New York: Plenum Press, 1979).

16. Flowers, *Women and Criminality,* p. 36.

17. Carol Nadelson and Malkah Notman, "Emotional Repercussions of Rape," *Medical Aspects of Human Sexuality,* Vol. 11 (1977), pp. 16–31.

18. Ibid., p. 5

19. DOJ, *Report to the Nation on Crime and Justice,* 2nd ed., p. 5

20. FBI, *Crime in the United States, 1991.* For UCR reporting purposes "minorities" are defined as blacks, Native American, Asians, Pacific Islanders, and Alaskan Natives.

21. Sometimes called "Assault with a Deadly Weapon with Intent to Kill" or AWDWWIK.

22. DOJ, *Report to the Nation on Crime and Justice,* 2nd ed., p. 6.

23. Ibid.

24. Ibid.

25. FBI, *Crime in the United States, 1991.*

26. Ibid., p. 5.

27. As indicated in the UCR definition of arson; see FBI, *Crime in the United States, 1991.*

28. Ibid.

29. While the old rule would have counted only one murder where a woman was raped and her husband murdered in the same criminal incident, the new rule would report both a murder and a rape.

30. FBI, *Crime in the United States, 1990* (Washington, D.C.: U.S. Government Printing Office, 1991), p. 5.

31. For additional information see BJS, *Criminal Victimization in the United States, 1985.*

32. This information is mostly derived from U.S. Department of Justice, Bureau of Justice Statistics, *BJS Data Report, 1986* (Washington: U.S. Government Printing Office, 1987).

33. U.S. Department of Justice, *BJS Bulletin: Criminal Victimization, 1986* (Washington, D.C.: Bureau of Justice Statistics, October 1987), p. 2.

34. DOJ, *Report to the Nation on Crime and Justice,* 2nd ed., p. 26.

35. U.S. Department of Justice, *The Risk of Violent Crime* (Washington, D.C.: Bureau of Justice Statistics, May 1985), p. 2.

36. Catherine J. Whitaker, *The Redesigned National Crime Survey: Selected New Data* (Washington, D.C.: U.S. Government Printing Office, 1989).

37. Ibid.

38. Bruce M. Taylor, *New Directions of the National Crime Survey* (Washington, D.C.: U.S. Government Printing Office, 1989).

39. DOJ, *Report to the Nation on Crime and Justice,* 2nd ed., p. 27.

40. Georgette Bennett, *Crimewarps: The Future of Crime in America* (Garden City, NY: Anchor/Doubleday, 1987).

41. Ibid.

42. Ibid., p. xiv.

43. DOJ, *Report to the Nation on Crime and Justice,* 2nd ed., p. 24.

44. U.S. Department of Justice, *Reactions to Crime Project: Executive Summary* (Washington, D.C.: National Institute of Justice, May 1982).

45. Ibid.

46. DOJ, *Report to the Nation on Crime and Justice,* 2nd ed., p. 32.

47. The definition of rape employed by the UCR, however, automatically excludes crimes of homosexual rape such as might occur in prisons and jails. As a consequence, the rape of males is excluded from the official count for crimes of rape.

48. DOJ, *Report to the Nation on Crime and Justice,* 2nd ed., p. 25.

49. See, for example, Elizabeth Stanko, "When Precaution Is Normal: A Feminist Critique of Crime Prevention," in Loraine Gelsthorpe and Allison Morris, *Feminist Perspectives in Criminology* (Philadelphia: Open University Press, 1990).

50. "Battered Women Tell Their Stories to the Senate," *The Charlotte Observer,* July 10, 1991, p. 3A.

51.   Caroline Wolf Harlow, *Female Victims of Violent Crime* (Washington, D.C.: Bureau of Justice Statistics, 1991).

52.   Nanci Koser Wilson, "Feminist Pedagogy in Criminology," *Journal of Criminal Justice Education,* Vol. 2, no. 1 (Spring 1991), pp. 81–93.

53.   "Suspect Is Charged in 1 of 7 Murders," *The Fayetteville Observer-Times,* January 19, 1991, p. 12A.

54.   "Fla. Slayings: Men Beware," *USA Today,* December 17, 1990, p. 3A.

55.   Otto Pollak, *The Criminality of Women* (Philadelphia: University. of Philadelphia Press, 1950).

56.   FBI, *Crime in the United States, 1991.*

57.   Timothy J. Flanagan and Kathleen Maguire, *Sourcebook of Criminal Justice Statistics, 1989,* (Washington, D.C.: Bureau of Justice Statistics, 1990).

58.   Rita Simon, *Women and Crime* (Lexington, MA: D. C. Heath, 1975).

59.   Freda Adler, *Sisters in Crime: The Rise of the New Female Criminal* (New York: McGraw-Hill, 1975).

60.   Jane Roberts Chapman, *Economic Realities and the Female Offender* (Lexington, MA: Lexington Books, 1980), p. 51, as cited in Flowers, *Women and Criminality,* p. 86.

61.   Darrell J. Steffensmeir, "Sex Differences in Patterns of Adult Crime, 1965–1977: A Review and Assessment," *Social Forces,* Vol. 58 (1980), pp. 1098–1099.

62.   Flowers, *Women and Criminality,* p. 87.

63.   DOJ, *Report to the Nation on Crime and Justice,* 2nd ed., p. 25

64.   Ibid.

65.   Ibid., p. 114.

66.   Katherine M. Jamieson and Timothy J. Flanagan, eds., *Sourcebook of Criminal Justice Statistics: 1986,* U.S. Department of Justice, Bureau of Justice Statistics (Washington: U.S. Government Printing Office, 1987), p. 449.

67.   DOJ, *Report to the Nation on Crime and Justice,* 2nd ed., p. 114.

68.   Bureau of Justice Statistics, *National Update* (Washington, D.C.: U.S. Government Printing Office, 1992.

69.   Ibid.

70.   J. M. Chaiken and M. R. Chaiken, *Varieties of Criminal Behavior* (Santa Monica, CA: The Rand Corporation, 1982).

71.   D. McBride, "Trends in Drugs and Death." Paper presented at the American Society of Criminology annual meeting, Denver, Colorado, 1983.

72.   B. Johnson et al., *Taking Care of Business: The Economics of Crime by Heroin Abusers* (Lexington, MA: Lexington Books, 1985). See also Bernard A. Grooper, *Research in Brief: Probing the Links Between Drugs and Crime* (Washington, D.C.: National Institute of Justice, February 1985).

73.   DOJ, *Report to the Nation on Crime and Justice,* 2nd ed., p. 114.

74. Ibid.

75. FBI, *Crime in the United States, 1991.*

76. Bennett, *Crimewarps*, p. 57.

77. Kristina Rose and Janet Rosenbaum, *BJS Information Package: Crime and Older Americans,* (Rockville, MD: Justice Statistics Clearinghouse, 1987), p. 17.

78. Ibid., p. 18.

79. Bennett, *Crimewarps*, p. 61.

80. Catherine J. Whitaker, *BJS Special Report: Elderly Victims* (Rockville, MD: Bureau of Justice Statistics, November 1987).

81. Ibid.

82. Ibid., p. 5.

83. Ibid.

84. Rose and Rosenbaum, *BJS Information Package.*

85. Ibid.

86. U.S. Department of Justice, *Bureau of Justice Statistics Annual Report: Fiscal 1987* (Washington, D.C.: Bureau of Justice Statistics, April 1988), p. 19.

87. DOJ, *Report to the Nation on Crime and Justice,* 2nd ed., p. 10.

88. Bureau of Justice Statistics, *Electronic Fund Transfer Fraud* (Rockville, MD: Bureau of Justice Statistics, March 1985).

CHAPTER 3

CRIMINAL LAW

Law is the art of the good and the Fair.
— Ulpian, Roman judge (circa 200 A.D.)

Every law is an infraction of liberty.
— Jeremy Bentham (1748–1832)

Law should be like death, which spares no one
— Montesquieu (1689–1755)

KEY CONCEPTS

jural postulates	procedural law	precedent
misdemeanor	felony	Code of Hammurabi
civil law	criminal law	tort
McNaughten rule	entrapment	substantial capacity
codification		*stare decisis*

□ SOURCES OF MODERN CRIMINAL LAW

Twenty years ago, as South American jungles were being cleared to make way for farmers and other settlers, a group of mercenaries brutally attacked and wiped out a small tribe of local Indians. About 20 Indian men, women, and children were hacked to death with machetes or shot. The Indians had refused to give up their land and would not move. At their arrest the killers uttered something that, to our ears, sounds frightening: "How can you arrest us?" they said. "We didn't know it was illegal to kill Indians!"

These men killed many people. But, they claimed, they were ignorant of the fact that the law forbade such a thing in this case.   Their ignorance of the law was rejected as a defense at their trial, and they were convicted of murder. All received lengthy prison sentences.

The men in this story were hardly literate, with almost no formal education. They knew very little about the law and, apparently, even less about basic moral principles. We, on the other hand, living in a modern society with highly developed means of communications, much formal schooling, and a large work force of professionals skilled in interpreting the law, usually know what the law *says*. But do we really know what the law *is?*

Most of us would probably agree that the law is whatever legislators tell us it is. If we hold to that belief, we would expect to be able to find the law unambiguously specified, in a set of books or codes.

Practically speaking, the laws of a nation or of a state are found in statutory provisions and constitutional enactments, as well as in the rulings of courts. According to the authoritative *Black's Law Dictionary,* the word *law* "generally contemplates both statutory and case law." If the law could be found entirely ensconced in written legal codes we would need far fewer lawyers than we find practicing today. Some laws (in the sense of precedents established by the courts) do not exist "on the books," but even those that do are open to interpretation.   A complete and accurate understanding of modern American criminal law can only be had by someone who is informed as to both its history and philosophical foundation.

> **Law:** A rule of conduct, generally enacted as a statute by a legislative body, and which is enforced by some designated authority.

THE CODE OF HAMMURABI

Modern law is the result of a long evolution of legal principles. The Code of Hammurabi is one of the first known bodies of law to survive and be available for study today. King Hammurabi ruled the ancient city of Babylon around the year 2000 B.C. The Code of Hammurabi is a set of laws engraved on stone tablets which were intended to establish property and other rights. Babylon was a commercial center, and the right of private property formed a crucial basis for prosperous growth. Hammurabi's laws spoke to issues of theft, ownership, sexual relationships, and interpersonal violence.   As Marvin Wolfgang has observed, "In its day, 1700 B.C., the Hammurabi Code, with its emphasis on retribution, amounted to a brilliant advance in penal philosophy mainly because it represented an attempt to keep cruelty within bounds."[1]   Prior to the Code, captured offenders often faced the most barbarous of punishments, frequently at the hands of revenge-seeking victims, no matter how minor their offenses had been.

EARLY ROMAN LAW

Of considerable significance for our own legal tradition is early Roman law. Roman legions under the Emperor Claudius conquered England in the mid-first century. Roman authority over "Britannia" was consolidated by later rulers who built walls and fortifications to keep out the still-hostile Scots.   Roman customs, law, and language were forced upon the English population during the succeeding three centuries under the *Pax Romana* — a peace imposed by the military might of Rome.[2]

Roman law derived from the Twelve Tables, which were written about 450 B.C. The Twelve Tables were a collection of basic rules related to family, religious, and economic life. The tables appear to have been based upon common and fair practices generally accepted among early tribes which existed prior to the establishment of the Roman Republic. Unfortunately, only fragments of the tables survive today.

The best known legal period in Roman history occurred under the rule of the Emperor Justinian I, who ruled between 527 and 565 A.D.   By the sixth century, the Roman Empire had declined substantially in size and influence and was near the end of its life. In what may have been an effort to preserve Roman values and traditions, Justinian undertook the laborious process of distilling Roman laws into a set of writings.   The Justinian Code actually consisted of three lengthy legal documents: (1) the Institutes, (2) the Digest, and (3) the Code itself. Justinian's code distinguished between two major legal categories: public and private laws. Public laws dealt with the organization of the Roman state, its Senate, and governmental offices. Private law concerned itself with contracts, personal possessions, the legal status of various types of persons (citizens, free persons, slaves, freedmen, guardians, husbands and wives, etc.), and injuries to citizens. It contained elements of both our modern civil and criminal law, and, no doubt, influenced Western legal thought through the Middle Ages.

COMMON LAW

Common law forms the basis of much of our modern statutory and case law. It has often been called *the* major source of modern criminal law. Common law refers to a traditional body of unwritten legal precedents created through everyday practice and supported by court decisions during the Middle Ages in English society. As novel situations arose and were dealt with by British justices, their declarations became the start for any similar future deliberation. These decisions generally incorporated the customs of society as it operated at the time.

Common law was given considerable legitimacy upon the official declaration that it was the law of the land by the English King Edward the Confessor in the eleventh century.

The authority of common law was further reinforced by the decision of William the Conqueror to use popular customs as the basis for judicial action following his subjugation of Britain in 1066 A.D.

> **Common Law:** A body of unwritten judicial opinion which was based on customary social practices of Anglo-Saxon society during the Middle Ages.

Eventually, court decisions were recorded and made available to barristers (the English word for trial lawyers) and judges. As Abadinsky says, "Common law involved the transformation of community rules into a national legal system. The controlling element (was) precedent."[3]

THE MAGNA CARTA

The Magna Carta (literally, "great charter") is another important source of modern laws and legal procedure. The Magna Carta was signed on June 15, 1215, by King John of England at Runnymede, under pressure from British barons who took advantage of John's military defeats at the hands of Pope Innocent III and King Philip Augustus of France. The barons demanded a pledge from the king to respect their traditional rights and forced the king to agree to be bound by law.

At the time of its signing, the Magna Carta, although 63 chapters in length, was little more than a feudal document[4] listing specific Royal concessions. It's wording, however, was later interpreted during a judicial revolt in 1613 to support individual rights. Sir Edward Coke, chief justice under James I, held that the Magna Carta guaranteed basic liberties for all British citizens and ruled that any acts of Parliament which contravened common law would be void. There is some evidence that this famous ruling became the basis for the rise of the U.S. Supreme Court, with its power to nullify laws enacted by Congress.[5] Similarly, one specific provision of the Magna Carta, designed originally to prohibit the king from prosecuting the barons without just cause, was expanded into the concept of "due process of law," a fundamental cornerstone of modern legal procedure. Because of these later interpretations the Magna Carta has been called "the foundation stone of our present liberties."[6]

THE U.S. CONSTITUTION

The U.S. Constitution is one of the most significant and enduring wellsprings of our modern criminal law. The Constitution was created through a long process of debate by the federal Constitutional Convention meeting in Philadelphia in 1787. The Constitution is the final authority in all questions pertaining to the rights of individuals, the power of the federal government and the states to create laws and prosecute offenders, and the limits of punishment which can be imposed for law violations.

Although the Constitution does not itself contain many prohibitions on behavior, it is the final authority in deciding whether existing laws are acceptable according to the principles upon which our country is founded. Historically, it has served to guide justices in gauging the merits of citizen's claims concerning the handling of their cases by the agencies of justice.

TABLE 3-1
Sources of the Law

Historical Sources of the Law	Modern Sources of American Law
Arguments from nature	The U.S. Constitution
Roman law	The Declaration of Independence
The Old and New Testaments	Statutes
The Magna Carta	Case law
Common law	
Religious belief and practice	

NATURAL LAW

Some people believe that the basis for many of our criminal laws can be found in immutable moral principles or some identifiable aspect of the natural order. The Ten Commandments, "inborn tendencies," the idea of sin, and perceptions of various forms of order in the universe and in the social world have all provided a basis for the assertion that a "natural law" exists. Natural law comes from outside the social group and is thought to be knowable through some form of revelation, intuition, or prophecy.

Natural law was used by the early Christian church as a powerful argument in support of its interests. Secular rulers were pressed to reinforce Church doctrine in any laws they decreed. Thomas Aquinas wrote in his *Summa Theologica* that any man-made law which contradicts natural law is corrupt in the eyes of God.[7] Religious practice, which strongly reflected natural law conceptions, was central to the life of early British society. Hence, natural law, as it was understood at the time, was incorporated into English common law throughout the Middle Ages.

The Constitution of the United States is built around an understanding of the natural law as held by Thomas Jefferson and other framers of that important document. When Jefferson wrote of inalienable rights to "life, liberty, property," he meant they were the natural due of all men and women. Truths which are held to be "self-evident" can be such only if they are somehow available to us all through reasoning or the promptings of conscience.

Students of natural law have set for themselves the task of uncovering just what that law encompasses. The modern debate over abortion is an example of the use of natural law arguments to support both sides in the dispute. Antiabortion forces, frequently called "prolifers," claim that the unborn fetus is a person, and that he or she is entitled to all the protections that we would give to any other living human being. Such protection, they suggest, is basic and humane, and lies in the natural relationship of one human being to another. They are striving for passage of a law, or a reinterpretation of past Supreme Court precedent which would support their position.

Supporters of the present law (which allows abortion upon request under certain conditions) maintain that abortion is a "right" of any pregnant woman because she is the one in control of her body. Such "prochoice" groups also claim that the legal system must address the abortion question, but only by way of offering protection to this "natural right" of women. Keep in mind, however, that what we refer to as "the present law" is not so much a law "on the books," but rather a consequence of a decision rendered by the U.S. Supreme Court in the case of *Roe* v. *Wade*.[8]

Mala in Se/Mala Prohibita

Natural law lends credence to the belief that certain actions are *wrong in themselves*. These behaviors are called *mala in se,* a Latin term which generally includes murder, rape, theft, arson, and other crimes of violence. Some states have legislated a special offense category called crime against nature. Crimes against nature, as specified in modern law, mostly encompass sexual deviance which is regarded as "contrary to the order of nature." Homosexuality, lesbianism, bestiality, and oral copulation are often prosecuted under these statutes, and may carry with them quite severe punishments.

Crimes which fall outside of this "natural" category are called *mala prohibita,* meaning that they are wrong only because they are prohibited by the law. Poaching on the king's land is an example of what was a *mala prohibita* crime under English common law.

It is easy to imagine that primitive societies, without a system of codified statutes, would still understand that some forms of behavior are wrong. This intuitive recognition of deviance forms the basis of both natural law and the classification of certain offenses as *mala in se.*

The terminology which distinguished *mala in se* from *mala prohibita* offenses derives from common law, and was an important consideration in deciding sentences in early England. *Mala prohibita* crimes were tried by justices of the peace and carried penalties which were generally far less severe than those for *mala in se* crimes.

PURPOSES OF THE LAW

Max Weber, an eminent sociologist of the early twentieth century, said the primary purpose of law was to regulate the flow of human interaction.[9] By creating enforceable rules, laws make the behavior of others predictable. This first, and most significant, purpose of the law can be simply stated: laws support social order.

Laws also serve a variety of other purposes. They ensure that the philosophical, moral, and economic perspectives of their creators are protected and made credible; they maintain values and uphold established patterns of social privilege; they sustain existing power relationships; and finally, they support a system for the punishment and rehabilitation of offenders.   Modifications of the law, when gradually induced, promote orderly change in the rest of society.

TABLE 3-2
What Does Law Do?

THE FUNCTIONS OF LAW

Laws Maintain Order in Society
Laws Regulate Human Interaction
Laws Enforce Moral Beliefs
Laws Define the Economic Environment
Laws Support the Powerful
Laws Promote Orderly Social Change
Laws Sustain Individual Rights
Laws Redress Wrongs
Laws Identify Evil-doers
Laws Mandate Punishment and Retribution

The question of *what the law does* is quite different from the question of *what the law should do*. Writing in the mid-1800s, John Stuart Mill questioned the liberal use of the criminal law as a tool for social reform.[10] Mill objected strongly to the use of law as a "way of compulsion and control" for any purpose other than to prevent harm to others. Behavior which might be thought morally "wrong" should not be contravened by law, said Mill, unless it was also harmful to others.   In similar fashion, Nigel Walker, a British criminologist of this century, applied what he called "a sociological eye" to the criminal codes of Western nations, and concluded that criminal statutes are not appropriate which seek to contravene behavior which lacks a clear and immediate harm to others; nor, he said, should laws be created for the purpose of compelling people to act in their own good.[11]

In reality, few legal codes live up to the Walker–Mill criteria. Most are influenced strongly by cultural conceptions of right and wrong and encompass many behaviors which are not immediately and directly harmful to anyone but those who choose to be involved in them. These illegal activities, often called victimless crimes, or social order offenses, include drug abuse, certain forms of "deviant" sexuality, gambling, and, various other legally proscribed consensual deeds. Advocates of legislation designed to curb these activities suggest that while such behavior is not always directly harmful to others, it may erode social cohesiveness, and ruin the lives of those who engage in it.

Standing in strong opposition to the Walker–Mills perspective are legislators and theorists who purposefully use the law as a tool to facilitate social change. Modifications in the legal structure of a society can quickly and dramatically produce changes in the behavior of entire groups. A change in the tax laws, for example, typically sends people scrambling to their accountants to devise spending and investment strategies which can take advantage of the change.

Our legal system, for example, not only condemns interpersonal violence, but also supports the dominant economic order (capitalism) and protects the powerful and the wealthy (through an emphasis on private property and the rights which attach to property).

Throughout American criminal law, Judeo-Christian principles hold considerable sway. Concepts such as sin and atonement provide for a view of men and women as willful actors in a world of personal and sensual temptations. Such ideas have made possible both the legal notion of *guilt* and the correctional ideal of individual *reformation*.

The realization that laws respond to the needs and interests of society at any given time was put into words by the popular jurist Oliver Wendell Holmes in an address he gave at Harvard in 1881. Holmes said: "The life of the law has not been logic: it has been experience. The felt necessities of the time, the prevalent moral and political theories, institutions of public policy, avowed or unconscious, even the prejudices which judges share with their fellowmen have had a good deal more to do than the syllogism in determining the rules by which men should be governed."[12] The "syllogism," as Holmes used the term, referred to idealized theorizing as the basis for law. The importance of such "theorizing" he thoroughly discounted. Once law has been created it is generally slow to change, because it is built upon years of tradition. The law can be thought of as a force which supports social order, but which is opposed to rapid social change. When law facilitates change, that change usually proceeds in an orderly and deliberate fashion. Revolutions, on the other hand, produce near-instantaneous legal changes, but bring with them massive social disorder.

Jural Postulates

One of the greatest legal scholars of modern times was Roscoe Pound, dean of the Harvard Law School during the years 1916–1936. Pound saw the law as a type of social engineering.[13] The law is a tool, he said, which meets the demands of men and women living together in society. Pound strongly believed that the law must be able to change with the times, and to reflect new needs as they arise.

Pound distilled his ideas into a set of jural postulates. Such postulates, claimed Pound, form the basis of all law because they reflect shared needs. In 1942 Pound published his postulates in the form of five propositions.[14] They are:

❶ In civilized society men must be able to assume that others will commit no intentional aggressions upon them.

❷ In civilized society men must be able to assume that they may control for beneficial purposes what they have discovered and appropriated to their own use, what they have created by their own labor, and what they have acquired under the existing social and economic order.

❸ In civilized society men must be able to assume that those with whom they deal in the general intercourse of society will act in good faith and hence:

➥ Will make good reasonable expectations which their promises or other conduct will reasonably create;

➥ Will carry out their undertakings according to the expectations which the moral sentiment of the community attaches thereto;

➥ Will restore specifically or by equivalent what comes to them by mistake or unanticipated or (via a) not fully intended situation whereby they receive at another's expense what they could not reasonably have expected to receive under the circumstances.

❹ In civilized society men must be able to assume that those who are engaged in some course of conduct will act with due care not to cause an unreasonable risk of injury upon others.

❺ In civilized society men must be able to assume that those who maintain things likely to get out of hand or to escape and do damage will restrain them or keep them within their proper bounds.

Pound's postulates form a theory of "consensus" about the origins of law — both civil and criminal. They suggest that most laws are the product of shared social needs experienced by the majority of members in the society where they arise. However, a number of writers have criticized Pound for failing to recognize the diversity of society. How, they ask, can the law address common needs in society when society consists of many different groups — each with their own set of interests and needs? As a consequence of such criticism Pound modified his theory to include a jurisprudence of interest. The concept of jurisprudence held that one of the basic purposes of law is to satisfy "as many claims or demands of as many people as possible."[15]

CONFLICT THEORY

Opposed to Pound's theory of consensus is William Chambliss's view of law as a tool of powerful individuals and groups acting in their own interests, and often in conflict with one another.[16] Conflict theory has its roots in the writings of Karl Marx, who explained all of social history as the result of an ongoing conflict between the "haves" and the "have-nots."

Chambliss believes we should not see the agencies of criminal justice as "neutral." Rather, he says, government is "a weapon of the dominant classes or interest groups in society."[17] Putting it more mildly, Chambliss also writes, "in one way or another, the laws which are passed, implemented, and incorporated into the legal system reflect the interests of those groups capable of having their views incorporated into the official (that is, legal) views of the society."[18]

❑ TYPES OF LAW

"Criminal" and "civil" law are the best known types of modern law.   However, scholars and philosophers have drawn numerous distinctions between categories of the law which rest upon their source, intent, and application.   Laws in modern societies can be usefully described in terms of the following groups:

➊ Criminal law
➋ Case law
➌ Procedural law
➍ Civil law
➎ Administrative law
➏ Constitutional law

CRIMINAL LAW

Criminal law is theoretically distinguishable from civil law primarily by the assertion that criminal acts injure not just individuals, but society as a whole.   Social order, as reflected in the values supported by statute, is reduced to some degree whenever a criminal act occurs.   In olden times offenders were said to violate the "King's Peace" when they committed a crime.   They offended not just the victim, but contravened the order established under the rule of the monarch.

In criminal cases, the state, as the injured party, begins the process of bringing the offender to justice.   Even if the victim is dead and has no one to speak on their behalf, the agencies of justice will investigate the crime and file charges against the offender.

> **Criminal Law:** That branch of modern law which concerns itself with offenses committed against society, members thereof, their property, and the social order.

Violations of the criminal law result in the imposition of punishment. Punishment is philosophically justified by the fact that the criminal *intended* the harm and is responsible for it. Punishment serves a variety of purposes, which we will discuss later in the chapter on sentencing. When punishment is imposed in a criminal case, however, it is for one basic reason: to express society's fundamental displeasure with the offensive behavior.

Criminal law functions to define offenses against individuals which are also offenses against the state. Because crimes injure the fabric of society, it is the state which becomes the plaintiff in criminal proceedings. Court cases reflect this fact by being cited as follows: *State of New York* v. *Smith* (where state law has been violated) or *U.S.* v. *Smith* (where the federal government is the injured party).

Criminal law is composed of statutory and case law. It is built upon constitutional principles and operates within the system established by procedural laws.

Statutory law is the "law on the books." It is the result of legislative action and is often thought of as the "law of the land." Written laws exist in both criminal and civil areas and are called codes. Federal statutes are compiled in the United States Code (U.S.C.) and the United States Code Annotated (U.S.C.A). State codes and municipal ordinances are also readily available in written, or statutory, form. The written form of the criminal law is called the penal code.

Written criminal law in this country is of two types: substantive and procedural. Substantive law deals directly with specifying the nature of, and appropriate punishments for, particular offenses. For example, every state in our country has laws against murder, rape, robbery, and assault. Differences in the law among these various jurisdictions can be studied in detail because each offense and the punishments associated with it are available in the substantive law in written form.

CASE LAW

Case law is also referred to as the law of precedent. It represents the accumulated wisdom of trial and appellate courts over the years. Once a court decision is rendered it is written down. At the appellate level, the reasoning behind the decision is recorded as well. Under the rule of precedent, this reasoning should then be taken into consideration by other courts in settling future cases.

Appellate courts have considerable power to influence new court decisions at the trial level. The court with the greatest influence, of course, is the U.S. Supreme Court. The precedents it establishes are incorporated as guidelines into the process of legal reasoning by which lower courts reach conclusions.

The principle of recognizing previous decisions as precedents to guide future deliberations is called *stare decisis* and forms the basis for our modern "law of precedent." Lief H. Carter has pointed out how precedent operates along two dimensions.[19] He calls them the vertical and the horizontal. The vertical rule requires that decisions made by a higher court be taken into consideration by lower courts in their deliberations. Under this rule, state appellate courts, for example, should be expected to follow the spirit of decisions rendered by their state supreme courts.

> **Precedent:** A legal principle which operates to insure that previous judicial decisions are authoritatively considered and incorporated into future cases.

The horizontal dimension means that courts on the same level should be consistent in their interpretation of the law. The U.S. Supreme Court, operating under the horizontal rule, for example, should not be expected to change its ruling in cases similar to those it has already decided.

Stare decisis makes for predictability in the law. Defendants walking into a modern courtroom will have the opportunity to be represented by lawyers who are trained in legal precedents as well as procedure. As a consequence, they will have a good idea of what to expect about the manner in which their trial will proceed.

PROCEDURAL LAW

Procedural law is another kind of statutory law. It is a body of rules which regulate the processing of an offender by the criminal justice system. Procedural law, for example, specifies in most jurisdictions that the testimony of one party to certain "victimless crimes" cannot be used as the sole evidence against the other party. General rules of evidence, search and seizure, procedures to be followed in an arrest, and other specified processes by which the justice system operates are contained in procedural law.

As a great jurist once said, however, the law is like a living thing. It changes and evolves over time. Legislatures enact new statutory laws, and justices set new precedents, sometimes overruling established ones. Many jurisdictions today, for example, are beginning to allow wives to bring charges of rape against their husbands. Similarly, wives may testify against their husbands in certain cases, even though both actions are contrary to years of previously created precedents.

CIVIL LAW

Civil law provides a formal means for regulating noncriminal relationships between persons. The body of civil law contains rules for divorce, child support and custody, the creation of wills, property transfers, negligence, libel, and many other contractual and social obligations. When the civil law is violated, a civil suit may follow.

Civil suits seek not punishment, but compensation, usually in the form of property or monetary damages. They may also be filed in order to achieve an injunction, or a kind of judicial cease-and-desist order. A violation of the civil law may be a tort (a breach of duty), or a contract violation, but it is not a crime. Because a tort is an injury to an individual, it is left to that individual to set the machinery of the court in motion.

Civil law is more concerned with assigning "blame" than it is with intent. Civil suits arising from automobile crashes, for example, do not allege that either driver intended to inflict bodily harm. Nor do they claim that it was the intent of the driver to damage either vehicle. However, when someone is injured, or property damage occurs, even in an accident, civil procedures make it possible to gauge responsibility and assign blame to one party or the other. The parties to a civil suit are referred to as the plaintiff and the defendant.

> **Civil Law:** That portion of the modern law which regulates contracts and other obligations involving primarily personal interests.

Civil law pertains to injuries suffered by individuals which are unfair or unjust according to the standards operative in the social group. Breeches of contract, unfair practices in hiring, the manufacture and sale of consumer goods with hidden hazards for the user, and slanderous comments made about others have all been common grounds for civil suits. Suits may, on occasion, arise as extensions of criminal action. Monetary compensation, for example, may be sought through our system of civil laws by a victim of a criminal assault after a criminal conviction has been obtained.

Following the murder a few years ago of Sandra Black, for example, her son and mother successfully sued *Soldier of Fortune* magazine, winning damages of $9.4 million.[20] *Soldier of Fortune* had printed a classified advertisement by a "mercenary" who, as a result of the ad, eventually contracted with Mrs. Black's husband to commit the murder. In a quite different type of civil suit, Robert McLaughlin was awarded $1.9 million by a New York state Court of Claims in October 1989, after having spent six and one-half years in prison for a murder and robbery he did not commit.[21]

ADMINISTRATIVE LAW

Administrative law refers to the body of regulations which have been created by governments to control the economic activities of industry, business, and individuals. Tax laws, health codes, restrictions on pollution and waste disposal, vehicle registration, building codes, and the like are examples of administrative law.

Other administrative laws cover practices in the areas of customs (imports/exports), immigration, agriculture, product safety, and most areas of manufacturing. Modern individualists claim that overregulation characterizes the American way of life, although they are in turn criticized for failing to recognize adequately the complexity of modern society. Overregulation has also been used on occasion as a rallying cry for political hopefuls who believe that many Americans wish to return to an earlier and simpler form of free enterprise.

Although the criminal law is, for the most part, separate from administrative regulations, the two may overlap. For instance, the rise in organized criminal activity in the area of toxic waste disposal has led to criminal prosecutions in several states. Denial of civil rights is another area which may lead to criminal sanctions through the federal system of laws.

Administrative agencies will sometimes issue consent decrees which fall short of court action, but which are considered binding on individuals or groups who have not lived up to the intent of federal regulations. Education, environmental protection, and discriminatory hiring practices are all areas in which consent decrees have been employed.

ELEMENTS OF CRIMINAL OFFENSES

Statutory law specifies exactly what constitutes a crime. The crime of first-degree murder, for example, in almost every jurisdiction in the United States involves four elements:

      ❶ An unlawful killing
      ❷ Of a human being
      ❸ Intentionally
      ❹ With malice

A CAREER WITH THE IMMIGRATION
AND NATURALIZATION SERVICE

Typical Positions. Special agent, immigration examiner, border patrol agent, immigration inspector, deportation officer.

Employment Requirements. Applicants for the position of special agent must meet the general requirements for a federal law enforcement officer and must (1) be a U.S. citizen; (2) hold a Bachelor's degree or have 3 years of responsible experience, or an equivalent combination of education and experience; (3) be in excellent physical condition, with good eyesight and hearing; (4) submit to urinalysis screening prior to employment; (5) possess emotional and mental stability; (6) be 21–34 years of age at the time of employment; (7) have no felony convictions or records of improper or criminal conduct.

Other Requirements. Border patrol agents are required to demonstrate proficiency in the Spanish language.

Salary. All positions provide for entry at GS-5 or GS-7 levels, depending upon qualifications. A Bachelor's degree qualifies applicants for appointment at the GS-5 level (earning $19,456 or more in mid-1993). Individuals with exceptional experience or education may be appointed at the GS-7 level. ($23,366 and higher in mid-1993).

Benefits. Paid annual vacation, sick leave, life and health insurance, and a liberal retirement plan.

Direct Inquiries to: Immigration and Naturalization Service, U.S. Department of Justice, 425 I Street, N.W., Washington, D.C. 20536. Phone: (202) 514-2000 or 2525.

The elements of a crime are the statutory minimum without which a crime cannot be said to have occurred. In any case that goes to trial, the task of the prosecution is to prove that all the elements were indeed present and that the accused was ultimately responsible for producing them.

Every element in a crime serves some purpose and is necessary. The crime of first-degree murder, for example, includes *an unlawful killing*. Even if all the other elements of first-degree murder are present, the act may still not be first-degree murder if the first element is not met. In a wartime situation, for instance, killings of human beings occur. They are committed with planning and, sometimes, with "malice." They are certainly intentional. Yet killing in war is not unlawful, so long as the belligerents wage war according to international conventions.

The second element of first-degree murder specifies that the killing must be of a "human being." People kill all the time. They kill animals for meat, they hunt, and they practice euthanasia upon aged and injured pets. Even if the killing of an animal is planned and involves malice (perhaps a vendetta against a neighborhood dog which wrecks trash cans), it does not constitute first-degree murder. Such a killing, however, may violate statutes pertaining to cruelty to animals.

The third element of first-degree murder, "intentionality," is the basis for the defense of accident. An unintentional killing is not necessarily first-degree murder, although it may violate some other statute.

Finally, murder has not been committed unless "malice" is involved. There are different kinds of malice. Second-degree murder involves malice in the sense of hatred or spite. A more extreme form of malice is necessary for a finding of first degree murder. Sometimes the phrase used to describe this type of feeling is "malice aforethought." This extreme kind of malice can be demonstrated by showing that planning was involved in the commission of the murder. Often, first-degree murder is described as "lying in wait," a practice which shows that thought and planning went into the illegal killing.

GENERAL CATEGORIES OF CRIME

Misdemeanors

Violations of the criminal law can be more or less serious. Misdemeanors are relatively minor crimes. They are usually thought of as any crime punishable by a year or less in prison. In fact, most misdemeanants receive suspended sentences involving a fine and supervised probation. If an "active sentence" is received for a misdemeanor violation of the law, it probably will involve time in a local jail, perhaps on weekends, rather than imprisonment in a long-term facility. Some misdemeanants have recently been sentenced to community service activities, requiring them to do such things as wash school buses, paint local government buildings, or clean parks and other public areas.

Normally, a police officer cannot arrest a person for a misdemeanor, unless the crime was committed in the officer's presence. If the in-presence requirement is missing, the officer will need to seek an arrest warrant from a magistrate or other judicial officer. Once a warrant has been issued, the officer may proceed with the arrest.

Felonies

Felonies are serious crimes. Under common law, felons could be sentenced to death and/or have their property confiscated. Many felons receive prison sentences, although the potential range of penalties can include anything from probation and a fine to capital punishment in many jurisdictions. The federal

Copyright 1990 by USA Today. Reprinted with permission.
In American society enforcement agents must adhere to the requirements of due process.

government and many states have moved to a scheme of classifying felonies, from most to least serious, using a number or letter designation. The federal system,[22] for example, for purposes of criminal sentencing, assigns a score of 43 to first-degree murder, while the crime of theft is only rated a "base offense level" of 4. Attendant circumstances and the criminal history of the offender are also taken into consideration in sentencing decisions.

> **Misdemeanor:** An offense punishable by incarceration, usually in a local confinement facility, for a period of which the upper limit is prescribed by statute in a given jurisdiction, typically limited to a year or less.

Because of differences between the states, a crime classified as a felony in one part of the country may be a misdemeanor in another. This is especially true of drug law violations and certain other "victimless" crimes such as homosexuality, prostitution, and gambling.

People who have been convicted of felonies usually lose certain privileges. Some states make conviction of a felony and incarceration grounds for uncontested divorce. Others prohibit offenders from running for public office or owning a firearm and exclude them from some professions such as medicine, law, and police work.

> **Felony:** A criminal offense punishable by death or by incarceration in a prison facility for at least a year.

Offenses

A third category of crime is the offense. Offenses are minor violations of the law such as jaywalking, spitting on the sidewalk, littering, and certain traffic violations, including the failure to wear a seat belt. Another word used to describe offenses is infraction. People committing infractions are typically ticketed and released, usually upon a promise to later appear in court. Court appearances may often be waived through payment of a small fine, which is often mailed in.

SPECIAL CATEGORIES

Treason

Felonies, misdemeanors, offenses, and the people who commit them comprise the daily work of the justice system. Special categories of crime, however, exist and should be recognized. Treason is one of these. Treason has been defined as "the act of a U.S. citizen's helping a foreign government to overthrow, make war against, or seriously injure the United States." Espionage, an offense akin to treason, refers to the "gathering, transmitting or losing"[23] of information related to the national defense in such a manner that the information becomes available to enemies of the United States and may be used to their advantage. In 1985, in what may have been the last widely publicized incident of espionage of the cold war period, John Walker, a retired Navy warrant officer, and his son Michael, a radio operator aboard the *U.S.S. Nimitz*, a nuclear-powered aircraft carrier, pled guilty to the charge of selling U.S. Navy secrets, including codes and details of tracking the movement of ships and submarines, to the Soviets. The father's espionage had gone undetected for 20 years, causing considerable damage to American's security network.

Treason and espionage may be committed for personal gain, for ideological reasons, or for both. They are crimes only under federal law, and they are often regarded as the most serious of felonies.

Inchoate Offenses

Another special category of crime is called inchoate. Inchoate offenses are those which have not been fully carried out. Conspiracies are an example. When a person conspires to commit a crime, any action undertaken in furtherance of the conspiracy is generally regarded as a sufficient basis for arrest and prosecution. For instance, a woman who intends to kill her husband may make a phone call in order to find a "hit man" to carry out her plan. The call itself is evidence of her intent and can result in her imprisonment for conspiring to murder.

Another type of inchoate offense is the attempt. Sometimes an offender is not able to complete the crime. Homeowners may arrive just as a burglar is beginning to enter their residence. The burglar may drop his tools and run. Even so, in most jurisdictions, this frustrated burglar can be arrested and charged with attempted burglary.

❏ THE ELEMENTS OF A CRIME

CORPUS DELICTI

Traditionally, a crime can be said to have occurred only if certain necessary elements are present. *Corpus delicti* is a Latin term which refers to the "body of the crime." It does *not* mean the body of the victim, as is sometimes thought. For a criminal definition to be imposed upon a social situation, it is necessary that the "body of the crime" be established. In other words, the elements which constitute a crime must be present. Each offense defined by law contains specific elements, as discussed earlier in the example of first-degree murder. All crimes, however, can be said to share certain general elements, which are described here.

THE CRIMINAL ACT

A necessary first element is some act in violation of the law. Such an act is termed the *actus reus* of a crime. The term means a "guilty act." Generally, a person must commit some act before they are subject to criminal sanctions. Someone who admits (perhaps on a TV talk show) that he or she is a drug user, for example, cannot be arrested on that basis. To *be* something is not a crime — to *do* something is. In the case of the admitted drug user, police who heard the admission might begin gathering evidence to prove some specific law violation in that person's past, or perhaps they might watch that individual for future behavior in violation of the law. An arrest might then occur. If it did, it would be based upon a specific action in violation of the law pertaining to controlled substances.

Vagrancy laws, popular in the early part of the twentieth century have generally been invalidated by the courts because they did not specify what act violated the law. In fact, the *less* a person did, the more vagrant they were.

An *omission to act*, however, may be criminal where the person in question is required by law to do something. Child neglect laws, for example, focus on parents and child guardians who do not live up to their responsibilities in caring for their children.

Threatening to act can itself be a criminal offense. Telling someone, "I'm going to kill you," might result in an arrest based upon the offense of "communicating threats." Threatening the president of the United States is taken seriously by the Secret Service, and individuals are regularly arrested for boasting about planned violence to be directed at the president.

Attempted criminal activity is also illegal. An attempt to murder or rape, for example, is a serious crime, even though the planned act was not accomplished.

Conspiracy statutes were mentioned earlier in this chapter. When a conspiracy unfolds, the ultimate act that it aims to bring about does not have to occur for the parties to the conspiracy to be arrested. When people plan to bomb a public building, for example, they can be legally stopped before the bombing. As soon as they take steps to "further" their plan, they have met the requirement for an act. Buying explosives, telephoning one another, or drawing plans of the building may all be actions in "furtherance of the conspiracy."

MENS REA

Mens rea is the second element of a crime. It literally means "guilty mind," and recognizes a mental component to crime. The modern interpretation of *mens rea,* however, does not focus so much on whether a person feels guilty about his or her act — but rather looks to whether or not the act was intended. As the famous Supreme Court Justice Oliver Wendell Holmes once wrote, "even a dog distinguishes between being stumbled over and being kicked."[24]

> **Mens Rea:** The state of mind which accompanies a criminal act. Also, guilty mind.

The idea of *mens rea* has undergone a gradual evolution during recent centuries such that today the term can be generally described as signifying blameworthiness. The question asked, at least theoretically, in criminal prosecutions, is whether or not the person charged with an offense *should be blamed* and held accountable for their actions.

Mens rea is said to be present when a person *should have known better*, even if they did not directly intend the consequences of their action. A person who acts recklessly, and thereby endangers others, may be found guilty of a crime when a harm occurs, even though no negative consequences were intended. For example, a mother who left her 15-month-old child alone in the tub can be later prosecuted for negligent homicide if the child drowns.

It should be recognized, however, that negligence in and of itself is not a crime. Negligent conduct can be evidence of a crime only when it falls below some acceptable standard of care. That standard is today applied in courts through the fictional creation of a *reasonable person*. The question to be asked in a given case is whether or not a reasonable person, in the same situation, would have known better, and acted differently, than the defendant. The reasonable person criteria provides a yardstick for juries faced with thorny issues of guilt or innocence.

CONCURRENCE

The concurrence of act and intent is the third element of a crime. A person may intend to kill a rival, for example. As they drive to the intended victim's house, gun in hand, fantasizing about how they will commit the murder, the victim may be crossing the street on the way home from grocery shopping. If the two collide, and the intended victim dies, there has been no concurrence of act and intent.

The three elements of a crime we have just outlined are regarded by some legal scholars as sufficient to constitute the *corpus delicti* of a crime. When all three are present in a given situation, a crime has occurred. Other scholars, however, see modern Western law as more complex. They argue that four additional principles are necessary before the *corpus delicti* can be established. They are (1) a harm, (2) a causal relationship between the act and the harm, (3) the principle of legality, and (4) the principle of punishment.

HARM

A harm occurs in any crime, although not all harms are crimes. When a person is murdered or raped, harm can clearly be identified. Some crimes, however, have come to be called "victimless." Perpetrators maintain that they are not harming anyone in committing such crimes. Rather, they say, the crime is pleasurable. Prostitution, gambling, homosexuality, "crimes against nature" (sexual deviance), and drug use are but a few crimes classified as "victimless." People involved in such crimes will argue that, if anyone is being hurt, it is only they. What these offenders fail to recognize is the social harm caused by their behavior. Areas afflicted with chronic prostitution, drug use, sexual deviance, and gambling usually will find property values falling, family life disintegrating, and other, more traditional crimes increasing as money is sought to support the "victimless" activities and law-abiding citizens flee the area.

CAUSATION

Causation refers to the fact that a clear link needs to be identifiable between the act and the harm occasioned by the crime. A classic example of this principle involves assault with a deadly weapon with intent to kill. If a person shoots another, but the victim is seriously injured and not killed, the victim might survive for a long time in a hospital. Death may occur, perhaps a year later, because pneumonia sets in or because blood clots form in the injured person from lack of activity. In such cases, defense attorneys will likely argue that the defendant did not cause the death, but rather that death occurred because of disease.

LEGALITY

The principle of legality is concerned with the fact that a behavior cannot be criminal if no law exists which defines it as such. It is OK to drink beer, if you are of "drinking age," because there is no statute "on the books" prohibiting it. During prohibition times, of course, the situation was quite different. (In fact, some parts of the United States are still "dry," and the purchase or public consumption of alcohol can be a law violation regardless of age.) The principle of legality also includes the notion that a law cannot be created tomorrow which will hold a person legally responsible for something he or she does today. These are called *ex post facto* laws. Laws are binding only from the date of their creation or from some future date at which they are specified as taking effect.

PUNISHMENT

Finally, the principle of punishment says that no crime can be said to occur where a punishment has not been specified in the law. Larceny, for example, would not be a crime in a jurisdiction where the law simply said, "It is illegal to steal." A punishment needs to be specified, so that if a person is found guilty of violating the law, a sanction can be imposed.

☐ DEFENSES

PERSONAL DEFENSES

When a person is charged with a crime, he or she will usually offer some defense. Our legal system has generally recognized two broad categories of defenses: personal and special. Personal defenses are based upon some characteristic of the individual who is charged with the crime. They include the following:

Infancy

The defense of infancy has its roots in the ancient belief that children cannot reason logically until around the age of 7. Early doctrine in the Christian church sanctioned that belief by declaring that rationality develops around the age of 7. As a consequence, only children past that age could be held responsible for their "crimes."

The defense of infancy today has been expanded to include people well beyond the age of 7. Many states set the 16th birthday as the age at which a person becomes an adult for purposes of criminal prosecution. Others use the age of 14, and still others 18. When a person below the age required for adult prosecution commits a "crime," it is termed a juvenile offense. He or she is not guilty of a criminal violation of the law by virtue of youth. In most jurisdictions, children below the age of 7 cannot be charged even with juvenile offenses, no matter how serious their actions may appear to others.

Insanity

Insanity is the second form of personal defense. It is important to realize that legal definitions of insanity often have very little to do with psychological or psychiatric understandings of mental illness. Legal insanity is a concept developed over time to meet the needs of the judicial system in assigning guilt or innocence to particular defendants. It is not primarily concerned with treatment, as is the idea of mental illness in psychiatry. Medical conceptions of mental illness do not always fit well into the legal categories created to deal with the phenomena. This difference has led to a situation in which mental health professionals often appear to give contradictory testimony in criminal trials.

⇨ The McNaughten Rule

Prior to the nineteenth century the insanity defense was nonexistent. Insane people who committed crimes were punished in the same way as other law violators. It was Daniel McNaughten (also spelled "M'Naghten"), a woodworker from Glasgow, Scotland, who, in 1844, became the first person to be found not guilty of a crime by reason of insanity. McNaughten had tried to assassinate Sir Robert Peel, the British prime minister. He mistook Edward Drummond, Peel's secretary, for Peel himself, and killed Drummond instead. At his trial, defense attorneys argued that McNaughten suffered from vague delusions centered on the idea that the Tories, a British political party, were persecuting him. Medical testimony at the trial agreed with the assertion of McNaughten's lawyers that he didn't know what he was doing at the time of the shooting. The judge accepted McNaughten's claim, and the insanity defense was born. The McNaughten rule, as it has come to be called, was defined later by the courts and still plays a major role in determining insanity in criminal prosecutions in 15 states today.[25]

The McNaughten Rule holds that a person is not guilty of a crime if, at the time of the crime, they either didn't know what they were doing, or didn't know that what they were doing was wrong. The inability to distinguish right from wrong must be the result of some mental defect or disability. The McNaughten case established a rule for the determination of insanity which is still followed in many U.S. jurisdictions today. However, in most states, the burden of proving insanity falls upon the defendant. Just as defendants are assumed innocent, in the majority of jurisdictions, they are also assumed to be sane at the outset of any criminal trial.

⇨ Irresistible Impulse

The McNaughten rule worked well for a time. Eventually, however, some cases arose in which defendants clearly knew what they were doing, and they knew it was wrong. Even so, they argued in their defense, they couldn't help themselves. They couldn't stop doing that which was wrong. Such people are said to suffer from an irresistible impulse, and may be found not guilty by reason of that particular brand of insanity in 18 of the United States. Some states which do not use the irresistible impulse test in determining insanity may still allow the successful demonstration of such an impulse to be considered in sentencing decisions.

The irresistible impulse test has been criticized on a number of grounds. Primary among them is the belief that all of us suffer from compulsions. Most of us, however, learn to control them. Should we give in to a compulsion, the critique goes, then why not just say it was unavoidable so as to escape any legal consequences.

⇨ **The Durham Rule**

A third rule for gauging insanity is called the Durham rule. It was originally created in 1871 by a New Hampshire court, and later adopted by Judge David Bazelon in 1954 as he decided the case of *Durham* v. *United States* for the Court of Appeals in the District of Columbia. The Durham rule states that a person is not criminally responsible for their behavior if their illegal actions were the result of some mental disease or defect.[26]

Courts which follow the Durham rule will typically hear from an array of psychiatric specialists as to the mental state of the defendant. Their testimony will inevitably be clouded by the need to address the question of cause. A successful defense under the Durham Rule necessitates that jurors be able to see the criminal activity in question as the *product* of mental deficiencies harbored by the defendant. And yet, many people who suffer from mental diseases or defects never commit crimes. In fact, low IQ, mental retardation, or general mental capacity are not allowable as excuses for criminal behavior. Because the Durham rule is especially vague, it provides fertile grounds for conflicting claims.

⇨ **The Substantial Capacity Test**

Nineteen states follow another guideline — the Substantial Capacity Test — as found in the Model Penal Code of the American Law Institute.[27] Also called the ALI rule or the MPC rule, it suggests that insanity should be defined as the lack of a substantial capacity to control one's behavior. This test requires a judgment to the effect that the defendant either had, or lacked, "the mental capacity needed to understand the wrongfulness of his act, or to conform his behavior to the requirements of the law."[28] The substantial capacity test is a blending of the McNaughten rule with the "irresistible impulse" standard. "Substantial capacity" does not require total mental incompetence nor does the rule require the behavior in question to live up to the criterion of total irresistibility. The problem, however, of establishing just what constitutes "substantial mental capacity" has plagued this rule from its inception.

⇨ **The Brawner Rule**

Judge Bazelon, apparently dissatisfied with the application of the Durham rule, created a new criterion for gauging insanity in the 1972 case of *U.S.* v. *Brawner*. The Brawner rule, as it has come to be called, places responsibility for deciding insanity squarely with the jury. Bazelon suggested that the jury should be concerned with whether or not the defendant could be *justly* held responsible for the criminal act in the face of any claims of insanity. Under this proposal, juries are left with few rules to guide them other than their own sense of fairness.

INSANITY AND SOCIAL REALITY

The insanity defense originated as a means of recognizing the social reality of mental disease. Unfortunately, the history of this defense has been rife with change, contradiction, and uncertainty. Psychiatric testimony is expensive, sometimes costing thousands of dollars per day for one medical specialist. Still worse is the fact that each "expert" is commonly contradicted by another.

Public dissatisfaction with the jumble of rules defining legal insanity peaked in 1982, when John Hinckley was acquitted of trying to assassinate then-President Reagan. At his trial, Hinckley's lawyers claimed that a series of delusions brought about by a history of schizophrenia left him unable to control his behavior. Government prosecutors were unable to counter defense contentions of insanity. The resulting acquittal shocked the nation and resulted in calls for a review of the insanity defense.

Guilty But Insane

A new finding of guilty but insane (in a few states the finding is "guilty but mentally ill," or GBMI) is now possible in some jurisdictions. It is one form the response to public frustration with the insanity issue has taken. Guilty but insane means that a person can be held responsible for a specific criminal act, even though a degree of mental incompetence may be present in his or her personality. Upon return of this verdict, a judge may impose any sentence possible under the law for the crime in question. However, mandated psychiatric treatment will generally be part of the commitment order. The offender, once cured, will usually be placed in the general prison population to serve any remaining sentence. In 1975 Michigan became the first state to pass a "guilty but mentally ill" statute, permitting a GBMI finding.[29]   At the time of this writing, eleven other states had also passed legislation making a verdict of "guilty but insane" possible.

As some authors have observed, the legal possibility of a guilty but mentally ill finding has three purposes: "[F]irst, to protect society; second, to hold some offenders who were mentally ill accountable for their criminal acts; [and] third, to make treatment available to convicted offenders suffering from some form of mental illness."[30]

The guilty but insane plea represents a conservative direction in criminal prosecution. The Supreme Court case of *Ford* v. *Wainwright*, however, recognized a problem of a different sort.[31]   The 1986 decision specified that prisoners who become insane while incarcerated cannot be executed. Hence, although insanity may not be a successful defense to criminal prosecution, it can later become a block to the ultimate punishment.

Temporary Insanity

Temporary insanity is another possible defense against a criminal charge. Widely used in the 1940s and 1950s, temporary insanity meant that the offender claimed to be insane only at the time of the commission of the offense. If a jury agreed, the defendant virtually went free. The suspect was not guilty of the criminal action by virtue of having been insane, and could not be ordered to undergo psychiatric counseling or treatment because the insanity was no longer present. This type of plea has become less popular as legislatures have regulated the circumstances under which it could be made.

THE INSANITY DEFENSE UNDER FEDERAL LAW

In 1984 the U.S. Congress passed the federal Insanity Defense Reform Act. The act created major revisions in the insanity defense, applicable to federal courts. Insanity under the law is now defined as a condition in which the defendant can be shown to have been suffering under a ". . . severe mental disease or defect [and, as a result] was unable to appreciate the nature and quality or the wrongfulness of his acts."[32]   This definition of insanity comes close to that set forth in the old McNaughten rule.

The act also places the burden of proving the insanity defense squarely on the defendant — a provision which has been challenged a number of times since the act was passed. Such a requirement was supported by the Supreme Court prior to the act's passage. In 1983, in the case of *Jones* v. *U.S.* (1983),[33] the Court ruled that defendants can be required to prove their insanity when it becomes an issue in their defense.   Shortly after the act became law, the Court, in *Ake* v. *Oklahoma* (1985),[34] held that the government must assure access to a competent psychiatrist whenever a defendant indicates that insanity will be an issue at trial.

CONSEQUENCES OF AN INSANITY RULING

The insanity defense today is not an "easy way out" of criminal prosecution, as some have assumed. Once a verdict of "not guilty by reason of insanity" is returned, the judge may order the defendant to undergo psychiatric treatment until cured. Because psychiatrists are reluctant to declare any potential criminal "cured," such a sentence may result in more time spent in an institution than would have resulted from a prison sentence.

Involuntary Drunkenness

Another personal defense is involuntary intoxication. Either drugs or alcohol may produce intoxication. Intoxication itself is rarely a defense to a criminal charge because it is a self-induced state. An altered mental condition which is voluntary cannot be used to exonerate guilty actions which follow from it.

Involuntary intoxication, however, is different. On occasion a person may be tricked into consuming an intoxicating substance. Secretly "spiked" punch, popular aphrodisiacs, or drug-laced desserts all might be ingested unknowingly. Because the effects and taste of alcohol are so widely known in our society, the defense of involuntary drunkenness can be difficult to demonstrate, however. A more unusual situation results from a disease caused by the yeast *Candida albicans,* occasionally found living in human intestines. A Japanese physician was the first to identify this disease, in which a person's digestive processes ferment the food they eat. Fermentation turns a portion of the food into alcohol, and people with this condition become intoxicated whenever they eat. First recognized about ten years ago, the disease has not yet been used successfully in this country to support the defense of involuntary intoxication.

Unconsciousness

A very rarely used form of personal defense is that of unconsciousness. An individual who is unconscious cannot be held responsible for anything he or she does. Because unconscious people rarely do anything at all, this defense is almost never seen. However, cases of sleepwalking, epileptic seizure, and neurological dysfunction may result in injurious, although unintentional, actions by people so afflicted. Under such circumstances the defense of unconsciousness might be argued with success.

Premenstrual Stress Syndrome

The use of premenstrual stress syndrome (PMS) as a defense against criminal charges is very new and demonstrates how changing social conceptions and advancing technology may change the way in which courts view illegal behavior. In 1980 British courts heard the case of Christine English, who killed her live-in lover when he threatened to leave her. An expert witness at the trial testified that English had been the victim of PMS for more than a decade. The witness, Dr. Katharina Dalton, advanced the claim that PMS had rendered Ms. English "irritable, aggressive, . . . and confused, with loss of self-control."[35] The jury, apparently accepting the claim, returned a verdict of "not guilty." PMS is not an officially acceptable defense in American criminal courts. However, in 1991 a Fairfax, Virginia, judge dismissed drunk-driving charges against a woman who cited the role PMS played in her behavior.[36] The woman, an orthopedic surgeon named Dr. Geraldine Richter, admitted to drinking four glasses of wine, and allegedly kicked and cursed a state trooper who stopped her car because it was weaving down the road. A Breathalyzer test showed a blood-alcohol level of 0.13% — higher than the 0.10% need to meet the requirement for drunken driving under Virginia law. But a gynecologist who testified on Dr. Richter's behalf said that the behavior she exhibited is characteristic of PMS. "I guess this is a new trend," said the state's attorney in commenting on the judge's ruling.

Other Biological Considerations

Modern nutritional science appears to be on the verge of establishing a new category of personal defense related to "chemical imbalances" in the human body produced by eating habits. Vitamins, food allergies, the consumption of stimulants (including coffee and nicotine), and the excessive ingestion of sugar all will probably soon be advanced by attorneys in defense of their clients.

The case of Dan White provides an example of this new direction in the development of personal defenses.[37] White, a former San Francisco police officer, walked into the office of Mayor Moscone and shot both the mayor and City Councilman Harvey Milk to death. It was established at the trial that White had spent the night before the murders drinking Coca-Cola and eating Twinkies, a packaged pastry. Expert witnesses testified that the huge amounts of sugar consumed by White prior to the crime substantially altered his judgment and ability to control his behavior. The jury, influenced by the expert testimony, and following California guidelines concerning diminished capacity, convicted White of a lesser charge. He eventually served a short prison sentence.

The strategy used by White's lawyers has come to be known as the "Twinkie defense." It may well be characteristic of future defense strategies now being developed in cases across the nation.

SPECIAL DEFENSES

A defense against criminal charges can be based on circumstances as well as personal attributes. Special defenses relate to circumstances surrounding the crime. They take into consideration external pressures, operating at the time the crime was committed, which might have lessened the responsibility or the resolve of the defendant in a way with which the rest of us could sympathize. Special defenses based on circumstance are nine in number.

Self-defense

Self-defense is probably the best known of the special defenses. This defense strategy makes the claim that the harm committed was not criminal because it was undertaken in order to ensure one's own safety in the face of certain injury. A person who harms an attacker can generally use this defense. However, the courts have held that where a "path of retreat" exists for a person being attacked, it should be taken. In other words, the safest use of self-defense is only when "cornered."

The extent of the injury inflicted in self-defense must be reasonable with respect to the degree of the perceived threat. In other words, although it may be acceptable for a person to defensively kill someone who is shooting at them, it would be inappropriate to shoot and kill someone who is just verbally insulting. Deadly force generally cannot be used to repel nondeadly force.

Self-defense extends to defense of others and to the defense of one's home. A person whose loved ones are being attacked can claim self-defense if they injure or kill the attacker. Similarly, a person can defend their home from invasion or forced entry, even to the point of using deadly force. However, the circumstances which surround the claim of self-defense are limited. The defense is useless where the person provoked an attack or where the attacker is justified. In cases of forcible arrest, for example, family members may not intervene to protect their relatives, providing the use of force by the police is legitimate.

Self-defense has been used recently in a spate of killings, by wives, of their abusive spouses. Killings which occur while the physical abuse is in process, especially where a history of such abuse can be shown, are likely to be excused by juries as self-defense. On the other hand, wives who suffer repeated abuse, but coldly plan the killing of their husbands, have not fared well in court. On the same day in 1988, for example, two women were adjudicated by state courts under similar circumstances, but with far different results. Caroline Decker of Broadalbin, New York, was acquitted of homicide charges in the shooting death of her abusive husband. Lana Anderson, of Kirksville, Missouri, however, was found guilty of hiring two men to kill her husband.[38] Even though a history of abuse could be demonstrated in both cases, the jury recommend that Ms. Anderson be sentenced to life in prison with no chance for parole, apparently because of the "cold-blooded" and preplanned nature of her actions.

Duress

Duress is another of the special defenses. People may act under duress if, for example, they steal their employers' payroll in order to meet a ransom demand by kidnappers holding their children. Should they later be arrested for larceny or embezzlement, they can claim that they felt compelled to commit the crime to help ensure the safety of their children. The defense of duress is sometimes also called coercion. Duress is generally not a useful defense when the crime committed involves serious physical harm.

Entrapment

Entrapment is a special defense which has become relatively popular in the news media and in the courts. It is a special defense which regulates the enthusiasm with which police officers may enforce the law. Entrapment defenses argue that enforcement agents effectively created a crime where there would otherwise have been none. Entrapment was claimed in the famous case of automaker John DeLorean. DeLorean was arrested on October 19, 1982, by federal agents near the Los Angeles airport.[39] An FBI videotape, secretly made at the scene, showed him allegedly "dealing" with undercover agents and holding packets of cocaine which he said were "better than gold." DeLorean was charged with narcotics smuggling violations involving a large amount of drugs.

At his 1984 trial, DeLorean claimed that he had been "set up" by the police to commit a crime which he would not have been involved in were it not for their urging. DeLorean's auto company had fallen upon hard times, and he was facing heavy debts. Federal agents, acting undercover, proposed to DeLorean a plan whereby he could make a great deal of money through drugs. Because the idea originated with the police, not with DeLorean, and because DeLorean was able to demonstrate successfully that he was repeatedly threatened not to "pull out" of the deal by a police informant, the jury returned a "not guilty" verdict.

The concept of entrapment is well summarized in a statement made by DeLorean's defense attorney to *Time* magazine before the trial: "This is a fictitious crime. Without the Government there would be no crime. This is one of the most insidious and misguided law-enforcement operations in history."[40]

Accident

The defense of accident claims that the action in question was not intended, but the result of some happenstance. Hunting accidents, for example, rarely result in criminal prosecution because the circumstances surrounding them clearly show the unintentional nature of the shootings. What appear as accidents, of course, may actually be disguised criminal behavior. A hunter in North Carolina, for example, was recently convicted of shooting at an airplane[41] (in which a passenger was seriously injured), even though he claimed that his gun accidentally discharged into the air. His defense fell apart when his girlfriend told authorities that he had confided in her as to what really happened.

Mistake

Mistake is a special defense with two components. One is mistake of law; the other is mistake of fact. Rarely is the defense of mistake of law acceptable. Most people realize that it is their responsibility to know the law as it applies to them. "Ignorance of the law is no excuse," is an old dictum still heard today. On occasion, however, humorous cases do arise in which such a defense is accepted by authorities. An elderly woman who raised marijuana plants because they could be used to make a tea which relieved her arthritis is within the author's memory. When her garden was discovered, she was not arrested, but advised as to how the law applied to her.

Mistake of fact is a much more useful form of the "mistake" defense. In 1987 Jerry Hall, fashion model and girlfriend of Mick Jagger, a well-known rock star, was arrested in Barbados as she attempted to leave a public airport baggage claim area after picking up a suitcase.[42] The bag contained 20 pounds of marijuana and was under surveillance by officials who were waiting for just such a pickup. Ms. Hall defended herself by arguing that she had mistook the bag for her own, which looked similar. She was released after a night in jail.

Necessity

Necessity is a useful defense in cases which do not involve serious bodily harm. One of the most famous uses of this defense occurred in *Crown* v. *Dudly & Stephens* in the late 1800s.[43] The case involved a shipwreck in which three sailors and a cabin boy were set adrift in a lifeboat. After a number of days at sea without rations, two of the men decided to kill and eat the cabin boy. At their trial, they argued that it was necessary to do so, or none of them would have survived. The court, however, reasoned that the cabin boy was not a direct threat to the survival of the men and rejected this defense. Convicted of murder, they were sentenced to death, although they were spared the gallows by royal intervention.

Although cannibalism is usually against the law, courts have sometimes recognized the necessity of consuming human flesh where survival was at issue. Those cases, however, involved only "victims" who had already died of natural causes.

Provocation

Provocation recognizes that a person can be emotionally enraged by another. Should they then strike out at their tormentor, some courts have held, they may not be guilty of any criminality. The defense of provocation is commonly used in barroom brawls where a person's parentage may have been called into question, although most states don't look very favorably upon verbal provocation alone. It has also been used in some recent spectacular cases where wives have killed their husbands, or children their fathers, citing years of verbal and physical abuse. In these latter instances, perhaps because of the degree of physical harm inflicted, the provocation defense has not been as readily accepted by the courts. As a rule, the defense of provocation is generally more acceptable in minor offenses than in serious violations of the law.

Consent

The defense of consent claims that whatever harm was done occurred only after the injured person gave his or her permission for the behavior in question. A recent trial saw Robert Chambers plead guilty to "first-degree manslaughter" in the killing of 18-year-old Jennifer Levin. In what was dubbed "the Preppy Murder Case,"[44] Chambers had claimed Levin died as a result of "rough sex" during which she had tied his hands behind his back and injured his testicles. Other cases, some involving sexual asphyxia (suffocation designed to heighten erotic pleasure) and bondage, culminated in a headline in *Time* magazine heralding the era of "The Rough Sex Defense."[45] The article suggested that such a defense works best with a good-looking defendant who appears remorseful: "[a] hardened type of character . . .,"[46] said the story, could not use the defense.

Alibi

A current reference book for criminal trial lawyers says, "Alibi is different from all of the other defenses . . . because . . . it is based upon the premise that the defendant is truly innocent."[47]   All the other defenses we have discussed are accepted ways to alleviate criminal responsibility. While they may produce findings of "Not Guilty," the defense of alibi, if believed, should support a ruling of "Innocent."

Alibi is best supported by witnesses and documentation. A person charged with a crime can use the defense of alibi to show that they were not present at the scene when the crime was alleged to have occurred.   Hotel receipts, eyewitness identification, and participation in social events have all been used to prove alibis.

PROCEDURAL DEFENSES

Chapter 5 describes the legal environment in which the police must operate. When police officers violate constitutional guarantees of due process, they may create a situation in which guilty defendants can go free. Defenses based upon improper procedures may also occur as a consequence of actions by prosecutors and judges.   Included among these procedural defenses are double jeopardy, collateral estoppel, prosecutorial misconduct, selective prosecution, and the denial of a speedy trial.

Double Jeopardy

The Fifth Amendment to the U.S. Constitution makes it clear that no person may be tried twice for the same offense. People who have been acquitted or found innocent may not be again put in "jeopardy of life or limb" for the same crime. Cases dismissed for a lack of evidence come under the double jeopardy rule and cannot result in a new trial.

Double jeopardy, however, does not apply in cases of trial error. Hence, convictions which are set aside because of some error in proceedings at a lower court level will permit a retrial on the same charges.   Similarly, when a defendant's motion for a mistrial is successful, a second trial may be held.

Collateral Estoppel

Collateral estoppel is similar to double jeopardy and applies to facts that have been determined by a "valid and final judgment."[48] Such facts cannot become the object of new litigation. Where a defendant, for example, has been acquitted of a multiple murder charge by virtue of an alibi, it would not be permissible to try that person again for the murder of a second person killed along with the first.

Some crimes violate the laws of two different jurisdictions. A bank robbery, for instance, may be both a state and federal offense. In such cases, the same defendant may be tried separately in courts of different jurisdiction without the double jeopardy rule coming into play.

Selective Prosecution

The procedural defense of selective prosecution is based upon the Fourteenth Amendment's guarantee of equal protection of the laws. The defense may be available where two or more individuals are suspected of criminal involvement, but not all are actively prosecuted. Selective prosecution based fairly upon the strength of available evidence is not the object of this defense. But when prosecution proceeds unfairly on the basis of some arbitrary and discriminatory attribute, such as race, sex, friendship, age, or religious preference, protection may be feasible under it.

Denial of Speedy Trial

The Sixth Amendment to the Constitution guarantees a right to a speedy trial. The purpose of the guarantee is to prevent unconvicted and potentially innocent people from languishing in jail. The federal government[49] and most states have laws (generally referred to as "speedy trial acts") which define the time limit necessary for a trial to be "speedy" and generally set a reasonable period such as 90 or 120 days following arrest. Excluded from the counting procedure are delays which result from requests by the defense to prepare their case. If the limit set by law is exceeded, the defendant must be set free, and no trial can occur.

Prosecutorial Misconduct

A final procedural defense may be found in prosecutorial misconduct. Prosecutors are expected to uphold the highest ethical standards in the performance of their roles. When they knowingly permit false testimony, when they hide information that would clearly help the defense, or when they make unduly biased statements to the jury in closing arguments, the defense of prosecutorial misconduct may be available to the defendant.

□ SUMMARY

Law serves many purposes. Primary among them is the maintenance of social order. Laws reflect the values held by society. The emphasis placed by law upon individual rights, personal property, and criminal reformation can tell us much about the cultural and philosophical basis of the society of which it is a part. Legal systems throughout the world reflect the experiences of the societies which created them. Islamic law, for example, has a strong religious component and requires judicial decisions in keeping with the Moslem Koran.

American law developed out of a long tradition of legal reasoning, extending back to the Code of Hammurabi — the earliest known codification of laws. The most recent historical source of modern law has been English "common law." Common law reflected the customs and daily practices of English citizens during the Middle Ages.

Western criminal law generally distinguishes between serious crimes (felonies) and those which are less grave (misdemeanors). Guilt can only be demonstrated if the *corpus delicti* of a crime can be proven in court.

Our judicial system has come to recognize a number of defenses to a criminal charge. Insanity and self-defense are two of the most important of the modern defenses. The insanity defense has met with considerable recent criticism. Efforts to reduce its blanket application are now underway in a number of states.

DISCUSSION QUESTIONS

1. Name some of the historical sources of modern law.

2. What kinds of concerns have influenced the development of the criminal law? How are social values and power arrangements in society represented in laws today?

3. Do you think there is a "natural" basis for laws? If so, what basis would you think it appropriate to build a system of laws upon? Do any of our modern laws appear to have a foundation in "natural law."

4. What is "common law"? Is there a modern form of the common law? If so, what is it?

5. What is the *corpus delicti* of a crime? Are there any elements of a crime which you think are unnecessary? Why?

6. What is the difference between *mala in se* and *mala prohibita* offenses? Do you think this difference is real or only theoretical?

7. Does the insanity defense serve a useful function today? If you could create your own rule for determining insanity in criminal trials, what would it be? How would it differ from

existing rules?

NOTES

1. Marvin Wolfgang, "The Key Reporter," *Phi Beta Kappa*, Vol. 52, no. 1 .

2. Roman influence in England had ended by 442 A.D., according to Crane Brinton, John B. Christopher, and Robert L. Wolff, *A History of Civilization*, 3rd ed., Volume 1 (Englewood Cliffs, NJ: Prentice Hall, 1967), p. 180.

3. Howard Abadinsky, *Law and Justice* (Chicago: Nelson-Hall, 1988), p. 6.

4. Edward McNall Burns, *Western Civilization* 7th ed. (New York: W. W. Norton, 1969), p. 339.

5. Ibid., p. 533.

6. Brinton, Christopher, and Wolff , *A History of Civilization*, p. 274.

7. Thomas Aquinas, *Summa Theologica* (Notre Dame, IN: University of Notre Dame Press, 1983).

8. *Roe* v. *Wade*, 410 U.S. 113 (1973).

9. Max Rheinstein, ed., *Max Weber on Law in Economy and Society* (Cambridge, MA: Harvard University Press, 1954).

10. John Stuart Mill, *On Liberty* (London: Parker, 1859).

11. Nigel Walker, *Punishment, Danger, and Stigma: The Morality of Criminal Justice* (Totowa, NJ: Barnes and Noble, 1980).

12. O. W. Holmes, *The Common Law* (Boston: Little, Brown., 1881).

13. Roscoe Pound, *Social Control Through the Law* (Hamden, CT: Archon, 1968), pp. 113–114.

14. As found in William Chambliss and Robert Seidman, *Law, Order, and Power* (Reading, MA: Addison-Wesley, 1971), pp. 154, 141–142.

15. Ibid., p. 140.

16. Ibid.

17. Ibid., p. 51.

18. Ibid.

19. Lief H. Carter, *Reason in Law*, 2nd ed. (Boston: Little Brown, 1984).

20. *Facts on File, 1988* (New York: Facts on File, 1988), p. 175.

21. Man Who Spent 6½ Years in Jail Is Awarded $1.9 Million by Judge, *The Fayetteville Times*, October 20, 1989, p. 7A.

22. U.S. Sentencing Commission, *Federal Sentencing Guidelines Manual* (St. Paul, MN: West, 1987).

23. Henry Campbell Black, *Black's Law Dictionary* (St. Paul, MN: West Publishing Co., 1990), 6th ed., p. 545.

24. Holmes, *The Common Law*, Volume 3.

25. *American Jurisprudence*, 21/2 Sections 55–57.

26. *American Law Review*, 9/4 Sections 1–8.

27. American Law Institute, *Model Penal Code: Official Draft and Explanatory Notes* (Philadelphia: The Institute, 1985).

28. Ibid.

29. John Klofas and Ralph Weisheit, "Guilty but Mentally Ill: Reform of The Insanity Defense in Illinois," *Justice Quarterly*, Vol. 4, no. 1 (March 1987), pp. 40–50.

30. Ibid.

31. *Ford* v. *Wainwright*, 477 U.S. 106 S.Ct. 2595 (1986).

32. 18 United States Code, Section 401.

33. *Jones* v. *U.S.*, U.S. Sup. Ct. 1983 33 CrL 3233.

34. *Ake* v. *Oklahoma*, U.S. Sup. Ct. (1985) 35 CrL 3159.

35. As reported in Arnold Binder, *Juvenile Delinquency: Historical, Cultural, Legal Perspectives* (New York: Macmillan, 1988), p. 494.

36. "Drunk Driving Charge Dismissed; PMS Cited," *The Fayetteville Observer-Times*, June 7, 1991, p. 3A.

37. *Facts on File, 1978* (New York: Facts on File, 1979).

38. *USA Today*, January 18, 1988, p. 3A.

39. *Time*, March 19, 1984, p. 26.

40. Ibid.

41. "Man Gets Prison, Must Pay $35,300 in Shooting of Jet," *The Fayetteville Times*, May 21, 1987, p. 14B.

42. *Facts on File, 1987* (New York: Facts on File, 1988).

43. *The Queen* v. *Dudly & Stephens*, 14 Q.B.D. 273, 286, 15 Cox C.C. 624, 636 (1884).

44. "The Rough-Sex Defense," *Time*, May 23, 1988, p. 55.

45. Ibid., p. 55

46. "The Preppie Killer Cops a Plea," *Time*, April 4, 1988, p. 22.

47. Patrick L. McCloskey and Ronald L. Schoenberg, *Criminal Law Deskbook* (New York: Matthew Bender, 1988), 20.03 [13].

48. Ibid., 20.02 [4].

49. Speedy Trial Act, 18 U.S.C. Section 3161. Some significant cases involving the U.S. Speedy Trial Act are those of *U.S.* v. *Carter* (1986) and *Henderson* v. *U.S.* (1986).

INDIVIDUAL RIGHTS VERSUS SOCIAL CONCERNS
✪ The Rights of the Accused Under Investigation ✪

Common law, constitutional, and humanitarian rights
of the accused:

A Right Against Unreasonable Searches
A Right Against Unreasonable Arrest
A Right Against Unreasonable Seizures of Property
A Right to Fair Questioning by Authorities
A Right to Protection from Personal Harm

The individual rights listed must be effectively balanced against
these community concerns:

The Efficient Apprehension of Offenders
The Prevention of Crimes

How does our system of justice work toward balance?

PART 2
The Police in America

Laws are generally not understood by three sorts of persons:
those that make them, those that execute them, and those
that suffer if they break them.
> — *Halifax* (1633–1695)

If we are to keep our democracy, there must be
one commandment: "Thou shalt not ration justice!
> — *Justice Learned Hand* (1872–1961)

There is no cruder tyranny than that which is perpetuated
under the shield of law and in the name of justice.
> — *Montesquieu* (1689–1755)

It is the spirit and not the form of law that
keeps justice alive.
> — *Justice Earl Warren* (1891–1974)

CHAPTER 4

POLICE ADMINISTRATION

The single most striking fact about the attitudes of citizens, black and white, toward the police is that in general these attitudes are positive, not negative.
— James Q. Wilson[1]

Crime is a community problem and stands today as one of the most serious challenges of our generation. Our citizens must . . . recognize their responsibilities in its suppression.
— O. W. Wilson[2]

KEY CONCEPTS

discretion	working personality	internal affairs
police culture	police ethics	POST
Knapp Commission	Wickersham Commission	professionalism

☐ CONTEMPORARY POLICING: THE ADMINISTRATIVE PERSPECTIVE

In a recent symposium, members of Harvard University's Kennedy School of Government divided the history of American policing into three different eras.[3] Each era was distinguished from the others by the apparent dominance of a particular administrative approach to police operations. The first period, the political era, was characterized by close ties between police and public officials. It began in the 1840s and ended around 1930. Throughout the period American police agencies tended to serve the interests of powerful politicians and their cronies, while providing community order maintenance services almost as an afterthought. The second period, the reform era, began in the 1930s and lasted until the 1970s. The reform era was characterized by pride in professional crime fighting. Police departments during this period focused most of their resources on solving "traditional" crimes such as murder, rape, and burglary and on capturing offenders. The final era — one which is just beginning — is the era of community problem solving. The problem solving approach to police work stresses the service role of police officers and envisions a partnership between police agencies and their communities.

STYLES OF POLICING

The influence of each historical phase identified by the Harvard team survives today in what James Q. Wilson calls policing styles.[4] Wilson's three types of policing — which he did not identify with a particular historical era — are (1) the watchman style (characteristic of the political era), (2) the legalistic style (professional crime fighting), and (3) the service style (which is becoming more commonplace today). These three styles, taken together, characterize nearly all municipal law enforcement agencies today, although some departments are more a mixture of two or more styles.

The Watchman Style

Police departments marked by the watchman style of policing are primarily concerned with achieving a goal that Wilson calls "order maintenance." They see their job as one of controlling illegal and disruptive behavior. The watchman style, however, as opposed to the legalistic, makes considerable use of discretion. Order in watchman style communities may be arrived at through informal police intervention, including persuasion, threats, or even by "roughing up" a few disruptive people from time to time. Some authors have condemned this style of policing, suggesting that it is unfairly found in lower-class, or lower middle-class communities, especially where interpersonal relations may include a fair amount of violence or physical abuse. Others, however, have pointed out that "[i]n responding to the mandate for order maintenance, the police create a sense of community that makes social life possible."[5]

The Legalistic Style

Departments operating under the legalistic model are committed to enforcing the "letter of the law." A few years ago, for example, when the speed limit on I-95 running north and south through North Carolina was 55 mph, a state highway patrol official was quoted by newspapers as saying that troopers would issue tickets at 56 mph. The law was the law, he said, and it would be enforced.

Conversely, legalistically oriented departments can be expected to routinely avoid involvement in community disputes arising from normative violations which do not break the law. Gary Sykes calls this enforcement style "laissez-faire policing," in recognition of its "hands-off" approach to behaviors which are simply bothersome or inconsiderate of community principles.

The Service Style

Departments which stress the goal of service reflect the felt needs of the community. In service-oriented departments, the police see themselves more as helpers than as embattled participants in a war against crime. Such departments work hand in hand with social service and other agencies to provide counseling for minor offenders and to assist community groups in preventing crimes and solving problems. Prosecutors may support the service style of policing by agreeing not to prosecute law violators who seek psychiatric help, or who voluntarily participate in programs like Alcoholics Anonymous, family counseling, drug treatment, and the like. The service style of policing is commonly found in wealthy neighborhoods, where the police are well paid and well educated. The service style is supported in part by citizen attitudes which seek to avoid the personal embarrassment which might result from a public airing of personal problems. Such attitudes reduce the number of criminal complaints filed, especially in the case of minor disputes.

Changing Styles

Historically, American police work has involved a fair amount of order maintenance activity. The United States a few decades ago consisted of a large number of immigrant communities, socially separated from one another by custom and language. Immigrant workers were often poorly educated, and some were prone toward displays of "manhood" which challenged police authority in the cities. Reports of police in "pitched battles" with bar-hopping laborers out for Saturday night "good times" were not uncommon. Arrests were infrequent, but "street justice" was often imposed through the use of the "billy stick" and blackjack. In these historical settings, the watchman style of policing must have seemed especially appropriate to both the police and many members of the citizenry.

As times have changed, so too have American communities. Even today, however, it is probably fair to say that the style of policing which characterizes a community tends to flow, at least to some degree, from the life-styles of those who live there. Rough-and-tumble life-styles encourage an oppressive form of policing; refined styles produce a service emphasis with stress on working together.

□ POLICE-COMMUNITY RELATIONS

In the 1960s, the legalistic style of policing, so common in America until then, began to yield to the newer service-oriented style of policing. The decade of the 1960s was one of unrest, fraught with riots and student activism. The war in Vietnam, civil rights concerns, and other burgeoning social movements produced large demonstrations and marches. The police, who were generally inexperienced in crowd control, all too often found themselves embroiled in tumultuous encounters with citizen groups. The police came to be seen by many as agents of "the establishment," and pitched battles between the police and the citizenry sometimes occurred.

As social disorganization increased, police departments across the nation sought ways to better understand and deal with the problems they faced. Significant outgrowths of this effort were the police-community relations (PCR) programs, which many departments created. Some authors have traced the development of the police-community relations concept to an annual conference begun in 1955.[6] Entitled the National Institute of Police and Community Relations, the meetings were sponsored jointly by the National Conference of Christians and Jews and the Michigan State University School of Police Administration and Public Safety. PCR represented a movement away from an exclusive police emphasis on the apprehension of law violators and meant increasing the level of positive police-citizen interaction. At the height of the PCR movement city police departments across the country opened storefront centers where citizens could air complaints and easily interact with police representatives. As Egon Bittner recognized,[7] for PCR programs to be truly effective, they need to reach to "the grassroots of discontent," where citizen dissatisfaction with the police exists.

Many contemporary PCR programs involve public relations officers, appointed to provide an array of services to the community. "Neighborhood Watch" programs, drug awareness workshops, "Project ID" — which uses police equipment and expertise to mark valuables for identification in the event of theft, and police-sponsored victim's assistance programs are all examples of services embodying the spirit of PCR. Modern PCR programs, however, often fail to achieve their goal of increased community satisfaction with police services because they focus on providing services to groups who already are well satisfied with the police. PCR programs which reach disaffected community groups are difficult to manage and may even alienate participating officers. Thus, as Bittner says, "while the first approach fails because it leaves out those groups to which the program is primarily directed, the second fails because it leaves out the police department."[8]

TEAM POLICING

During the 1960s and 1970s a number of communities began to experiment with the concept of team policing. An idea thought to have originated in Aberdeen, Scotland,[9] team policing rapidly became an extension of the PCR movement. Some authors have called team policing a "technique to deliver total police services to a neighborhood."[10] Others, however, have dismissed it as "little more than an attempt to return to the style of policing that was prevalent in the United States over a century ago."[11] Team policing assigned officers on a semi-permanent basis to particular neighborhoods, where it was expected they would become familiar with the inhabitants and with their problems and concerns. Patrol officers were given considerable authority in processing complaints from receipt through to resolution. Crimes were investigated and solved at the local level, with specialists called in only if the needed resources to continue an investigation were not locally available.

COMMUNITY POLICING

In recent years the police-community relations concept has undergone a substantial shift in emphasis. The old PCR model was built around the unfortunate self-image held by many police administrators of themselves as enforcers of the law who were isolated from, and often in opposition to, the communities they policed. Under such jaded administrators, PCR easily became a shallowly disguised and insincere effort to overcome public suspicion and community hostility.

In contrast, an increasing number of law enforcement administrators today are embracing the role of service provider. Modern police departments are frequently called upon to help citizens resolve a vast array of personal problems — many of which involve no direct law enforcement activity. Such requests may involve help for a sick child or the need to calm a distraught person, open a car with the keys locked inside, organize a community crime prevention effort, investigate a domestic dispute, and regulate traffic or give a talk to a class of young people on the dangers of drug abuse. Calls for service today far exceed the number of calls received by the police which directly relate to law violations. As a consequence, the referral function of the police is crucial in producing effective law enforcement. Officers may make referrals, rather than arrests, for interpersonal problems to agencies as diverse as Alcoholics Anonymous, departments of social service, domestic violence centers, drug rehabilitation programs, and psychiatric clinics.

In contemporary America, according to Harvard University's Executive Session on Policing, three "corporate strategies" guide American policing:[12] (1) strategic policing, (2) problem-solving policing, and (3) community policing.

The first, strategic policing, is something of a holdover from the reform era of the mid-1900s. Strategic policing "emphasizes an increased capacity to deal with crimes that are not well controlled by traditional methods."[13] Strategic policing retains the traditional police goal of professional crime fighting, but enlarges the enforcement target to include nontraditional kinds of criminals such as serial offenders, gangs and criminal associations, drug distribution networks, and sophisticated white-collar and computer criminals. In order to meet its goals, strategic policing generally makes use of innovative enforcement techniques, including intelligence operations, undercover stings, electronic surveillance, and sophisticated forensic methods.

The other two strategies give greater cognizance to the service style described by Wilson. Problem-solving (or problem-oriented) policing takes the view that many crimes are caused by existing social conditions in the communities served by the police. In order to control crime, problem-oriented police managers attempt to uncover and effectively address underlying social problems. Problem-solving policing makes thorough use of other community resources such as counseling centers, welfare programs, and job training facilities. It also attempts to involve citizens in the job of crime prevention through education, negotiation, and conflict management. Residents of poorly maintained housing areas, for example, might be asked to clean up litter, install better lighting, and provide security devices for their homes and apartments, in the belief that clean, secure, and well-lighted areas are a deterrent to criminal activity.

According to Herman Goldstein, five concerns have "strongly influenced the development of problem-oriented policing:"[14] 1. An historical preoccupation, among police managers, with internal procedures and efficiency, "to the exclusion of appropriate concern for effectiveness in dealing with substantive problems." 2. The fact that police, in the past, have developed too little initiative on their own — instead responding mostly to public calls for service. 3. A growing recognition that the "community is a major resource with an enormous potential, largely untapped, for reducing the number and magnitude of problems that otherwise become the problems of the police." 4. A new willingness to utilize the time and talent of the large numbers of rank-and-file officers, which, up until now, has not been effectively utilized. 5. An increasing consciousness that internal police policies and organizational structures must change if policing is to be improved.

The third, and newest, police strategy goes a step beyond the other two. Community policing attempts to involve the community actively with the police in the task of crime control by creating an effective working partnership between the community and the police.[15] In the words of Jerome Skolnick, community policing is "grounded on the notion that, together, police and public are more effective and more humane coproducers of safety and public order than are the police alone."[16] Skolnick says that, under the community policing model, the police and the public are "co-producers of safety and order."[17] According to Skolnick, community policing involves at least one of four elements: (1) community-based crime prevention, (2) the reorientation of patrol activities to emphasize the importance of nonemergency services, (3) increased police accountability to the public, and (4) a decentralization of command, including a greater use of civilians at all levels of police decision making.[18] Supporting Skolnick's view, Wesley Skogan[19] points out that "Community policing is not an operational shopping list of specific policing programs. Neither is it a particular tactical *product* to be adopted. Rather, it involves reforming organizational decision-making *processes* . . . A key to community policing is a shift in orientation from crime fighting to problem solving."

Each of these three conceptual approaches to policing has produced a number of innovative programs in recent years. In the early 1980s, for example, Houston's DART Program (Directed Area Responsibility Teams) emphasized problem-oriented policing; the Baltimore County, Maryland, Police Department began project COPE (Citizen Oriented Police Enforcement) in 1982; and Denver, Colorado, initiated its Community Service Bureau, one of the first major community policing programs. By the late 1980s, Jerome H. Skolnick and David Bayley's study of six American cities, entitled *The New Blue Line: Police Innovation in Six American Cities,*[20] documented the growing strength of community-police cooperation throughout the nation, giving further credence to the continuing evolution of service-oriented styles of policing.

Unfortunately, many problems remain.   There is some evidence that not all police officers are ready to accept new images of police work. Some authors have warned that police subculture is so committed to a traditional view of police work that efforts at change can demoralize an entire department, rendering it ineffective at its basic tasks.[21]   As some analysts of the modern situation warn, only when the formal values espoused by today's innovative police administrators begin to match those of rank and file officers can any police organization begin to be high performing.[22]

Nor are all citizens ready to accept a greater involvement of the police in their personal lives. Although the turbulent protest-prone years of the 1960s and early 1970s are gone, some groups remain suspicious of the police.   No matter how inclusive community policing programs become, it is doubtful that the gap between the police and the public will ever be entirely bridged. The police role of restraining behavior which violates the law will always produce friction between police departments and some segments of the community.

☐ CONTEMPORARY POLICING: THE INDIVIDUAL OFFICER

Regardless of the "official" policing style espoused by a department, individual officers retain considerable discretion in what they do. As one author has observed, "police authority can be, at once, highly specific and exceedingly vague."[23] The determination to stop and question suspects, the choice to arrest, and many other police practices are undertaken solely by individual officers acting in a decision-making capacity. Kenneth Culp Davis says, "The police make policy about what law to enforce, how much to enforce it, against whom, and on what occasions."[24]   The discretionary authority exercised by individual law enforcement officers is of potentially greater significance to the individual who has contact with the police than are all department manuals and official policy statements combined.

Patrolling officers will often decide against a strict enforcement of the law, preferring instead to handle situations informally. Minor law violations, crimes committed out of the officer's presence where the victim refuses to file a complaint, and certain violations of the criminal law where the officer suspects sufficient evidence to guarantee a conviction is lacking, may all lead to discretionary action short of arrest. Although the widest exercise of discretion is more likely in routine situations involving relatively less serious violations of the law, serious and clear-cut criminal behavior may occasionally result in discretionary decisions to avoid an arrest. Drunk driving, possession of controlled substances, and assault are but a few examples of crimes in which on the scene officers may decide warnings or referrals are more appropriate than arrest.

> **Discretion:** The exercise of choice, by enforcement agents, in the disposition of suspects, in the carrying out of official duties, and in the application of sanctions.

A summation of various studies of police discretion tells us that a number of factors influence the discretionary decisions of individual officers.   Some of these factors include the following:

The Background of the Officer: Law enforcement officers bring to their job all of life's previous experiences. Values shaped through early socialization in family environments, as well as attitudes acquired from ongoing socialization, impact the decisions an officer will make. If the officer has learned prejudice against certain ethnic groups, it is likely that such prejudices will manifest themselves in enforcement decisions. Officers who place a high value on the nuclear family may handle spouse abuse, child abuse, and other forms of domestic disputes in predetermined ways.

Characteristics of the Suspect: Some officers may treat men and women differently. A police friend of the author has voiced the belief that women "are not generally bad . . . but when they do go bad, they go *very* bad." His official treatment of women has been tempered by this belief. Very rarely will this officer arrest a woman, but when he does, he spares no effort to see her incarcerated. Other characteristics of the suspect which may influence police decisions include demeanor, style of dress, and grooming. Belligerent suspects are often seen as "asking for it" and as challenging police authority. Well-dressed suspects are likely to be treated with deference, but poorly groomed suspects can expect less exacting treatment. Suspects sporting personal styles with a "message" — biker's attire, unkempt beards, strange haircuts, and other nonconformist styles are more likely to be arrested than others.

The
Police
Chief

Department Policy: Discretion, while not entirely subject to control by official policy, can be influenced by it. If a department has targeted certain kinds of offenses, or if especially close control of dispatches and communications is held by supervisors who adhere to strict enforcement guidelines, discretionary release of suspects will be quite rare.

Community Interest: Public attitudes toward certain crimes will increase the likelihood of arrest for suspected offenders. Contemporary attitudes toward crimes involving children, including child sex abuse, the sale of drugs to minors, domestic violence involving children, and child pornography, have all led to increased and strict enforcement of laws governing such offenses across the nation. Communities may identify particular problems affecting them and ask law enforcement to respond. Fayetteville, North Carolina, adjacent to a major military base, was plagued a few years ago by a downtown area notorious for prostitution and "massage" parlors. Once the community voiced its concern over the problem, and clarified the economic impact on the city, the police responded with a series of highly effective arrests which eliminated massage parlors within the city limits. Departments which require officers to live in the areas they police are operating in recognition of the fact that community interests impact citizens and officers alike.

Pressures from Victims: Victims who refuse to file a complaint are commonly associated with certain crimes such as spouse abuse, the "robbery" of drug merchants, and assault on customers of prostitutes. When victims refuse to cooperate with the police, there is often little that can be done. On the other hand, some victims are very vocal in insisting that their victimization be recognized and dealt with. Modern victim's assistance groups, including People Assisting Victims, the Victim's Assistance Network, and others, have sought to keep pressure on police departments and individual investigators to ensure the arrest and prosecution of suspects.

Disagreement with the Law: Some laws lack a popular consensus. Among them are many "victimless" offenses such as homosexuality, lesbianism, drug use, gambling, pornography, and some crimes involving alcohol. Not all of these behaviors are even crimes in certain jurisdictions. Gambling is legal in Atlantic City, New Jersey, on board cruise ships, and in Las Vegas, Nevada. Many states have now legalized homosexuality and lesbianism and most forms of sexual behavior between consenting adults. Prostitution is officially sanctioned in portions of Nevada, and some drug offenses have been "decriminalized," with offenders being ticketed rather than arrested. Unpopular laws are not likely to bring much attention from law enforcement officers. Sometimes such crimes are regarded as just "part of the landscape," or as the consequence of laws which have not kept pace with a changing society. When arrests do occur, it may be because individuals investigated for more serious offenses were caught in the act of violating an unpopular statute. Drug offenders, for example, arrested in the middle of the night, may be "caught in the act" of an illegal sexual performance when the police break in. Charges may include "crime against nature" as well as possession or sale of drugs.

On the other hand, certain behaviors that are not law violations, and that may even be protected by guarantees of free speech, may be annoying, offensive, or disruptive according to the normative standards of a community or the personal standards of an officer. Where the law has been violated, and the guilty party known to the officer, the evidence necessary for a conviction in court may be "tainted" or in other ways not usable. Sykes, in recognizing these possibilities, says, "One of the major ambiguities of the police task is that officers are caught between two profoundly compelling moral systems: justice as due process . . . and conversely, justice as righting a wrong as part of defining and maintaining community norms."[25] In such cases, discretionary police activity may take the form of "street justice," and approach vigilantism.

Available Alternatives: Police discretion can be impacted by the officer's awareness of alternatives to arrest. Community treatment programs, including out-patient drug and alcohol counseling, psychiatric or psychological services, domestic dispute resolution centers, and other options may all be kept in mind by officers looking for a "way out" of official action.

Personal Practices of the Officer: Some officers, because of actions undertaken in their personal lives, view potential law violations more or less seriously than other officers. The police officer who has an occasional marijuana cigarette with friends at a party may be inclined to deal less harshly with minor drug offenders than nonuser officers. The officer who routinely exceeds speed limits while driving the family car may be prone to discretionary action toward speeders encountered while on duty.

☐ CONTEMPORARY POLICING: ISSUES

A number of issues hold special interest for today's police administrators and officers. Some concerns, such as police stress, danger, and the use of deadly force, derive from the very nature of police work. Others have arisen over the years due to commonplace practice, characteristic police values, and public expectations surrounding the enforcement of laws. Included here are such negatives as the potential for corruption, as well as positive efforts which focus on ethics and recruitment strategies to increase professionalism.

POLICE CULTURE

A few years ago Jerome Skolnick described what he called the "working personality" of police officers.[26] Skolnick's description was consistent with William Westley's classic study[27] of the Gary, Indiana, Police Department, in which he found a police culture with its own "customs, laws, and morality," and with Niederhoffer's observation that cynicism was pervasive among officers in New York City.[28]   More recent authors[29] have claimed that the "blue curtain of secrecy" surrounding much of police work shields knowledge of the nature of the police personality from outsiders.

Skolnick found that a process of informal socialization, occurring when new officers begin to work with seasoned veterans, is often far more important than formal police academy training in determining how rookies will see police work. In everyday life, formal socialization occurs through schooling, church activities, job training, and so on. Informal socialization is acquired primarily from one's peers in less institutionalized settings and provides an introduction to value-laden subcultures. The information that passes between officers in the locker room, in a squad car, over a cup of coffee, or in many other relatively private moments produces a shared view of the world that can be best described as street-wise. The streetwise cop may know what official department policy is, but he or she also knows the most efficient way to get a job done. By the time they become streetwise, the officers will know just how acceptable various informal means of accomplishing the job will be to other officers. The police subculture creates few real "mavericks," but it also produces few officers who view their job exclusively in terms of public mandates and official dictums.

Skolnick says that the police working personality has at least six recognizable characteristics. Additional writers[30] have identified others. Taken in concert, they create the picture of the police personality shown in Table 4-1.

Some components of the police working personality are essential for survival and effectiveness. Officers are exposed daily to situations which are charged with emotions and potentially threatening. The need to gain control over belligerent people quickly leads to the development of authoritarian strategies for handling people. Eventually such strategies become "second nature," and the cornerstone of the police personality is firmly set. Cynicism evolves from a constant flow of experiences which demonstrate that people and events are not always what they seem to be. The natural tendency of most suspects, even when they are clearly guilty in the eyes of the police, is denial. Repeated attempts to mislead the police in the performance of their duty creates an air of suspicion and cynicism in the minds of most officers.

The origin of the police personality is at least bidimensional. On the one hand, some aspects of the world-view that comprise that personality can be attributed to the socialization which occurs when rookie officers are inducted into police ranks. On the other, it may be that some of the components of the police personality already exist in some individuals and lead them into police work.[31]   Supporting such a view are studies which indicate that police officers who come from conservative backgrounds continue to view themselves as defenders of middle-class morality.[32]

Police methods and the police culture are not static, however. Lawrence Sherman, for example, has reported on the modification of police tactics surrounding the use of weapons which characterized the period from 1970 to the 1980s.[33] Firearms, Sherman tells us, were routinely brought into play 20 years ago; although not often fired, they would be frequently drawn and pointed at suspects. Few departmental restrictions were placed on the use of weapons, and officers employed them almost as they would their badge in the per-formance of duties. Today the situation has changed. It is a rare officer who will unholster a weapon during police work, and those who do know that only the gravest of situations can justify the public display of firearms.

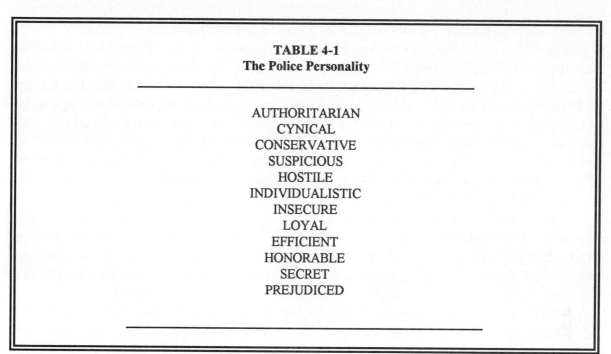

TABLE 4-1
The Police Personality

AUTHORITARIAN
CYNICAL
CONSERVATIVE
SUSPICIOUS
HOSTILE
INDIVIDUALISTIC
INSECURE
LOYAL
EFFICIENT
HONORABLE
SECRET
PREJUDICED

Some authors attribute this shift in thinking about firearms to increased training and the growth of restrictive policies.[34] Changes in training, however, are probably more a response to a revolution in social understandings about the kind of respect due citizens. For example, the widespread change in social consciousness regarding the worth of individuals, which has taken place over the past few decades, appears to have had considerable impact upon police subculture itself.

CORRUPTION

The police role carries considerable authority, and officers are expected to exercise a well-informed discretion in all their activities. The combination of authority and discretion, however, produces great potential for abuse.

Police deviance has been a problem in American society since the early days of policing. It is probably an ancient and natural tendency of human beings to attempt to placate or "win over" those in positions of authority over them. This tendency is complicated in today's materialistic society by greed and by the personal and financial benefits to be derived from evading the law. Hence, the temptations toward illegality offered to police range all the way from a free cup of coffee given by a small restaurant owner in the thought that one day it may be necessary to call upon the goodwill of the officer, perhaps for something as simple as a traffic ticket, to huge monetary bribes arranged by drug dealers to guarantee the police will look the other way as an important shipment of contraband arrives.

Police corruption ranges from minor "offenses" to those that are themselves serious violations of the law. Barker and Carter distinguish between occupational deviance and abuse of authority in describing police deviance.[35] Occupational deviance, they say, is motivated by the desire for personal benefit. Abuse of authority, however, occurs most often in order to further the organizational goals of law enforcement — including arrest, ticketing, and the successful conviction of suspects. Examples of police deviance, ranked in what the author judges to be an increasing level of severity, are shown in Table 4-2.

Two decades ago Frank Serpico made headlines as he testified before the Knapp Commission on police corruption in New York City.[36] Serpico, an undercover operative within the police department, revealed a complex web of corruption in which money and services routinely changed hands in "protection rackets" created by unethical officers. The Knapp Commission Report distinguished between two types of corrupt officers which they termed grass eaters and meat eaters.[37] "Grass eating," the most common form of police deviance, was described as illegitimate activity which occurs from time to time in the normal course of police work. It involves mostly small bribes or relatively minor services offered by citizens seeking to avoid arrest and prosecution. "Meat eating" is a much more serious form of corruption, involving as it does the active *seeking* of illicit money-making opportunities by officers. Meat eaters solicit bribes through threat or intimidation, whereas grass eaters make the simpler mistake of not refusing those which are offered.

Popular books often tell the story of police misbehavior. Some years ago Robert Daley's best seller *Prince of the City*[38] detailed the adventures of New York City detective Robert Leuci who walked among corrupt cops with a tape recorder hidden on his body. The more recent best-seller *Buddy Boys*,[39] by Mike McAlary, is subtitled "When Good Cops Turn Bad." McAlary, an investigative reporter with New York *Newsday*, began his efforts to uncover police corruption with a list of 13 names of officers who had been suspended in New York's 77th Precinct. His book describes organized criminal activity among police in the "Big Apple," involving holdups of drug dealers, organized burglaries, fencing operations, and numerous other illegal activities conducted from behind the shield. McAlary says New York's criminal officers saw themselves as a kind of "elite" within the department and applied the name "Buddy Boys" to their gang.[40]

Corruption, of course, is not unique to New York. In 1991 Detroit Police Chief William Hart was indicted by a federal grand jury and charged with the disappearance of $2.6 million from a secret police department fund.[41] The fund, which was to be used for undercover drug buys and to pay informants, had secretly paid out nearly $10 million since its creation in 1980. Hart, who was 67 years old at the time of the indictment, had been police chief in Detroit since 1976. The indictment came on the heels of other problems for Detroit police. Two years earlier, a city police officer was arrested for allegedly committing five robberies in one evening, and eight other officers were arrested for breaking and entering as well as assault. The *Detroit News*, a major newspaper in the city, conducted a study in which it found that Detroit police are "accused of committing crimes more often than officers in any other major U.S. city."[42] Convicted in 1992, Hart was sentenced to a number of years in prison.

The police personality provides fertile ground for the growth of corrupt practices. Police "cynicism" develops out of continued association with criminals and problem-ridden people. The cop who is "streetwise" is also ripe for corrupt influences to take root. Edwin Sutherland years ago applied the concept of differential association to deviant behavior.[43]

Sutherland suggested that continued association with one type of person, more frequently than with any other, would make the associates similar.

TABLE 4-2
Types of Police Deviance
by Category and Example

High-Level
Corruption
↑

Violent Crimes: The physical abuse of suspects, including torture and nonjustifiable homicide
Denying Civil Rights: Routinized schemes to circumvent constitutional guarantees
Criminal Enterprise: The resale of confiscated drugs, stolen property, etc.
Property Crimes: Burglary, theft, etc., committed by police
Major Bribes: Accepting $1000 to "overlook" contraband shipments and other law violations
Role Malfeasance: Destroying evidence, offering biased testimony, and protecting "crooked" cops
Being "Above" Inconvenient Laws: Speeding, smoking marijuana
Minor Bribes: Accepting $20 to "look the other way" on a ticket
Playing Favorites: Not ticketing friends, etc.
Gratuities: Accepting free coffee, meals, etc.
↓

Low-Level
Corruption

Sutherland was talking about criminals, not police officers. Consider, however, the dilemma of the average officer: a typical day is spent running down petty thieves, issuing traffic citations to citizens who try to talk their way out of the situation, dealing with prostitutes who feel "hassled" by the police presence, and arresting drug users who think it should be their right to do what they want as long as it "doesn't hurt anyone." The officer encounters personal hostility and experiences a constant, and often quite vocal, rejection of society's formalized norms. Bring into this environment low pay and the resulting sense that police work is not really valued, and it is easy to understand how an officer might develop a jaded attitude about the double standards of the civilization he or she is sworn to protect.

Corruption is not unique to American police. During the 1960s and 1970s the formerly prestigious London Metropolitan Police force was beset by a series of scandals. In 1969 the *London Times* pictured the "Met" as protecting a "firm within a firm," from which payoffs and corrupt practices emanated. The Royal Commission on Criminal Procedures was formed in 1977 to investigate allegations of routine and intentional mistreatment of suspects, and public opinion polls following 1985 saw the level of citizen satisfaction with the police decline substantially.[44]

Money — The Root of Police Evil?

Salaries paid to police officers in this country have been notoriously low when compared to those of other professions involving personal dedication, extensive training, high stress, and the risk of bodily harm. As police professionalism increases, salaries will rise. No matter how much police pay grows, however, it will never be able to compete with the staggering amounts of money to be made through dealing in contraband. In *The Underground Empire: Where Crime and Governments Embrace*, James Mills[45] tells the story of a man he calls a "young American entrepreneur," who, he writes, has "criminal operations on four continents and a daily income greater than U.S. Steel's."[46] Mills' book is about "Centac," a semisecret arm of the Drug Enforcement Administration, which coordinates the operations of various agencies in the ongoing battle against illicit drugs. Although international drug trafficking is the focus of *The Underground Empire*, the book contains details of international police corruption purchased with the vast resources available to the trade.

Working hand in hand with monetary pressures toward corruption are the moral dilemmas produced by the unenforceable laws which provide the basis for criminal profit. The Wickersham Commission warned during the Prohibition Era of the potential for official corruption inherent in the legislative taboo on alcohol. The demand for drink, immense as it was, called into question the wisdom of the law, while simultaneously providing vast resources designed to circumvent that law.   Today's drug scene bears some similarities to the Prohibition Era. As long as substantial segments of the population are willing to make large financial and other sacrifices to feed the drug trade, the pressures on the police to embrace corruption will remain substantial.

Combating Corruption

High moral standards, embedded in the principles of the police profession, and effectively communicated to individual officers through formal training and peer group socialization, would undoubtedly be the most effective way to combat corruption in police work. There are, of course, many officers of great personal integrity who hold to the highest of professional ideals, and there is evidence that law enforcement training programs are becoming increasingly concerned with instruction designed to reinforce the high ideals many recruits bring to police work. Practical efforts to combat corruption are also being brought to bear in many police organizations.

Most large law enforcement agencies have their own Internal Affairs Divisions which are empowered to investigate charges of wrongdoing made against officers. Where necessary, state police agencies may be called upon to examine reported incidents. Federal agencies, including the FBI and the DEA, involve themselves when corruption goes far enough to violate federal statutes. The U.S. Department of Justice, through various investigative offices, has the authority to examine possible violations of civil rights which may result from the misuse of police authority and is often supported by the American Civil Liberties Union, the NAACP, and other "watchdog" groups in such endeavors.

A little over a decade ago a U.S. Department of Justice–sponsored report studied scandals involving police corruption in New York City; Oakland, California; Newburgh,

New York; and an anonymous area termed "Central City" (somewhere in the Midwest).[47] A new police chief had been appointed in each city, and each arrived armed with a mandate to reform his department. Three major strategies for controlling corruption evolved in the reorganized departments. The first of these, termed "managerial strategies" by the report, involved a four-pronged attack on corruption: (1) New officers were hired and personnel were "turned over," on the theory that corruption cannot survive where the people perpetrating it are removed. (Personnel turnover can also be accomplished by simply shifting agents from one division to another, or from one geographical area to another.) (2) "Accountability" was clearly expected of supervisors. Those who wouldn't accept responsibility for combating corruption were asked to retire early or were removed from their command positions. (3) Closer supervision was required of commanders, especially sergeants, and other "first-line" supervisors. Sergeants were expected to spend more time with their officers and to create procedures for making any work performed more visible within the context of the department. (4) "Corrupting practices" were ended. Quotas for vice arrests and reimbursements for out-of-pocket, job-related expenses (such as lunches, office supplies, etc.), were eliminated. Drug arrests through "buys" were well financed, ending the pressure to hold back money from other drug arrests to effect new ones.

A second strategy for reducing corruption was termed "changing the task environment." City officials made public pleas asking that citizens refrain from offering "gifts" to law enforcement officers. The chief of the Newburgh force asked for the repeal of a local ordinance allowing officers to accept gifts of under $25.00 in value. Special teams of officers concentrated on making highly visible arrests of citizens who attempted to bribe the police.

The last strategy identified in the report was called "changing the political environment." One police chief clearly communicated a new policy of enforcing "all the laws against all the people, including City Council Members." The Newburgh, New York, police executive tried to organize a federal investigation of political officials in the county. Corrupt politicians were either forced out of office or encouraged to retire.

A final technique to combat corruption, which was used by all the departments in the study, relied upon "internal policing strategies." Each department either created an Internal Affairs Division (IAD) or increased the numbers of officers participating in internal investigations. The New York Police Department, for example, originally had only one officer assigned to internal affairs for every 533 other officers. Following reorganization, Internal Affairs increased in size almost ten times. One officer was assigned to IAD for every 64 enforcement officers. Each department also encouraged the Internal Affairs Division to become more active in seeking out information about corruption. Complaints were taken from numerous sources, including citizens who wished to remain anonymous, and former "reactive" strategies were turned into "proactive" efforts to gather information on corruption. The report revealed that Internal Affairs Divisions found especially useful wiretaps of known offenders (which sometimes implicated police "on the take"), "corruption patrolling" (in which IAD agents patrolled areas in which the potential for police corruption was high), and "integrity tests" (which provided officers with an easy opportunity to commit criminal or corrupt acts).

Drug Testing of Police Employees

The widespread potential for corruption created by illicit drugs has led to focused efforts to combat drug use by officers. Drug testing programs at the department level are an example of such efforts. In 1986 the National Institute of Justice (NIJ) conducted a telephone survey of 33 large police departments across the nation to determine what measures were being taken to identify officers and civilian employees who were using drugs.[48] The NIJ learned that almost all departments had written procedures to test employees who were reasonably suspected of drug abuse. Applicants for police positions were being tested by 73% of the departments surveyed, and 21% of the departments were actively considering testing all officers. In what some people found a surprisingly low figure, 21% reported that they might offer treatment to identified violators rather than dismiss them, depending upon their personal circumstances.

The International Association of Chiefs of Police has made available to today's police managers a "Model Drug Testing Policy." It is directed toward the needs of local departments and suggests:[49]

❶ Testing all applicants and recruits for drug or narcotics use.
❷ Testing current employees when performance difficulties or documentation indicate a potential drug problem.
❸ Testing current employees when they are involved in the use of excessive force or suffer or cause on-duty injury.
❹ Routine testing of all employees assigned to special "high risk" areas such as narcotics and vice.

Drug testing based upon a reasonable suspicion that drug abuse has or is occurring has been supported by the courts (*Maurice Turner* v. *Fraternal Order of Police*, 1985),[50] although random testing of officers was banned by the New York State Supreme Court in the case of *Philip Caruso, President of P.B.A.* v. *Benjamin Ward, Police Commissioner* (1986).[51] Citing overriding public interests, a 1989 decision by the U.S. Supreme Court upheld the testing of U.S. Customs personnel applying for transfer into positions involving drug law enforcement or carrying a firearm.[52] Many legal issues surrounding employee drug testing, however, remain to be resolved in court.

Complicating the situation is the fact that drug and alcohol addiction are "handicaps" protected by the Federal Rehabilitation Act of 1973. As such, federal law enforcement employees, as well as those working for agencies with federal contracts, are entitled to counseling and treatment before action toward termination can be taken.

The issue of employee drug testing in police departments, as in many other agencies, is a sensitive one. Some claim that existing tests for drug use are inaccurate, yielding a significant number of "false positives." Repeated testing and high "threshold" levels for narcotic substances in the blood may eliminate many of these concerns. Less easy to address, however, is the belief that drug testing intrudes upon the personal rights and professional dignity of individual employees.

☐ THE DANGERS OF POLICE WORK

Police work is, by its very nature, dangerous. While it is true that most officers throughout their careers never draw their weapons in the line of duty, it is also plain that some officers meet death while in the performance of their duties. On-the-job police deaths occur from stress, training accidents, and auto crashes. However, it is violent death at the hands of criminal offenders that police officers and their families fear most.

At 3:25 on a Friday morning in March 1988, New York City Police Officer Edward Byrne was gunned down while he sat in his patrol car protecting the home of a witness in a major narcotics case. Officer Byrne was 22 years old and had decided to make policing his career. The cold-blooded killing motivated then-Mayor Ed Koch to place a large advertisement in *The New York Times* condemning the world of drug peddling and American policies which support countries where drugs are produced.[53] The ad, accompanied by a large picture of Officer Byrne in uniform, called for New Yorkers to exert political pressures to end economic and other forms of U.S. aid to countries from which drugs are smuggled.

Execution-style killings like those of Officer Byrne are rare. More common are line-of-duty deaths in battles with fleeing felons, in domestic disturbances, and while apprehending criminal suspects. Table 4-3 shows the number of law enforcement officers killed during 1990 by circumstances.

For statistics on police killings to have meaning beyond the personal tragedy they entail, however, it is necessary to place them within a larger framework. Official statistics show that in 1991 there were 535,629 sworn state and local police officers in this country, and another 65,000 federal agents employed nationwide.[54] Such numbers show that the rate of violent death among law enforcement officers in the line of duty is small indeed.

TABLE 4-3
Law Enforcement Officers Killed
by Circumstances at Scene of Incident, 1990

Circumstance	Number Killed
Arrest situations	33
Investigations	22
Disturbance calls	7
Ambush	7
Traffic pursuits	6
Handling prisoners	2
Mentally deranged	1

Source: Bureau of Justice Statistics, *Sourcebook of Criminal Justice Statistics, 1990* (Washington, D.C.: U.S. Government Printing Office, 1991), p. 393.

Infected Evidence

Not all of the dangers facing law enforcement officers are as direct as outright violence and assault. The increasing incidence of serious diseases capable of being transmitted by blood and other bodily fluids, combined with the fact that crime and accident scenes are inherently dangerous, has made "caution" a necessary byword among investigators and "first on the scene" officers.   Potential for minor cuts and abrasions abounds in the broken glass and torn metal of a wrecked car, in the sharp edge of weapons remaining at the scene of an assault or murder, and in drug implements such as razor blades and hypodermic needles secreted in vehicles, apartments, and pockets.   Such minor injuries, previously shrugged off by many police personnel, have become a focal point for warnings about the dangers of AIDS (Acquired Immune Deficiency Syndrome), hepatitis B, tuberculosis, and other diseases spread through contact with infected blood.

In 1988 Sonoma County, California, Sheriff Dick Michaelson became the first law enforcement supervisor to announce a clear-cut case of AIDS infection in an officer caused by interaction with a suspect. A deputy in Michaelson's department apparently contracted AIDS a few years earlier when he was pricked by a hypodermic needle during a "pat down" search.[55]

Understandably, there is much concern among officers as to how to deal with the threat of AIDS and other bloodborne diseases. However, as a new manual of the New York City Police Department reminds its officers, "Police officers have a professional responsibility to render assistance to those who are in need of our services. We cannot refuse to help. Persons with infectious diseases must be treated with the care and dignity we show all citizens."[56]

The FBI has also become concerned with the use of breath alcohol instruments on infected persons, the handling of evidence of all types, seemingly innocuous implements such as staples, the emergency delivery of babies in squad cars, and the risk of attack (especially bites) by infected individuals who are being questioned or who are in custody. The following are among the 16 recommendations made by the FBI as "defenses against exposure" to infectious substances:[57]

❶ The first line of defense against infection at the crime scene is protecting the hands and keeping them away from the eyes, mouth, and nose.

❷ Any person with a cut, abrasion, or any other break in the skin on the hands should never handle blood or other body fluids without protection.

❸ Use gloves, and replace them whenever you leave the crime scene. Wash hands thoroughly.

❹ No one at the crime scene should be allowed to smoke, eat, drink, or apply makeup.

❺ Use the utmost care when handling knives, razors, broken glass, nails, and the like to prevent a puncture of the skin.

❻ If a puncture of the skin does occur cleanse it thoroughly with rubbing alcohol and wash with soap and water. Then seek immediate medical assistance.

❼ When possible, use disposable items at the crime scene, such as pencils, gloves, and throw-away masks. These items should be incinerated after use.

❽ Nondisposable items, such as cameras, notebooks, and so on, should be decontaminated using bleach mixed with water.

The National Institute of Justice adds to this list the recommendations that suspects should be asked to empty their own pockets, where possible, and that punctures wounds should be "milked" as in the case of snakebites to help flush infectious agents from the wound.[58]

It is sometimes necessary for local police agencies to send evidence out for analysis by well-equipped laboratories. When using the U.S. Mail, Part 72 of the Code of Federal Regulations requires that packages containing potentially contaminated bodily fluids be labeled with warnings and that they be tightly sealed and wrapped. The National Bureau of Standards is working on a process to sterilize evidence using gamma radiation. If the process is perfected, blood proteins and other substances crucial in forensic analysis will be preserved. In the meantime, the FBI Laboratory will accept evidence from AIDS cases for analysis only if:

❶ The contributor knows that the evidence will be "autoclaved," destroying its worth in serological analysis.

❷ Letters from the prosecuting and defense attorneys accompany the evidence, acknowledging that it will be autoclaved.

❸ The evidence is securely packaged and warnings labels have been applied.

Police departments will face an increasing number of legal challenges in the years to come in cases involving infectious diseases such as AIDS. Some predictable areas of concern will involve (1) the need to educate officers and other police employees relative to AIDS and other serious infectious diseases, (2) the responsibility of police departments to prevent the spread of AIDS in police lockups, and (3) the necessity of effective and nondiscriminatory enforcement activities and life-saving measures by police officers in AIDS environments. With regard to nondiscriminatory activities, the National Institute of Justice has suggested that legal claims in support of an officer's refusal to render assistance to AIDS victims would probably not be effective in court.[59] The reason is twofold: the officer has a basic duty to render assistance to individuals in need of it, and the possibility of AIDS transmission by casual contact has been scientifically established as extremely remote. A final issue of growing concern involves activities by police officers infected with the AIDS virus. A recent issue of *Law Enforcement News* reports, "Faced with one of the nation's largest populations of AIDS sufferers — and perhaps one of the largest cadres of AIDS-infected officers — the New York City Police Department has debuted its own AIDS awareness effort."[60] Few statistics are currently available on the number of officers with AIDS, but public reaction to those officers may be a developing problem area which police managers will soon need to address.

Police Stress

Perhaps the most insidious and least visible of all threats facing law enforcement personnel today is debilitating stress. While some degree of stress can be a positive motivator, serious stress, over long periods of time, is generally regarded as destructive, even life threatening.

Stress is a natural component of police work. The American Institute of Stress, based in Yonkers, New York, ranks policing among the top ten stress-producing jobs in the country.[61] Danger, frustration, paper work, the daily demands of the job, and a lack of understanding from family members and friends contribute to the negative stresses officers experience.

Joseph Victor has identified four sources of police stress:[62] (1) external stress, which results from "real dangers," such as responding to calls involving armed suspects, (2) organizational stress, generated by the demands of police organizations themselves, such as scheduling, paperwork, training requirements, and so on, (3) personal stress, produced by interpersonal relationships among officers themselves, and (4) operational stress, which Victor defines as "the total effect of the need to confront daily the tragedies of urban life."

Some of the stressors in police work are particularly destructive. One is frustration brought on by the inability to be effective, regardless of the amount of personal effort expended. From the point of view of the individual officer, the police mandate is to bring about some change in society for the better. The crux of police work involves making arrests based upon thorough investigations which lead to convictions and the removal of individuals who are damaging to the social fabric of the community — all under the umbrella of the criminal law. Unfortunately, reality is often far from the ideal. Arrests may not lead to convictions. Evidence which is available to the officer may not be allowed in court. Sentences which are imposed may seem too "light" to the arresting officer. The feelings of powerlessness and frustration which come from seeing repeat offenders back on the streets, and from experiencing numerous injustices worked upon seemingly innocent victims, may greatly stress police officers and cause them to question the purpose of their professional lives.

Another source of stress — that of living with constant danger — is incomprehensible to most of us, even to the family members of many officers. As James Mills says, "I kick in a door and I've gotta talk some guy into putting a gun down . . . and I go home, and my wife's upset because the lawn isn't cut and the kids have been bad. Now, to *her* that's a real problem."[63]

Stress is not unique to the police profession, but because of the "macho" attitude that has traditionally been associated with police work, denial of the stress experience may be found more often among police officers than in other occupational groups. Certain types of individuals are probably more susceptible to the negative effects of stress than others. The "Type A" personality was popularized a few years ago as the category of person more likely to perceive life in terms of pressure and performance. "Type B" personalities were said to be more "laid back" and less likely to suffer from the negative effects of stress. Police ranks, drawn as they are from the general population, are filled with both stress-sensitive and stress-resistant personalities.

People who are susceptible to stress tend to react in characteristic ways. They become agitated, nervous, depressed, and argumentative. Stress may lead to alcoholism, drug abuse, divorce, high blood pressure, other serious physical illnesses, and sometimes suicide.

Stress Reduction

Natural reactions to stress include attempts at its control. Health care professionals, for example, have long been noted for their ability to joke around patients who may be seriously ill or even dying, and humor is a well recognized technique for stress management. Maintaining an emotional distance from stressful events is another way of coping with them, although such distance is not always easy to maintain. Police officers who have had to deal with serious cases of physical child abuse have often reported on the emotional turmoil they experienced as a consequence of what they saw.

The support of family and friends can be crucial in developing other strategies to handle stress. Exercise, meditation, abdominal breathing, biofeedback, self-hypnosis, guided imaging, induced relaxation, subliminal conditioning, music, prayer, and diet have all been cited as techniques which can be useful in stress reduction. Devices to measure stress levels are available in the form of hand-held heart rate monitors, blood pressure devices, "biodots" (which change color according to the amount of blood flow in the extremities), and psychological inventories.

POLICE CIVIL LIABILITY

An area of growing concern among police managers today is that of civil liability for official misconduct. Police officers may become involved in a variety of situations, as shown by Table 4-4, which create the potential for civil suits against the officers, their superiors, and their departments.

Swanson says that the most common sources of lawsuits against the police involve "assault, battery, false imprisonment, and malicious prosecution."[64] A classic case of police assault involved Henry Z. Spell, who was arrested a few years ago by the Fayetteville, North Carolina, Police Department and charged with driving while impaired and possession of methaqualone. During the booking process, Spell was beaten by officers and kicked in the groin, which left him sterile. Spell brought suit against the police department, and was able to show that at the time he was attacked he was not offering any resistance and, in fact, was restrained with his hands "cuffed" behind his back. In addition, Spell's lawyers offered evidence to demonstrate that the treatment of their client was characteristic of police operations in the city at the time. Spell's award of $1.4 million, with accumulated interest, left him a wealthy man.

TABLE 4-4
Major Sources of Police Civil Liability

Failure to Protect Property in Police Custody
Negligence in the Care of Persons in Police Custody
Failure to Render Proper Emergency Medical Assistance
Failure to Prevent a Foreseeable Crime
Failure to Aid Private Citizens
Lack of Due Regard for the Safety of Others
False Arrest
False Imprisonment
Inappropriate Use of Deadly Force
Unnecessary Assault or Battery
Malicious Prosecution
Violations of Constitutional Rights

Of all complaints brought against the police, assault charges are the best known, being, as they are, subject to high media visibility. Less visible, but not uncommon, are civil suits charging the police with false arrest or false imprisonment. In the 1986 case of *Malley* v. *Briggs*,[65] the U.S. Supreme Court held that a police officer who effects an arrest or a conducts a search on the basis of an improperly issued warrant may be liable for monetary damages when a reasonably well-trained officer, under the same circumstances, "would have known that his affidavit failed to establish probable cause and that he should not have applied for the warrant." Significantly, the Court, in *Malley,* also ruled that an officer "cannot excuse his own default by pointing to the greater incompetence of the magistrate."[66] When an officer makes an arrest without probable cause, or simply impedes an individual's right to leave the scene without good reason, he or she may well be liable for the charge of false arrest. Officers who enjoy "throwing their weight around" are especially subject to this type of suit, grounded as it is on the abuse of police authority. Because employers may generally be sued for the negligent or malicious actions of their employees, many police departments are finding themselves named as co-defendants in lawsuits today.

Negligent actions by officers may also provide the basis for suits. High-speed chases are especially dangerous because of the potential they entail for injury to innocent bystanders. Flashing blue or red lights (the color of police vehicle lights varies by state) legally only *request* the right-of-way on a highway, they do not demand it. Officers who drive in such a way as to place others in danger may find themselves the subject of suits. In the case of *Biscoe* v. *Arlington* (1984),[67] for example, Alvin Biscoe was awarded $5 million after he lost both legs as a consequence of a high-speed chase while he was waiting to cross the street. Biscoe was an innocent bystander and was struck by a police car that had gone out of control. The fact that the police department in *Biscoe* had sanctioned high-speed chases as a part of official policy made the department especially liable. Departments may protect themselves to some degree through regulations limiting the authority of their personnel. In a recent case, for example, a Louisiana police department was exonerated in an accident which occurred during a high-speed chase because of its policy limiting emergency driving to no more than 20 miles over the posted speed limit. The officer, however, who drove 75 mph in a 40 mph zone was found to be negligent and held liable for damages.[68]

Law enforcement supervisors may find themselves the object of lawsuits by virtue of the fact that they are responsible for the actions of their officers. Where it can be shown that supervisors were negligent in hiring (as when someone with a history of alcoholism, mental problems, sexual deviance, or drug abuse is employed), or if supervisors failed in their responsibility to train officers properly before they armed and deployed them, findings of supervisory liability may result.

In the 1989 case of the *City of Canton, Ohio* v. *Harris*,[69] the U.S. Supreme Court ruled that a "failure to train" can become the basis for legal liability on the part of a municipality where the "failure to train amounts to deliberate indifference to the rights of persons with whom the police come into contact."[70] In that case, Geraldine Harris was arrested and taken to the Canton, Ohio, police station. While at the station she slumped to the floor several times. Officers finally decided to leave her on the floor and never called for qualified medical assistance. Upon release, Ms. Harris was taken by family members to a local hospital. She was hospitalized for a week and received follow-up outpatient treatment for the next year. The Court ruled that although municipalities could not justifiably be held liable for limited instances of unsatisfactory training, they could be held accountable where the failure to train results from a deliberate or conscious choice.

Civil suits brought against law enforcement personnel are of two types: state or federal. Suits brought in state courts have generally been the most common form of civil litigation involving police officers. In recent years, however, an increasing number of suits are being brought in federal courts on the legal rationale that the civil rights of the plaintiff, as guaranteed by federal law, have been denied.

Federal suits are often called 1983 lawsuits because they are based upon Section 1983 of Title 42 of the United States Code, an act passed by Congress in 1871 to ensure the civil rights of men and women of all races. That act requires due process of law before any person can be deprived of life, liberty, or property, and specifically provides redress for the denial of these constitutional rights by officials acting under color of *state* law. For example, a 1983 suit may be brought against officers who shoot suspects under questionable circumstances — thereby denying them of their right to life — without due process. The 1981 case of *Prior* v. *Woods*[71] resulted in a $5.7 million judgment against the Detroit Police Department after David Prior — who was mistaken for a burglar — was shot and killed in front of his home.

Another type of liability action, this one directed specifically at federal officials or enforcement agents, is called a Bivens suit. The case of *Bivens* v. *Six Unknown Federal Agents* (1971)[72] established a path for legal action against agents enforcing federal laws which is similar to that found in a 1983 suit. Bivens actions may be addressed against individuals, but not the United States. Federal officers have generally been granted a court-created qualified immunity and have been protected from suits where they were found to have acted in the belief that their action was consistent with federal law.[73]

Title 42, United States Code
Section 1983

Every person who, under color of any statute, ordinance, regulation, custom, or usage, of any State or Territory, subjects, or causes to be subjected, any citizen of the United States or other person within the jurisdiction thereof to the deprivation of any rights, privileges, or immunities secured by the Constitution and laws, shall be liable to the party injured in an action at law, suit in equity, or other proper proceeding for redress.

In times past, the doctrine of sovereign immunity barred legal actions against state and local governments. Sovereign immunity was a legal theory that held that a governing body could not be sued because it made the law and therefore could not be bound by it. Immunity is a much more complex issue today. Some states have officially abandoned any pretext at immunity through legislative action. New York state, for example, has declared that public agencies are equally as liable as private agencies for violations of constitutional rights. Other states, like California, have enacted statutory provisions which define and place limits on governmental liability.[74] A number of state immunity statutes have been struck down by court decision. In general, states are moving in the direction of setting dollar limits on liability and adopting federal immunity principles to protect individual officers, including "good faith" and "reasonable belief" rules.

Most departments carry liability insurance to protect them against the severe financial damage which can result from the loss of a large suit. Some officers make it a point to acquire private policies which provide coverage in the event they are named as individuals in such suits. Both types of insurance policies generally provide for a certain amount of legal fees to be paid by the policy for defense against the suit, regardless of the outcome of the case. Police departments who face civil prosecution because of the actions of an officer, however, may find that legal and financial liability extends to supervisors, city managers, and the community itself. Where insurance coverage does not exist (as in the case of the city of Fayetteville, or is inadequate, city coffers may be nearly drained to meet the damages awarded.[75]

Deadly Force

The use of deadly force by police officers is one area of potential civil liability which has received considerable attention in recent years. Historically, the fleeing felon rule applied to most U.S. jurisdictions. It held that officers could use deadly force to prevent the escape of a suspected felon, even when that person represented no immediate threat to the officer or to the public. The fleeing felon rule probably stemmed from early common law punishments which specified death for a large number of crimes. Today, however, the death penalty is far less frequent in application, and the fleeing felon rule has been called into question in a number of courts.

The 1985 Supreme Court case of *Tennessee* v. *Garner*[76] specified the conditions under which deadly force could be used in the apprehension of suspected felons. Edward Garner, a 15-year-old suspected burglar, was shot to death by Memphis police officers after he refused their order to halt and attempted to climb over a chain link fence. In an action initiated by Garner's father, who claimed that his son's constitutional rights had been violated, the Court held that the use of deadly force by the police to prevent the escape of a fleeing felon might be justified only where the suspect could reasonably be thought to represent a significant threat of serious injury or death to the public or to the officer. In reaching its decision, the Court declared that "The use of deadly force to prevent the escape of all felony suspects, whatever the circumstances, is constitutionally unreasonable."[77]

Studies of killings by the police have often focused on claims of discrimination, that is, that black and minority suspects are more likely to be shot than whites. Research in the area, however, has not provided solid support for such claims. While individuals shot by police are more likely to be minorities, James Fyfe[78] found that police officers will generally respond with deadly force when mortally threatened and that minorities are considerably more likely to use weapons in assaults on officers than are whites. Complicating the picture further were Fyfe's data showing that minority officers are involved in the shooting of suspects more often than other officers, a finding that may be due to the assignment of such officers to inner-city and ghetto areas. However, a more recent study by Fyfe,[79] which analyzed police shootings in Memphis, Tennessee, found that black property offenders were twice as likely as whites to be shot by police.

Although relatively few police officers will ever feel the need to draw their weapon during the course of their careers, those who do may find themselves embroiled in a web of social, legal, and personal complications. It is estimated that an average year sees 600 suspects killed by gunfire from public police in America, while another 1,200 are shot and wounded, and 1,800 individuals are shot at and missed.[80]

The personal side of police shootings is well summarized in the title of an article in *Police Magazine*, "I've Killed That Man Ten Thousand Times."[81] The article demonstrated how police officers who have to use their weapon may be haunted by years of depression and despair. Not long ago, according to Anne Cohen, author of the article, all departments did to help officers who had shot someone was to "give him enough bullets to reload his gun." The stress and trauma which result from shootings by officers in defense of themselves or others are only now beginning to be realized, and most departments have yet to develop mechanisms for dealing with them adequately.[82]

PROFESSIONALISM AND ETHICS

Police administrators have responded in a variety of ways to issues of danger, liability, and the potential for corruption. Among the most significant responses have been increased calls for professionalism at all levels of policing. A profession is characterized by a body of specialized knowledge, acquired through extensive education,[83] and by a well-considered set of internal standards and ethical guidelines which hold members of the profession accountable to one another and to society. Associations of like-minded practitioners generally serve to create and disseminate standards for the profession as a whole.

Contemporary policing evidences many of the attributes of a profession. Specialized knowledge in policing includes a close familiarity with criminal law, laws of procedure, constitutional guarantees, and relevant Supreme Court decisions; a working knowledge of weapons and hand-to-hand tactics; driving skills and vehicle maintenance; a knowledge of radio communications; report-writing abilities; interviewing techniques; and media and human relations skills. Other specialized knowledge may include Breathalyzer operation, special weapons firing, polygraph operation, conflict resolution, and hostage negotiation skills. Supervisory personnel require an even wider range of skills, including administrative knowledge, management techniques, personnel administration, and deployment strategies for optimum utilization of officers and physical resources.

The Law Enforcement Code of Ethics

As a Law Enforcement Officer, my fundamental duty is to serve mankind; to safeguard lives and property; to protect the innocent against deception, the weak against oppression or intimidation, and the peaceful against violence or disorder; and to respect the Constitutional rights of all men to liberty, equality and justice.

I will keep my private life unsullied as an example to all; maintain courageous calm in the face of danger, scorn, or ridicule; develop self-restraint; and be constantly mindful of the welfare of others. Honest in thought and deed in both my personal and official life, I will be exemplary in obeying the laws of the land and the regulations of my department. Whatever I see or hear of a confidential nature or that is confided to me in my official capacity will be kept secret unless revelation is necessary in the performance of my duty.

I will never act officiously or permit personal feelings, prejudices, animosities or friendships to influence my decisions. With no compromise for crime and with relentless prosecution of criminals, I will enforce the law courteously and appropriately without fear or favor, malice or ill will, never employing unnecessary force or violence and never accepting gratuities.

I recognize the badge of my office as a symbol of public faith, and I accept it as a public trust to be held so long as I am true to the ethics of the police service. I will constantly strive to achieve these objectives and ideals, dedicating myself before God to my chosen profession . . . law enforcement.

Source: International Association of Chiefs of Police. Reprinted with permission.

Basic law enforcement training requirements were begun in the 1950s by the state of New York, and through a voluntary system of Peace Officer Standards and Training (POST) in California. Today, such requirements are mandated by law in every state in the nation, although they vary considerably from region to region. Modern police education involves, at a minimum, more than 100 classroom contact hours (Missouri), and in some places nearly 1,000 hours of intensive training (Hawaii),[84] in subject areas which include human relations, firearms and weapons, communications, legal aspects of policing, patrol, criminal investigations, administration, report writing, and criminal justice systems.

Federal law enforcement agents receive schooling at the Federal Law Enforcement Training Center (FLETC) in Glynco, Georgia. The Center provides training for about 60 federal law enforcement agencies (excluding the FBI, which has its own training center at Quantico, Virginia) and has begun offering advanced training to state and local police organizations, where such training is not available under other auspices. Specialized schools, such as Northwestern University's Traffic Institute, have also been credited with raising the level of police practice from purely operational concerns to a more professional level.[85]

Police work is guided by an ethical code originated in 1956 by the Peace Officer's Research Association of California (PORAC) in conjunction with Dr. Douglas M. Kelley of Berkeley's School of Criminology.[86] The *Law Enforcement Code of Ethics* is reproduced in the accompanying box. Ethics training is still not well integrated into most basic law enforcement training programs, but a movement in that direction has begun, and calls for expanded training in ethics are on the increase.

Professional associations abound in police work. The Fraternal Order of Police (FOP) is one of the best known organizations of public service workers in the United States. The International Association of Chiefs of Police (IACP) has done much to raise professional standards in policing and continually strives for improvements in law enforcement nationwide.

Accreditation provides another channel toward police professionalism. The Commission on Accreditation for Law Enforcement Agencies was formed in 1979. Police departments wishing to apply for accreditation through the Commission must meet hundreds of standards relating to areas as diverse as day-to-day operations, administration, review of incidents involving the use of a weapon by officers, and evaluation and promotion of personnel. To date, few police agencies are accredited, although a number have applied to begin the process. Those agencies are now conducting self-evaluations as part of the application process. Although accreditation makes possible the identification of high-quality police departments, it is often undervalued because it carries few incentives. Accreditation is still only "icing on the cake," and does not guarantee a department any rewards beyond the recognition of peers.

Education

As the concern for quality policing builds, increasing emphasis is being placed on the education of police officers. As early as 1931, the National Commission on Law Observance and Enforcement (the Wickersham Commission) highlighted the importance of a well-educated police force by calling for "educationally sound" officers.[87] In 1967 the President's Commission on Law Enforcement and the Administration of Justice voiced the belief that "[t]he ultimate aim of all police departments should be that all personnel with general enforcement powers have baccalaureate degrees." At the time, the average educational level of police officers in the United States was 12.4 years — slightly beyond a high school degree. In 1973 the National Advisory Commission on Criminal Justice Standards and Goals made the following rather specific recommendation:[88] "Every police agency should, no later than 1982, require as a condition of initial employment the completion of at least 4 years of education . . . at an accredited college or university."[89]

Recommendations, of course, do not always translate into practice. Today, the average level of educational achievement among law enforcement officers stands at almost 14 years — nearly the equivalent of an associate's degree from a "two-year" or community college.[90] Female officers (with an average level of educational achievement of 14.6 years) tend to be better educated than their male counterparts (who report an average attainment level of 13.6 years). Only 3.3% of male officers hold graduate degrees, while almost one-third (30.2%) of women officers hold such degrees. On the down side, 34.8% of male officers have no college experience, and 24.1% of female officers have none.

A report by the Police Executive Research Forum (PERF) explains the difference between male and female educational achievement by saying that "[w]omen tend to rely on higher education more than men as a springboard for a law enforcement career . . . [and] [p]olice departments may utilize higher standards — consciously or unconsciously — for selecting women officers."[91]

The PERF report stresses the need for educated police officers, citing the following benefits which accrue to police agencies from the hiring of educated officers:[92] (1) better written reports, (2) enhanced communications with the public, (3) more effective job performance, (4) fewer citizens' complaints, (5) greater initiative, (6) a wiser use of discretion, (7) a heightened sensitivity to racial and ethnic issues, and (8) fewer disciplinary problems. On the other hand, a greater likelihood that educated officers will leave police work, and their tendency to question orders and request reassignment with relative frequency, are some of the education-induced drawbacks which the report lists.[93]

To meet the growing needs of police officers for college level training, the International Association of Police Professors (IAPP) was formed in 1963. The IAPP later changed its name to the Academy of Criminal Justice Sciences (ACJS) and widened its focus to include criminal justice education.

A number of agencies now require the completion of at least some college-level work for officers seeking promotion. The San Diego Police Department, for example, requires two years of college work for promotion to the rank of sergeant.[94] In 1988 the Sacramento, California, police department set completion of a four-year college degree as a requirement for promotion to lieutenant, and, in the same year, the New York City police department announced a requirement of at least 64 college credits for promotion to supervisory ranks. At the state level, a variety of plans exist for integrating college work into police careers. Minnesota now requires a college degree for new candidates taking the state's Peace Officer Standards and Training Board's licensing examination. Successful completion of all POST requirements permits employment as a fully certified law enforcement officer in the state of Minnesota. Beginning in 1991, the state of New York set 60 semester hours of college-level work as a mandated minimum for hiring into the New York State Police. Finally, many federal agencies require college degrees for entry-level positions. Among them are the FBI, DEA, ATF, Secret Service, the U.S. Customs Service, and the Immigration and Naturalization Service.

RECRUITMENT AND SELECTION

Any profession needs informed, dedicated, and competent personnel. When the National Advisory Commission on Criminal Justice Standards and Goals issued its report on the "Police," it bemoaned the fact that "many college students are unaware of the varied, interesting, and challenging assignments and career opportunities that exist within the police service."[95] In the intervening years the efforts made by police departments to correct such misconceptions have had a considerable effect. Today police organizations actively recruit new officers from college campuses, professional organizations, and two-year junior colleges and technical institutes. Education is an important criterion in selecting today's police recruits.[96] Some departments require a minimum number of college credits for entry-level work. A policy of the Dallas, Texas, Police Department requiring a minimum of 45 semester hours of successful college-level study for new recruits was upheld in 1986 by the U.S. Supreme Court in the case of *Davis* v. *Dallas.*[97]

A CAREER WITH THE DRUG ENFORCEMENT ADMINISTRATION

Typical Positions. Criminal investigator, diversion investigator, and intelligence research specialist.

Employment Requirements. Applicants for GS-5 levels must (1) be U.S. citizens, (2) hold a four-year college degree, (3) be in good health, (4) pass a comprehensive background investigation, (5) possess effective oral and written communications skills, and (6) have three years of general job experience. Applicants for GS-7 levels must also demonstrate one of the following: (1) a 2.9 overall college average, (2) a 3.5 grade point average in the applicant's major field of study, (3) a standing in the upper one-third of the applicant's graduating class, (4) membership in a national honorary scholastic society, (5) one year of successful graduate study, or (6) one year of specialized experience (defined as "progressively responsible investigative experience").

Other Requirements. Applicants must (1) be willing to travel frequently, (2) submit to a urinalysis test designed to detect the presence of controlled substances, and (3) successfully complete a two-month formal training program at the FBI's training center in Quantico, Virginia.

Salary. Starting salary in 1993 for individuals with four-year college degrees was $26,289. Appointments are made at higher pay grades for individuals possessing additional education and experience.

Benefits. Benefits include (1) 13 days of sick leave annually, (2) 2½ to 5 weeks of annual paid vacation and 10 paid federal holidays each year, (3) federal health and life insurance, and (4) a comprehensive retirement program.

Direct inquiries to: Drug Enforcement Administration, Office of Personnel, Recruitment, and Placement, 1405 I Street, N.W., Washington, D.C. 20537. Phone: (202) 307-4000.

The National Commission report stressed the setting of high standards for police recruits and recommended a strong emphasis on minority recruitment, an elimination of residence requirements for new officers, a decentralized application and testing procedure, and various recruiting incentives. The Commission also suggested that a four-year college degree should soon become a reasonable expectation for police recruits. A recent survey of 699 police departments by the Police Executive Research Forum (PERF) found that the average level of education among both black and white officers was 14 years of schooling. Hispanic officers averaged 13 years spent in school. The survey also found that 62% of responding agencies had at least one formal policy in support of officers pursuing higher education.[98]

Effective policing, however, may depend more upon personal qualities than it does upon educational attainment. O. W. Wilson once enumerated some of the "desirable personal qualities for patrol officers."[99] They included (1) initiative; (2) the capacity for responsibility; (3) the ability to deal alone with emergencies; (4) the capacity to communicate effectively with persons of diverse social, cultural, and ethnic backgrounds; (5) the ability to learn a variety of tasks quickly; (6) the attitude and ability necessary to adapt to technological changes; (7) the desire to help people in need; (8) an understanding of others; (9) emotional maturity; and (10) sufficient physical strength and endurance.

Standard procedures employed by modern departments in selecting trainees usually include basic skills tests, physical agility measurements, interviews, physical examinations, eye tests, psychological evaluations, and background investigations into the personal character of applicants. After training, successful applicants are typically placed on a period of probation approximately one year in length. The probationary period in police work has been called the "first true job-related test . . . in the selection procedure,"[100] providing as it does the opportunity for supervisors to gauge the new officer's response to real-life situations.

Ethnic Minorities and Women

In 1967 the National Advisory Commission on Civil Disorders conducted a survey of supervisory personnel in police departments.[101] They found a marked disparity between the number of black and white officers in leadership positions. One of every 26 black police officers had been promoted to the rank of sergeant, while the ratio among whites was 1 in 12. Only 1 of every 114 black officers had become a lieutenant, while among whites the ratio was 1 out of 26. At the level of captain the disparity was even greater — 1 out of every 235 black officers had achieved the rank of captain, while 1 of every 53 whites had climbed to that rank.

Since then, the emphasis placed upon minority recruitment by task forces, civil rights groups, courts, and society in general has done much to rectify the situation. In 1979, for example, one of the first affirmative action disputes involving a police department was settled out of court. The settlement required the San Francisco Police Department to ensure that over the next ten years minorities would receive 50% of all promotions and that 20% of all new officers hired would be women.[102] Today the situation is improving. Many departments, through dedicated recruitment efforts, have dramatically increased their complement of officers from underrepresented groups. The metropolitan Detroit police department, for example, now has a force which is more than 50% black.

Unfortunately, although ethnic minorities have moved into policing in substantial numbers, females are still substantially underrepresented. A recent study by the Police Foundation[103] found that women accounted for nearly 9% of all officers in municipal departments serving populations of 50,000 or more, but that they comprised only 3% of all supervisors in city agencies and 1% of supervisors in state police agencies. Female officers made up 10.1% of the total number of officers in departments which were functioning under court order to increase their proportion of women officers, while women constituted 8.3% of officers in agencies with voluntary affirmative action programs and only 6.1% of officers in departments without such programs.

A 1991 report[104] on women police officers in Massachusetts found that female officers (1) are "extremely devoted to their work;" (2) "see themselves as women first, and then police officers;" and (3) were more satisfied when working in non-uniformed capacities. Two groups of women officers were identified: those who felt themselves to be well integrated into their departments and were confident in their jobs, and those who experienced strain and on-the-job isolation. The officers' children were cited as a significant influence on their self-perceptions and on the way in which they viewed their jobs. The demands which attend child rearing in contemporary society were found to be major factors contributing to the resignation of female officers. The study also found that the longer women officers stayed on the job, the greater stress and frustration they tended to experience — primarily as a consequence of the noncooperative attitudes of male officers. Some of the female officers interviewed identified networking as a potential solution to the stresses encountered by female officers, but also said that when women get together to solve problems they are seen as "crybabies" rather than professionals. Said one of the women in the study, "[w]e've lost a lot of good women who never should have left the job. If we had helped each other maybe they wouldn't have left."[105] Networking is a concept which is quickly taking root among the nation's women police officers, as attested to by the growth of organizations like the International Association of Women Police, based in New York City. Mentoring, another method for introducing women to police work, has been suggested by some authors.[106] Mentoring would create semiformal relationships between experienced women officers and rookies entering the profession. Through such relationships, problems could be addressed as they arose, and the experienced officer could serve to guide her junior partner through the maze of formal and informal expectations which surround the job of policing.

Other studies, like those already discussed, have found that female officers are often underutilized, and that many departments are hesitant to assign women to patrol and other potentially dangerous field activities. As a consequence, some women in police work experience frustrations and a lack of satisfaction with their jobs.[107] Other women are hesitant to consider a police career, and a few departments complain that it is difficult to find significant numbers of well-qualified minority recruits interested in police work. Also, harassment on the job continues to be a reality for some minority officers. For example, in the late 1980s a black FBI agent complained to his superiors and to the Justice Department's Office of Professional Responsibility about death threats, obscene mail, and threats against his family, apparently generated by fellow agents because he is black. An Equal Employment Opportunity Commission decision in the case concluded that the agent had indeed been the victim of a series of discriminatory activities, and the officer filed suit against the FBI alleging violation of his civil rights.[108]

In a continuing effort to increase the representation of women and ethnic minorities in police work, the Police Foundation recommends: (1) involving underrepresented groups in affirmative action and long-term planning programs which are undertaken by police departments; (2) encouraging the development of an open system of promotions whereby women can feel free to apply for promotion, and in which qualified individuals of any race or gender will face equity in the promotion process; and (3) using periodic audits to ensure that women officers are not being underutilized by being ineffectively tracked into clerical and support positions.[109]

◻ SUMMARY

Police work today is characterized by the opportunity for individual officers to exercise considerable discretion, by a powerful subculture which communicates select values in support of a "police personality," and by the very real possibility of corruption and deviance. Opposed to the illegitimate use of police authority, however, are increased calls for an ethical awareness in police work and continuing growth of the professionalism ideal. Professionalism, with its emphasis on education, training, high ethical values, and personal accountability, should soon lead to greater public recognition of the significance of police work, and to higher salaries for career police personnel. Increased salaries and a clear public appreciation for the police should do much to decrease corruption and deviance in law enforcement ranks.

DISCUSSION QUESTIONS

1. What are the central features of the police "working personality"? How does the police working personality develop? What programs might be initiated to "shape" the police personality in a more desirable way?

2. Do you think police officers exercise too much discretion in the performance of their duties? Why or why not? If it is desirable to limit discretion, how would you do it?

3. What themes run through the findings of the Knapp Commission and the Wickersham Commission? What innovative steps might police departments take to reduce or eliminate corruption among their officers?

4. Is police work a profession? Why do you think it is, or why do you think it is not? What advantages are there to viewing policing as a profession? How do you think most police officers today see their work — as a "profession" or as just a "job?"

5. Reread the *Law Enforcement Code of Ethics* found in this chapter. Do you think most police officers make conscious efforts to apply the code in the performance of their duty? How might ethics training in police departments be improved?

NOTES

1. James Q. Wilson, *Thinking About Crime* (New York: Basic Books, 1975), p. 99.

2. O. W. Wilson, "Reorganization in Chicago," in *The Police Yearbook* (Washington, D.C.: The International Association of Chiefs of Police, 1962), pp. 56–64.

3. Francis X. Hartmann, "Debating the Evolution of American Policing," *Perspectives on Policing*, No. 5 (Washington, D.C.: National Institute of Justice, November 1988).

4. James Q. Wilson, *Varieties of Police Behavior: The Management of Law and Order in Eight Communities* (Cambridge, MA: Harvard University Press, 1968).

5. Gary W. Sykes, "Street Justice: A Moral Defense of Order Maintenance Policing," *Justice Quarterly* (October 1986), p. 505.

6. Louis A. Radelet, *The Police and the Community* (Encino, CA: Glencoe, 1980).

7. Egon Bittner, "Community Relations," in *Police Community Relations: Images, Roles, Realities* by Alvin W. Cohn and Emilio C. Viano (Philadelphia: J. B. Lippincott, 1976), pp. 77–82.

8. Ibid.

9. Charles Hale, *Police Patrol: Operations and Management* (New York: John Wiley and Sons, 1981), p. 112.

10. Paul B. Weston, *Police Organization and Management* (Pacific Palisades, CA: Goodyear, 1976), p. 159.

11. Hale, *Police Patrol*.

12. Mark H. Moore and Robert C. Trojanowicz, "Corporate Strategies for Policing," in *Perspectives on Policing*, No. 6 (Washington, D.C.: National Institute of Justice, November 1988).

13. Ibid., p. 6.

14. Herman Goldstein, *Problem-Oriented Policing* (Philadelphia: Temple University Press, 1990), p. 14.

15. Ibid., p. 8.

16. See Jerome H. Skolnick and David H. Bayley, *Community Policing: Issues and Practices Around the World* (Washington, D.C.: National Institute of Justice, 1988), and Jerome H. Skolnick and David H. Bayley, "Theme and Variation in Community Policing," in Norval Morris and Michael Tonry, eds., *Crime and Justice: An Annual Review of Research*, Volume 10 (Chicago: University of Chicago Press, 1988), pp. 1–37.

17. Ibid.

18. Ibid.

19. Wesley G. Skogan, *Disorder and Decline: Crime and the Spiral of Decay in American Neighborhoods* (New York: The Free Press, 1900), pp. 90–91.

20. Jerome H. Skolnick and David H. Bayley, *The New Blue Line: Police Innovation in Six American Cities* (New York: The Free Press, 1986).

21. Malcolm K. Sparrow, "Implementing Community Policing," *Perspectives on Policing*, Vol. 9 (Washington, D.C.: National Institute of Justice, 1988).

22. Robert Wasserman and Mark H. Moore, "Values in Policing," *Perspectives in Policing*, No. 8 (Washington, D.C.: National Institute of Justice, November 1988), p. 7.

23. Howard Cohen, "Overstepping Police Authority," *Criminal Justice Ethics* (Summer/Fall 1987), pp. 52–60.

24. Kenneth Culp Davis, *Police Discretion* (St. Paul, MN: West, 1975).

25. Sykes, *Street Justice*, p. 505.

26. Jerome H. Skolnick, *Justice Without Trial: Law Enforcement in A Democratic Society* (New York: Wiley, 1966).

27. William A. Westley, *Violence and the Police: A Sociological Study of Law, Custom, and Morality* (Cambridge, MA: MIT Press, 1970) and William A. Westley "Violence and the Police," *American Journal of Sociology*, Vol. 49 (1953), pp. 34–41.

28. Arthur Niederhoffer, *Behind the Shield: The Police in Urban Society* (Garden City, NY: Anchor Press, 1967).

29. Thomas Barker and David L. Carter, *Police Deviance* (Cincinnati, OH: Anderson, 1986).

30. See, for example, Michael Brown, *Working the Street: Police Discretion and the Dilemmas of Reform* (New York: Russell Sage Foundation, 1981).

31. Richard Bennett and Theodore Greenstein, "The Police Personality: A Test of the Predispositional Model," *Journal of Police Science and Administration*, Vol. 3 (1975), pp. 439–445.

32. James Teevan and Bernard Dolnick, "The Values of the Police: A Reconsideration and Interpretation," *Journal of Police Science and Administration* (1973), pp. 366–369.

33. Lawrence Sherman and Robert Langworthy, "Measuring Homicide by Police Officers," *Journal of Criminal Law and Criminology*, Vol. 4, 1979, pp. 546–560, and Lawrence W. Sherman et al., *Citizens Killed by Big City Police, 1970–1984* (Washington, D.C.: Crime Control Institute, 1986).

34. Joel Samaha, *Criminal Justice* (St. Paul, MN: West, 1988), p. 235.

35. Thomas Barker and David L. Carter, *Police Deviance* (Cincinnati, OH: Anderson, 1986).

36. *Knapp Commission Report on Police Corruption* (New York: George Braziller, 1973).

37. Ibid.

38. Robert Daley, *Prince of the City: The Story of a Cop Who Knew Too Much* (Boston: Houghton Mifflin, 1978).

39. Mike McAlary, *Buddy Boys: When Good Cops Turn Bad* (New York: G. P. Putnam's Sons, 1987).

40. Ibid.

41. "Detroit's Top Cop Indicted," *USA Today*, February 12, 1991, p. 1A.

42. Ibid., p. 5A.

43. Edwin H. Sutherland and Donald Cressey, *Principles of Criminology*, 8th ed. (Philadelphia: J. B. Lippincott, 1970).

44. See Robert Reiner, "Where Does the Met Go Now?" in *Criminal Justice International*, Vol. 4, no. 2 (March/April 1988), p. 23.

45. James Mills, *The Underground Empire: Where Crime and Governments Embrace* (New York: Dell, 1986), p. 15.

46. Ibid.

47. National Institute of Law Enforcement and Criminal Justice, *Controlling Police Corruption: The Effects of Reform Policies*, Summary Report (Washington, D.C.: U.S. Department of Justice, 1978).

48. See National Institute of Justice, "Employee Drug Testing Policies in Police Departments," *NIJ Research in Brief* (Washington, D.C.: U.S. Department of Justice, 1986).

49. Ibid.

50. *Maurice Turner* v. *Fraternal Order of Police*, No 83-1213, D.C. Court of Appeals (November 13, 1985).

51. *Philip Caruso, President of P.B.A.* v. *Benjamin Ward, Police Commissioner*, New York State Supreme Court, Pat. 37, Index No. 12632-86, 1986.

52. *National Treasury Employees Union* v. *Von Raab*, 44 CrL 3192 (1989) .

53. *The New York Times*, February 29, 1988, p. B7.

54. Federal Bureau of Investigation, *Crime in the United States, 1991* (Washington, D.C.: United States Government Printing Office, 1992), p. 290.

55. As reported by The Headline News Network, April 26, 1988.

56. "AIDS and Our Workplace," New York City Police Department pamphlet (November 1987).

57. "Collecting and Handling Evidence Infected with Human Disease-Causing Organisms," *FBI Law Enforcement Bulletin* (July 1987).

58. Theodore M. Hammett, "Precautionary Measures and Protective Equipment: Developing a Reasonable Response," *National Institute of Justice Bulletin* (Washington, D.C.: U.S. Government Printing Office, 1988).

59. *National Institute of Justice Reports,* No. 206 (November/December 1987).

60. "Taking Aim at a Virus: NYPD Tackles AIDS on the Job and in the Ranks," *Law Enforcement News*, March 15, 1988, p. 1.

61. "Stress on the Job" *Newsweek*, April 25, 1988, p. 43.

62. Joseph Victor, "Police Stress: Is Anybody Out There Listening?" *New York Law Enforcement Journal,* (June 1986), pp. 19–20.

63. Ibid.

64. Charles R. Swanson, Leonard Territo, and Robert W. Taylor, *Police Administration: Structures, Processes, and Behavior,* 2nd ed. (New York: Macmillan, 1988).

65. *Malley* v. *Briggs,* 475 U.S. 335, 106 S.Ct. 1092 (1986).

66. *Malley* at 4246.

67. *Biscoe* v. *Arlington* (1984), 80-0766 *National Law Journal,* May 13, 1985.

68. *Kaplan* v. *Lloyd's Insurance Co.,* 479 So. 2d 961 (La. App. 1985).

69. *City of Canton, Ohio* v. *Harris,* U.S. 109 S.Ct. 1197 (1989).

70. *Harris,* at 1204.

71. *Prior* v. *Woods,* (1981), *National Law Journal,* November 2, 1981.

72. *Bivens* v. *Six Unknown Federal Agents,* 403 U.S. 388 (1971).

73. *Wyler* v. *U.S.* 725 F.2d 157 (2d Cir. 1983).

74. California Government Code, Section 818.

75. For more information on police liability, see Daniel L. Schofield, "Legal Issues of Pursuit Driving," *FBI Law Enforcement Bulletin* (May 1988), pp. 23–29.

76. *Tennessee* v. *Garner,* 471 U.S. 1 (1985).

77. Ibid.

78. James Fyfe, *Shots Fired: An Examination of New York City Police Firearms Discharges* (Ann Arbor, Mich: University Microfilms, 1978).

79. James Fyfe, "Blind Justice? Police Shootings in Memphis," (paper presented at the annual meeting of the Academy of Criminal Justice Sciences, Philadelphia, March 1981).

80. It is estimated that American police shoot at approximately 3,600 people every year. See William Geller, "Deadly Force" study guide Crime File Series (Washington, D.C.: National Institute of Justice, no date).

81. Anne Cohen, "I've Killed That Man Ten Thousand Times," *Police Magazine* (July 1980).

82. For more information, see Joe Auten, "When Police Shoot," in *North Carolina Criminal Justice Today* Vol. 4, no. 4 (Summer 1986), pp. 9–14.

83. As quoted by Michael Siegfried, "Notes on the Professionalization of Private Security," in *The Justice Professional* (Spring 1989).

84. *Sourcebook of Criminal Justice Statistics,* p. 16.

85. See Edward. A. Farris, "Five Decades of American Policing, 1932–1982: The Path to Professionalism," *The Police Chief* (November 1982), p. 31.

86. Ibid., p. 34.

87. National Commission on Law Observance and Enforcement, *Report on Police,* 1931.

88. National Advisory Commission on Criminal Justice Standards and Goals, *Report on the Police* (Washington, D.C.: U.S. Government Printing Office, 1973).

89. Ibid.

90. David L. Carter, Allen D. Sapp, and Darrel W. Stephens, *The State of Police Education: Policy Direction for the 21st Century* (Washington, D.C.: Police Executive Research Forum, 1989).

91. Ibid., p. xiv.

92. Ibid., p. xxii-xxiii.

93. Ibid., xxiii.

94. Carter, Sapp, and Stephens, *The State of Police Education,* p. 84.

95. National Advisory Commission on Criminal Justice Standards and Goals, *Police* (Washington, D.C.: U.S. Government Printing Office, 1973), p. 238.

96. "Dallas PD College Rule Gets Final OK," *Law Enforcement News,* July 7, 1986, pp. 1, 13.

97. *Davis* v. *Dallas,* 1986.

98. David L. Carter and Allen Sapp, *The State of Police Education: Critical Findings* (Washington, D.C.: Police Executive Research Forum, no date).

99. O. W. Wilson and Roy Clinton McLaren, *Police Administration,* 4th ed. (New York: McGraw-Hill, 1977), p. 259.

100. Ibid., p. 270.

101. National Advisory Commission on Civil Disorders, *Police,* p. 332.

102. As reported in Charles Swanson and Leonard Territo, *Police Administration: Structures, Processes, and Behavior* (New York: Macmillan, 1983), p. 203, from *Affirmative Action Monthly* (February 1979), p. 22.

103. The Police Foundation, *On the Move: The Status of Women in Policing* (Washington, D.C.: The Police Foundation, 1990).

104. C. Lee Bennett, "Interviews with Female Police Officers in Western Massachusetts," paper presented at the annual meeting of the Academy of Criminal Justice Sciences, Nashville, TN, March 1991.

105. Ibid., p. 9.

106. See, for example, Pearl Jacobs, "Suggestions for the Greater Integration of Women into Policing," paper presented at the annual meeting of the Academy of Criminal Justice Sciences, Nashville, TN, March 1991, and Cynthia Fuchs Epstein, *Deceptive Distinctions: Sex, Gender and the Social Order* (New Haven, CT: Yale University Press, 1988).

107. Carole G. Garrison, Nancy K. Grant, and Kenneth L. J. McCormick, "Utilization of Police Women," unpublished manuscript.

108. "Foot-Dragging Charged in FBI Racism Probe," *The Fayetteville Times*, March 27, 1988.

109. The Police Foundation, *On the Move*.

CHAPTER 5

POLICE: THE LEGAL ENVIRONMENT

"Yeah," the detective mumbled. "Fifteen guys. You might want to think about that. Only two of us." . . . "On the other hand . . ." He shook his head. "Sneaking a bunch of cops into a neighborhood like this is going to be like trying to sneak the sun past a rooster." . . . As he started up the stairs, Angelo reached not for his gun but for his wallet. He took out a Chase Manhattan calendar printed on a supple but firm slip of plastic. He flicked the card at Rand. "I'll open the door with this. You step in and freeze them."

"Jesus Christ, Angelo," the agent almost gasped. "We can't do that. We haven't got a warrant."

"Don't worry about it, kid," Angelo said, drawing up to the second door on the right on the second floor. "It ain't a perfect world."

> — Larry Collins
> and Dominique Lapierre
> *The Fifth Horseman*[1]

The police in the United States are not separate from the people. They draw their authority from the will and consent of the people, and they recruit their officers from them. The police are the instrument of the people to achieve and maintain order; their efforts are founded on principles of public service and ultimate responsibility to the public.

> — The National Advisory
> Commission on Criminal Justice Standards
> and Goals[2]

KEY CONCEPTS

Bill of Rights	landmark cases	*Miranda* rights
due process	Warren court	Burger court
search and seizure	exclusionary rule	good faith
probable cause	plain view	

☐ THE ABUSE OF POLICE POWER

New Report
Critical of
L.A. Police

In the spring of 1991 Rodney King, an unemployed 25-year-old black man, was apprehended by Los Angeles police for an alleged violation of motor vehicle laws. Police said King had been speeding and refused to stop for a pursuing patrol car. Officers claimed to have clocked King's 1988 Hyundai at 115 mph on suburban Los Angeles' Foothill Freeway — even though the car's manufacturer later said the vehicle was not capable of speeds over 100 mph and recordings of police radio communications surrounding the incident never mentioned excessive speed.

Eventually King did stop, but then officers of the Los Angeles Police Department attacked him — shocking him twice with electronic stun guns, and striking him with nightsticks and fists. Kicked in the stomach, face and back, he was left with 11 skull fractures, missing teeth, a crushed cheekbone, and a broken ankle. A witness told reporters she heard King begging officers to stop the beating, but that they "were all laughing, like they just had a party."[3] King eventually underwent surgery for brain injuries.

Twenty-five police officers — 21 from the LAPD, 2 California Highway Patrol officers, and 2 school district officers — were involved in the incident. Four of them, who were later indicted, beat King, as the others watched. Los Angeles County District Attorney Ira Reiner called the behavior of the officers who watched, "irresponsible and offensive," but not criminal.[4]

There are two important differences between this incident and the other crime stories related in this textbook: (1) this time the suspects wore police uniforms, and (2) the entire incident was captured on videotape by an amateur photographer from a nearby balcony who was trying out his new night-sensitive video camera. The 2 minute videotape was repeatedly broadcast over national TV and picked up by hundreds of local television stations. The furor which erupted over the tape embroiled LAPD then-Chief Daryl Gates in resignation calls, and eventually led to a Justice Department review of law enforcement violence across the country.[5] The immediate goal of the review, announced by then-U.S. Attorney General Richard Thornburg, was "to determine whether there is a pattern of abuse to a high degree in any particular region or police department."[6] Some defended the police, citing the "war zone" mentality of today's inner-city crime fighters as fostering a violent mind-set. Officers involved in the beating claimed that King, at 6-foot-3 and 225 pounds, appeared strung out on PCP and that he and his two companions made officers feel threatened.[7]

King filed an $56 million lawsuit against the city — $1 million for each time he was struck. Although King himself may not have been a model citizen (he was on parole at the time of the beating, after having served time for robbery, came under investigation for another robbery after the beating, and was arrested again three months after his release from the hospital — for allegedly picking up a male prostitute dressed as a woman, and for trying to run over police who confronted him[8]), investigative reporters began to highlight a history of police abuse in Los Angeles. The month before the videotaped beating took place, baseball Hall of Famer Joe Morgan won $540,000 in damages against the city of Los Angeles for mistreatment at the hands of the police who mistook him for a drug runner,[9] and the southern California branch of the American Civil Liberties Union reported receiving 55 complaints each week about police brutality from black and Hispanic citizens.

In 1992 the officers involved in King's beating were acquitted in state courts by a jury which lacked any black members. Within hours the city of Los Angeles erupted in rioting, and many stores and businesses in the city's south-central area were looted and destroyed. Some social commentators at the time claimed that the moral bankruptcy of the justice system, combined in this particular instance with poverty and hopelessness, propelled many disenfranchised inner-city residents into an orgy of destructive social protest. Others said the acquittal was simply an excuse for the expression of pent-up hostilities, or provided the opportunity for expressions of greed. By fall 1992, however, the officers had been indicted by a federal grand jury investigating civil rights aspects of the case at the behest of the U.S. Attorney General's Office. In the spring of 1993 two of the officers, Sergeant Staccy Koon and Officer Laurence Powell, were found guilty by a jury in federal court of depriving King of his constitutional right "not to be deprived of liberty without due process of law, including the right to be . . . free from the intentional use of unreasonable force."[10] Officers Theodore Briseno and Timothy Wind were found not guilty of the same charge. As controversy over the case continued, the American Civil Liberties Union, in heated debated, voted to protest the convictions, claiming that "repeat prosecution by different jurisdictions for the same act amounted to double jeopardy."[11]

☐ A CHANGING CLIMATE

The Constitution of the United States — especially in the Bill of Rights — is designed to protect citizens against abuses of police power. Long after it occurred, the King incident served as a rallying point for individual rights activists concerned with ensuring that citizens would remain protected from such abuses in an increasingly conservative society. However, the legal environment surrounding the police in modern America is much more complex than it was just 30 years ago. In the interim the U.S. Supreme Court, under the direction of Chief Justice Earl Warren, forcefully guaranteed individual rights in the face of criminal prosecution. Most Supreme Court decisions of the past three decades in the area of criminal justice derive from the first ten amendments to the U.S. Constitution — otherwise known as the Bill of Rights. Warren court rulings bound the police to strict procedural requirements in the areas of investigation, arrest, and interrogation.   Later rulings scrutinized trial court procedure and enforced humanitarian standards in sentencing and punishment. The Fourteenth Amendment provided a basis for requiring that state criminal justice agencies adhere to the interpretations of the Constitution rendered by the U.S. Supreme Court.   The apex of the individual rights emphasis in Supreme Court decisions was reached in the 1965 case of *Miranda* v. *Arizona,* which established the famous requirement of a police "right's advisement" of suspects. In wielding its brand of idealism, the Warren court recognized the fact that a few guilty people would go free in order that the rights of the majority of Americans, as it understood them, would be protected.

Court decisions of the last few years, however, the product of a new and still emerging Court philosophy, have begun what some call a "reversal" of previous advances in the area of individual rights. By creating exceptions to the exclusionary rule such as the "plain view doctrine" and "stop and frisk authority," and in allowing for the "emergency questioning" of suspects prior to rights advisements, the Court has recognized the realities attending day-to-day police work and the need to ensure public safety. This practical approach to justice, characteristic of the Reagan-Bush political era, was all the more interesting for the fact that it had to struggle within the confines of earlier Court decisions.

CONSTRAINTS ON POLICE ACTION

The Constitution of the United States provides for a system of checks and balances. By this we mean that one branch of government is always held accountable to other branches. The system is designed to ensure that no one individual or agency can become powerful enough to usurp the rights and freedoms guaranteed under the Constitution. Without accountability, it is possible to imagine a police state in which the power of law enforcement is absolute and is related to political considerations and personal vendettas more than to any objective considerations of guilt or innocence.

Under our system of government, courts become the arena for dispute resolution, not just between individuals, but between citizens and the agencies of government itself. After handling by the justice system, people who feel they have not received the respect and dignity due them under law can appeal to the courts for redress. Such appeals are usually based upon procedural issues and are independent of more narrow considerations of guilt or innocence.

THE DUE PROCESS ENVIRONMENT

The police environment is infused with due process requirements. Most pertain to three major areas of activity: (1) evidence and investigation (often called "search and seizure"), (2) arrest, and (3) interrogation. Each of these areas has been addressed by a history of landmark U.S. Supreme Court decisions. Landmark cases are recognizable by the fact that they produce substantial changes in both the understanding of the requirements of due process, and in the practical day-to-day operations of the justice system.

Another way to think of landmark decisions is that they help significantly in clarifying the "rules of the game" — the procedural guidelines by which the police and the rest of the justice system must abide.

The three areas we will discuss have been well defined by decades of court precedent. Keep in mind, however, that judicial interpretations of the constitutional requirement of due process are constantly evolving. As new decisions are rendered, and as the composition of the Court itself changes, additional refinements will occur.

> **Due Process of Law:** A right guaranteed by the Fifth, Sixth, and Fourteenth Amendments of the U.S. Constitution, and generally understood, in legal contexts, to mean the due course of legal proceedings according to the rules and forms which have been established for the protection of private rights.

☐ SEARCH AND SEIZURE

The U.S. Constitution declares that people must be secure in their homes and in their persons against unreasonable searches and seizures. This right is asserted by the Fourth Amendment, which reads: "The right of the people to be secure in their persons, houses, papers, and effects, against unreasonable searches and seizures shall not be violated, and no warrants shall issue but upon probable cause, supported by oath or affirmation, and particularly describing the place to be searched, and the persons or things to be seized." This amendment, a part of the Bill of Rights, was adopted by Congress, and became effective on December 15, 1791.

The language of the Fourth Amendment is familiar to all of us. "Warrants," "probable cause," and other phrases from the amendment are frequently cited in editorials, TV news shows, and daily conversation. It is the interpretation of these phrases over time by the U.S. Supreme Court, however, which has given them the impact they have on the justice system today (see Table 5-1).

THE WARREN COURT

Prior to the decade of the 1960s, the U.S. Supreme Court intruded only infrequently upon the overall operation of the criminal justice system. As some authors have observed, however, the 1960s provided a time of youthful idealism, and "without the distraction of a depression or world war, individual liberties were examined at all levels of society."[12]

The Bill of Rights was given lip service in proceedings around the country, but in practice, law enforcement, especially on the state and local levels, revolved around tried and true methods of search, arrest, and interrogation, which left little room for the practical recognition of individual rights.

The Warren court, led by Chief Justice Earl Warren, an Eisenhower nominee, permanently changed the day-to-day practice of American policing. The Court, in *Mapp* v. *Ohio* (1961),[13] quickly let it be known that past and future Supreme Court decisions were to be binding upon state law enforcement agents and state courts. Beginning with the now-famous *Mapp* case, the Court set out to chart a course which would guarantee nationwide recognition of individual rights, as it understood them, by agencies at all levels of the justice system.

The Exclusionary Rule

The first landmark case in the area of search and seizure was that of *Weeks* v. *U.S.*[14] (1914). Freemont Weeks was suspected of using the U.S. mail to sell lottery tickets, a federal crime. Weeks was arrested and federal agents went to his home to conduct a search. They had no search warrant; at the time warrants were not routinely used by investigators. They confiscated many incriminating items of evidence, as well as personal possessions of the defendant including clothes, papers, books, and even candy.

TABLE 5-1
Constitutional Amendments
of Special Significance to the American System of Justice,
from the "Bill of Rights"

This Right Is Guaranteed	By This Amendment
The Right Against Unreasonable Searches and Seizures	Fourth
No Arrest Without Probable Cause	Fourth
The Right Against Self-incrimination	Fifth
The Right Against "Double Jeopardy"	Fifth
The Right to Due Process of Law	Fifth, Fourteenth
The Right to a Speedy Trial	Sixth
The Right to a Jury Trial	Sixth
The Right to Know the Charges	Sixth
The Right to Cross-examine Witnesses	Sixth
The Right to a Lawyer	Sixth
The Right to Compel Witnesses on One's Behalf	Sixth
The Right to Reasonable Bail	Eighth
The Right Against Excessive Fines	Eighth
The Right Against Cruel and Unusual Punishments	Eighth
The Applicability of Constitutional Rights to All Citizens, Regardless of State Law or Procedure (not part of the Bill of Rights)	Fourteenth

---

Prior to the trial, Weeks' attorney asked that the personal items be returned, claiming that they had been illegally seized. A judge agreed and ordered the materials returned. On the basis of the evidence which was retained, however, Weeks was convicted in federal court and sentenced to prison. His appeal eventually reached the Supreme Court. There his lawyer reasoned that if some of his client's belongings had been illegally seized, then the remainder of them were also taken improperly. The Supreme Court agreed, and overturned Weeks' earlier conviction.

The *Weeks* case forms the basis of what is now called the exclusionary rule. The exclusionary rule means that evidence illegally seized by the police cannot be used in a trial.

Contrary to much popular belief, Freemont Weeks could have been retried on the original charges following the Supreme Court decision in his case. He would not have faced double jeopardy because he was in fact not *finally convicted* on the earlier charges. His conviction was nullified on appeal, resulting in neither a conviction nor an acquittal. Double jeopardy becomes an issue only when a defendant faces retrial on the same charges following acquittal at his or her original trial or when the defendant is retried after having been convicted.

> **Exclusionary Rule:** The understanding, operative in contemporary American criminal justice as a result of Supreme Court precedent, that incriminating information must be seized according to constitutional specifications of due process, or it will not be allowable as evidence in criminal trials.

It is important to recognize that the decision of the Supreme Court in the *Weeks* case was binding, at the time, only upon federal officers, because it was federal agents who were involved in the illegal seizure.

Problems with Precedent

The *Weeks* case demonstrates the power of the Supreme Court in *enforcing* what we have called the "rules of the game." It also lays bare the much more significant role of rule creation by the Court. Until the *Weeks* case was decided, federal law enforcement officers had little reason to think they were acting in violation of due process. Common practice had not required that they obtain a warrant before conducting searches. The rule which resulted from *Weeks* was new, and it would forever alter the enforcement activities of federal officers. Yet the *Weeks* case was also retroactive, in the sense that it was applied to Weeks himself.

There is a problem in the way in which our system generates and applies principles of due process which may be obvious from our discussion of the *Weeks* case. The problem is that the present appeals system, focusing as it does upon the "rules of the game," presents a ready-made channel for the guilty to go free. There can be little doubt but that Freemont Weeks had violated federal law. A jury had convicted him. Yet he escaped punishment because of the illegal behavior of the police — behavior which, until the Court ruled, had not been regarded as anything but legitimate.

Even if the police knowingly violate the principles of due process, which they sometimes do, our sense of justice is compromised when the guilty go free. Famed Supreme Court Justice Benjamin Cardozo once complained, "The criminal is to go free because the constable has blundered."

Students of criminal justice have long considered three possible solutions to this problem. The first solution suggests that rules of due process, especially when newly articulated by the courts, should be applied only to future cases, but not to the initial case in which they are stated. In other words, the justices in the *Weeks* case, for example, might have said, "We are creating the 'exclusionary rule,' based upon our realization in this case. Law enforcement officers are obligated to use it as a guide in all future searches. However, insofar as the guilt of Mr. Weeks was decided by a jury under rules of evidence existing at the time, we will let that decision stand."

A second solution would punish police officers or other actors in the criminal justice system who act illegally, but would not allow the guilty defendant to escape punishment. This solution would be useful in applying established precedent where officers and officials had the benefit of clearly articulated rules and should have known better. Under this arrangement, any officer today who intentionally violates due process guarantees might be suspended, reduced in rank, lose pay, or be fired. Some authors have suggested that "decertification" might serve as "an alternative to traditional remedies for police misconduct."[15] Departments which employed the decertification process would punish violators by removing their certification as police officers. Because officers in every state except Hawaii must meet the certification requirements of state boards (usually called Training and Standards Commissions or Peace Officer Standards and Training Boards) in order to hold employment, some authors[16] argue that decertification would have a much more personal (and therefore more effective) impact on individual officers than the exclusionary rule ever could.

A third possibility would allow for theoretical questions involving issue of due process to be addressed by the Supreme Court. Concerned supervisors and officials could put questions to the Court, inquiring as to what the Court would rule "*if . . .*". As things now work, the Court can only address real cases, and does so on a writ of *certiorari*, in which the Court orders the record of a lower court case to be prepared for review.

The obvious difficulty with these solutions, however, is that they would substantially reduce the potential benefits available to defendants through the appeals process   and, hence, would eliminate the process itself.

The Fruit of the Poisoned Tree Doctrine

In 1926 Frederick Silverthorne and his sons operated a lumber company and were accused of avoiding payment of federal taxes. When asked to turn over the company's books to federal investigators, the Silverthornes refused, citing their privilege against self-incrimination.

Shortly thereafter, federal agents, without a search warrant, descended on the lumber company and seized the wanted books. The Silverthorne's lawyer appeared in court and asked that the materials be returned, citing the need for a search warrant as had been established in the *Weeks* case. The prosecutor agreed to defense requests, and the books were returned to the Silverthornes.

The Silverthornes came to trial thinking they would be acquitted because the evidence against them was no longer in the hands of prosecutors. In a surprise move, however, the prosecution introduced photocopies of incriminating evidence which they had made from the returned books. The Silverthornes were convicted in federal court. Their appeal eventually reached the Supreme Court of the United States. The Court ruled that just as illegally seized evidence cannot be used in a trial, neither can evidence be used which *derives* from an illegal seizure.[17] The conviction of the Silverthornes was overturned and they were set free.

The Silverthorne case articulated a new principle of due process which we today call the fruit of the poisoned tree doctrine. This doctrine is potentially far reaching. Complex cases developed after years of police investigative effort may be ruined if defense attorneys are able to demonstrate that the prosecution's case, no matter how complex, was originally based upon a search or seizure which violated due process. In such cases, it is likely that all evidence will be declared "tainted" and become useless.

> **Fruit of the Poisoned Tree Doctrine:** A legal principle which excludes from introduction at trial any evidence eventually developed as a result of an originally illegal search or seizure.

The Exclusionary Rule and the States

While the exclusionary rule became an overriding consideration in federal law enforcement from the time that it was first defined by the Supreme Court, it was not until 1961 that it became applicable to criminal prosecutions at the state level.[18] In that year, the case of Dolree Mapp was reviewed by the Supreme Court, and her conviction on charges of possessing obscene material was overturned.

Mapp was suspected of harboring a fugitive wanted in a bombing. When officers arrived at her house she refused to admit them. Eventually, they forced their way in. During the search which ensued, pornographic materials including photographs were uncovered. Mapp was arrested, and eventually convicted, under an Ohio law which made possession of such materials illegal.

Prior decisions by the U.S. Supreme Court, including *Wolf* v. *Colorado*,[19] had led officers to expect that the exclusionary rule did not apply to agents of state and local law enforcement. The precedent established in *Mapp* v. *Ohio*, however, firmly applied the principles developed in *Weeks* and *Silverthorne* to trials in state courts.

The case of *Chimel* v. *California* (1969)[20] involved both arrest and search activities by local law enforcement officers. Ted Chimel was convicted of the burglary of a coin shop, based upon evidence gathered at the scene of his arrest — his home. Officers, armed with a warrant, arrested Chimel at his residence and proceeded with a search of his entire three bedroom house, including the attic, a small workshop, and the garage. The justification later provided for the search, was that it was conducted incidental to arrest, and the officers involved believed that such a search, conducted for their own protection, was lawful. Coins taken from the burglarized coin shop were found at various places in Chimel's residence, including the garage, and provided the evidence used against him.

Chimel's appeal eventually reached the U.S. Supreme Court, which ruled that the search conducted by officers, without a warrant, and incidental to arrest, became invalid when it went beyond the person arrested and the area subject to that person's "immediate control." The thrust of the Court's decision was that searches during arrest can be made to protect the arresting officers, but that, without a search warrant, their scope must be strongly circumscribed.

TABLE 5-2
Implications of *Chimel* v. *California*

What Arresting Officers May Search
  The defendant
  The physical area within easy reach of the defendant

Valid Reasons for Conducting a Search
  To protect the arresting officers
  To prevent evidence from being destroyed
  To keep the defendant from escaping

When a Search Becomes Illegal
  When it goes beyond the defendant and the area within the defendant's immediate
    control
  When it is conducted for other than a valid reason

The decision in the case of Ted Chimel followed earlier reasoning by the Court in the case of *U.S.* v. *Rabinowitz* (1950).[21]   Rabinowitz, a stamp collector, had been arrested and charged by federal agents with selling altered postage stamps in order to defraud other collectors.   Employing a valid arrest warrant, officers arrested Rabinowitz at his place of employment and then proceeded to search his desk, file cabinets, and safe.   They did not have a search warrant, but his office was small — only one room — and the officers conducted the search with a specific object in mind, the illegal stamps.   Eventually, 573 altered postage stamps were seized in the search, and Rabinowitz was convicted in federal court of charges related to selling altered stamps.

Rabinowitz's appeal to the U.S. Supreme Court, based upon the claim that the warrantless search of his business was illegal, was denied. The Court ruled that the Fourth Amendment provides protection against unreasonable searches but that the search, in this case, followed legally from the arrest of the suspect. In the language used by the Court: "It is not disputed that there may be reasonable searches, incident to arrest, without a search warrant. Upon acceptance of this established rule that some authority to search follows from lawfully taking the person into custody, it becomes apparent that such searches turn upon the reasonableness under all the circumstances and not upon the practicability of procuring a search warrant, for the warrant is not required."[22]

Since the early days of the exclusionary rule, other court decisions have highlighted the fact that "the Fourth Amendment protects people, not places."[23]   In other words, although the commonly heard claim that "a person's home is his or her castle" has a great deal of validity within the context of constitutional law, persons can have a reasonable expectation to privacy in "homes" of many descriptions.   Apartments, duplex dwellings, motel rooms — even the cardboard boxes or make-shift tents of the "homeless" — can all become protected places under the Fourth Amendment. In *Minnesota* v. *Olson* (1990)[24], the U.S. Supreme Court extended the protection against warrantless searches to overnight guests residing in the home of another.   The capacity to claim the protection of the Fourth

Amendment, said the Court, depends upon whether the *person* who makes that claim has a legitimate expectation of privacy in the place searched.

THE BURGER AND REHNQUIST COURTS

The swing toward conservatism which our country experienced during the late 1970s and the 1980s gave rise to the "yuppie generation," designer jeans, and a renewed concern with protecting the financial and other interests of the well-to-do. The Reagan years and the popularity of a president in whom many saw the embodiment of "old-fashioned" values reflected the tenor of a nation seeking a return to simpler times.

The U.S. Supreme Court mirrored the conservative decade of the 1980s by distancing itself from certain earlier decisions of the Warren court. The underlying theme of the new Court, the Burger court, was its apparent adherence to the principle that criminal defendants need to bear the bulk of the responsibility in showing that the police went beyond the law in the performance of their duties.

Good Faith Exceptions to the Exclusionary Rule

The Burger court began what some have called a "chipping away" at the strict application of the exclusionary rule originally set forth in the *Weeks* and *Silverthorne* cases. In the case of *Illinois* v. *Gates* (1983),[25] the Court was asked to modify the exclusionary rule to permit the use of evidence in court which had been seized in "reasonable good faith" by officers, even though the search was later ruled illegal. The Court, however, chose not to the address the issue at that time.

The 1984 case of *U.S.* v. *Leon*[26] marked the first time the Court recognized what has now come to be called the good faith exception to the exclusionary rule. The *Leon* case involved the Burbank, California, Police Department and its investigation of a drug trafficking suspect. The suspect, Leon, was placed under surveillance following a tip from a confidential informant. Investigators applied for a search warrant based upon information gleaned through the surveillance. The affidavit in support of the warrant was reviewed by numerous deputy district attorneys, and a warrant was issued by a state judge. A search of Leon's three residences yielded a large amount of drugs and other evidence. A later ruling, in a federal district court, resulted in the suppression of the evidence gathered, on the basis that the original affidavit had not been adequate to establish probable cause.

The government petitioned the U.S. Supreme Court to consider whether evidence gathered by officers acting in good faith as to the validity of a warrant, should fairly be excluded at trial. The impending modification of the exclusionary rule was intoned in the first sentence of that court's written decision: "This case presents the question whether the Fourth Amendment exclusionary rule should be modified so as not to bar the use in the prosecution's case-in-chief of evidence obtained by officers acting in reasonable reliance on a search warrant issued by a detached and neutral magistrate but ultimately found to be unsupported by probable cause." The Court continued: ". . . when law enforcement officers have acted in objective good faith or their transgressions have been minor, the magnitude of the benefit conferred on such guilty defendants offends basic concepts of the criminal justice system." The Court found for the government and reinstated the conviction of Leon.

In the same year the Supreme Court case of *Massachusetts* v. *Sheppard*[27] (1984) further reinforced the concept of "good faith." In the *Sheppard* case officers executed a search warrant which failed to describe accurately the property to be seized. Although they were aware of the error, they had been assured by a magistrate that the warrant was valid. After the seizure was complete and a conviction had been obtained, the Massachusetts Supreme Judicial Court reversed the finding of the trial court. Upon appeal the U.S. Supreme Court reiterated the good faith exception and let the original conviction stand.

Some people have cited the cases of *Leon* and *Sheppard* as beginning an erosion of personal rights guaranteed under the Constitution, and in particular as a reversal of U.S. Supreme Court philosophy in the face of growing conservative tendencies.

There is mounting evidence of such a tendency in the Court. A series of recent decisions appears to continue the trend begun in *Leon* and *Sheppard.* In the 1987 case of *Illinois* v. *Krull*,[28] for example, the Court found that the good faith exception applied to a warrantless search supported by state law even where the statute was later found to violate the Fourth Amendment.

Another 1987 Supreme Court case, *Maryland* v. *Garrison*,[29] supported the use of evidence obtained with a search warrant which was inaccurate in its specifics. Officers had procured a warrant to search an apartment believing it was the only one on a third floor. After searching the entire floor, they discovered that it housed more than one apartment. Evidence acquired in the search was held to be admissible based upon the reasonable mistake of the officers.

In the 1990 case of *Illinois* v. *Rodriguez*[30] the Supreme Court further diminished the scope of the exclusionary rule. In *Rodriguez*, a badly beaten woman named Gail Fischer complained to police that she had been assaulted in a Chicago apartment. Fischer led police to the apartment — which she indicated she shared with the defendant — produced a key, and opened the door to the dwelling. Inside, investigators found the defendant, Edward Rodriguez, asleep on a bed, with drug paraphernalia and cocaine spread around him. Rodriguez was arrested and charged with assault and possession of a controlled substance.

Upon appeal, Rodriguez demonstrated that Fischer had not lived with him for at least a month — and argued that she could no longer be said to have legal control over the apartment. Hence, the defense claimed, Fischer had no authority to provide investigators with access to the dwelling. According to arguments made by the defense, the evidence, which had been obtained without a warrant, had not been properly seized. The Supreme Court disagreed, ruling that "even if Fischer did not possess common authority over the premises, there was no Fourth Amendment violation if the police *reasonably believed* at the time of their entry that Fischer possessed the authority to consent."

Legal scholars have suggested that the exclusionary rule may undergo even further modification in the near future. Erickson, for example, points to the fact that ". . . the Court's majority is clearly committed to the idea that the exclusionary rule is not directly part of the Fourth Amendment (and Fourteenth Amendment due process), but instead is an evidentiary device instituted by the Court to effectuate it."[31] In other words, if the Court should be persuaded that the rule is no longer effective, or that some other strategy could better achieve the aim of protecting individual rights, the rule could be abandoned.

The Plain View Doctrine

Police officers have the opportunity to begin investigations or confiscate evidence, without the need for a warrant, based upon what they find in plain view and open to public inspection. The plain view doctrine was first stated in the Supreme Court case of *Harris* v. *U.S.*,[32] in which a police officer inventorying an impounded vehicle discovered evidence of a robbery. In the *Harris* case the Court ruled that, "...objects falling in the plain view of an officer who has a right to be in the position to have that view are subject to seizure and may be introduced in evidence."[33]

The plain view doctrine applies only to sightings by the police under legal circumstances, that is, in places where the police have a legitimate right to be, and typically only if the sighting was coincidental. Similarly, the incriminating nature of the evidence seized must have been "immediately apparent" to the officers making the seizure.[34] If officers conspired to avoid the necessity for a search warrant by helping to create a plain view situation through surveillance, duplicity, or other means, the doctrine likely would not apply.

Common situations in which the plain view doctrine is applicable include emergencies such as crimes in progress, fires, and accidents. A police officer responding to a call for assistance, for example, might enter a residence intending to provide aid to an injured person and find drugs or other contraband in plain view. If so, the officer would be within his or her legitimate authority to confiscate the materials and effect an arrest if the owner of the substance could be identified.

The plain view doctrine, however, has recently been restricted by federal court decisions. In the 1982 case of *U.S.* v. *Irizarry*,[35] the First Circuit of Appeals held that officers could not move objects to gain a view of evidence otherwise hidden from view. Agents had arrested a number of men in a motel room in Isla Verde, Puerto Rico. A valid arrest warrant formed the legal basis for the arrest, and some quantities of plainly visible drugs were seized from the room. An agent, looking through a window into the room prior to the arrest, had seen one of the defendants with a gun. After the arrest was complete, and no gun had been found on the suspects, another officer noticed a bathroom ceiling panel out of place. The logical conclusion was that a weapon had been secreted there. Upon inspection, a substantial quantity of cocaine and various firearms were found hidden in the ceiling. The Court, however, refused to allow these weapons and drugs to be used as evidence because, it said, "the items of evidence found above the ceiling panel were not plainly visible to the agents standing in the room."[36]

In the Supreme Court case of *Arizona* v. *Hicks* (1987)[37], the requirement that evidence be in plain view, without the need for officers to move or dislodge evidence, was reiterated. In the *Hicks* case, officers responded to a shooting in an apartment. A bullet had been fired in a second floor apartment and had gone through the floor, injuring a man in the apartment below.

The quarters of James Hicks were found to be in considerable disarray when entered by investigating officers. As officers looked for the person who might have fired the weapon, they discovered and confiscated a number of guns and a stocking mask such as might be used in robberies. In one corner, however, officers noticed two expensive stereo sets. One of the officers, suspecting that the sets were stolen, went over to the equipment, and was able to read the serial numbers of one of the components from where it rested.

TABLE 5-3
Established Exceptions to the Exclusionary Rule

Police Powers	Supported by
Stop and frisk	*Terry* v. *Ohio* (1968)
Warrantless searches incident to a lawful arrest	*U.S.* v. *Rabinowitz (1950)*
Seizure of evidence in "good faith," even in the face of some exclusionary rule violations	*U.S.* v. *Leon* (1984) *Illinois* v. *Krull* (1987)
Warrantless vehicle searches where probable cause exists that the vehicle contains contraband and/or the occupants have been lawfully arrested	*Carroll* v. *U.S.* (1925) *New York* v. *Belton* (1981) *U.S.* v. *Ross* (1982) *California* v. *Carney* (1985) *California* v. *Acevedo (1991)*
Gathering of incriminating evidence during interrogation in noncustodial circumstances	*Beckwith* v. *United States* (1976)
Authority to search incidental to arrest and/or to conduct a protective sweep in conjunction with an in-home arrest	*Chimel* v. *California* (1969) *U.S.* v. *Edwards* (1974) *Maryland* v. *Buie* (1990)
Authority to enter and/or search an "open field" without a warrant	*Hester* v. *U.S.* (1924) *Oliver* v. *U.S.* (1984) *U.S.* v. *Dunn* (1987)
Permissibility of warrantless naked-eye aerial observation of open areas and/or greenhouses	*California* v. *Ciraolo* (1986) *Florida* v. *Riley* (1989)
Warrantless seizure of abandoned materials and refuse	*California* v. *Greenwood* (1988)
Prompt action in the face of threats to public safety	*Warren* v. *Hayden* (1967) *Borchardt* v. *U.S.* (1987) *New York* v. *Quarles* (1984)
Evidence in "plain view" may be seized	*Harris* v. *New York* (1968) *Coolidge* v. *New Hampshire* (1971) *Horton* v. *California* (1990)
Use of police informants in jail cells	*Kuhlman* v. *Wilson* (1986) *Illinois* v. *Perkins* (1990) *Arizona* v. *Fulminante* (1991)

Some of the serial numbers, however, were not clearly visible, and the investigating officer moved some of the components in order to read the numbers. When he called the numbers into headquarters he was told that the equipment indeed had been stolen. The stereo components were seized and James Hicks was arrested. Hicks was eventually convicted on a charge of armed robbery, based upon the evidence seized.

Upon appeal, the Hicks case reached the U.S. Supreme Court, which ruled that the officer's behavior had become illegal when he moved the stereo equipment in order to record serial numbers. The Court held that persons have a "reasonable expectation to privacy,"[38] which means that officers, lacking a search warrant, even when invited into a residence, must act more like guests than inquisitors.

Most evidence seized under the plain view doctrine is discovered "inadvertently" — that is, by accident.[39] However, in 1990, the U.S. Supreme Court, in the case of *Horton* v. *California,* ruled that "even though inadvertence *is* a characteristic of most legitimate 'plain view' seizures, it *is not* a necessary condition."[40] In the *Horton* case, a warrant was issued authorizing the search of a defendant's home for stolen jewelry. The affidavit, completed by the officer who requested the warrant, alluded to an Uzi submachine gun and a stun gun — weapons purportedly used in the jewel robbery. It did not request that those weapons be listed on the search warrant. Officers searched the defendant's home, but did not find the stolen jewelry. They did, however, seize a number of weapons — among them the Uzi, two stun guns, and a .38-caliber revolver. Horton was convicted of robbery, in a trial where the seized weapons were introduced into evidence. He appealed his conviction, claiming that officers had reason to believe that the weapons were in his home at the time of the search, and were therefore not seized inadvertently.

As a result of the *Horton* case, "inadvertence" is no longer considered a condition necessary to ensure the legitimacy of a seizure which results when evidence other than that listed in a search warrant is discovered.

Emergency Searches

Certain emergencies may justify a police officer in searching a premises, even without a warrant. Recent decisions by U.S. Appeals Courts have resulted in such activities being termed exigent circumstances searches. According to the Legal Counsel Division of the FBI, there are three threats which "provide justification for emergency warrantless action.[41]" They are clear dangers: (1) to life, (2) of escape, and (3) of the removal or destruction of evidence. Any one of these situations may create an exception to the Fourth Amendment's requirement of a search warrant. Where emergencies necessitate a quick search of a premises, however, it will be the responsibility of law enforcement officers to demonstrate that a dire situation did exist which justified their actions. Failure to do so in court successfully, will, of course, taint any seized evidence and make it unusable.

The need for emergency searches was first recognized by the U.S. Supreme Court in 1967 in the case of *Warden* v. *Hayden.*[42] The Court approved the search of a residence which was conducted without a warrant, but which followed reports that an armed robber had fled into the building. In *Mincey* v. *Arizona*(1978)[43], the Supreme Court held that, "the Fourth Amendment does not require police officers to delay in the course of an investigation if to do so would gravely endanger their lives or the lives of others."[44] A 1990 decision, rendered in the case of *Maryland* v. *Buie*, extended the authority of police to search locations in a house where a potentially dangerous person could hide, while an arrest warrant is being served. The *Buie* decision was meant primarily to protect the investigators from potential danger and can apply even when officers lack a warrant, probable cause, or even reasonable suspicion.

□ ARREST

Most people think of arrest in terms of what they see on popular television crime shows. The suspect is chased, subdued, and "cuffed" after committing some loathsome act in view of the camera. Some arrests do occur that way. In reality, however, most instances of arrest are far more mundane.

In technical terms, an arrest occurs whenever a law enforcement officer restricts a person's freedom to leave. There may be no yelling "You're under arrest!"; no *Miranda* warnings may be offered; and, in fact, the suspect may not even consider himself to be in custody. Such arrests, and the decision to enforce them, evolve as the situation between the officer and suspect develops. They usually begin with polite conversation and a request by the officer for information. Only when the suspect tries to leave, and tests the limits of the police response, may the person discover that he or she is really in custody.

Arrests which follow the questioning of a suspect are probably the most common type of arrest. When the decision to arrest is reached, the officer has come to the conclusion that a crime has been committed and that the suspect is the one who probably committed it. The presence of these mental elements constitutes the probable cause needed for an arrest. Probable cause is the basic minimum necessary for an arrest under any circumstances.

Arrests may also occur when the officer comes upon a crime in progress. Such situations often require apprehension of the offender to ensure the safety of the public. Most arrests made during crimes in progress are for misdemeanors. In fact, many states do not allow arrest for a misdemeanor unless it is committed in the presence of an officer. In any event, crimes in progress clearly provide the probable cause necessary for an arrest.

> **Probable Cause:** A set of facts and circumstances which would induce a reasonably intelligent and prudent person to believe that a particular person had committed a specific crime; reasonable grounds to make or believe an accusation.

Most jurisdictions allow arrest for a felony without a warrant when a crime is not in progress, as long as probable cause can be established. Some, however, require a warrant. Arrest warrants are issued by magistrates upon a demonstration of probable cause by police officials. Magistrates[45] are low-level judges and, under our system of checks and balances, act to ensure that the police have established the probable cause needed for an arrest. Magistrates will usually require that the officers seeking an arrest warrant submit a written affidavit outlining their reason for seeking an arrest.

SEARCHES INCIDENT TO ARREST

The U.S. Supreme Court has established a clear rule that police officers have the right to conduct a search of a person being arrested, and to search the area under the immediate control of that person, in order to protect themselves from attack. This is true even if the officer and the arrestee are of different sexes.

This "rule of the game" was created in the *Rabinowitz* and *Chimel* cases cited earlier. It became firmly established in cases involving personal searches, such as the 1973 case of *Robinson* v. *U.S.*.[46] Robinson was stopped for a traffic violation, when it was learned that his driver's license was expired. He was arrested for operating a vehicle without a valid license. Officers subsequently searched the defendant thoroughly and discovered a substance which later proved to be heroin. When Robinson's appeal reached the U.S. Supreme Court, the Court upheld the officer's right to conduct a search for purposes of personal protection. In the words of the Court, "A custodial arrest of a suspect based upon probable cause is a reasonable intrusion under the Fourth Amendment; that intrusion being lawful, a search incident to the arrest requires no additional justification."[47]

The Court's decision in *Robinson* provided reinforcement for an earlier ruling involving a seasoned officer who conducted a "pat down" of two men whom he suspected were "casing" a store, about to commit a robbery.[48] The officer in the case was a 39-year veteran of police work, who testified that the men "did not look right." When he approached them, he suspected they might be armed. Fearing for his life, he quickly spun the men around, put them up against a wall, patted down their clothing, and found a gun on one of the men. The man, Terry, was later convicted in Ohio courts of carrying a concealed weapon.

Terry's appeal was based upon the argument that the suspicious officer had no probable cause to arrest him, and therefore no cause to search him. The search, he argued, was illegal, and the evidence obtained should not have been used against him. The Supreme Court disagreed. Chief Justice Earl Warren wrote: "In view of these facts, we cannot blind ourselves to the need for law enforcement officers to protect themselves and other prospective victims of violence in situations where they may lack probable cause for an arrest."[49]

The *Terry* case has become the basis for what we today refer to as field interrogation. A popular name for on-the-street interrogation is stop and frisk. The *Terry* case, for all the authority it conferred on officers, also made it clear that officers must have reasonable grounds for any stop or frisk that they conduct.

In 1989, the Supreme Court, in the case of *U.S.* v. *Sokolow*,[50] clarified the basis upon which law enforcement officers, lacking probable cause to believe that a crime has occurred, may stop and briefly detain a person for investigative purposes. In *Sokolow* the Court ruled that the legitimacy of such a stop must be evaluated according to a "totality of circumstances" criteria — in which all aspects of the defendant's behavior, taken in concert, may provide the basis for a legitimate stop. In this case, the defendant, Sokolow, appeared suspicious to police because, while traveling under an alias from Honolulu, he had paid $2,100 in $20 bills (from a large roll of money) for two airplane tickets after spending a surprisingly small amount of time in Miami. In addition, the defendant was obviously nervous and checked no luggage. A warrantless airport investigation by DEA agents uncovered more than 1,000 grams of cocaine in the defendant's belongings. The Court, in upholding Sokolow's conviction, ruled that, although no single activity was proof of illegal activity, taken together they created circumstances under which suspicion of illegal activity was justified.

Just as arrest must be based on probable cause, officers may not stop and question an unwilling citizen whom they have no reason to suspect of a crime. In the case of *Brown* v. *Texas*[51] (1979), two Texas law enforcement officers stopped the defendant and asked for identification. Brown, they later testified, had not been acting suspiciously, nor did they think he might have a weapon. The stop was made simply because officers wanted to know who he was. Brown was arrested under a Texas statute which required a person to identify himself properly and accurately when requested to do so by peace officers. Eventually, his appeal reached the U.S. Supreme Court, which ruled that, under circumstances found in the *Brown* case, a person "may not be punished for refusing to identify himself."

In *Smith* v. *Ohio* (1990)[52], the Court held that an individual has the right to protect his or her belongings from unwarranted police inspection. In *Smith*, the defendant was approached by two officers in plainclothes who observed that he was carrying a brown paper bag. The officers asked him to "come here a minute" and, when he kept walking, identified themselves as police officers. The defendant threw the bag onto the hood of his car and attempted to protect it from the officer's intrusion. Marijuana was found inside the bag, and the defendant was arrested. Since there was little reason to stop the suspect in this case, and because control over the bag was not thought necessary for the officer's protection, the Court found that the Fourth Amendment protects both "the traveler who carries a toothbrush and a few articles of clothing in a paper bag," as well as "the sophisticated executive with the locked attaché case."[53]

The following year, however, in what some Court observers saw as a turnabout, the U.S. Supreme Court ruled in *California* v. *Hodari* (1991)[54] that suspects who flee from the police and throw away evidence as they retreat may later be arrested based upon the incriminating nature of the abandoned evidence. The case, which began in Oakland, California, centered on the behavior of a group of juveniles who had been standing around a parked car. Two city police officers, driving an unmarked car, but with the word "Police" emblazoned in large letters on their jackets, approached the youths. As they came close, the juveniles apparently panicked and fled. One of them tossed away a "rock" of crack cocaine, which was retrieved by the officers. The juvenile was later arrested and convicted of the possession of a controlled substance, but the California Court of Appeals reversed his conviction, reasoning that the officers did not have sufficient reasonable suspicion to make a "Terry-type stop." The Supreme Court, in reversing the finding of the California court, found that reasonable suspicion was not needed, since no "stop" was made. The suspects had not been "seized" by the police, the Court ruled. Therefore, the evidence taken was not the result of an illegal seizure within the meaning of the Fourth Amendment. The significance of *Hodari* for future police action was highlighted by California prosecutors who pointed out that cases like *Hodari* occur "almost everyday in this nation's urban areas."[55]

In a sharply worded dissenting opinion, Justices John Paul Stevens and Thurgood Marshall wrote: "It is too early to know the consequences of the court's holding. If carried to its logical conclusion, it will encourage unlawful displays of force that will frighten countless innocent citizens into surrendering whatever privacy rights they may still have."[56]

EMERGENCY SEARCHES OF PERSONS

It is possible to imagine emergency situations in which officers may have to search people based upon quick decisions. A person who matches the description of an armed robber; a woman who is found lying unconscious; a man who has what appears to be blood on his shoes. Such searches can save lives by disarming fleeing felons or by uncovering a medical reason for an emergency situation. They may also prevent the escape of criminals or the destruction of evidence.

Searches performed on an emergency basis fall under the exigent circumstances exception to the warrant requirement of the Fourth Amendment. The Supreme Court, in the 1979 case of *Arkansas* v. *Sanders*,[57] recognized the need for exigent searches of persons. The Court indicated such searches would be approved, "where the societal costs of obtaining a warrant, such as danger to law officers or the risk of loss or destruction of evidence, outweigh the reasons for prior recourse to a neutral magistrate."[58]

The 1987 case of *Borchardt* v. *U.S.*,[59] decided by the Fifth Circuit Court of Appeal, held that Borchardt could be prosecuted for heroin uncovered during medical treatment, even over the defendant's objections. Borchardt was a federal inmate at the time he was discovered unconscious in his cell. He was taken to a hospital where tests revealed heroin in his blood. His heart stopped and he was revived using CPR. Borchardt was given three doses of Narcan, a drug used to counteract the effects of heroin, and he improved, regaining consciousness. The patient refused requests to pump his stomach, but began to become lethargic, indicating the need for additional Narcan. Eventually he vomited nine plastic bags full of heroin, along with two bags which had burst. The heroin was turned over to federal officers, and Borchardt was eventually convicted of heroin possession. Attempts to exclude the heroin from evidence were unsuccessful, and the appeals court ruled that the necessity of the emergency situation overruled the defendant's objections to search his person.

The Legal Counsel Division of the FBI provides the following guidelines in conducting emergency warrantless searches of individuals, where the possible destruction of evidence is at issue (keep in mind that there may be no probable cause to *arrest* the individual being searched):[60]

♦ There was probable cause to believe at the time of the search that there was evidence concealed on the person searched.

♦ There was probable cause to believe an emergency threat of destruction of evidence existed at the time of the search.

♦ The officer had no prior opportunity to obtain a warrant authorizing the search.

♦ The action was no greater than necessary to eliminate the threat of destruction of evidence.

VEHICLE SEARCHES

Vehicles present a special law enforcement problem. They are highly movable and, when an arrest of a driver or an occupant occurs, the need to search them may be immediate.

The first significant Supreme Court case involving an automobile was that of *Carroll* v. *U.S.*[61] in 1925. In the *Carroll* case a divided Court ruled that a warrantless search of an automobile or other vehicle is valid if it is based upon a reasonable belief that contraband is present.

In 1964, however, in the case of *Preston* v. *U.S.*,[62] the limits of warrantless vehicle searches were defined. Preston was arrested for vagrancy and taken to jail. His vehicle was impounded, towed to the police garage, and later searched. Two revolvers were uncovered in the glove compartment, and more incriminating evidence was found in the trunk. Preston was convicted on weapons possession and other charges, and eventually appealed to the U.S. Supreme Court. The Court held that the warrantless search of Preston's vehicle had occurred while the automobile was in secure custody and had been, therefore, illegal. Time and circumstances would have permitted, the Court reasoned, acquisition of a warrant to conduct the search.

When the search of a vehicle occurs after it has been impounded, however, that search may be legitimate if it is undertaken for routine and reasonable purposes. In the case of *South Dakota* v. *Opperman* (1976),[63] for example, the Court held that a warrantless search undertaken for purposes of the inventorying and safekeeping of personal possessions of the car's owner was not illegal, even though it turned up marijuana. The intent of the search had not been to discover contraband, but to secure the owner's belongings from possible theft. Again, in *Colorado* v. *Bertine* (1987), the Court reinforced the idea that officers may open closed containers found in a vehicle while conducting a routine search for inventorying purposes. In the words of the Court, such searches are "now a well-defined exception to the warrant requirement."[64] In 1990, however, in the precedent-setting case of *Florida* v. *Wells*,[65] the Court agreed with a lower court's suppression of marijuana discovered in a locked suitcase in the trunk of a defendant's impounded vehicle. In *Wells* the Court held that standardized criteria authorizing the search of a vehicle for inventorying purposes were necessary before such a discovery could be legitimate. Standardized criteria, said the Court, might take the form of department policies, written general orders, or established routines.

Warrantless vehicle searches may extend to any area of the vehicle, and may include sealed containers, the trunk area, and the glove compartment if officers have probable cause to conduct a purposeful search, or if officers have been given permission to search the vehicle. In the 1991 case of *Florida* v. *Jimeno*,[66] arresting officers stopped a motorist who gave them permission to search his car. The defendant was later convicted on a drug charge, when a bag on the floor of the car was found to contain cocaine. Upon appeal to the Supreme Court, however, he argued that the permission given to search his car did not extend to bags and other items within the car. In a decision which may have implications beyond vehicle searches, the Court held that "[a] criminal suspect's Fourth Amendment right to be free from unreasonable searches is not violated when, after he gives police permission to search his car, they open a closed container found within the car that might reasonably hold the object of the search. The Amendment is satisfied when, under the circumstances, it is objectively reasonable for the police to believe that the scope of the suspect's consent permitted them to open the particular container."[67] In *United States* v. *Ross* (1982),[68] the Court found that officers had not exceeded their authority in opening a bag in the trunk which was found to contain heroin. The search was held to be justifiable on the basis of information developed from a search of the passenger compartment. The Court said, "if probable cause justifies the search of a lawfully stopped vehicle, it justifies the search of every part of the vehicle and its contents that may conceal the object of the search."[69]

The 1983 case of *U.S.* v. *Villamonte-Marquez*[70] widened the Carroll doctrine to include watercraft. The case involved an anchored sailboat occupied by Villamonte-Marquez which was searched by a U.S. Customs officer after one of the crew members appeared unresponsive to being hailed. The officer thought he smelled burning marijuana after boarding the vessel and saw burlap bales through an open hatch which he suspected might be contraband. A search proved him correct, and the ship's occupants were arrested. Their conviction was overturned upon appeal, but the U.S. Supreme Court reversed the appeals court. The Court reasoned that a vehicle on the water can easily leave the jurisdiction of enforcement officials, just as a car or truck can.

Finally, in *California* v. *Carney* (1985),[71] the Court extended police authority to conduct warrantless searches of vehicles to include motor homes. Earlier arguments had been advanced that a motor home, because it is more like a permanent residence, should not be considered a vehicle in the same sense of an automobile for purposes of search and seizure. The Court, in a 6 to 3 decision, rejected those arguments, reasoning that a vehicle's appointments and size do not alter its basic function of providing transportation.

Houseboats were brought under the automobile exception to the Fourth Amendment warrant requirement in the 1988 Tenth Circuit Court case of *U.S.* v. *Hill*.[72] In the *Hill* case, DEA agents developed evidence which led them to believe that methamphetamine was being manufactured on board a houseboat traversing Lake Texoma in Oklahoma. Because a storm warning had been issued for the area, agents decided to board and search the boat prior to obtaining a warrant. During the search an operating amphetamine laboratory was discovered, and the boat seized. In an appeal, the defendants argued that the houseboat search had been illegal because agents lacked a warrant to search their home. The appellate court, however, in rejecting the claims of the defendants, ruled that a houseboat, because it is readily mobile, may be searched without a warrant where probable cause exists to believe that a crime has been or is being committed.

The 1991 Supreme Court case of *Florida* v. *Bostick*,[73] which permitted warrantless "sweeps" of intercity buses, moved the Court deeply into conservative territory. The *Bostick* case came to the attention of the Court as a result of the Broward County, Florida, Sheriff Department's routine practice of boarding buses at scheduled stops and asking passengers for permission to search their luggage. Terrance Bostick, a passenger on one of the buses, gave police permission to search his luggage, which was found to contain cocaine. Bostick was arrested and eventually pled guilty to charges of drug trafficking. The Florida Supreme Court, however, found merit in Bostick's appeal, which was based upon a Fourth Amendment claim that the search of his luggage had been unreasonable. The Florida court held that "a reasonable passenger in (Bostick's) situation would not have felt free to leave the bus to avoid questioning by the police" and overturned the conviction.

The state appealed to the U.S. Supreme Court, which held that the Florida Supreme Court erred in interpreting Bostick's *feelings* that he was not free to leave the bus. In the words of the Court, "Bostick was a passenger on a bus that was scheduled to depart. He would not have felt free to leave the bus even if the police had not been present. Bostick's movements were 'confined' in a sense, but this was the natural result of his decision to take the bus." In other words, Bostick was constrained not so much by police action, as by his own feelings that might miss the bus were he to get off. Following this line of reasoning, the Court concluded that police warrantless, suspicionless "sweeps" of buses, "trains, planes and city streets" are permissible so long as officers (1) ask individual passengers for permission before searching their possessions, (2) do not coerce passengers to consent to a search, and (3) do not convey the message that citizen compliance with the search request is mandatory. Passenger compliance with police searches must be voluntary for the searches to be legal.

The
Police
Chief

In contrast to the tone of Court decisions a decade earlier, the justices did not require officers to inform passengers that they were free to leave, nor that they had the right to deny officers the opportunity to search (although Bostick himself was so advised by Florida officers). Any reasonable person, the Court ruled, should feel free to deny the police request. In the words of the Court, "[t]he appropriate test is whether, taking into account all of the circumstances surrounding the encounter, a reasonable passenger would feel free to decline the officers' requests or otherwise terminate the encounter." The Court continued: "[r]ejected, however, is Bostick's argument that he must have been seized because no reasonable person would freely consent to a search of luggage containing drugs, since the 'reasonable person' test presumes an innocent person."

Critics of the decision saw it as creating new "Gestapo-like" police powers in the face of which citizens on public transportation will feel compelled to comply with police requests for search authority. Dissenting Justices Blackmun, Stevens, and Marshall held that "the bus sweep at issue in this case violates the core values of the Fourth Amendment." However, in words which may presage a significant change of direction for other Fourth Amendment issues, the Court defended its ruling by intoning "[t]he Fourth Amendment proscribes unreasonable searches and seizures; it does not proscribe voluntary co-operation."

☐ THE INTELLIGENCE FUNCTION

The police role includes the need to gather information through the questioning of both suspects and informants. Even more often, the need for information leads police investigators to question potentially knowledgeable citizens who may have been witnesses or victims. Data gathering is a crucial form of intelligence, without which enforcement agencies would be virtually powerless to plan and effect arrests.

The importance of gathering information in police work cannot be overstressed. Studies have found that the one factor most likely to lead to arrest in serious crimes is the presence of a witness who can provide information to the police. Undercover operations, neighborhood watch programs, "crime stoppers" groups, and organized detective work, all contribute information to the police.

Many ethical questions have been raised about the techniques employed by police to gather information. Police use of paid informants, for example, is an area of concern to ethicists who believe that informants are often paid to get away with crimes. The police practice (endorsed by some by prosecutors) of agreeing not to charge one offender out of a group if he or she will "talk," and to testify against others, is another concern of students of justice ethics.

The Fourth Amendment specifies, "No warrants shall issue, but upon probable cause." As a consequence, the successful use of informants in supporting requests for a warrant depends upon the demonstrable reliability of their information. The use of informants was clarified by the case of *Aguilar* v. *Texas*[74] in 1964. That case established a two-pronged test to the effect that informant information could establish probable cause if *both* of the following criteria are met:

♦   The source of the informant's information is made clear.
♦   The police officer has a reasonable belief that the informant is reliable.

The two-pronged test of *Aguilar* v. *Texas* was intended to prevent the issuance of warrants on the basis of false or fabricated information. Two later cases provided exceptions to the two-pronged test. *Harris* v. *United States* (1971)[75] recognized the fact that information which was damaging to the informant probably had to be true when provided by the informant. In *Harris* an informant told police that he had purchased non-tax-paid whiskey from another person. Since the information also implicated the informant in a crime, it was held to be accurate, even though it could not meet the second prong of the *Aguilar* test. The 1969 Supreme Court case of *Spinelli* v. *United States*[76] created an exception to the requirements of the first prong. In *Spinelli*, the Court held that some information can be so highly specific that it must be accurate, even if its source is not revealed. In 1983, in the case of *Illinois* v. *Gates*,[77] the Court adopted a totality of circumstances approach, which held that sufficient probable cause for issuing a warrant exists where an informer can be reasonably believed on the basis of everything that is known by the police. The *Gates* case involved an anonymous informant who provided incriminating information about another person through a letter to the police. Although the source of the information was not stated, and the police were unable to say whether or not the informant was reliable, the overall *sense* of things, given what was already known to the police, was that the information supplied was probably valid.

Finally, in the 1990 case of *Alabama* v. *White*,[78] the Supreme Court ruled that an anonymous tip, even in the absence of other, corroborating information about a suspect, could form the basis for an investigatory stop where the informant accurately predicts the *future* behavior of the suspect. The ability to predict a suspect's behavior demonstrates, the Court reasoned, a significant degree of familiarity with the suspect's affairs. In the words of the Court: "Because only a small number of people are generally privy to an individual's itinerary, it is reasonable for the police to believe that a person with access to such information is likely to also have access to reliable information about that individual's illegal activities."[79]

POLICE INTERROGATION

Physical Abuse

Landmark decisions by the U.S. Supreme Court have clearly focused on issues of police interrogation. The first in a series of significant cases was that of *Brown* v. *Mississippi*,[80] decided in 1936. The *Brown* case began with the robbery of a white store owner in Mississippi in 1934. During the robbery the victim was killed.

A posse formed spontaneously, and went to the home of a local black man rumored to have been one of the perpetrators. They dragged the suspect from his home, put a rope around his neck, and hoisted him into a tree. They repeated this process a number of times, hoping to get a confession from the man, but failing. The posse was joined by a deputy sheriff who led them to the home of other suspects, where they repeated their "interrogation" technique. Finally, they were able to get a confession from one of the men. The remaining defendants were laid over chairs in the jail and whipped with belts and buckles until they also "confessed." These confessions were used in the trial which followed, and the three defendants were convicted of murder. Their convictions were upheld by the Mississippi Supreme Court. One of the defendants, named Brown, made further appeals. In 1936 his case was reviewed by the U.S. Supreme Court, which overturned Brown's conviction, saying that it was difficult to imagine techniques of interrogation more "revolting" to the sense of justice than those used in this case.

Inherent Coercion

Interrogation need not involve physical abuse for it to be contrary to constitutional principles. In the case of *Ashcraft* v. *Tennessee*,[81] the Court found that inherently coercive interrogation was not acceptable. Ashcraft had been charged with the murder of his brother-in-law. He was arrested on a Friday night, and interrogated by relays of skilled interrogators until Monday morning, when he finally confessed to the murder. During questioning he had been faced by a blinding light, but not physically mistreated. Investigators later testified that when the suspect requested cigarettes, food, or water, they "kindly" provided them. The Supreme Court's ruling in this case made it plain that the Fifth Amendment guarantee against self-incrimination excludes *any* form of official coercion or pressure during interrogation.

A similar case, involving four black defendants, occurred in Florida in 1940.[82] The four men, including one whose name was Chambers, were arrested without warrants as suspects in a robbery and murder of an aged white man. After several days of questioning in a hostile atmosphere, the men confessed to the murder. The confessions were used as the primary evidence against them at a trial which ensued, and all four were sentenced to die. Upon appeal to the Supreme Court, the Court held that "the very circumstances surrounding their confinement and their questioning without any formal charges having been brought, were such as to fill petitioners with terror and frightful misgivings."[83]

Psychological Manipulation

Interrogation must not only be free of coercion and hostility, it cannot involve sophisticated trickery designed to ferret out a confession. While interrogators do not necessarily have to be scrupulously honest in confronting suspects, and while the expert opinions of medical and psychiatric practitioners may be sought in investigations, the use of professionals skilled in psychological manipulation to gain confessions was banned by the Court in the case of *Leyra* v. *Denno*[84] in 1954.

The early 1950s were the "heyday" of psychiatric perspectives on criminal behavior. In the *Leyra* case, detectives employed a psychiatrist to question Leyra, who had been charged with the hammer slayings of his parents. Leyra had been led to believe that the medical doctor to whom he was introduced in an interrogation room had actually been sent to help him with a sinus problem.   Following a period of questioning, including subtle suggestions by the psychiatrist that he would feel better if he confessed to the murders, Leyra did indeed confess.

The Supreme Court, on appeal, ruled that the defendant had been effectively, and improperly, duped by the police. In the words of the Court, "Instead of giving petitioner the medical advice and treatment he expected, the psychiatrist by subtle and suggestive questions simply continued the police effort of the past days and nights to induce petitioner to admit his guilt. For an hour and a half or more the techniques of a highly trained psychiatrist were used to break petitioner's will in order to get him to say he had murdered his parents."[85] After a series of three trials, each with less and less evidence permitted into the courtroom by appeals courts, and following convictions in each, Leyra was finally set free by a state appeals court which found insufficient evidence for the final conviction.

During the 1991 Supreme Court term, the case of *Arizona* v. *Fulminante*[86] threw a blanket of uncertainty over the use of sophisticated techniques to gain a confession. Oreste Fulminante was an inmate in a federal prison when he was approached secretly by a fellow inmate who was an FBI informant. The informant told Fulminante that other inmates were plotting to kill him because of a rumor that he had killed a child. He offered to protect Fulminante if he was told the details of the crime. Fulminante then described his role in the murder of his 11-year-old stepdaughter. Fulminante was arrested for that murder, tried and convicted. Upon appeal to the U.S. Supreme Court, his lawyers argued that Fulminante's confession had been coerced because of the threat of violence communicated by the informant. The Court agreed that the confession had been coerced, and ordered a new trial at which the confession could not be admitted into evidence. Simultaneously, however, the Court found that the admission of a coerced confession should be considered a harmless "trial error" which need not necessarily result in reversal of a conviction, if other evidence still proves guilt. The decision was especially significant because it partially reversed the Court's earlier ruling, in *Chapman* v. *California*,[87] where it was held that forced confessions were such a basic form of constitutional error that they could never be used and automatically invalidated any conviction to which they related.

The Right to a Lawyer at Interrogation

In 1964, in the case of *Escobedo* v. *Illinois*,[88] the right to have legal counsel present during police interrogation was recognized. Danny Escobedo was arrested without a warrant for the murder of his brother-in-law and was interrogated. He made no statement, and was released the same day. A few weeks later another person identified Escobedo as the killer. Escobedo was rearrested and taken back to the police station. During the interrogation which followed, officers told him that they "had him cold" and that he should confess. Escobedo asked to see his lawyer, but was told that an interrogation was in progress, and that he couldn't just go out and see his lawyer. Soon the lawyer arrived and asked to see Escobedo. Police told him that his client was being questioned and could be seen after questioning concluded. Escobedo later claimed that while he repeatedly asked for his lawyer, he was told, "Your lawyer doesn't want to see you."

Eventually Escobedo confessed and was convicted at trial on the basis of his confession. Upon appeal to the U.S. Supreme Court, the Court overturned Escobedo's conviction, ruling that counsel is necessary at police interrogations to protect the rights of the defendant and should be provided when the defendant desires.

In 1981, the case of *Edwards* v. *Arizona*[89] established a "bright-line rule" for investigators to use in interpreting a suspect's right to counsel. In *Edwards* the Supreme Court reiterated its *Miranda* concern that once a suspect, who is in custody and who is being questioned, has requested the assistance of counsel, all questioning must cease until an attorney is present. In 1990 the Court refined the rule in *Minnick* v. *Mississippi*, when it held that interrogation may *not* resume after the suspect has had an opportunity to consult his or her lawyer, when the lawyer is no longer present. Similarly, according to *Arizona* v. *Roberson* (1988),[90] the police may not avoid the defendant's request for a lawyer by beginning a new line of questioning, even if it is about an unrelated offense.

THE *MIRANDA* DECISION

In the area of suspect rights, no case is as well known as that of *Miranda* v. *Arizona*,[91] which was decided in 1965. Ernesto Miranda was arrested in Phoenix, Arizona, and accused of having kidnapped and raped a young woman. At police headquarters he was identified by the victim. After being interrogated for two hours, Miranda signed a confession which formed the basis of his later conviction on the charges.

Upon eventual appeal to the U.S. Supreme Court, the Court rendered what some regard as the most far-reaching opinion to have impacted criminal justice in the last few decades. The Court ruled that Miranda's conviction was unconstitutional because, "The entire aura and atmosphere of police interrogation without notification of rights and an offer of assistance of counsel tends to subjugate the individual to the will of his examiner."

The Court continued, saying that the defendant, "must be warned prior to any questioning that he has the right to remain silent, that anything he says can be used against him in a court of law, that he has the right to the presence of an attorney, and that if he cannot afford an attorney one will be appointed for him prior to any questioning if he so desires. Opportunity to exercise these rights must be afforded to him throughout the interrogation. After such warnings have been given, and such opportunity afforded him, the individual may knowingly and intelligently waive these rights and agree to answer the questions or make a statement.   But unless and until such warnings and waiver are demonstrated by the prosecution at the trial, no evidence obtained as a result of interrogation can be used against him."[92]

ADULT RIGHTS WARNING

Persons 18 years old or older who are in custody must be given this advice of rights before any questioning:

1. You have the right to remain silent.
2. Anything you say can be used against you in a court of law.
3. You have the right to talk to a lawyer and to have a lawyer present while you are being questioned.
4. If you want a lawyer before or during questioning but cannot afford to hire a lawyer, one will be appointed to represent you at no cost before any questioning.
5. If you answer questions now without a lawyer here, you still have the right to stop answering questions at any time.

WAIVER OF RIGHTS

After reading and explaining the rights of a person in custody, an officer must also ask for a waiver of those rights before any questioning. The following waiver questions must be answered affirmatively, either by express answer or by clear implication. Silence alone is not a waiver.

1. Do you understand each of these rights I have explained to you? (Answer must be YES.)
2. Having these rights in mind, do you now wish to answer questions? (Answer must be YES.)
3. Do you now wish to answer questions without a lawyer present? (Answer must be YES.)

For juveniles ages 14, 15, 16, and 17, the following question must be asked:

4. Do you now wish to answer questions without your parents, guardians, or custodians present? (Answer must be YES.)

To ensure that proper advice is given to suspects at the time of their arrest, the now-famous *Miranda* rights are read before any questioning begins. These rights, as they appear on a *Miranda* warning card commonly used by police agencies, appear in the accompanying box.

Once suspects have had a *Miranda* rights advisement, they are commonly asked to sign a paper which lists each right, in order to confirm that they were advised of their rights, and that they understand each right. Questioning may then begin, but only if suspects waives their rights not to talk, or to have a lawyer present during interrogation.

Some hailed the *Miranda* case as one which ensured the protection of individual rights guaranteed under the Constitution. To guarantee those rights, they suggested, what better agency is available than the police themselves, since the police are present at the initial stages of the criminal justice process.

Critics of the *Miranda* decision have argued that *Miranda* puts police agencies in the uncomfortable and contradictory position of not only enforcing the law, but also of having to offer defendants advice on how potentially to circumvent conviction and punishment. Under *Miranda* the police partially assume the role of legal advisor to the accused.   During the last years of the Reagan administration, then-Attorney General Edwin Meese focused on the *Miranda* decision as the antithesis of "law and order."   He pledged the resources of his office to an assault upon the *Miranda* rules in order to eliminate what he saw as the frequent release of guilty parties on the basis of "technicalities."

A Waiver of Rights

Suspects in police custody may waive their *Miranda* rights. The legal standard for the waiver of rights has been held to be a *voluntary* "knowing and intelligent" waiver. A *knowing waiver* can only be made if a suspect has had the benefit of a rights advisement, and if they were in a condition to understand the advisement. A rights advisement made in English, for example, to a Spanish-speaking defendant, cannot produce a knowing waiver. Likewise, an *intelligent waiver* of rights requires that the defendant be able to understand the consequences of not invoking the *Miranda* rights. In the case of *Moran* v. *Burbine* (1986),[93] the Supreme Court defined an intelligent and knowing waiver as one "made with a full awareness both of the nature of the right being abandoned and the consequences of the decision to abandon it."[94] Similarly, in *Colorado* v. *Spring* (1987),[95] the Court has held that an intelligent and knowing waiver can be made even though a suspect has not been informed of all the alleged offenses about which he or she is about to be questioned.

Exceptions to *Miranda*

A good example of the change in Supreme Court philosophy, alluded to earlier in this chapter as a movement from "Warren" to "Burger" court doctrine, can be had in the case of *Nix* v. *Williams* (1984).[96] The *Nix* case epitomizes what some have called a "nibbling away" at the advances in defendant rights which reached their apex in *Miranda*. The case had its beginnings in 1969 when Robert Anthony Williams was convicted of murdering a 10-year-old girl, Pamela Powers, around Christmastime. Although Williams had been advised of his rights, detectives searching for the girl's body were riding in a car with the defendant, when one of them made what has since come to be known as the "Christian burial speech."   The detective told Williams that, since Christmas was almost upon them, it would be "the Christian thing to do" to see to it that Pamela could have a decent burial, rather than having to lay in a field somewhere. Williams relented and led detectives to the body. However, because Williams had not been reminded of his right to have a lawyer present during his conversation with the detective, the Supreme Court overturned Williams' conviction, saying that the detective's remarks were "a deliberate eliciting of incriminating evidence from an accused in the absence of his lawyer."[97]

That was in 1975. In 1977, Williams was retried for the murder, but his remarks in leading detectives to the body were not entered into evidence. The discovery of the body was itself used, however, prompting another appeal to the Supreme Court based upon the argument that the body should not have been used as evidence since it was discovered on the basis of the illegally gathered statements. This time the Supreme Court affirmed

Williams' conviction, holding that the body would have been found anyway, since detectives were searching in the direction where it lay. That ruling came in 1984 and clearly demonstrates a tilt by the Court away from suspect's rights and an accommodation with the imperfect world of police procedure. The *Nix* case, as it was finally resolved, is said to have created the inevitable discovery exception to the *Miranda* requirements.

Public Safety Exceptions to *Miranda*

In 1984 the U.S. Supreme Court also established what has come to be known as the public safety exception to the *Miranda* rule. The case, *New York* v. *Quarles*,[98] centered upon an alleged rape in which the victim told police her assailant had fled, with a gun, into a nearby A&P supermarket. Two police officers entered the store and apprehended the suspect. One officer immediately noticed that the man was wearing an empty shoulder holster and, apparently fearing that a child might find the discarded weapon, quickly asked, "Where's the gun?"

Quarles was convicted of rape, but appealed his conviction, requesting that the weapon be suppressed as evidence because officers had not advised him of his *Miranda* rights prior to asking a question about the gun. The Supreme Court disagreed, stating that considerations of public safety were overriding and negated the need for rights advisement prior to limited questioning which focused on the need to prevent further harm.

Where coercive conduct on the part of the police is lacking, and *Miranda* warnings have been issued, the Supreme Court has held that even a later demonstration that a person may have been suffering from mental problems will not necessarily negate a confession. *Colorado* v. *Connelly* (1986)[99] involved a man who approached a Denver police officer and said he wanted to confess to the murder of a young girl. The officer immediately informed him of his *Miranda* rights, but the man waived them and continued to talk. When a detective arrived, the man was again advised of his rights, and again waived them. After being taken to the local jail, the man began to hear "voices," and later claimed that it was these voices which had made him confess. At the trial the defense moved to have the earlier confession negated on the basis that it was not voluntarily nor freely given, because of the defendant's mental condition. Upon appeal, the Supreme Court disagreed, saying that "no coercive government conduct occurred in this case."[100] Hence, "self-coercion," be it through the agency of a guilty conscience or faulty thought processes, does not appear to bar prosecution based on information revealed willingly by the defendant.

In a final refinement of *Miranda*, the lawful ability of a police informant, placed in a jail cell along with a defendant to gather information for later use at trial, was upheld in the 1986 case of *Kuhlmann* v. *Wilson*.[101] The passive gathering of information was judged to be acceptable, provided that the informant did not make attempts to elicit information.

In the case of *Illinois* v. *Perkins* (1990), the Court expanded its position to say that, under appropriate circumstances, even the active questioning of a suspect by an undercover officer posing as a fellow inmate does not require *Miranda* warnings. In *Perkins*, the Court found that, lacking other forms of coercion, the fact that the suspect was not aware of the questioner's identity as a law enforcement officer ensured that his statements were freely given. In the words of the Court, "[t]he essential ingredients of a 'police-dominated atmosphere' and compulsion are not present when an incarcerated person speaks freely to someone that he believes to be a fellow inmate."[102]

Miranda and the Meaning of Interrogation

Modern interpretations of the applicability of "*Miranda* warnings" turn upon an understanding of *interrogation*. The *Miranda* decision, as originally rendered, specifically recognized the necessity for police investigators to make inquiries at crime scenes in order to determine facts or establish identities. So long as the individual questioned is not yet in custody, and so long as probable cause to arrest is lacking in the investigator's mind, such questioning can proceed unencumbered by the need for *Miranda* warnings. In such cases, interrogation, within the meaning of *Miranda*, has not yet begun.

THE *MIRANDA* "TRIGGERS"

Custody
Interrogation

Custodial interrogation triggers the need for *Miranda* warnings.

The case of *Rock* v. *Zimmerman*[103] (1982) provides a different sort of example — one in which a suspect willingly made statements to the police before interrogation began. The suspect had burned his own house and shot and killed a neighbor. When the fire department arrived he began shooting again and killed the fire chief. Cornered later in a field, the defendant, gun in hand, spontaneously shouted at police, "How many people did I kill; how many people are dead?"[104] This spontaneous statement was held to be admissible evidence at the suspect's trial.

It is also important to recognize that the Supreme Court in the *Miranda* decision required that officers provide warnings only in those situations involving *both* arrest and custodial interrogation. In other words, it is generally permissible for officers to take a suspect into custody, and listen, without asking questions, while he or she tells a story. Similarly, they may ask questions without providing a *Miranda* warning, even within the confines of a police station house, as long as the person questioned is not a suspect and is not under arrest.[105] Warnings are required only when officers begin to actively solicit responses from the defendant. Recognizing this fact, the FBI, in some of its training literature, has referred to interrogation as the *Miranda* trigger.

Interrogation was itself the subject of definition by the Court in 1980 in the case of *Rhode Island* v. *Innis*.[106] Interrogation was defined to include any behaviors by the police "that the police should know are reasonably likely to elicit an incriminating response from the suspect." In the *Innis* case, the Court held that interrogation included "staged line-ups, reverse line-ups, positing guilt, minimizing the moral seriousness of crime, and casting blame on the victim or society...."

It is noteworthy that the Court has held that "police words or actions normally attendant to arrest and custody do not constitute interrogation."[107] Officers were found to have acted properly in the case of *South Dakota* v. *Neville* (1983),[108] in informing a DWI suspect, without reading him his rights, that he would stand to lose his driver's license if he did not submit to a Breathalyzer test. When the driver responded, "I'm too drunk. I won't pass the test," his answer became evidence of his condition and was not subject to exclusion at trial.

A CAREER WITH THE U.S. MARSHALS SERVICE

Typical Positions. U.S. marshals are involved in the following activities: (1) court security, (2) fugitive investigations, (3) personal and witness security, (4) asset seizure, (5) special operations, and (6) transportation and custody of federal prisoners.

Employment Requirements. General employment requirements with the Marshals Service include (1) a comprehensive written exam, (2) a complete background investigation, (3) an oral interview, (4) excellent physical condition, and (5) a Bachelor's degree or three years of "responsible experience." Applicants must be between 21 and 35 years of age and be U.S. citizens with a valid driver's license.

Other Requirements. Successful applicants must complete 13 weeks of training.

Salary. At midyear 1993, starting salary was $23,545 per year (for individuals hired at GS-7 level positions).

Benefits. Benefits include (1) 13 days of sick leave annually, (2) 2½ to 5 weeks of annual paid vacation and 10 paid federal holidays each year, (3) federal health and life insurance, and (4) a comprehensive retirement program.

Direct inquiries to: U.S. Marshals Service, 600 Army-Navy Drive, Arlington, Virginia 22202. Phone: (202) 307-9402.

Finally, a third-party conversation recorded by the police after a suspect has invoked the *Miranda* right to remain silent may be used as evidence, according to the 1987 ruling in *Arizona* v. *Mauro*.[109] A man who willingly conversed with his wife in the presence of a police tape recorder, even after invoking his right to keep silent, had effectively abandoned that right.

☐ GATHERING NONTESTIMONIAL EVIDENCE

RIGHT TO PRIVACY

The police environment is complicated by the fact that suspects are often privy to evidence of a nontestimonial sort. The gathering of nontestimonial evidence from suspects is an area rich in precedent. The Fourth Amendment guarantee that persons should be secure in their homes and in their persons has been interpreted by the courts to generally mean that the involuntary seizure of physical evidence is illegal and will result in exclusion of that evidence at trial.

Two cases, *Hayes* v. *Florida*[110] and *Winston* v. *Lee*,[111] are examples of limits placed by the courts upon the seizure of nontestimonial evidence. The *Hayes* case established the right of suspects to refuse to be fingerprinted when probable cause necessary to effect an arrest does not exist. *Winston* demonstrated the inviolability of the body against surgical and other substantially invasive techniques which might be ordered by authorities against a suspect's will.

In the *Winston* case, Rudolph Lee, Jr., was found a few blocks from a store robbery with a gunshot wound in his chest. The robbery had involved an exchange of gunshots by the store owner and the robber, with the owner noting that the robber had apparently been hit by a bullet. At the hospital, the store owner identified Lee as the robber. The prosecution sought to have Lee submit to surgery to remove the bullet in his chest, arguing that the bullet would provide physical evidence linking him to the crime. Lee refused the surgery, and the Supreme Court in *Winston* v. *Lee* (1985) ruled that Lee could not be ordered to undergo surgery because such a magnitude of intrusion into his body was unacceptable under the right to privacy guaranteed by the Fourth Amendment. The *Winston* case was based upon precedent established in *Schmerber* v. *California* (1966).[112] The *Schmerber* case turned upon the extraction of a blood sample to be measured for alcohol content against the defendant's will. In *Schmerber* the Court ruled that warrants must be obtained for bodily intrusions unless fast action is necessary to prevent the destruction of evidence by natural physiological processes.

Body Cavity Searches

Body cavity searches are among the most problematic for police today. "Strip" searches of convicts in prisons, including the search of body cavities, have generally been held permissible. The 1985 Supreme Court case of *U.S.* v. *Montoya de Hernandez*[113] focused on the issue of "alimentary canal smuggling," in which the suspect typically swallows male prophylactics filled with cocaine or heroin and waits for nature to take its course in order to recover the substance.

In the *Montoya* case, a woman known to be a "balloon swallower" arrived in the United States on a flight from Colombia. She was detained by U.S. Customs officials, and given a "pat down" search by a female agent. The agent reported that the woman's abdomen was firm, and suggested that X-rays be taken. The suspect refused and was given the choice of submitting to further tests or taking the next flight back to Colombia. No flight was immediately available, however, and the suspect was placed in a room for 16 hours, where she refused all food and drink. Finally, a court order for an X-ray was obtained. The procedure revealed "balloons," and the woman was detained another 4 days, during which time she passed numerous cocaine-filled plastic condoms. The Court ruled that the woman's confinement was not unreasonable, based as it was upon the supportable suspicion that she was "body-packing" cocaine. Any discomfort she experienced, the court ruled, "resulted solely from the method that she chose to smuggle illicit drugs."[114]

☐ SUMMARY

The principles of individual liberty and social justice are the cornerstones upon which the American way of life rests. Ideally, the work of the criminal justice system is to ensure justice while guarding liberty. The liberty/justice issue is the dual thread which weaves the tapestry of the justice system together — from the simplest daily activities of police on the beat, to the often complex and lengthy renderings of the U.S. Supreme Court.

For the criminal justice system, the question becomes: "How can individual liberties be maintained in the face of the need for official action, including arrest, interrogation, incarceration, and the like?" The answer is far from simple, but it begins with a recognition of the fact that "liberty" is a double-edged sword, entailing obligations as well as rights. For police action to be "just," it must recognize the rights of individuals while simultaneously holding them accountable to the social obligations defined by law.

DISCUSSION QUESTIONS

1. How has the "Rodney King case" impacted American criminal justice? Has the American system of criminal justice changed substantially as a result of this case? If so, how?

2. Are there any U.S. Supreme Court decisions discussed in this chapter with which you disagree? Which ones? Why do you disagree?

3. Do you agree with the theme of this chapter's summary that "for police action to be just, it must recognize the rights of individuals, while holding citizens to the social obligations defined by law?" What is the basis for your agreement or disagreement?

4. In your opinion, should the U.S. Supreme Court have created exceptions to the exclusionary rule? To *Miranda*? Why or why not?

5. What does the due process environment mean to you? How do you think we should try to ensure due process in our legal system?

6. Justice Benjamin Cardozo once complained, "The criminal is to go free because the constable has blundered." Can we afford to let some guilty people go free in order to ensure that the rights of the rest of us are protected? Is there some other (better) way to achieve the same goal?

NOTES

1. Larry Collins and Dominique Lapierre, *The Fifth Horseman* (New York: Simon & Schuster, 1980).

2. National Advisory Commission on Criminal Justice Standards and Goals, *Police* (Washington, D.C.: U.S. Government Printing Office, 1973), p. 9.

3. "Police Brutality!" *Time,* March 25, 1991, p. 18.

4. "21 L.A. Officers Not Indicted," *The Fayetteville Observer-Times,* May 11, 1991, p. 10C.

5. 'Police Brutality!' p. 16–19.

6. Ibid., p. 16.

7. "Police Charged in Beating Case Say They Feared for Their Lives," *The Boston Globe,* May 22, 1991, p. 22.

8. "Rodney King's Run-ins," *USA Today,* May 30, 1991, p. 2A.

9. "Morgan Awarded $540,000 by Jurors," *Los Angeles Times,* February 15, 1991, p. B1.

10. "Cries of Relief," *Time,* April 26, 1993, p. 18.

11. "A.C.L.U. — Not all That Civil," *Time,* April 26, 1993, p. 31.

12. Clemmens Bartollas, *American Criminal Justice* (New York: Macmillan, 1988), p. 186.

13. *Mapp* v. *Ohio,* 367 U.S. 643 (1961).

14. *Weeks* v. *U.S.,* 232 U.S. 383 (1914).

15. Roger Goldman and Steven Puro, "Decertification of Police: An Alternative to Traditional Remedies for Police Misconduct," *Hastings Constitutional Law Quarterly,* Vol. 15, pp. 45–80.

16. Ibid.

17. *Silverthorne Lumber Co.* v. *U.S.,* 251 U.S. 385 (1920).

18. *Mapp* v. *Ohio.*

19. *Wolf* v. *Colorado,* 338 U.S. 25 (1949).

20. *Chimel* v. *California,* 395 U.S. 752 (1969).

21. *U.S.* v. *Rabinowitz,* 339 U.S. 56 (1950).

22. Ibid.

23. *Katz* v. *U.S.,* 389 U.S. 347, 88 S.Ct. 507 (1967).

24. *Minnesota* v. *Olson,* 110 S.Ct. 1684 (1990).

25. *Illinois* v. *Gates,* 426 U.S. 318 (1982).

26. *U.S.* v. *Leon,* 468 U.S. (1984); 104 S.Ct. 3405.

27. *Massachusetts* v. *Sheppard,* 104 S.Ct. 3424(1984).

28. *Illinois* v. *Krull,* 107 S.Ct. 1160 (1987).

29. *Maryland* v. *Garrison,* 107 S.Ct. 1013 (1987).

30. *Illinois* v. *Rodriguez,* 110 S.Ct. 2793 (1990).

31. William H. Erickson, William D. Neighbors, and B. J. George, Jr., *United States Supreme Court Cases*

and Comments (New York: Matthew Bender, 1987), Section 1.13 [7].

32. *Harris* v. *U.S.*, 390 U.S. 234 (1968).

33. As cited in Kimberly A. Kingston, "Look but Don't Touch: The Plain View Doctrine," *FBI Law Enforcement Bulletin*, December 1987, p. 18.

34. *Horton* v. *California*, 110 S. Ct. 2301, 47 CrL 2135 (No. 88–7164, 1990).

35. *U.S.* v. *Irizarry* (1982).

36. Kingston, "Look but Don't Touch," p. 20.

37. *Arizona* v. *Hicks*, 107 S.Ct. 1149 (1987).

38. See *Criminal Justice Today*, North Carolina Justice Academy, Fall 1987, p. 24.

39. "Inadvertency" as a requirement of legitimate plain view seizures was first cited in the U.S. Supreme Court case of *Coolidge* v. *New Hampshire*, 403 U.S. 443, 91 S. Ct. 2022, in 1971.

40. *Horton* v. *California*, 110 S.Ct. 2301, 47 CrL 2135 (No. 88-7164, 1990).

41. John Gales Sauls, "Emergency Searches of Premises," Part 1, *FBI Law Enforcement Bulletin*, March 1987, p. 23.

42. *Warden* v. *Hayden*, 387 U.S. 294 (1967).

43. *Mincey* v. *Arizona*, 437 U.S. 385, 392 (1978).

44. Sauls, "Emergency Searches of Premises," p. 25.

45. Judicial titles vary between jurisdictions. Many lower-level state judicial officers are referred to as "magistrates." Federal magistrates, however, are generally regarded as functioning at a significantly higher level of judicial authority.

46. *Robinson* v. *U.S.*, 414 U.S. 218 (1973).

47. Ibid.

48. *Terry* v. *Ohio*, 392 U.S. 1 (1968).

49. Ibid.

50. *U.S.* v. *Sokolow*, 109 S.Ct. 1581 (1989).

51. *Brown* v. *Texas*, 443 U.S. 47 (1979).

52. *Smith* v. *Ohio*, 110 S.Ct. 1288 (1990).

53. *Smith*, 110 S.Ct. at 1289.

54. *California* v. *Hodari D.*, No. 89-1632 (1991).

55. *Criminal Justice Newsletter*, May 1, 1991, p. 2.

56. Dissenting opinion in *California* v. *Hodari D.*

57. *Arkansas* v. *Sanders*, 442 U.S. 753 (1979).

58. Ibid.

59. *Borchardt* v. *U.S.*, 809 F.2d 1115 (5th Cir. 1987).

60. *FBI Law Enforcement Bulletin*, January 1988, p. 28.

61. *Carroll* v. *U. S.*, 267 U.S. 132 (1925).

62. *Preston* v. *U. S.*, 376 U.S. 364 (1964).

63. *South Dakota* v. *Opperman*, 428 U.S. 364 (1976).

64. *Colorado* v. *Bertine*, 479 U.S. 367, 107 S.Ct. 741 (1987).

65. *Florida* v. *Wells,* 110 S.Ct. 1632 (1990).

66. *Florida* v. *Jimeno*, No. 90-622 (1991).

67. *Jimeno,* on-line syllabus.

68. *United States* v. *Ross,* 456 U.S. 798 (1982).

69. Ibid.

70. *U.S.* v. *Villamonte-Marquez*, 462 U.S. 579 (1983).

71. *California* v. *Carney*, 471 U.S. (1985).

72. *U.S.* v. *Hill* 855 F.2d 664 (10th Cir. 1988).

73. *Florida* v. *Bostick,* No. 89-1717, 1991.

74. *Aguilar* v. *Texas*, 378 U.S. 108 (1964).

75. *Harris* v. *United States*, 403 U.S. 573 (1971).

76. *Spinelli* v. *United States*, 393 U.S. 410 (1969).

77. *Illinois* v. *Gates,* 426 U.S. 318 (1982).

78. *Alabama* v. *White,* 110 S.Ct. 2412 (1990).

79. *White* at 2417.

80. *Brown* v. *Mississippi*, 297 U.S. 278 (1936).

81. *Ashcraft* v. *Tennessee*, 322 U.S. 143 (1944).

82. *Chambers* v. *Florida*, 309 U.S. 227 (1940).

83. Ibid.

84. *Leyra* v. *Denno*, 347 U.S. 556 (1954).

85. *Leyra*, op cit.

86. *Arizona* v. *Fulminante*, No. 89-839 (1991).

87. *Chapman* v. *California*, 386 U.S. 18 (1967).

88. *Escobedo vs. Illinois*, 378 U.S. 478 (1964).

89. *Edwards* v. *Arizona*, U.S. 477, 101 S.Ct. 1880 (1981).

90. *Arizona* v. *Roberson*, 486 U.S. 675, 108 S.Ct. 2093 (1988).

91. *Miranda* v. *Arizona*, 384 U.S. 436 (1966).

92. Ibid.

93. *Moran* v. *Burbine*, 475 U.S., 106 S.Ct. 1135 (1986).

94. Ibid.

95. *Colorado* v. *Spring*, 479 U.S. 564, 107 S.Ct. 851 (1987).

96. *Nix* v. *Williams*, 104 S.Ct. 2501 (1984).

97. Ibid.

98. *New York* v. *Quarles*, 104 S.Ct. 2626, 81 L.Ed. 2d 550 (1984).

99. *Colorado* v. *Connelly*, 107 S.Ct. 515, 93 L.Ed. 2d 473 (1986).

100. Ibid.

101. *Kuhlmann* v. *Wilson*, 477 U.S., 106 S.Ct. 2616 (1986).

102. *Perkins* at 2397.

103. *Rock* v. *Zimmerman*, 543 F.Supp. 179 (M.D. Penna. 1982).

104. Ibid.

105. See *Oregon* v. *Mathiason*, 429 U.S. 492, 97 S.Ct. 711 (1977).

106. *Rhode Island* v. *Innis*, 446 U.S. 291 (1980).

107. *South Dakota* v. *Neville*, 103 S.Ct. 916 (1983).

108. Ibid.

109. *Arizona* v. *Mauro*, 107 S.Ct. 1931, 95 L.Ed. 2d 458 (1987).

110. *Hayes* v. *Florida*, 470 U.S., 105 S.Ct. 1643 (1985).

111. *Winston* v. *Lee*, 470 U.S., 105 S.Ct. 1611 (1985).

112. *Schmerber* v. *California*, 384 U.S. 757 (1966).

113. *U.S.* v. *Montoya de Hernandez*, 473 U.S. 105 S.Ct. 3304 (1985).

114. Ibid.

INDIVIDUAL RIGHTS VERSUS SOCIAL CONCERNS
✪ The Rights of the Accused Before The Court ✪

Common law, constitutional, and humanitarian rights of the accused:

The Right to a Speedy Trial
The Right to Legal Counsel
The Right Against Self-incrimination
A Right Not to Be Tried Twice for the Same Offense
A Right to Know the Charges
A Right to Cross-examine Witnesses
A Right to Speak and Present Witnesses
A Right Against Excessive Bail

The individual rights listed must be effectively balanced against these community concerns:

Conviction of the Guilty
Exoneration of the Innocent
The Imposition of Appropriate Punishment
Protection of Society
Efficient and Cost-effective Procedures

How does our system of justice work toward balance?

PART 3
Adjudication and Sentencing

When a man wants to murder a tiger, he calls it sport;
when the tiger wants to murder him, he calls it ferocity.
The distinction between crime and justice is no greater.
— *G. B. Shaw* (1856–1950)

The love of justice in most men is only the fear of
suffering injustice.
— *La Rochefoucauld* (1613–1680)

The concept of desert is the only connecting link between
punishment and justice. It is only as deserved or undeserved
that a sentence can be just or unjust.
— *C. S. Lewis* (1898–1963)

CHAPTER 6

THE COURTS

There is no such thing as justice — in or out of court.
— Clarence Darrow (1857–1938)

KEY CONCEPTS

judicial review	dual court system	jurisdiction
circuit courts	impeach	pretrial release
writ of *certiorari*	trial court	lower court
court of last resort	plea bargaining	bond
court administrator	release on recognizance	

☐ INTRODUCTION

Between the often enthralling police quest for suspects and the sometimes hopeless incarceration of offenders, stands the system of federal and state courts. Courts dispense justice on a daily basis and work to ensure that all official actors in the justice arena carry out their duties in recognition of the rule of law.

At many points in this volume we take a close look at court precedents which have defined the "legality" of enforcement efforts and correctional action. A separate chapter explores the law-making function of courts. This chapter is primarily descriptive of the American court system at both the state and federal levels. The steps characteristic of a criminal trial are described in the chapter which follows.

☐ AMERICAN COURT HISTORY

Two criminal court systems coexist in America today: (1) state courts and (2) federal courts. Today's dual court system is the result of general agreement among the nation's founders about the need for individual states to retain significant legislative authority, and autonomy from federal control. Under this concept, the United States developed as a relatively loose federation of semi-independent provinces. New states joining the union were assured of limited federal intervention into local affairs. Under this arrangement, state legislatures were free to create laws, and state court systems were needed to hear cases in which violations of those laws occurred. The last 200 years have seen a slow ebbing of state's rights relative to the power of the federal government. Even today, however, state courts do not hear cases involving alleged violations of federal law, nor do federal courts involve themselves in deciding issues of state law, unless there is a conflict between local statute and federal constitutional guarantees.

In this chapter we will describe both federal and state court systems in terms of their historical development and current structure. It is to state courts that we first turn our attention.

STATE COURT DEVELOPMENT

Each of the original American colonies had its own system for resolving disputes, both civil and criminal. As early as 1629 the Massachusetts Bay Colony had created a "General Court," composed of the governor, his deputy, 18 assistants, and 118 elected officials. The General Court was a combined legislature/court, which made laws, held trials, and imposed sentences.[1] By 1639, as the colony grew, county courts were created, and the General Court took on as its primary job the hearing of appeals, retaining original jurisdiction only in cases involving "tryalls of life, limm, or banishment" (and divorce).[2]

Pennsylvania began its colonial existence with the belief that "every man could serve as his own lawyer."[3] The Pennsylvania system utilized "common peacemakers" who served as referees. Parties to a dispute, including criminal suspects, could choose one person who would then hear the case pled by the aggrieved and the accused. The decision of the peacemaker was binding upon the suspect and the colony. Although the Pennsylvania referee system ended in 1766, lower-level judges, called magistrates in many other jurisdictions, are still referred to as "justices of the peace" in Pennsylvania and a few other states.

Prior to 1776 all American colonies had established fully functioning court systems. The practice of law, however, was substantially inhibited by a lack of trained lawyers. A number of the early colonies even displayed a strong reluctance to recognize the practice of law as a profession. A Virginia statute, for example, enacted in 1645, provided for the removal of "mercenary attorneys" from office and prohibited the practice of law for a fee. Most other colonies retained strict control over the number of authorized barristers by requiring formal training in English law schools and gubernatorial appointments. New York, which provided for the appointment of "counsellors at law," permitted a total of only 41 lawyers to practice law between 1695 and 1769.[4]

The tenuous status of lawyers in the colonies was highlighted by the 1735 New York trial of John Zenger. Zenger was editor of the *New York Journal*, a newspaper, and was accused of slandering then-governor Cosby. Cosby blatantly threatened to disbar any lawyer who defended Zenger, prompting Zenger to hire Pennsylvania lawyer Andrew Hamilton. Hamilton, by virtue of his out-of-state residence, was immune to the governor's threats. Zenger's acquittal resulted in the country's first landmark decision supporting freedom of the press.[5]

Following the American Revolution, colonial courts provided the organizational basis for the growth of fledgling state court systems. As there had been considerable diversity in the structure of colonial courts, state courts were anything but uniform.

Initially, most states made no distinction between original and appellate jurisdiction, and many had no provisions for appeal. Delaware, for example, did not allow for appeals in criminal cases until 1897. States which did permit appeals often lacked any established appellate courts and sometimes used state legislatures for that purpose.

> **Appellate Jurisdiction:** The lawful authority of a court to review a decision made by a lower court; the lawful authority of a court to hear an appeal from a judgment of a lower court.

By the late 1800s a dramatic increase in population and far-reaching changes in the American way of life had led to a tremendous increase in civil litigation and criminal arrests. Law-making bodies tried to keep pace with the rising tide of suits. They created a multiplicity of courts at the trial, appellate, and supreme court levels, calling them by a diversity of names, and assigning them functions which sometimes bore little resemblance to like-sounding courts in neighboring states. City courts arose to handle the special problems of urban life and were limited in their jurisdiction by community boundaries. Other tribunals, such as juvenile courts, developed to handle special kinds of problems or special clients. Some, like magistrates' or small claims courts, handled only petty disputes and minor law violations. Others, like traffic courts, were very narrow in focus. The result was a patchwork quilt of hearing bodies, some only vaguely resembling modern notions of a trial court.

State court systems did, however, have several models to follow during their development. One was the New York state Field Code of 1848, which was eventually copied by most other states. The Field Code clarified jurisdictional claims and specified matters of court procedure, but was later amended so extensively that its usefulness as a model dissolved. Another court systems model was provided by the federal Judiciary Act of 1789 and the later federal Reorganization Act of 1801. States which followed the federal model developed a three-tiered structure of (1) trial courts of limited jurisdiction, (2) trial courts of general jurisdiction, and (3) appellate courts.

STATE COURT SYSTEMS TODAY

The federal model was far from a panacea, however. Within the three-tiered structure it provided, many local and specialized courts proliferated. Traffic courts, magistrates' courts, municipal courts, recorder's courts, probate courts, and courts held by justices of the peace were but a few which functioned at the lower levels. A movement toward simplification of state court structures, led primarily by the American Bar Association and the American Judicature Society, began in the early 1900s. Proponents of state court reform sought the unification of redundant courts which held overlapping jurisdiction. Most reform-minded thinkers suggested a uniform model for states everywhere which would build upon (1) a centralized court structure composed of a clear hierarchy of trial and appellate courts; (2) the consolidation of numerous lower-level courts holding overlapping jurisdiction; and (3) a centralized state court authority which would be responsible for budgeting, financing, and management of all courts within a state.

The court reform movement is still operative today. It has made a substantial number of inroads in many states. However, a large number of differences continue to exist between and among state court systems. Reform states, which early on embraced the reform movement, are now characterized by streamlined judicial systems consisting of precisely conceived trial courts of limited and general jurisdiction, supplemented by one or two appellate court levels. Nonreform, or traditional states, retain judicial systems which are a conglomeration of multilevel and sometimes redundant courts with poorly defined jurisdiction. Even in nonreform states, however, most criminal courts can be classified within the three-story structure of two trial court echelons and an appellate tier.

Trial Courts

Trial courts are where criminal cases begin. The trial court conducts arraignments, sets bail, takes pleas, and conducts trials. If the defendant is found guilty (or pleads guilty) the trial court imposes sentence. Trial courts of limited or special jurisdiction are also called lower courts. Lower courts are authorized to hear only less serious criminal cases, usually involving misdemeanors or to hear special types of cases such as traffic violations, family disputes, small claims, and so on. Courts of limited jurisdiction rarely hold jury trials, depending instead on the hearing judge to make determinations of both fact and law. At the lower court level a detailed record of the proceedings is not maintained. Case files will only include information on the charge, the plea, the finding of the court, and the sentence.

Lower courts are much less given to formality than courts of general jurisdiction. In an intriguing analysis of court characteristics, Thomas Henderson[6] found that misdemeanor courts process cases according to a decisional model. The decisional model is informal, personal, and decisive. It depends upon the quick resolution of relatively uncomplicated issues of law and fact.

Courts of general jurisdiction, called variously, high courts, circuit courts, or superior courts, are authorized to hear any criminal case. In many states they also provide the first appellate level for courts of limited jurisdiction. In most cases, superior courts offer defendants whose cases originated in lower courts the chance for a new trial instead of a review of the record of the earlier hearing. When a new trial is held it is referred to as trial de novo.

Henderson[7] describes courts of general jurisdiction according to a procedural model. Such courts make full use of juries, prosecutors, defense attorneys, witnesses, and all the other actors we usually associate with American courtrooms. The procedural model is fraught with numerous court appearances to ensure that all of a defendant's due process rights are protected. The procedural model makes for a long, expensive, relatively impersonal, and highly formal series of legal maneuvers involving many professional participants.

Trial courts of general jurisdiction operate within a fact-finding framework called the adversarial process. That process pits the interests of the state, represented by prosecutorial resources, against the professional skills and abilities of defense attorneys. The adversarial process is not a free-for-all, but is, rather, constrained by procedural rules specified in law and sustained through tradition.

Appellate Courts

Most states today have an appellate division, consisting of a intermediate appellate court (often called the court of appeals) and a high-level appellate court (generally termed the state supreme court). High-level appellate courts are referred to as courts of last resort, to indicate that no other appellate route remains to a defendant within the state court system once the high court rules on a case. All states have supreme courts, although only 36 have intermediate appellate courts.[8]

An appeal by a convicted defendant asks that a higher court review the actions of a lower one. Courts within the appellate division, once they accept an appeal, do not conduct a new trial. Instead they provide a review of the case on the record. In other words, appellate courts examine the written transcript of lower court hearings to ensure that those proceedings were carried out fairly and in accordance with proper procedure and state law. They may also allow brief oral arguments to be made by attorneys for both sides, and will generally consider other briefs or information filed by the appellant (the party initiating the appeal) or appellee (the side opposed to the appeal). State statutes generally require that sentences of death or life imprisonment be automatically reviewed by the state supreme court.

Most convictions are affirmed upon appeal. Occasionally, however, an appellate court will determine that the trial court erred in allowing certain kinds of evidence to be heard or that it failed to interpret properly the significance of a relevant statute. When that happens, the verdict of the trial court will be reversed, and the case may be remanded, or sent back for a new trial. Where a conviction is overturned by an appellate court because of constitutional issues, or where a statute is determined to be invalid, the state usually has recourse to the state supreme court or the U.S. Supreme Court (when a state law is held to contravene the U.S. Constitution).

Defendants who are not satisfied with the resolution of their case within a state court system may attempt an appeal to the U.S. Supreme Court. For such an appeal to have any chance of being heard, it must be based upon claimed violations of the defendant's rights as guaranteed under federal law or the U.S. Constitution.

> **Appeal:** Generally, the request that a court with appellate jurisdiction review the judgment, decision, or order of a lower court and set it aside (reverse it) or modify it.

STATE COURT ADMINISTRATION

To function efficiently, courts require uninterrupted funding, adequate staffing, trained support personnel, a well-managed case flow, and coordination between levels and among jurisdictions. To oversee these and other aspects of judicial management, every state today has its own mechanism for court administration. Most make use of state court administrators.

The first state court administrator was appointed in New Jersey in 1948.[9] Although other states were initially slow to follow the New Jersey lead, increased federal funding for criminal justice administration during the 1970s, and a growing realization that some form of coordinated management was necessary for effective court operation, eventually led most states to create similar administrative offices. The following tasks are typical of state court administrators today:

♦ The preparation, presentation, and monitoring of a budget for the state court system[10]

♦ The analysis of case flows and backlogs in order to determine where additional resources such as judges, prosecutors, and other court personnel are needed

♦ The collection and publication of statistics describing the operation of state courts

♦ Efforts to streamline the flow of cases through individual courts and the system as a whole

♦ Service as a liaison between state legislatures and the court system

♦ The development and/or coordination of requests for federal and other
outside funding

♦ The management of state court personnel, including promotions for
support staff, and the handling of retirement and other benefits
packages for court employees

♦ The creation and the coordination of plans for the training of judges
and other court personnel (in conjunction with local chief judges and
supreme court justices)

♦ The assignment of judges to judicial districts (especially in states that
use rotating judgeships)

♦ The administrative review of payments to legal counsel for indigent
defendants

Dispute Resolution Centers

Some communities have begun to recognize that it is possible to resolve at least
minor disputes without the need for a formalized process of adjudication.   Dispute resolution centers, which function to hear victim's claims of minor wrongs, such as bad checks,
trespass, shoplifting, and petty theft, operate today in over 200 locations throughout the
country.[11]   Frequently staffed by volunteer mediators, such programs work to resolve
disagreements without the need to assign blame.   Dispute resolution programs began in the
early 1970s, with the earliest being the Community Assistance Project in Chester,
Pennsylvania; the Columbus, Ohio, Night Prosecutor Program; and the Arbitration as an
Alternative program in Rochester, New York. Following the lead of these programs, the
U.S. Department of Justice helped promote the development of three experimental
"neighborhood justice centers" in Los Angeles, Kansas City, and Atlanta.   Each center
accepted both minor civil and criminal cases.

Mediation centers are often closely integrated with the formal criminal justice
process, and may substantially reduce the caseload of lower-level courts. Some centers are,
in fact, run by the courts in various jurisdictions, and work only with court-ordered
referrals. Others are semiautonomous, but may be dependent upon courts for endorsement
of their decisions, while others function with complete autonomy. Rarely however, do
dispute resolution programs entirely supplant the formal criminal justice mechanism, and
defendants who appear before a community mediator may also later be charged with a
crime.

Mediation centers have been criticized for the fact that they typically work only with
minor offenses, thereby denying the opportunity for mediation to victims and offenders in
more serious cases, and for the fact that they may be seen by defendants as just another
form of criminal sanction.[12] Other critiques claim that community dispute resolution centers
do little other than provide a forum for shouting matches between the parties involved.

☐ THE RISE OF THE FEDERAL COURTS

State courts had their origins in early colonial arrangements. Federal courts, however, were created by the U.S. Constitution. Section I of Article III of the Constitution provides for the establishment of "one supreme Court, and . . . such inferior Courts as the Congress may from time to time ordain and establish." Article III, Section II, specifies that such courts are to have jurisdiction over cases arising under the Constitution, federal laws, and treaties. Federal courts are also to settle disputes between states and to have jurisdiction in cases where one of the parties is a state.

> **Original Jurisdiction:** The lawful authority of a court to hear or act upon a case from its beginning and to pass judgment on the law and the facts.

The federal court system of today represents the culmination of a series of congressional mandates which have expanded the federal judicial infrastructure so that it can continue to carry out the duties envisioned by the Constitution. Notable federal statutes which have contributed to the present structure of the federal court system include the Judiciary Act of 1789, the Judiciary Act of 1925, and the Magistrate's Act of 1968.

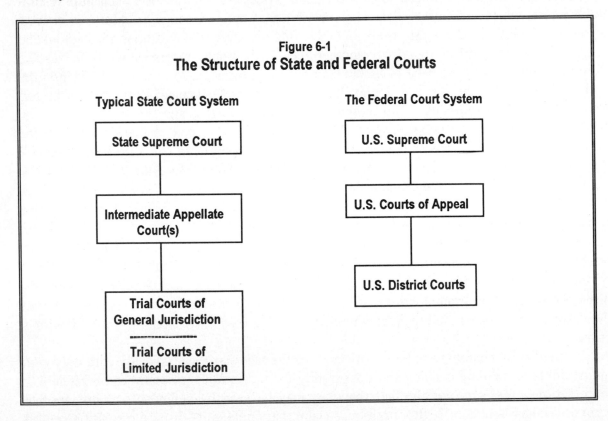

Figure 6-1
The Structure of State and Federal Courts

Typical State Court System

- State Supreme Court
- Intermediate Appellate Court(s)
- Trial Courts of General Jurisdiction
- Trial Courts of Limited Jurisdiction

The Federal Court System

- U.S. Supreme Court
- U.S. Courts of Appeal
- U.S. District Courts

The Judiciary Act of 1789 created, in addition to the U.S. Supreme Court, 13 federal court districts, grouped into three circuits. Under those early arrangements, judges would ride the circuit, a practice especially useful in dispensing justice to the widely scattered populations of the American West. In each circuit, federal appeals courts composed of two Supreme Court justices and one federal district judge were designated to hear appeals from district courts. The act also required states to enforce the Constitution and Federal laws.

By the mid-1800s Supreme Court justices had been relieved of circuit duties, and in 1891 Congress established nine intermediate federal appellate courts to reduce the number of appeals deluging the Supreme Court. The 1891 act also gave the Supreme Court the authority to choose only those cases for hearing which represented a significant legal principle.

Today's federal judiciary consists of three levels: (1) U.S. district courts, (2) U.S. courts of appeals, and (3) the U.S. Supreme Court (see Figure 6-1). Each is described in turn.

FEDERAL DISTRICT COURTS

The lowest level of the federal court system consists of 94 district courts located in the 50 states (except for the District of Wyoming) which includes the Montana and Idaho portions of Yellowstone National Park), Puerto Rico, the District of Columbia, and the U.S. territories of Guam, the Virgin Islands, and the Northern Mariana Islands. Each state has at least one U.S. district court, and some, like New York and California, have as many as four. District courts were first authorized by Congress through the 1789 Judiciary Act, which allocated one federal court to each state. Population increases over the years have necessitated the addition of new courts in a number of states. District courts are the trial courts of the federal judicial system. They have original jurisdiction over all cases involving alleged violations of federal statutes.

Nearly 600 district court judges staff federal district courts. District court judges are appointed by the president, confirmed by the Senate, and serve for life. An additional 460 U.S. magistrates serve the district court system and assist federal judges. Magistrates have the power to conduct arraignments and may set bail, issue warrants, and try petty offenders and some misdemeanants.[13]

U.S. district courts handle thousands of criminal cases per year. Some courts are much busier than others. As a consequence the number of district court judges varies from a low of 2 in some jurisdictions, to a high of 27 in others. In a recent year, the Southern District of California adjudicated 134 criminal cases per judgeship, the highest number of any district.[14] During the past 20 years the number of cases handled by the entire federal district court system has grown exponentially. The hiring of new judges has not kept pace with the increase in caseload, and questions persist as to the quality of justice that can be delivered by overworked judges. One of the most pressing issues facing district court judges is the fact that their pay, which at a minimum of $89,500 in mid-1989 placed them in the top 1% of income-earning Americans, is small compared to what most could earn in private practice.[15] On the other hand, financial disclosure statements filed by all federal judges in 1989 found that, excluding the investment portfolios of spouses and children, 176 qualified as millionaires.[16] Many judges made substantial amounts of money from private practice before assuming the bench, while others had income from investments or held family fortunes.

U.S. COURTS OF APPEALS

U.S. Courts of Appeals are the intermediate-level appellate courts of the federal system. Federal appellate courts are also called circuit courts because the federal system is divided into thirteen circuits (see Figure 6-2). Note that in Figure 6-2 only 11 of the 13 circuit courts are officially numbered. Those courts, plus the District of Columbia judicial circuit, are jurisdictionally organized according to the territory they serve. The jurisdiction of the U.S. Court of Appeals for the Federal Circuit (in effect, the "Thirteenth Circuit"), however, is defined by the nature of the cases heard.

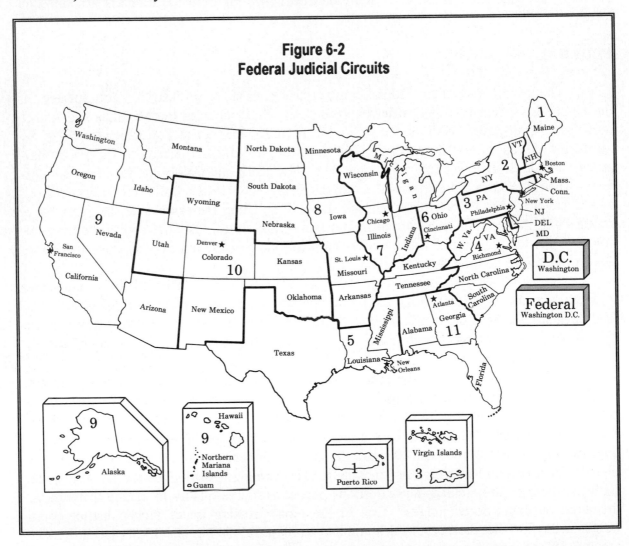

Figure 6-2
Federal Judicial Circuits

Federal appellate courts have mandatory jurisdiction over the decisions of district courts within their circuits. Mandatory jurisdiction means that U.S. courts of appeals are required to hear the cases brought to them. Criminal appeals from federal district courts are usually heard by panels of three judges sitting on a courts of appeals, rather than by all the judges of each circuit.

Federal appellate courts operate under the *Federal Rules of Appellate Procedure,* although each has also created its own separate "local rules." Local rules may mean that one circuit, such as the Second, will depend heavily upon oral arguments, while others may substitute written summary dispositions in their place. Appeals generally fall into one of three categories:[17] (1) frivolous appeals, which have little substance and raise no significant new issues — they are generally quickly disposed of; (2) ritualistic appeals, which are brought primarily because of the demands of litigants, even though the probability of reversal is negligible; and (3) nonconsensual appeals, which entail major questions of law and policy, and on which there is considerable professional disagreement among the courts and within the legal profession. The probability of reversal is, of course, highest in the case of nonconsensual appeals.

Because the Constitution guarantees a right to an appeal, federal circuit courts have found themselves facing an ever-increasing work load. Almost all appeals from federal district courts go to the court of appeals serving the circuit in which the case was first heard. A defendant's right to appeal, however, has been interpreted to mean the right to *one* appeal. Hence, the U.S. Supreme Court need not necessarily hear the appeals of defendants who are dissatisfied with the decision of a federal appeals court.

Copyright 1991 by USA Today. Reprinted with permission.
During the early 1990s many civil libertarians became concerned that the U.S. Supreme Court was taking a dramatic turn towards the political right.

THE SUPREME COURT OF THE UNITED STATES

At the apex of the federal court system stands the U.S. Supreme Court. The Supreme Court consists of nine justices, eight of whom are referred to as associate justices. Presiding over the Court is the chief justice of the United States. Supreme Court justices are nominated by the President, confirmed by the Senate, and serve for life. Lengthy terms of service are a tradition among justices. One of the earliest chief justices, John Marshall, served the Court for 34 years, from 1801 to 1835. The same was true of Justice Stephen J. Field who sat on the bench for 34 years, between 1863 and 1897. Justice Hugo Black passed the 34-year milestone, serving an additional month, before he retired in 1971. Justice William O. Douglas set a record for longevity on the bench, retiring in 1975, after 36 years and 6 months of service.

The Supreme Court of the United States wields immense power. The Court's greatest authority lies in its capacity for judicial review of lower court decisions and state and federal statutes. By exercising its power of judicial review, the Court decides what laws and lower court decisions are in keeping with the intent of the U.S. Constitution. The power of judicial review is not explicit in the Constitution, but was anticipated by its framers. In the *Federalist Papers*, which urged adoption of the Constitution, Alexander Hamilton wrote that, through the practice of judicial review, the Court would ensure that "the will of the whole people," as grounded in the Constitution, would be supreme over the "will of the legislature" which might be subject to temporary whims.[18]

It was not until 1803, however, that the Court forcefully asserted its power of judicial review. In an opinion written for the case of *Marbury* v. *Madison* (1803),[19] Chief Justice John Marshall established the Court's authority as final interpreter of the U.S. Constitution, declaring that, "It is emphatically the province of the judicial department to say what the law is."

Increasing Complexity and the Supreme Court

The evolution of the U.S. Supreme Court provides one of the most dramatic examples of institutional development in American history. Sparsely described in the Constitution, the Court has grown from a handful of circuit riding justices into a modern organization which wields tremendous legal power over all aspects of American life. Much of the Court's growth has been due to its increasing willingness to mediate fundamental issues of law and to act as a resort from arbitrary and capricious processing by the justice system of the states and national government.

The *Marbury* decision, described earlier, established the Court as a mighty force in federal government by virtue of the power of judicial review. It was the Court's willingness to apply that power during the 1960s to issues of crime and justice at the state and local levels, however, which has created a burdensome work load for the Court, which even today shows few signs of abatement. The Court's change in orientation was signaled in 1961 by the case of *Mapp* v. *Ohio*.[20] The *Mapp* case, described in detail in an earlier chapter, extended the exclusionary rule to the states. Such extension, combined with the near-simultaneous end of the hands-off doctrine which had previously exempted state prison systems from Court scrutiny, placed the authority of the Court squarely over the activities of state criminal justice systems.

Is the Supreme Court's Liberal Hour Over?

The Supreme Court Today

The Supreme Court has limited original jurisdiction and does not conduct trials, except in disputes between states and some cases of attorney disbarment. The Court, rather, reviews the decisions of lower courts and may accept cases from both U.S. courts of appeals and state supreme courts. The decision to review a case depends upon a vote of at least four justices who must be in favor of a hearing. When at least four justices agree that a case should be heard, the Court will issue a writ of *certiorari* to a lower court, ordering it to send the records of the case forward for review. Once having granted *certiorari*, the Justices can revoke the decision. In such cases a writ is dismissed by ruling it improvidently granted.

The U.S. Supreme Court may review any decision appealed to it which it decides is worthy of review. In fact, however, the Court elects to review only cases which involve a substantial federal question. Of approximately 5,000 requests for review received by the Court yearly, only about 200 are actually heard.

A term of the Supreme Court begins, by statute, on the first Monday in October and lasts until early July. The term is divided between sittings, when cases will be heard, and time for the writing and delivering of opinions. Between 22 and 24 cases will be heard at each sitting, with each side allocated 30 minutes for arguments before the justices. Intervening recesses allow justices time to study arguments and supporting documentation and to work on their opinions.

A CAREER WITH THE ADMINISTRATIVE OFFICE OF THE U.S. COURTS

Typical Positions. U.S. probation officer, pretrial services officer, statistician, defender services officer, and defense investigator.

Employment Requirements. To qualify for the position of probation officer at the GS-5 level, an applicant must possess a baccalaureate degree from an accredited college or university and have a minimum of two years of general work experience. General experience must have been acquired after obtaining the baccalaureate degree, and cannot include experience as a police, custodial, or security officer unless work in such positions involved criminal investigative experience. In lieu of general experience a baccalaureate degree from an accredited college or university in an accepted field of study (including criminology, criminal justice, penology, correctional administration, social work, sociology, public administration, and psychology) will qualify an applicant for immediate employment at the GS-5 level providing that at least 32 semester hours or 48 quarter hours were taken in one or more of the accepted fields of study. One year of study qualifies applicants for appointment at the GS-7 level, while a master's degree in an appropriate field or a law degree may qualify the applicant for advanced placement.

Other Requirements. Applicants must be less than 37 years of age at the time of hiring and be in excellent physical health.

Salary. Appointees at the GS-5 level were earning $19,456 or more in mid-1993, and GS-7 appointees earned $23,366 or more. Experienced statisticians with Bachelor's degrees earned between $31,116 and $57,650.

Benefits. U.S. probation and pretrial services officers are included in the federal hazardous-duty law enforcement classification and are covered by liberal federal health and life insurance programs. A comprehensive retirement program is available to all federal employees.

Direct Inquiries to: Administrative Office of the U.S. Courts, Personnel Office, Washington, D.C. 20544. Phone: (202) 273-1297.

Rarely are the decisions rendered by the Supreme Court unanimous. Opinions agreed upon by a majority of the Court's justices, make for the judgment of the Court. Concurring opinions are written by justices who agree with the Court's judgment, but for a different reason, or who feel that they have some new light to shed on a particular legal issue involved in the case. Dissenting opinions are provided by justices who do not agree with the decision of the Court. Dissenting opinions may offer new possibilities for successful appeals made at a later date.

Ideas for Change

Increasing caseloads at the federal appellate court level, combined with the many requests for Supreme Court review, have led to proposals to restructure the federal appellate court system. In 1973, a study group appointed by Chief Justice Burger, suggested the creation of a national court of appeals, which would serve as a kind of "mini-Supreme Court."[21] Under the proposal, the national court of appeals would be staffed on a rotating basis by judges who now serve the various circuit courts of appeal. The purpose of the new court was suggested to include a review of cases awaiting hearings before the Supreme Court, so that the high court's work load might be reduced.

A similar national court of appeals was proposed in 1975 by the Congressional Commission on Revision of the Federal Court Appellate System. The national court proposed by the Commission would have heard cases sent to it via transfer jurisdiction, from lower appellate courts, and through reference jurisdiction— when the Supreme Court decided to forward cases to it. The most recent version of a mini-Supreme Court was proposed by the Senate Judiciary Committee in 1986 when it called for the creation of an intercircuit tribunal of the U.S. courts of appeals. To date, however, no legislation to establish such a court has passed both houses of Congress.

☐ PRETRIAL ACTIVITIES

The stages in criminal processing, from investigation and arrest through sentencing and punishment are described in overview fashion in Chapter 1. Because magistrates and other judges issue search and arrest warrants, court involvement may be present at a very early stage in the justice process. Most defendants, however, will not come into contact with an officer of the court until their first appearance before a magistrate.[22]

THE MAGISTRATE'S REVIEW

Following an arrest in the absence of a warrant, many states require a magistrate's review to determine whether or not there is cause to *detain* the suspect. The magistrate's review of the arrest proceeds in an relatively informal fashion, with the judge seeking to decide whether, at the time of apprehension, the arresting officer had reason to believe both that (1) a crime had been or was being committed and (2) the defendant was the person who committed it. Most of the evidence presented to the magistrate comes either from the arresting officer or the victim. At this stage in the criminal justice process the suspect generally is not afforded an opportunity to present evidence. In cases where the suspect is unruly, intoxicated, or uncooperative, the magistrate's review may occur in their absence.

Some states waive a magistrate's review and proceed directly to arraignment, especially when the defendant has been arrested on a warrant. In those states the procedures undertaken to obtain a warrant are regarded as sufficient to demonstrate a basis for detention.

FIRST APPEARANCE

According to the procedural rules of all jurisdictions, defendants must be offered an in-court appearance before a magistrate "without unnecessary delay."   The 1943 Supreme Court case of *McNabb* v. *U.S.*[23] established that any unreasonable delay in an initial court appearance would render inadmissible confessions obtained by interrogating officers during the delay.   Based upon the *McNabb* decision, 48 hours following arrest became the rule of thumb for reckoning the maximum time by which a first appearance should have been held.   The 48 hour rule was formalized by the U.S. Supreme Court in a 1991 class action suit, entitled the *County of Riverside (California)* v. *McLaughlin.*[24]   In *McLaughlin*, the Court held that "a jurisdiction that provides judicial determinations of probable cause within 48 hours of arrest will, as a general matter, comply with the promptness requirement."   The Court specified, however, that weekends and holidays could not be excluded from the 48-hour requirement (as they had been in Riverside County) and that, depending upon the specifics of the case, delays of fewer than two days may still be unreasonable.   In a dissenting opinion, Justice Thurgood Marshall spurned the idea that an appropriate time limit of any kind could be usefully specified.   He wrote, a "probable cause hearing is sufficiently 'prompt' . . . only when provided immediately upon completion of the administrative steps incident to arrest ."[25]

At the first appearance, the accused is brought before a magistrate and apprised of the charges on which he or she is being held.   The U.S. Supreme Court has held that defendants are entitled to representation by counsel at their first appearance.[26]   Indigent defendants may have counsel appointed to represent them, and proceedings may be adjourned until counsel can be obtained.

Bail

A highly significant aspect of the first appearance hearing is consideration of bail or pretrial release.   Defendants charged with very serious crimes, or those thought likely to escape or injure others will usually be held in jail until trial.   Such a practice is called pre-trial detention.

> **Bail Bond:** A document guaranteeing the appearance of the defendant in court as required, and recording the pledge of money or property to be paid to the court if he or she does not appear, which is signed by the person to be released and any other persons acting in his or her behalf.

The majority of defendants, however, will be afforded the opportunity for release. The most commonly used means to ensure that released defendants will return for further court processing is bail.   Bail serves two purposes: (1) it helps ensure reappearance of the accused, and (2) it prevents unconvicted persons from suffering imprisonment unnecessarily.

Bail involves the posting of a bond as a pledge that the accused will return for further hearings. Bail bonds are usually cash deposits, but may consist of property or other valuables. A fully secured bond requires the defendant to post the full amount of bail set by the court. The usual practice, however, is for a defendant to seek privately secured bail through the services of a professional bail bondsman.   The bondsman will assess a percentage (usually 15%) of the required bond as a fee which the defendant will have to pay up front. Those who "skip bail" by hiding or fleeing will sometimes find their bond ordered forfeit by the court. Forfeiture hearings must be held before a bond can be taken, and most courts will not order bail forfeit unless it appears that the defendant intends to avoid prosecution permanently. Bail forfeiture will often be reversed where the defendant later willingly appears to stand trial.

In many states bondsmen are empowered to hunt down and bring back defendants who have fled. In some jurisdictions bondsmen hold virtually unlimited powers, and have been permitted by courts to pursue, arrest, and forcibly extradite their charges from foreign jurisdiction without concern for the due process considerations or statutory limitations which apply to law enforcement officers.[27]   Recently, however, a number of states have enacted laws which eliminate for-profit bail bond businesses, replacing them instead with state-operated pretrial service agencies.

Alternatives to Bail

The Eighth Amendment to the U.S. Constitution, while it does not guarantee the opportunity for bail, does state that "Excessive bail shall not be required."   Some studies, however, have found that many defendants who are offered the opportunity for bail are unable to raise the needed money.   A report by the National Advisory Commission on Criminal Justice Standards and Goals found that as many as 93% of felony defendants in some jurisdictions were unable to make bail.[28]

To extend the opportunity for pretrial release to a greater proportion of nondangerous arrestees, a number of states and the federal government now make available various alternatives to the cash bond system.   Alternatives include (1) release on recognizance, (2) conditional release, (3) third party custody, (4) attorney affidavit, (5) unsecured or signature bond, (6) property bond, and (7) deposit bail.

Release on recognizance (ROR) involves no cash bond, requiring as a guarantee only that the defendant agree in writing to return for further hearings as specified by the court. As an alternative to cash bond, release on recognizance was tested during the 1960s in a social experiment called the Manhattan Bail Project.[29]   In the experiment not all defendants were eligible for release on their own recognizance. Those arrested for serious crimes including murder, rape, robbery, and defendants with extensive prior criminal records were excluded from project participation.   Remaining defendants were scored and categorized according to a number of "ideal" criteria used as indicators of both dangerousness and the likelihood of pretrial flight.   Criteria included (1) no previous convictions, (2) residential stability, and (3) a good employment record. Those with too high a score were not released.

Studies of the bail project revealed that it released four times as many defendants prior to trial as had been freed under the traditional cash bond system.[30]   Even more surprising was the finding that only 1% of those released fled from prosecution — a figure which was the same as for those set free on cash bond.[31]   Later studies, however, were unclear as to the effectiveness of release on recognizance, with some finding a no-show rate as high as 12%.[32]

Property bonds also avoid the use of cash in order to secure release. Property bonds, however, substitute other items of value in place of cash. Land, houses, automobiles, stocks, and so on may be consigned to the court as collateral against pretrial flight.

An alternative form of cash bond available in some jurisdictions is deposit bail. Deposit bail places the court in the role of the bondsman, allowing the defendant to post a percentage of the full bail with the court. Unlike private bail operatives, court-run deposit bail programs usually return the amount of the deposit except for a small (perhaps one percent) administrative fee. If the defendant fails to appear for court, the entire amount of court-ordered bail is forfeit.

Conditional release imposes a set of requirements upon the defendant. Requirements might include attendance at drug treatment programs, staying away from specified others such as potential witnesses, and regular job attendance. Release under supervision is similar to conditional release, but adds the stipulation that defendants report to an officer of the court or a police officer at designated times.

Third party custody is a bail bond alternative which assigns custody of the defendant to an individual or agency which promises to assure his or her later appearance in court.[33] Some pretrial release programs allow attorneys to assume responsibility for their clients in this fashion. If clients fail to appear, however, the attorney's privilege to participate in the program may be ended.[34]

An unsecured bond is based upon a court-determined dollar amount of bail. Like a credit contract, it requires no monetary deposit with the court. The defendant agrees in writing that failure to appear will result in forfeiture of the entire amount of the bond, which might then be taken in seizures of land, personal property, bank accounts, and so on.

A signature bond allows release based upon the defendant's written promise to appear. Signature bonds involve no particular assessment of the defendant's dangerousness or likelihood of later appearance in court. They are used only in cases of minor offenses such as traffic law violations and some petty drug law violations. Signature bonds may be issued by the arresting officer acting on behalf of the court.

Pretrial release is common practice. Approximately 85% of state-level defendants[35] and 82% of federal defendants[36] are released prior to trial. A growing movement, however, stresses the fact that defendants released prior to trial may be dangerous to themselves or others, and seeks to reduce the number of defendants released under any conditions. This conservative policy has been prompted by an increasing concern for public safety in the face of a number of studies documenting crimes committed by defendants released on bond. One such study found that 16% of defendants released before trial were rearrested, and, of those, 30% were arrested more than once.[37] Another determined that as many as 41% of those released prior to trial for serious crimes, such as rape and robbery, were rearrested before their trial date.[38] Not surprisingly, such studies generally find that the longer the time spent on bail prior to trial, the greater the likelihood of misconduct.

In response to claims like these, some states have enacted danger laws, which limit the right to bail for certain kinds of offenders.[39] Others, including Arizona, California, Colorado, Florida, and Illinois, have approved constitutional amendments restricting the use of bail.[40]　Most such provisions exclude persons charged with certain crimes from bail eligibility and demand that other defendants being considered for bail meet stringent conditions.　Some states combine these strictures with tough release conditions designed to keep close control over defendants prior to trial.

The 1984 federal Bail Reform Act allows judges to assess the danger represented by an accused to the community and to deny bail to persons who are thought dangerous.　In the words of the act, a suspect held in pretrial custody on federal criminal charges is required to be detained if, "after a hearing . . . he is found to pose a risk of flight and a danger to others or the community and if no condition of release can give reasonable assurances against these contingencies."[41]　Defendants seeking bail are faced with the necessity of demonstrating a high likelihood of later court appearance.　The act also requires that a defendant is entitled to a speedy first appearance and, if he or she is to be detained, that a detention hearing must be held in consort with the initial appearance.　In the 1990 case of *U.S.* v. *Montalvo-Murillo*,[42] however, a defendant who was not provided with a detention hearing at the time of his first appearance, and was subsequently released, was found to have no "right" to freedom because of this "minor" statutory violation.　The Supreme Court held that "unless it has a substantial influence on the outcome of the proceedings . . . failure to comply with the Act's prompt hearing provision does not require release of a person who should otherwise be detained" because "[a]utomatic release contravenes the statutory purpose of providing fair bail procedures while protecting the public's safety and assuring a defendant's appearance at trial."[43]

Court challenges to the constitutionality of pretrial detention legislation have not met with much success.　The U.S. Supreme Court case of *U.S.* v. *Hazzard* (1984),[44] decided only a few months after enactment of federal bail reform, held that Congress was justified in providing for denial of bail to offenders who represent a danger to the community.　Later cases have supported the presumption of flight which federal law presupposes for certain types of defendants.[45]

THE PRELIMINARY HEARING

Although the preliminary hearing is not nearly as elaborate as a criminal trial, it has many of the same characteristics.　The defendant is taken before a lower court judge who will summarize the charges and review the rights to which all criminal defendants are entitled.　The prosecution may present witnesses and will offer evidence in support of the complaint.　The defendant will be afforded the right to testify and may also call witnesses. The purpose of the preliminary hearing is to afford the defendant an opportunity to challenge the legal basis for his or her detention.　The hearing will turn on a determination of whether there is probable cause to believe that a crime has been committed and that the defendant committed it.

At this stage in the criminal justice process the defendant's guilt need not be proved beyond a reasonable doubt.　All that is required for the wheels of justice to grind forward is a demonstration "sufficient to justify a prudent man's belief that the suspect has committed or was committing an offense."[46]　If the magistrate finds enough evidence to justify a trial, the defendant is bound over to the grand jury — or sent directly to the trial court in those states which do not require grand jury review.　If the complaint against the defendant cannot be substantiated the defendant is released. A release is not a bar to further prosecution, and the defendant may be rearrested if further evidence comes to light.

THE GRAND JURY

The federal government and about half of the states use grand juries as part of the pretrial process. Grand juries are composed of private citizens (often 23 in number) who hear evidence presented by the prosecution. Grand juries serve primarily as filters to eliminate from further processing cases for which there is not sufficient evidence. In early times grand juries served a far different purpose. The grand jury system was begun in England in 1166 as a way of identifying law violators. Lacking a law enforcement agency with investigative authority, the government looked to the grand jury as a source of information on criminal activity in the community. Even today, grand juries in most jurisdictions may initiate prosecution independently of the prosecutor, although they rarely do.

Grand jury hearings are held in secret, and the defendant is not afforded the opportunity to appear before the grand jury.[47] Similarly, the opportunity to cross-examine prosecution witnesses is absent. Grand juries have the power to subpoena witnesses, and to mandate a review of books, records, and other documents crucial to their investigations.

After hearing the evidence, the grand jury votes on the indictment, presented to it by the prosecution. The indictment is a formal listing of proposed charges. If the majority of grand jury constituents agree to forward the indictment to the trial court, it becomes a true bill upon which further prosecution will turn. Jurisdictions which do not make use of the grand jury system depend instead upon an information, or complaint, filed by the prosecutor with the trial court.

ARRAIGNMENT

Once an indictment has been returned, or an information filed, the accused will be formally arraigned before the trial court. The arraignment is generally a brief process which serves two purposes: (1) it informs the defendant of the specific charges against him or her, and (2) it allows the defendant to enter a plea. The Federal Rules of Criminal Procedure allow for one of three types of pleas to be entered: (1) guilty, (2) not guilty, and (3) *nolo contendere* (no contest). Some defendants refuse to enter any plea and are said to "stand mute."

PLEA BARGAINING

Guilty pleas often are not as straightforward as they might seem, typically being arrived at only after complex negotiations referred to as plea bargaining. Plea bargaining is an out-of-court process of negotiation which usually involves the defendant, prosecutor, and defense counsel. It is founded upon the mutual interests of all involved. Defense attorneys and their clients will generally agree to a plea of guilty when they are unsure of their ability to win acquittal at trial. Prosecutors may be willing to bargain because the evidence they have against the defendant is weaker than they would like it to be. From the prosecutorial perspective, plea bargaining results in a quick conviction, without the need to commit the time and resources necessary for trial. Benefits to the accused include the possibility of reduced or combined charges, lessened defense costs, and a lower sentence than might have otherwise been anticipated. The U.S. Supreme Court has held that a guilty plea constitutes conviction.[48] To validate the conviction, negotiated pleas require judicial consent. Judges are likely to often accept pleas which are the result of a bargaining process because such pleas reduce the work load of the court. Although few judges are willing to guarantee a sentence before a plea is entered, most prosecutors and criminal trial lawyers know what sentences to expect from typical pleas.

In the past, plea bargaining, though apparently common, had often been veiled in secrecy. Judicial thinking held that, for pleas to be valid, they had to be freely given. Pleas struck as the result of bargains seemed to depend upon the state's coercive power to encourage the defendant's cooperation. The 1973 National Advisory Commission on Criminal Justice Standards and Goals recommended abolishing the practice of plea negotiation. That recommendation came in the midst of a national debate over the virtues of trading pleas for reductions in sentences. However, in 1970, even before the Commission's recommendation, the U.S. Supreme Court had given its consent to the informal decision-making processes of bartered pleas. In the case of *Brady* v. *U.S.*,[49] the court reasoned that such pleas were voluntarily and knowingly made. A year later, in *Santobello* v. *New York* (1971),[50] the high court forcefully ruled that plea bargaining is an important and necessary component of the American system of justice. In the words of the Court, "The disposition of criminal charges by agreement between the prosecutor and the accused, sometimes loosely called 'plea bargaining,' is an essential component of the administration of justice. Properly administered, it is to be encouraged. If every criminal charge were subjected to a full-scale trial, the States and the Federal Government would need to multiply by many times the number of judges and court facilities."[51]

Today, bargained pleas are commonplace. Some surveys have found that 90% of all criminal cases prepared for trial are eventually resolved through a negotiated plea.[52] In a study of 37 big-city prosecutors,[53] the Bureau of Justice Statistics found that for every 100 adults arrested on a felony charge, half were eventually convicted of either a felony or a misdemeanor. Of all convictions, fully 94% were the result of a plea. Only 6% of convictions were the result of a criminal trial.

After a guilty plea has been entered it may be withdrawn with the consent of the court. In the case of *Henderson* v. *Morgan* (1976),[54] for example, the U.S. Supreme Court permitted a defendant to withdraw a plea of guilty nine years after it had been given. In *Henderson* the defendant had originally entered a plea of guilty to second-degree murder, but attempted to withdraw it before trial. Reasons for wanting to withdraw the plea included the defendant's belief that he had not been completely advised as to the nature of the charge or the sentence he might receive as a result of the plea.

Recent Supreme Court decisions, however, have enhanced the prosecutor's authority in the bargaining process by declaring that negotiated pleas cannot be capriciously withdrawn by defendants.[55] Other rulings have supported discretionary actions by prosecutors in which sentencing recommendations were retracted even after bargains had been struck.[56] Some lower court cases have upheld the government's authority to withdraw from a negotiated plea where the defendant fails to live up to certain conditions.[57]

Conditions may include requiring the defendant to provide information on other criminal involvement, criminal cartels, the activities of smugglers, and so on. Because it is a process of negotiation involving many interests, plea bargaining may have unintended consequences. For example, while it is generally agreed that bargained pleas should relate in some way to the original charge, actual practice may not adhere to such expectations. Many plea negotiations turn on the acceptability of the anticipated sentence, rather than on a close relationship between the charge and the plea. Entered pleas may be chosen for the punishments likely to be associated with them rather than for their accuracy in describing the criminal offense in which the defendant was involved.[58] This is especially true where the defendant is concerned with minimizing the socially stigmatizing impact of the offense. A charge of "indecent liberties," for example, in which the defendant is accused of sexual misconduct, may be plead out as assault. Such a plea, which takes advantage of the fact that "indecent liberties" can be thought of as a form of sexual assault, would effectively disguise the true nature of the offense. Even though plea bargaining has been endorsed by the Supreme Court, the public continues to view it suspiciously. "Law and order" advocates, who generally favor harsh punishments and long jail terms, claim that plea bargaining results in unjustifiably light sentences. As a consequence, prosecutors who regularly engage in the practice rarely advertise it. Often unrealized is the fact that plea bargaining can be a powerful prosecutorial tool.

> **Plea:** In criminal proceedings, a defendant's formal answer in court to the charge contained in a complaint, information, or indictment, that he or she is guilty or not guilty of the offense charged, or does not contest the charge.

Power carries with it, however, the potential for misuse. Plea bargains, because they circumvent the trial process, hold the possibility of abuse by prosecutors and defense attorneys who are more interested in a speedy resolution of cases than they are in seeing justice done. Carried to the extreme, plea bargaining may result in defendants being convicted of crimes they did not commit. Although it probably happens only rarely, it is conceivable that innocent defendants (especially those with prior criminal records) who — for whatever reason — think a jury will convict them, may plead guilty to lessened charges in order to avoid a trial. In an effort to protect defendants against hastily arranged pleas, the new Federal Rules of Criminal Procedure require judges to: (1) inform the defendant of the various rights he or she is surrendering by pleading guilty, (2) determine that the plea is voluntary, (3) require disclosure of any plea agreements, and (4) make sufficient inquiry to ensure there is a factual basis for the plea.[59]

Other Types of Pleas

A no-contest (*nolo contendere*) plea is much the same as a plea of guilty. A defendant who pleads no contest is immediately convicted and may be sentenced just as though he or she had entered a plea of guilty. A no-contest plea, however, is no admission of guilt and provides one major advantage to defendants: it may not be used as a later basis for civil proceedings which seek monetary or other damages against the defendant.

Standing mute is a defense strategy rarely employed by an accused. Defendants who choose this alternative simply do not answer the request for a plea. However, for procedural purposes, a defendant who stands mute is considered to have entered a plea of not guilty.

Another plea, acceptable in some jurisdictions, is that of once in jeopardy. The plea of once in jeopardy is based upon the constitutional right against double jeopardy. Double jeopardy is a guarantee against more than one trial for the same charge. Where a defendant has previously been acquitted of criminal charges, those same charges may not be used as the basis for renewed prosecution. However, hung juries and appellate reversals of conviction are not generally allowable as a basis for a claim of double jeopardy.

◻ SUMMARY

American criminal courts present an intriguing contrast. On the one hand, they exude an aura of highly formalized judicial procedure, while on the other, they demonstrate a surprising lack of organizational uniformity. Courts in one jurisdiction may bear little resemblance to those of another, especially when different states are compared. The separate systems of federal and state courts can lead to further confusion. Court reform, because it has not equally impacted all areas of the country, has in some instances exacerbated the differences between court systems.

This chapter has concerned itself mainly with pretrial practices. Prior to trial, courts often act to shield the accused from the punitive power of the state through the use of pretrial release. In doing so, they must balance the rights of the unconvicted defendant against the potential for future harm which that person may represent. A significant issue facing pretrial decision makers is how to ensure that all defendants, rich and poor, are afforded the same degree of protection.

DISCUSSION QUESTIONS

1. What is the "dual court system?" Why do we have a dual court system in America? Could the drive toward court unification eventually lead to a monolithic court system? Would such a system be effective?

2. According to data reported on in this chapter, 90% of all criminal cases carried beyond the initial stages are finally resolved through bargained pleas. What are some of the problems associated with plea bargaining? Given those problems, do you believe that plea bargaining is an acceptable practice in today's criminal justice system? Give reasons for your answer.

3. People who are accused of crimes are often granted pretrial release. Do you think all defendants accused of crimes should be so released? If not, what types of defendants might

you keep in jail? Why?

4. What inequities exist in today's system of pretrial release? How might the system be improved?

NOTES

1. Law Enforcement Assistance Administration, *Two Hundred Years of American Criminal Justice* (Washington, D.C.: U.S. Government Printing Office, 1976), p. 31.

2. Ibid.

3. Ibid.

4. Ibid.

5. Ibid.

6. Thomas A. Henderson, Cornelium M. Kerwin, Randall Guynes, Carl Baar, Neal Miller, Hildy Saizow, and Robert Grieser, *The Significance of Judicial Structure: The Effects of Unification on Trial Court Operations* (Washington, D.C.: National Institute of Justice, 1984).

7. Ibid.

8. Bureau of Justice Statistics, *Report to the Nation on Crime and Justice,* 2nd ed. (Washington, D.C.: U.S. Government Printing Office, 1988), p. 82.

9. H. Ted Rubin, *The Courts: Fulcrum of the Justice System* (Pacific Palisades, CA: Goodyear, 1976), p. 200.

10. Ibid., p. 198.

11. Martin Wright, *Justice for Victims and Offenders* (Bristol, PA: Open University Press, 1991), p. 56.

12. Ibid., pp. 104, 106.

13. Administrative Office of the U.S. Courts, *The United States Courts: A Pictorial Summary for the Twelve Month Period Ended June 30, 1985* (Washington, D.C.: The Administrative Office, 1985), p. 16.

14. Timothy J. Flanagan and Katherine M. Jamieson, *Sourcebook of Criminal Justice Statistics — 1988* (Washington, D.C.: U.S. Government Printing Office, 1989), p. 100.

15. "Up to 176 Federal Judges Are Millionaires, Study Finds," *The Fayetteville Times*, June 6, 1989, p. 17A.

16. Ibid.

17. Stephen L. Wasby, *The Supreme Court in the Federal Judicial System*, 3rd ed. (Chicago: Nelson-Hall, 1988), p. 58.

18. *The Supreme Court of the United States* (Washington, D.C.: U.S. Government Printing Office, no date), p. 4.

19. 1 *Cranch* 137 (1803).

20. *Mapp* v. *Ohio,* 367 U.S. 643 (1961).

21. Wasby, *The Supreme Court in the Federal Judicial System*, pp. 58–59.

22. "Arraignment" is also a term used to describe an initial appearance, although we will reserve use of that word to describe a later court appearance following the defendant's indictment by a grand jury or the filling of an information by the prosecutor.

23. *McNabb* v. *United States,* 318 U.S. 332 (1943).

24. *County of Riverside and Cois Byrd, Sheriff of Riverside County* v. *Donald Lee McLaughlin et al.,* No. 89-1817 (1991).

25. *McLaughlin,* dissenting opinion.

26. *White* v. *Maryland,* 373 U.S. 59 (1963).

27. *Taylor* v. *Taintor,* 83 U.S. 66 (1873).

28. National Advisory Commission on Criminal Justice Standards and Goals, *The Courts* (Washington, D.C.: U.S. Government Printing Office, 1973), p. 37.

29. C. Ares, A. Rankin, and H. Sturz, "The Manhattan Bail Project: An Interim Report on the Use of Pre-Trial Parole," *New York University Law Review,* Vol. 38 (January 1963), pp. 68–95.

30. H. Zeisel, "Bail Revisited," *American Bar Foundation Research Journal,* Vol. 4 (1979), pp. 769–789.

31. Ibid.

32. "12% of Those Freed on Low Bail Fail to Appear," *The New York Times*, December 2, 1983, p. 1.

33. BJS, *Report to the Nation on Crime and Justice,* p. 76.

34. Joseph B. Vaughn and Victor E. Kappeler, "The Denial of Bail: Pre-Trail Preventive Detention," *Criminal Justice Research Bulletin* (Huntsville, TX: Sam Houston State University), Vol. 3, no. 6 (1987), p. 1.

35. M. A. Toborg, *Pretrial Release: A National Evaluation of Practice and Outcomes,* (McLean, VA: Lazar Institute, 1981).

36. BJS, *Report to the Nation on Crime and Justice,* p. 77.

37. Donald E. Pryor and Walter F. Smith, "Significant Research Findings Concerning Pretrial Release," *Pretrial Issues* (Washington, D.C.: Pretrial Services Resource Center, February 1982), Volume 4, no. 1.

38. BJS, *Report to the Nation on Crime and Justice,* p. 77.

39.   According to Vaughn and Kappeler "The Denial of Bail: Pre-Trial Preventive Detention," *Criminal Justice Research Bulletin*, Vol. 3, no. 6 (1987), the first such legislation was the 1970 District of Columbia Court Reform and Criminal Procedure Act.

40. Ibid.

41. Bail Reform Act of 1984, 18 U.S.C. 3142(e).

42. *U.S.* v. *Montalvo-Murillo,* No. 89-163 (1990).

43. *U.S.* v. *Montalvo-Murillo* (1990), on-line syllabus.

44. *U.S.* v. *Hazzard,* 35 CrL 2217 (1984).

45. See, for example, *U.S.* v. *Motamedi,* 37 CrL 2394, CA 9 (1985).

46. *Federal Rules of Criminal Procedure* 5.1 (a).

47.   A few states now have laws that permit the defendant to appear before the grand jury.

48. *Kercheval* v. *U.S.,* 274 U.S. 220, 223, 47 S.Ct. 582, 583 (1927); *Boykin* v. *Alabama,* 395 U.S. 238 (1969); and *Dickerson* v. *New Banner Institute, Inc.,* 460 U.S. 103 (1983).

49. *Brady* v. *United States,* 397 U.S. 742 (1970).

50. *Santobello* v. *New York,* 404 U.S. 257, 92 S. Ct. 495, 30 L.Ed.2d 427 (1971).

51. Ibid.

52.   U.S. Department of Justice, Bureau of Justice Statistics, *The Prosecution of Felony Arrests* (Washington, D.C.: U.S. Government Printing Office, 1983).

53. Barbara Boland, Wayne Logan, Ronald Sones, and William Martin, *The Prosecution of Felony Arrests, 1982* (Washington, D.C.: U.S. Government Printing Office, May 1988).

54.   *Henderson* v. *Morgan,* 426 U.S. 637 (1976).

55. *Santobello* v. *New York.*

56. *Mabry* v. *Johnson,* 467 U.S. 504 (1984).

57.   *U.S.* v. *Baldacchino,* 762 F.2d 170 (1st Cir. 1985); *U.S.* v. *Reardon,* 787 F.2d 512 (10th Cir. 1986); and *U.S.* v. *Donahey,* 529 F.2d 831 (11th Cir. 1976).

58.   For a now classic discussion of such considerations, see David Sudnow, "Normal Crimes: Sociological Features of the Penal Code in a Public Defender Office," *Social Problems,* Vol. 12 (1965), p. 255.

59. *Federal Rules of Criminal Procedure,* No. 11.

CHAPTER 7

THE CRIMINAL TRIAL

To hear patiently, to weigh deliberately and dispassionately, and to decide impartially: these are the chief duties of a judge.
— Albert Pike (1809–1891)

In civil jurisprudence it too often happens that there is so much law, there is no room for justice, and that the claimant expires of wrong, in the midst of right, as mariners die of thirst in the midst of water.

— Colton (1780–1832)

KEY CONCEPTS

prosecutor	impeachment	bailiff
confidentiality	public defender	subpoena
judge	advocacy model	Speedy Trial Act
expert witness	lay witness	victim compensation
hearsay	perjury	criminal trial

☐ THE CRIMINAL TRIAL

From arrest through sentencing, the criminal justice process is carefully choreographed. Arresting officers must follow proper procedure in the gathering of evidence and in the arrest and questioning of suspects. Magistrates, prosecutors, jailers, and prison officials are all subject to similar strictures. Nowhere, however, is the criminal justice process more closely circumscribed than at the stage of the criminal trial.

Procedures in a modern courtroom are highly formalized. Rules of evidence and other procedural guidelines determine the course of a criminal hearing and trial. Rules of evidence are partially based upon tradition. All U.S. jurisdictions, however, have formalized rules of evidence in written form. Criminal trials at the federal level generally adhere to the requirements of *Federal Rules of Evidence.*

Trials are also circumscribed by informal rules and professional expectations. An important component of law school education is the teaching of rules which structure and define appropriate courtroom demeanor. In addition to statutory rules, law students are thoroughly exposed to the ethical standards of their profession as found in the *American Bar Association Standards* and other writings.

In the next few pages we will describe the chronology of a criminal trial and comment on some of the widely accepted rules of criminal procedure. Before we begin the description, however, it is good to keep two points in mind. One is that the primary purpose of any criminal trial is the determination of the defendant's guilt or innocence. In this regard, it is important to recognize the crucial distinction made by legal scholars between legal guilt and factual guilt. Factual guilt deals with the issue of whether or not the defendant is actually responsible for the crime of which he or she stands accused. If the defendant "did it" then they are, in fact, guilty. Legal guilt is not so clear. Legal guilt is established only when the prosecutor presents evidence which is sufficient to convince the judge (where the judge determines the verdict) or jury that the defendant is guilty as charged. Legal guilt necessitates the adequate presentation of proof by the prosecution that the defendant is the guilty party. The distinction between legal guilt and factual guilt is crucial, because it points to the fact that the burden of proof rests with the prosecution, and it indicates the possibility that guilty defendants may, nonetheless, be found "not guilty."

The second point to remember is that criminal trials under our system of justice are built around an adversary system, and that central to such a system is the advocacy model. Participating in the adversary system are advocates for the state (the prosecution or district attorney) and for the defendant (defense counsel, public defender, etc.). The philosophy behind the adversary system holds that the greatest number of just resolutions in all foreseeable criminal trials will occur when both sides are allowed to argue their case effectively and vociferously before a fair and impartial jury. The system requires that advocates for both sides do their utmost, within the boundaries set by law and professional ethics, to protect and advance the interests of their client. The advocacy model makes clear that it is not the job of the defense attorney nor the prosecution to judge the guilt of any defendant. Hence, even defense attorneys who are convinced that their client is guilty are still exhorted to offer the best possible defense and to counsel their client as effectively as possible.

The adversarial model has been criticized by some thinkers who point to fundamental differences between law and science in the way the search for truth is conducted.[1] While proponents of traditional legal procedure accept the belief that truth can best be uncovered through an adversarial process, scientists adhere to a painstaking process of research and replication in order to acquire knowledge. Most of us would agree that scientific advances in recent years may have made factual issues less difficult to ascertain. For example, some of the new scientific techniques in evidence gathering, such as DNA fingerprinting, are now able to link suspects unequivocally to criminal activity. Whether scientific findings should continue to serve a subservient role to the adversarial process itself is a question which is now being raised. The ultimate answer will probably be couched in terms of the results either process is able to produce. If the adversarial model results in the acquittal of too many demonstrably guilty people because of legal "technicalities," or the scientific approach inaccurately identifies too many suspects, either could be restricted.

We turn now to a discussion of the steps in a criminal trial. Trial chronology consists of 11 stages (1) Trial initiation (2) Jury selection (3) Opening statements (4) Presentation of the prosecution's case (5) Defense motions to dismiss (6) Presentation of the defense (7) Closing arguments (8) The judge's charge to the jury (9) Jury deliberations (10) The verdict (11) Sentencing. For purposes of brevity, stages 3 and 5 will be discussed jointly. Sentencing is reviewed in detail in a separate chapter.

TRIAL INITIATION: THE SPEEDY TRIAL ACT

The Sixth Amendment to the U.S. Constitution guarantees that "In all criminal prosecutions, the accused shall enjoy the right to a speedy and public trial." Clogged court calendars, limited judicial resources, and general inefficiency, however, often combine to produce what appears to many to be unreasonable delays in trial initiation. The attention of the Supreme Court was brought to bear on trial delays in three precedent-setting cases: *Klopfer* v. *North Carolina* (1967),[2] *Baker* v. *Wingo* (1972),[3] and *Strunk* v. *United States* (1973).[4] The *Klopfer* case involved a Duke University professor and focused on civil disobedience in a protest against segregated facilities. In Klopfer's long-delayed trial the Court asserted that the right to a speedy trial is a fundamental guarantee of the Constitution. In the *Baker* case the Court held that Sixth Amendment guarantees to a quick trial could be violated even in cases where the accused did not explicitly object to delays. In *Strunk* it found that denial of a speedy trial should result in a dismissal of all charges.

In 1974, against the advice of the Justice Department, the U.S. Congress passed the federal Speedy "Trial Act."[5] The act, which was phased in gradually, and became fully effective in 1980, allows for the dismissal of federal criminal charges in cases where the prosecution does not seek an indictment or information within 30 days of arrest (a 30-day extension is granted when the grand jury is not in session) or where trial does not commence within 70 working days after indictment for defendants who plead not guilty. Delays brought about by the defendant, through requests for a continuance, or because of escape, are not counted in the specified time periods. The Speedy Trial Act has been condemned by some as shortsighted. One federal trial court judge, for example, wrote: "The ability of the criminal justice system to operate effectively and efficiently has been severely impeded by the Speedy Trial Act. Resources are misdirected, unnecessary severances required, cases proceed to trial inadequately prepared, and in some indeterminate number of cases, indictments against guilty persons dismissed."[6]

In an important 1988 decision, *U.S.* v. *Taylor,*[7] the U.S. Supreme Court applied the requirements of the Speedy Trial Act to the case of a drug defendant who had escaped following arrest. The Court made it clear that trial delays, when they derive from the willful actions of the defendant, do not apply to the 70-day period. The Court also held that trial delays, even when they result from government action, do not necessarily provide grounds for dismissal if they occur "without prejudice." Delays without prejudice are those which are due to circumstances beyond the control of criminal justice agencies.

Pre- and Posttrial Motions

A **motion** is defined by the *Dictionary of Criminal Justice Data Terminology*[1] as "[a]n oral or written request made to a court at any time before, during, or after court proceedings, asking the court to make a specified finding, decision, or order." Written motions are called **petitions.** This box lists the typical kinds of motions that may be made by both sides in a criminal case before and after trial.

Motion for Discovery: A motion for discovery, filed by the defense, asks the court to allow the defendant's lawyers to view the evidence which the prosecution intends to present at trial. Physical evidence, lists of witnesses, documents, photographs, and on so on, which the prosecution plans to introduce in court will usually be made available to the defense as a result of such a motion.

Motion to Suppress Evidence: In the preliminary hearing, or through pretrial discovery the defense may learn of evidence which the prosecution intends to introduce at the trial. If some of that evidence has been, in the opinion of the defense counsel, unlawfully acquired, a motion to suppress the evidence may be filed.

Motion to Dismiss Charges: A variety of circumstances may result in the filing of a motion to dismiss. They include (1) an opinion, by defense counsel, that the indictment or information is not sound, (2) violations of speedy trial legislation, (3) a plea bargain with the defendant (which may require testimony against codefendants), (4) the death of an important witness or the destruction or disappearance of necessary evidence, (5) the confession, by a supposed victim, that the facts in the case have been fabricated, and (6) the success of a motion to suppress evidence which effectively eliminates the prosecution's case.

Motion for Continuance: This motion seeks a delay in the start of the trial. Defense motions for continuance are often based on the inability to locate important witnesses, the illness of the defendant, or a change in defense counsel immediately prior to trial.

Motion for Change of Venue: In well-known cases, pretrial publicity may lessen the opportunity for a case to be tried before an unbiased jury. A motion for a change of venue asks that the trial be moved to some other area where prejudice against the defendant is less likely to exist.

Motion for Severance of Offenses: Defendants charged with a number of crimes may ask to be tried separately on all or some of the charges. Although consolidating charges for trial saves time and money, some defendants may think that it is more likely to make them appear guilty.

Motion for Severance of Defendants: Similar to the foregoing motion, this request asks the court to try the accused separately from any co-defendants. Motions for severance are likely to be filed where the defendant believes that the jury may be prejudiced against him or her by evidence applicable only to other defendants.

Motion to Determine Present Sanity: "Present sanity," even though it may be no defense against the criminal charge, can delay trial. A person cannot be tried, sentenced, or punished while insane. If a defendant is insane at the time a trial is to begin, this motion may halt the proceedings until treatment can be arranged.

Motion for a Bill of Particulars: This motion asks the court to order the prosecutor to provide detailed information about the charges which the defendant will be facing in court. Defendants charged with a number of offenses, or with a number of counts of the same offense may make such a motion. They may, for example, seek to learn which alleged instances of an offense will become the basis for prosecution, or which specific items of contraband allegedly found in their possession are held to violate the law.

Motion for a Mistrial: A mistrial may be declared at any time, and a motion for mistrial may be made by either side. Mistrials are likely to be declared where highly prejudicial comments are made by either attorney. Defense motions for a mistrial do not provide grounds for a later claim of double jeopardy.

Motion for Arrest of Judgment: After the verdict of the jury has been announced, but before sentencing, the defendant may make a motion for arrest of judgment. Such a motion means the defendant believes that some legally acceptable reason exists as to why sentencing should not occur. Defendants who are seriously ill, hospitalized, or have gone insane prior to judgment being imposed may file such a motion.

Motion for a New Trial: After a jury has returned a guilty verdict a defense motion for a new trial may be entertained by the court. Acceptance of such a motion is most often based upon the discovery of new evidence which is of significant benefit to the defense, and will set aside the conviction.

[1]U.S. Department of Justice, *Dictionary of Criminal Justice Data Terminology*, 2nd ed. (Washington, D.C.: National Institute of Justice, 1982).

The Speedy Trial Act is applicable only to federal courts. However, the *Klopfer* case effectively made constitutional guarantees of a speedy trial applicable to state courts. In keeping with the trend toward reduced delays, many states have since enacted their own speedy trial legislation. Typical state legislation sets limits of 120 or 90 days as a reasonable period of time for a trial to commence.

JURY SELECTION

The Sixth Amendment also guarantees the right to an impartial jury. An impartial jury is not necessarily an ignorant one. In other words, jurors will not always be excused from service on a jury if they have some knowledge of the case which is before them.[8] Jurors, however, who have already formed an opinion as to the guilt or innocence of a defendant are likely to be excused.

A number of different types of juror challenges are available to both prosecution and defense attorneys. Challenges are intended to ensure the impartiality of the jury which is being empaneled. Three types of challenges are recognized in criminal courts:

Picking the
Kennedy
Jury

   ♦ Challenges to the array
   ♦ Challenges for cause
   ♦ Peremptory challenges

Challenges to the array signify the belief, generally by the defense attorney, that the pool from which potential jurors are to be selected is not representative of the community, or is biased in some significant way. A challenge to the array is argued before the hearing judge before jury selection begins. The jury selection process includes the questioning of potential jurors by both prosecution and defense attorneys. This questioning is known as *voir dire*.

A depiction of the first jury trial in which blacks and whites served together. Circa 1867. Courtesy of the Library of Congress.

Jurors are expected to be unbiased and free of preconceived notions of guilt or innocence. Challenges for cause, which may arise during *voir dire* examination make the claim that an individual juror cannot be fair or impartial. One special issue of juror objectivity has concerned the Supreme Court. It is whether jurors with philosophical opposition to the death penalty should be excluded from juries whose decisions might result in the imposition of capital punishment. In the case of *Witherspoon* v. *Illinois* (1968),[9] the Court ruled that a juror opposed to the death penalty could be excluded from such juries if it were shown that (1) the juror would automatically vote against conviction without regard to the evidence or (2) the juror's philosophical orientation would prevent an objective consideration of the evidence. The *Witherspoon* case has left unresolved a number of issues, among them the concern that how a juror would "automatically vote" is difficult to demonstrate and may not even be known to the juror before the trial begins.

Another area of concern, which has been addressed by the Supreme Court, involves the potential bias which jurors may experience as a result of exposure to stories about a case which appears in the news media prior to the start of trial. One such case in which the

Court addressed the issue is that of *Mu'Min* v. *Virginia*[10] (1991). Mu'Min was a Virginia inmate who was serving time for first-degree murder. While accompanying a work detail outside of the institution he committed another murder. At the ensuing trial, 8 of the 12 jurors who were eventually seated admitted that they had heard or read something about the case, although none indicated that they had formed an opinion in advance as to Mu'Min's guilt or innocence. Following his conviction, Mu'Min appealed to the Supreme Court, claiming that his right to a fair trial had been denied due to pretrial publicity. The Court disagreed, however, citing the admittedly unbiased nature of the original jurors.

A Word on Peremptory Challenges

Peremptory challenges, intended originally to ensure impartiality in the selection of jurors, sometimes conflict with the goal they were meant to serve. In 1965 a black defendant in Alabama was convicted of rape by an all-white jury. The local prosecutor had used his peremptory challenges to exclude blacks from the jury. The case eventually reached the Supreme Court, where the conviction was upheld.[1] The Court refused to limit the practice of peremptory challenges, reasoning that to do so would place them under the same judicial scrutiny as challenges for cause.

In 1986, following what many claimed were widespread abuses of peremptory challenges, the Supreme Court was forced to overrule its earlier decision.   It did so in the case of *Batson* v. *Kentucky*.[2] Batson, a black man, had been convicted of second-degree burglary and other offenses by an all white jury. The prosecutor had used his peremptory challenges to remove all blacks from jury service at the trial. The Court agreed that the use of peremptory challenges for apparently purposeful discrimination constitutes a violation of the defendant's right to an impartial jury.

The *Batson* decision established requirements which defendants seeking to address the discriminatory use of peremptory challenges must establish. They include the need to prove that the defendant is a member of a recognized racial group which has been intentionally excluded from the jury and the need to raise a reasonable suspicion that the prosecutor used peremptory challenges in a discriminatory manner.

[1]*Swain* v. *Alabama*, 380 U.S. 202 (1965).
[2]*Batson* v. *Kentucky*, 106 S.Ct. 1712, 90 L.Ed. 2d 69 (1986).

The third kind of challenge, the peremptory challenge, effectively removes potential jurors without need for a reason. Peremptory challenges are limited in number. Federal courts allow each side up to 20 peremptory challenges in capital cases, and as few as three in minor criminal cases.[11]

A developing field, which seeks to take advantage of peremptory challenges, is that of scientific jury selection.   Scientific jury selection uses correlational techniques from the social sciences to gauge the likelihood that potential jurors will vote for conviction or acquittal.   It makes predictions based on the economic, ethnic, and other personal and social characteristics of each member of the juror pool. There have been some recent indications, however, that scientific jury selection may soon run afoul of the requirement established by the Supreme Court in *Thiel* v. *Southern Pacific Co.*[12]

Criticisms of jury selection techniques have focused on the end result of the process. Such techniques generally remove potential jurors who have any knowledge or opinions about the case to be tried. Also removed are persons trained in the law or in criminal justice. Anyone working for a criminal justice agency, or anyone who has a family member working for such an agency, or for a defense attorney will likely be dismissed through peremptory challenges, on the chance that they may be biased in favor of one side or the other. Scientific jury selection techniques may result in the additional dismissal of educated or professionally successful individuals, to eliminate the possibility of such individuals exercising undue control over jury deliberations. The end result of the jury selection process may be to produce a jury composed of people who are uneducated, uninformed, and generally inexperienced at making any type of well-considered decision. Such a jury may not understand the charges against the defendant or comprehend what is required for a finding of guilt or innocence. Some of the selected jurors may not even possess the span of attention needed to hear all the testimony that will be offered in the case. As a consequence, decisions rendered by such a jury may be based more upon emotion than findings of fact.

Intentional jury selection techniques appear to have played a significant role in the outcome of the trial of Larry Davis. Davis, who was black, was charged with the 1986 shooting of seven white New York City police officers as they attempted to arrest the heavily armed defendant for the alleged murder of four drug dealers.[13] None of the officers died and Davis was later apprehended. At the trial, defense attorney William Kunstler assembled a jury of ten blacks and two Hispanics. On two occasions Judge Bernard Fried had dismissed previous juries before the trial could begin, saying that Kunstler was packing the panel with blacks.[14] Although many of the wounded officers testified against Davis, and no one seriously disputed the contention that Davis was the trigger man in the shooting of the officers, the jury found him innocent. The finding prompted one of the injured policemen to claim, "It was a racist verdict."[15] Explaining the jury's decision another way, a spokesperson for the NAACP Legal Defense Fund said after the trial, "The experience of blacks in the criminal justice system may make them less prone to accept the word of a police officer."[16]

Juries intentionally selected so that they are racially imbalanced may soon be a thing of the past. As long ago as 1880, the U.S. Supreme Court held that "a statute barring blacks from service on grand or petit juries denied equal protection of the laws to a black man convicted of murder by an all-white jury."[17] Even so, peremptory challenges continued to provide an avenue toward racial imbalance. In 1965, for example, a black defendant in Alabama was convicted of rape by an all-white jury. The local prosecutor had used his peremptory challenges to exclude blacks from the jury. The case eventually reached the Supreme Court, where the conviction was upheld.[18] At that time, the Court refused to limit the practice of peremptory challenges, reasoning that to do so would place them under the same judicial scrutiny as challenges for cause.

However, in 1986, following what many claimed were widespread abuses of peremptory challenges by prosecution and defense alike, the Supreme Court was forced to overrule its earlier decision. It did so in the case of *Batson* v. *Kentucky*.[19] Batson, a black man, had been convicted of second-degree burglary and other offenses by an all-white jury. The prosecutor had used his peremptory challenges to remove all blacks from jury service at the trial. The Court agreed that the use of peremptory challenges for apparently purposeful discrimination constitutes a violation of the defendant's right to an impartial jury.

A CAREER WITH THE BUREAU OF
ALCOHOL, TOBACCO, AND FIREARMS

Typical Positions. Explosives expert, firearms specialist, bomb scene investigator, and liquor law violations investigator.

Employment Requirements. ATF special agent applicants must meet the same employment requirements as most other federal agents, including (1) successful completion of the Treasury Enforcement Agent Examination, (2) a field interview, and (3) a thorough background investigation. See the box on employment with the U.S. Secret Service for additional details on Treasury agent general employment requirements.

Other Requirements. Other general requirements for employment as a federal officer apply. They include (1) U.S. citizenship, (2) an age between 21 and 35, (3) good physical health, and (4) eyesight of no less than 20/40 uncorrected. New agents undergo eight weeks of specialized training at the Federal Law Enforcement Training Center in Glynco, Georgia.

Salary. A Bachelor's degree qualifies applicants for appointment at the GS-5 level (earning $18,340 or more in mid-1993), although some appointments are made at the GS-7 level ($22,717 and higher in mid-1993).

Benefits. Benefits include (1) 13 days of sick leave annually, (2) 2½ to 5 weeks of annual paid vacation and 10 paid federal holidays each year, (3) federal health and life insurance, and (4) a comprehensive retirement program.

Direct inquiries to: Bureau of Alcohol, Tobacco, and Firearms, U.S. Treasury Department, 1200 Pennsylvania Ave., N.W., Washington, D.C. 20226. Phone: (202) 566-7321.

The *Batson* decision established requirements which defendants seeking to address the discriminatory use of peremptory challenges must establish. They include the need to prove that the defendant is a member of a recognized racial group which has been intentionally excluded from the jury, and the need to raise a reasonable suspicion that the prosecutor used peremptory challenges in a discriminatory manner. Justice Thurgood Marshall, writing a concurring opinion in *Batson* presaged what was to come. "The inherent potential of peremptory challenges to destroy the jury process," he wrote, "by permitting the exclusion of jurors on racial grounds should ideally lead the Court to ban them entirely from the criminal justice system."

A few years later, in *Ford* v. *Georgia* (1991),[20] the Court moved much closer to Justice Marshall's position when it remanded a case for a new trial, based upon the fact that the prosecutor had used peremptory challenges to remove potential minority jurors. Nine of the ten peremptory challenges available to the prosecutor under Georgia law had been used to eliminate prospective black jurors. Following his conviction on charges of kidnapping, raping, and murdering a white woman, the black defendant, James Ford, argued that the prosecutor had demonstrated a systematic and historical racial bias, in other cases as well as his own. Specifically, Ford argued that his Sixth Amendment right to an impartial jury had been violated by the prosecutor's racially based method of jury selection. His defense attorney's written appeal to the Supreme Court made the claim that, "The exclusion of members of the black race in the jury when a black accused is being tried is done in order that the accused will receive excessive punishment if found guilty, or to inject racial prejudice into the fact finding process of the jury."[21] While the Court did not find a basis for such a Sixth Amendment claim, it did determine that the civil rights of the jurors were violated under the Fourteenth Amendment due to a pattern of discrimination based on race.

In another 1991 case, *Powers* v. *Ohio*,[22] the Court found in favor of a white defendant who claimed that his constitutional rights were violated by the intentional exclusion of blacks from his jury through the use of peremptory challenges. In *Powers,* the Court held that "[a]lthough an individual juror does not have the right to sit on any particular petit jury, he or she does possess the right not to be excluded from one on account of race." In a civil case with significance for the criminal justice system, the Court held in *Edmonson* v. *Leesville Concrete Co., Inc.* (1991),[23] that peremptory challenges in *civil* suits were not acceptable if based upon race: "The importance of . . . lies in the Court's significant expansion of the scope of state action — the traditionally held doctrine that private attorneys are immune to constitutional requirements because they do not represent the government." Justice Kennedy, writing for the majority, said that race-based juror exclusions are forbidden in civil lawsuits because jury selection is a "unique governmental function delegated to private litigants" in a public courtroom.

Given the direction in which the Court has chosen to move in recent years, it should not be long before private defense attorneys in criminal trials are prohibited from exercising racially motivated peremptory challenges. In the near future the banning of all peremptory challenges may be the price the judicial system will have to pay to achieve racial equity in its juries. After wrangling over jury selection has run its course, the jury is sworn in and alternates are selected. At this point the judge will decide whether the jury is to be sequestered during the trial. Members of sequestered juries are not permitted to have contact with the public and are often housed in a motel or hotel until completion of the trial. Anyone who attempts to contact a sequestered jury or to influence members of a nonsequestered jury may be held accountable for jury tampering. Following jury selection the stage is set for opening arguments[24] to begin.

OPENING STATEMENT

The presentation of information to the jury begins with opening statements made by the prosecution and defense. The purpose of opening statements is to advise the jury of what the attorneys intends to prove and to describe how such proof will be offered. In cases where a defendant maintains innocence the jury will have to weigh the evidence and decide between the effectiveness of the arguments made by both sides. Where a defendant may in fact be guilty, it will be the job of the defense attorney to dispute the veracity of the prosecution's version of the facts. Under such circumstances defense attorneys may chose not to present any evidence, focusing instead on the burden of proof requirement facing the prosecution. During opening arguments the defense attorney is likely to stress the human qualities of the defendant and to remind jurors of the awesome significance of their task.

Lawyers for both sides are bound by a "good faith" ethical requirement in their opening statements. That requirement limits the content of such statements to only that evidence which the attorneys actually believe can and will be presented as the trial progresses. Allusions to evidence which an attorney has no intention of offering are regarded as unprofessional and have been defined as "professional misconduct" by the Supreme Court.[25]

THE PRESENTATION OF EVIDENCE

Although procedural rules proscribe almost every routine activity within the courtroom, the area most closely scrutinized is the introduction of evidence at a criminal trial. Evidence is of two types: direct and circumstantial. Direct evidence is that which, if believed by the judge or jury, proves a fact without the need for inferences to be drawn. Direct evidence may consist, for example, of the information contained on a photograph or videotape. It might also consist of testimonial evidence provided by a witness on the stand. A straightforward statement by a witness, such as, "I saw him do it!" is a form of direct evidence.

> **Direct Evidence:** Evidence which, if believed, directly proves a fact. Eyewitness testimony (and, more recently, videotaped documentation) account for the majority of all direct evidence heard in the criminal courtroom.

Circumstantial evidence requires the judge or jury to make inferences and draw conclusions. At a murder trial, for example, a person who heard gunshots, and moments later saw someone run by with a smoking gun in their hand, might testify to those facts. Even though there may have been no eyewitness to the actual homicide, the jury might later conclude that the person seen with the gun was the one who pulled the trigger and committed homicide. Contrary to popular belief, circumstantial evidence is sufficient to produce a verdict and conviction in a criminal trial. In fact, some prosecuting attorneys claim to prefer working entirely with circumstantial evidence, weaving a tapestry of the criminal act in their arguments to the jury.

Real evidence consists of physical material or traces of physical activity. Weapons, tire tracks, ransom notes, and fingerprints all fall into the category of physical evidence. Physical evidence is introduced into the trial process by means of exhibits. Exhibits are objects or displays which, once formally accepted as evidence by the judge, may be shown to members of the jury. Documentary evidence includes writings such as business records, journals, written confessions, and letters. Documentary evidence can extend beyond the media of paper and pen, to include magnetic and optical storage devices used in computer operations and video and voice recordings.

One of the most significant decisions made by a trial court judge is deciding what evidence can be presented to the jury. In making that decision, judges will examine the relevance of the information in question to the case at hand. Relevant evidence is that which has a bearing on the facts at issue. For example, a decade or two ago it was not unusual for a woman's sexual history to be brought out in rape trials. Under "rape shield statutes," most states today will not allow such a practice, recognizing that these details often have no bearing on the case. Rape shield statutes have been strengthened by recent U.S. Supreme Court decisions, including the 1991 case of *Michigan* v. *Lucas.*[26] In this case, the defendant, Lucas, had been charged with criminal sexual conduct involving his ex-girlfriend. Lucas had forced the woman into his apartment at knifepoint, beat her, and forced her to engage in several nonconsensual sex acts. At his trial, Lucas asked to have evidence introduced demonstrating that a prior sexual relationship had existed between the two. At the time, however, Michigan law required that a written motion to use such information had to be made within 10 days following arraignment — a condition Lucas failed to meet. Lucas was convicted and sentenced to a term of from 44 to 180 months in prison, but appealed his conviction, claiming that the Sixth Amendment to the U.S. Constitution guaranteed him the right to confront witnesses against him.   The U.S. Supreme Court disagreed, however, and ruled that the Sixth Amendment guarantee does not necessarily extend to evidence of a prior sexual relationship between a rape victim and a criminal defendant.

> **Circumstantial Evidence:** Evidence which requires interpretation, or which requires a judge or jury to reach a conclusion based upon what the evidence indicates. From the close proximity of a smoking gun to the defendant, for example, the jury might conclude that she pulled the trigger.

On occasion, some evidence will be found to have only limited admissibility. Limited admissibility means that the evidence can be used for a specific purpose, but that it might not be accurate in other details. Photographs, for example, may be admitted as evidence for the narrow purpose of showing spatial relationships between objects under discussion, even though the photographs themselves may have been taken under conditions that did not exist (such as daylight) when the offense was committed.

THE TESTIMONY OF WITNESSES

Witness testimony is generally the chief means by which evidence is introduced at trial. Witnesses may include victims, police officers, the defendant, specialists in recognized fields, and others with useful information to provide.   Some of these witnesses may have been present during the commission of the alleged offense, while most will have had only a later opportunity to investigate the situation or to analyze evidence.

Before a witness will be allowed to testify to any fact, it is necessary that the questioning attorney establish the competence of the witness.   Competency to testify requires that the witness have personal knowledge of the information about to be discussed and that he or she understands the duty of a witness to tell the truth.

One critical decision which has to be made by the defense is whether or not to put the defendant on the stand. Defendants have a Fifth Amendment right to remain silent and to refuse to testify.   In the precedent-setting case of *Griffin* v. *California* (1965),[27] the U.S. Supreme Court declared that if a defendant refuses to testify, prosecutors and judges are enjoined from even commenting on the fact, other than to instruct the jury that such a failure cannot be held to indicate guilt. Griffin was originally arrested for the beating death of a woman whose body was found in an alley. Charged with first-degree murder, he refused to take the stand when his case came to trial. At the time of the trial Article I, Section 13, of the California constitution provided in part: "in any criminal case, whether the defendant testifies or not, his failure to explain or to deny by his testimony any evidence or facts in the case against him may be commented upon by the court and by counsel, and may be considered by the court or the jury."   The prosecutor, remarking on the evidence in closing arguments to the jury, declared: "These things he has not seen fit to take the stand and deny or explain. Essie Mae is dead, she can't tell you her side of the story. The defendant won't." The judge then instructed the jury that they might infer from the defendant's silence his inability to deny the evidence which had been presented against him. Griffin was convicted of first degree murder and his appeal reached the Supreme Court. The Court ruled that the Fifth Amendment, made applicable by the Fourteenth Amendment to the states, protected the defendant from any inferences of guilt based upon a failure to testify. The verdict of the trial court was voided.

"Pleading the Fifth"

The Fifth Amendment to the U.S. Constitution is one of the best known items of the Bill of Rights. Television shows and crime novels have popularized phrases such as "pleading the Fifth," or "taking the Fifth." As these media recognize, the Fifth Amendment is a powerful ally of any criminal defendant. When the accused, generally upon the advice of counsel, decides to invoke the Fifth Amendment right against self-incrimination, the state cannot require the defendant to testify. In the past, defendants who refused to take the stand were often denigrated by comments the prosecution made to the jury. In 1965 the U.S. Supreme Court, in the case of *Griffin* v. *California*,[1] ruled that the defendant's unwillingness to testify could not be interpreted as a sign of guilt. The Court reasoned that such interpretations forced the defendant to testify and effectively negated Fifth Amendment guarantees. Defendants who chose to testify, however, but who fail to answer adequately the questions put to them, may lawfully find themselves the target of prosecutorial comment.

[1]*Griffin* v. *California*, 380 U.S. 609 (1965).

Direct examination of a witness takes place when a witness is first called to the stand. If the prosecutor calls the witness, the witness is referred to as a witness for the prosecution. Where the direct examiner is a defense attorney, witnesses are called witnesses for the defense.

The direct examiner may ask questions which require a "yes or no" answer, but can also employ narrative questions which allow the witness to tell a story in his or her own words. During direct examination courts generally prohibit the use of leading questions, or those which suggest answers to the witness.[28] Many courts also consider questions which call for "yes or no" answers to be inappropriate since they are inherently suggestive.

Cross-examination refers to the examination of a witness by anyone other than the direct examiner. Anyone who offers testimony in a criminal court has the duty to submit to cross-examination.[29] The purpose of cross-examination is to test the credibility and memory of a witness.

Most states and the federal government restrict the scope of cross-examination to material covered during direct examination. Questions about other matters, even though they may relate to the case before the court, are not allowed. A small number of states allow the cross-examiner to raise any issue as long as it is deemed relevant by the court. Leading questions, generally disallowed in direct examination, are regarded as the mainstay of cross-examination. Such questions allow for a concise restatement of testimony which has already been offered and serve to focus efficiently on potential problems that the cross-examiner seeks to address. Some witnesses offer perjured testimony, or statements which they know to be untrue. Reasons for perjured testimony vary, but most witnesses who lie on the stand probably do so in an effort to help friends accused of crimes. Witnesses who perjure themselves are subject to impeachment, in which either the defense counsel or prosecution demonstrates that they have intentionally offered false testimony. Such a demonstration may occur through the use of prior inconsistent statements, whereby previous statements made by the witness are shown to be at odds with more recent declarations. Perjury is a serious offense in its own right, and dishonest witnesses may face fines or jail time. When it can be demonstrated that a witness has offered inaccurate or false testimony, the witness has been effectively impeached.

Behavior in the courtroom must be respectful and appropriate, as this cartoon depicts.

At the conclusion of the cross-examination the direct examiner may again question the witness. This procedure is called redirect examination and may be followed by a recross-examination and so on, until both sides are satisfied that they have exhausted fruitful lines of questioning.

Children as Witnesses

An area of special concern involves the use of children as witnesses in a criminal trial, especially where the children may have been victims. Currently, in an effort to avoid what may be traumatizing direct confrontation between child witnesses and the accused, 37 states allow the use of videotaped testimony in their criminal courtrooms, and 32 permit the use of closed-circuit television — which allows the child to testify out of the presence of the defendant. In 1988, however, the U.S. Supreme Court, in the case of *Coy* v. *Iowa*,[30] ruled that a courtroom screen, used to shield child witnesses from visual confrontation with a defendant in a child sex-abuse case, had violated the confrontation clause of the Constitution.

On the other hand, in the 1990 case of *Maryland* v. *Craig*,[31] the Court upheld the use of closed-circuit television to shield children who testify in criminal courts. The Court's decision was partially based upon the realization that "a significant majority of States has enacted statutes to protect child witnesses from the trauma of giving testimony in child-abuse cases [which] attests to the widespread belief in the importance of such a policy." The case involved Sandra Craig, a former preschool owner and administrator in Clarksville, Maryland, who had been found guilty by a trial court with 53 counts of child abuse, assault, and perverted sexual practices which she had allegedly performed on the children under her care. During the trial, four young children, none past the age of 6, had testified against Ms.

Craig while separated from her in the judges chambers. Questioned by the district attorney the children related stories of torture, burying alive, and sexual assault with a screwdriver.[32] Sandra Craig watched the children reply over a television monitor which displayed the process to the jury seated in the courtroom. Following the trial, Craig appealed, arguing that her ability to communicate with her lawyer (who had been in the judge's chambers and not the courtroom during questioning of the children) had been impeded and her right to a fair trial under the Sixth Amendment to the U.S. Constitution had been denied since she was not given the opportunity to be "confronted with the witnesses" against her. In finding against Craig, Justice Sandra Day O'Connor, writing for the Court's majority, stated, "if the State makes an adequate showing of necessity, the state interest in protecting child witnesses from the trauma of testifying in a child-abuse case is sufficiently important to justify the use of a special procedure that permits a child witness in such cases to testify . . . in the absence of face-to-face confrontation with the defendant."[33]

Although a face-to-face confrontation with a child victim may not be necessary in the courtroom, the Supreme Court has been reluctant to allow into evidence descriptions of abuse and other statements made by children, even to child care professionals, when those statements are made outside of the courtroom. The Court, in *Idaho* v. *Wright* (1990),[34] reasoned that such "statements [are] fraught with the dangers of unreliability which the Confrontation Clause is designed to highlight and obviate."

The Hearsay Rule

One aspect of witness testimony bears special mention. Hearsay is anything not based upon the personal knowledge of a witness. A witness may say, for example, "John told me that Fred did it!" Such a witness becomes a hearsay

Courtroom trauma

Copyright 1990 by USA Today. Reprinted with permission.
Because children often feel threatened by official proceedings, courtroom procedure often allows for special treatment of witnesses who are juveniles.

declarant, and, following a likely objection by counsel, the trial judge will have to decide whether the witness's statement will be allowed to stand as evidence. In most cases the judge will instruct the jury to disregard such comments from the witness, thereby enforcing the hearsay rule. The hearsay rule does not permit the use of "secondhand" evidence.

There are some exceptions to the hearsay rule, however, that have been established by both precedent and tradition. One is the dying declaration. Dying declarations are statements made by a person who is about to die. When heard by a second party, they may be repeated in court, providing that certain conditions have been met. Dying declarations are generally valid exceptions to the hearsay rule when they are made by someone who knows that he or she is about to die, and when the statements made relate to the cause and circumstances of the impending death.

> **Hearsay:** Something which is not based upon the personal knowledge of a witness. Witnesses who testify, for example, about something they have heard, are offering hearsay by repeating information about a matter of which they have no direct knowledge.

Spontaneous statements provide another exception to the hearsay rule. Statements are considered spontaneous when they are made in the heat of excitement before time for fabrication exists. For example, a defendant who is just regaining consciousness following a crime, may make an utterance which could later be repeated in court by those who heard it.

Out of court statements made by a witness, especially when they have been recorded in writing or by some other means, may also become exceptions to the hearsay rule. The use of such statements usually requires the witness to testify that at the time they were made, the statements were accurate. This past recollection recorded exception to the hearsay rule is especially useful in drawn-out court proceedings which occur long after the crime. Under such circumstances, witnesses may no longer remember the details of an event. Their earlier statements to authorities, however, can be introduced into evidence as past recollection recorded.

The
Judge

CLOSING ARGUMENTS

At the conclusion of a criminal trial both sides have the opportunity for a final narrative presentation to the jury. This summation provides a review and analysis of the evidence. Its purpose is to persuade the jury to draw a conclusion favorable to the presenter. Testimony can be quoted, exhibits referred to, and attention drawn to inconsistencies in the evidence which has been presented by the other side.

States vary as to the order of closing arguments. Nearly all allow the defense attorney to speak to the jury before the prosecution makes its final points. A few permit the prosecutor the first opportunity for summation. Some jurisdictions and the *Federal Rules of Criminal Procedure*[35] authorize a defense rebuttal. Rebuttals are responses to the closing arguments of the other side.

Some specific issues may need to be addressed during summation. If, for example, during the trial the defendant has not taken the stand, the defense attorney's closing argument will inevitably stress that the failure of the accused to testify can not be regarded as indicative of guilt. Where the prosecution's case rests entirely upon circumstantial evidence, the defense can be expected to stress the lack of any direct proof, while the prosecutor is likely to argue that circumstantial evidence can be stronger than direct evidence, since it is not as easily affected by human error or false testimony.

THE JUDGE'S CHARGE TO THE JURY

With the completion of closing arguments, the judge will charge the jury to "retire and select one of your number as a foreman . . . and deliberate upon the evidence which has been presented until you have reached a verdict."   The words of the charge will vary somewhat between jurisdictions and among judges, but all judges will remind members of the jury of their duty to consider objectively only the evidence which has been presented, and of the need for impartiality.   Most judges will also remind jury members of the statutory elements of the alleged offense, of the burden of proof which rests upon the prosecution, and of the need for the prosecution to have proven guilt beyond a reasonable doubt before a guilty verdict can be returned.

In their charge many judges will also provide a summary of the evidence presented, usually from notes they have taken during the trial, as a means of refreshing the juror's memories of events.   About half of all the states allow judges the freedom to express their own views as to the credibility of witnesses and the significance of evidence.   Other states only permit judges to summarize the evidence in an objective and impartial manner.

Following the charge the jury will be removed from the courtroom and permitted to begin its deliberations.   In the absence of the jury, defense attorneys may choose to challenge portions of the judge's charge.   If they feel that some oversight has occurred in the original charge, they may also request that the judge provide the jury with additional instructions or information.   Such objections, if denied by the judge, often become the basis for appeals when a conviction is returned.

JURY DELIBERATIONS AND THE VERDICT

In cases where the evidence is either very clear or very weak, jury deliberations may be brief, lasting only a matter of hours or even minutes.   Some juries, however, deliberate days or sometimes weeks, carefully weighing all the nuances of the evidence they have seen and heard.   Many jurisdictions require that juries reach a unanimous verdict, although the U.S. Supreme Court has ruled that unanimous verdicts are not required in noncapital cases.[36] Even so, some juries are unable to agree upon any verdict. Such juries are referred to as deadlocked or hung.   Where a unanimous decision is required, juries may be deadlocked by the strong opposition of only one member to a verdict agreed upon by all the others.

In some states, judges are allowed to add a boost to nearly hung juries by re-charging them under a set of instructions agreed upon by the Supreme Court in the 1896 case of *Allen* v. *United States.*[37] The "Allen charge," as it is known in those jurisdictions, urges the jury to vigorous deliberations and suggests to obstinate jurors that their objections may be ill founded if they make no impression upon the minds of other jurors.

Problems with the Jury System

The jury system has received much criticism as an inefficient and outmoded method for determining guilt or innocence.[38]   Jurors cannot be expected to understand modern legal complexities and to appreciate all the nuances of trial court practice.   Many instructions to the jury are probably poorly understood and rarely observed by even the best-meaning jurors.[39]   Emotions are difficult to separate from fact.   During deliberations many juries are probably dominated by one or two forceful personalities.   Jurors may also become confused over legal technicalities, suffer from inattention, or be unable to understand fully the testimony of expert witnesses or the significance of technical evidence.

Many such problems became evident in the trial of Raymond Buckey and his mother, Peggy McMartin Buckey, who were tried in Los Angeles for allegedly molesting dozens of children at their family-run preschool.[40]   The trial, which comprised 65 counts of child sexual molestation and conspiracy, included 61 witnesses and ran for more than three years. Many jurors were stressed to the breaking point by the length of time involved.   Family relationships suffered as the trial droned on and jurors were unable to accompany their spouses and children on vacation.   Small-business owners, who were expected to continue paying salaries to employees serving as jurors faced financial ruin and threatened their absent employees with termination.   Careers were put on hold, and at least one juror had to be dismissed for becoming inattentive to testimony.   The trial cost taxpayers more than $12 million but was nearly negated as jury membership and the number of alternate jurors declined due to sickness and personal problems.

Opponents of the jury system have argued that it should be replaced by a panel of judges who would both render a verdict and impose sentence.   Regardless of how well considered such a suggestion may be, however, such a change could not occur without modification of the Constitution's Sixth Amendment right to trial by jury.

An alternative suggestion to improving the process of trial by jury has been the call for professional jurors.   Professional jurors would be paid by the government, just as are judges, prosecutors, and public defenders.   Sitting on any jury would be their job, and they would be expected to carry out that job with acquired expertise.   Professional jurors would be trained to listen objectively and would be schooled with the kinds of decision-making skills necessary to function effectively within an adversarial context.   They could be expected to hear one case after another, perhaps moving between jurisdictions in cases of highly publicized crimes.

The advantages a professional jury system offers include:

- ◆ **Dependability.** Professional jurors could be expected to report to the courtroom in a timely fashion and to be good listeners, since both would be expected by the nature of the job.

- ◆ **Knowledge.** Professional jurors would be trained in the law, would understand what a finding of guilt requires, and would know what to expect from other actors in the courtroom.

- ◆ **Equity.** Professional jurors would understand the requirements of due process and would be less likely to be swayed by the emotional content of a case, having been schooled in the need to separate matters of fact from personal feelings.

A professional jury system would not be without difficulties.   Jurors under such a system might become jaded, deciding cases out of hand as routines lead to boredom and suspects are categorized according to whether they "fit the type" for guilt or innocence developed on the basis of previous experiences. Job requirements for professional jurors would be difficult to establish without infringing on the jurors' freedom to decide cases as they understood them. For the same reason, any evaluation of the job performance of professional jurors would be a difficult call. Finally, professional jurors might not truly be peer jurors, since their social characteristics could conceivably be skewed by education, residence, and politics.

IMPROVING THE ADJUDICATION PROCESS

Courts today are coming under increasing scrutiny. Researchers and concerned citizens have identified a number of aspects of court activity which might benefit from reform.   Court unification is one area which many consider to hold the promise of better justice and greater economy through the efficient handling of cases.

Today's multiplicity of jurisdictions frequently leads to what many believe are avoidable conflicts and overlaps in the handling of criminal defendants.   Problems are exacerbated by the lack of any centralized judicial authority in some states which might resolve jurisdictional and procedural disputes.[41] Proponents of unification suggest the elimination of overlapping jurisdictions, the creation of special purpose courts, and the formulation of administrative offices in order to achieve economies of scale.[42]

Court-watch citizens groups are rapidly growing in number. Such organizations focus on the trial court level, but they are part of a general trend toward seeking greater openness in government decision making at all levels.[43] Court-watch groups monitor court proceedings on a regular basis and attempt to document and often publicize inadequacies. They frequently focus on the handling of indigents, fairness in the scheduling of cases for trial, unnecessary court delays, the reduction of waiting time, the treatment of witnesses and jurors, and the adequacy of rights advisements for defendants throughout judicial proceedings.

The statistical measurement of court performance is another area which is receiving increased attention. Research has looked at the efficiency with which prosecutors schedule cases for trial, the speed with which judges resolve issues, the amount of time judges spend on the bench, and the economic and other costs to defendants, witnesses, and communities involved in the judicial process.[44]   Statistical studies of this type often attempt to measure elements of court performance as diverse as sentence variation, charging accuracy, fairness in plea bargaining, evenhandedness, delays, and attitudes toward the court by lay participants.[45]

☐ SUMMARY

The criminal trial, which owes its legacy to the evolution of democratic principles, stands as a centerpiece of American criminal justice. It has long been seen as a peer-based fact-finding process intended to protect the rights of the accused while sifting out disputed issues of guilt or innocence. The adversarial environment, which has served American courts for over 200 years, however, is now itself being questioned.   A plethora of far-reaching social and technological changes, many of them unanticipated by the framers of our judicial system, have recently transpired. In many cases   new technologies, such as DNA fingerprinting, may soon unequivocally link suspects to criminal activity. Newspapers and the electronic media can rapidly and widely disseminate findings. This combination, of investigative technologies and readily available information, may eventually make courtroom debates about guilt or innocence obsolete.   Whether the current adversarial system can continue to serve the interests of justice in an information rich and technologically advanced society will be a central question for the future.

DISCUSSION QUESTIONS

1. What is a dying declaration? Under what circumstances might it be a valid exception to the hearsay rule? Why do most courts seem to believe that a person who is about to die is likely to tell the truth?

2. Do you think the present jury system is outmoded? Might "professional jurors" be more effective than the present system of "peer jurors"? On what do you base your opinion?

3. What is an expert witness? A lay witness? What different kinds of testimony may both provide? What are some of the difficulties in expert testimony?

4. What are the three forms of indigent defense used throughout various regions of the United States? Why might defendants prefer private attorneys over public counsel?

NOTES

1. Marc G. Gertz and Edmond J. True, "Social Scientists in the Courtroom: The Frustrations of Two Expert Witnesses," in Susette M. Talarico, ed., *Courts and Criminal Justice: Emerging Issues* (Beverly Hills, CA: Sage, 1985), pp. 81–91.

2. *Klopfer* v. *North Carolina*, 386 U.S. 213 (1967).

3. *Barker* v. *Wingo*, 407 U.S. 514 (1972).

4. *Strunk* v. *U.S.*, 412 U.S. 434 (1973).

5. *The Federal Speedy Trial Act*, 18 U.S.C., Section 3161 (1974).

6. *U.S.* v. *Brainer*, 515 F.Supp. 627 (D.Md.1981).

7. *U.S.* v. *Taylor*, U.S. 108, S.Ct. 2413 (1988).

8. See, for example, the U.S. Supreme Court's decision in the case of *Murphy* v. *Florida*, 410 U.S. 525 (1973).

9. *Witherspoon* v. *Illinois*, 391 U.S. 510 (1968).

10. *Mu'Min* v. *Virginia* No. 90-5193 (1991).

11. *Fed. R. Crim. Procedure* 24 (b).

12. Ibid.

13. "Are Juries Colorblind?" *Newsweek*, December 5, 1988, p. 94.

14. Ibid.

15. Ibid.

16. Ibid.

17. Supreme Court majority opinion in *Powers* v. *Ohio*, No. 89-5011 (1991), citing *Strauder* v. *West Virginia*, 100 U.S. 303 (1880).

18. *Swain* v. *Alabama*, 380 U.S. 202 (1965).

19. *Batson* v. *Kentucky*, 476 U.S. 79, 106 S.Ct. 1712 (1986).

20. *Ford* v. *Georgia*, No. 87-6796 (1991), footnote 2.

21. *Ford* v. *Georgia*, footnote 2.

22. *Powers* v. *Ohio*.

23. *Edmonson* v. *Leesville Concrete Co., Inc.*, No. 89-7743 (1991).

24. Although the words "argument" and "statement" are sometimes used interchangcably in alluding to opening remarks, defense attorneys are enjoined from drawing conclusions or "arguing" to the jury at this stage in the trial. Their task, as described in the section which follows, is simply to provide information to the jury as to how the defense will be conducted.

25. *U.S.* v. *Dinitz*, 424 U.S. 600, 612 (1976).

26. *Michigan* v. *Lucas*, No. 90-149 (1991).

27. *Griffin* v. *California*, 380 U.S. 609 (1965).

28. Leading questions may, in fact, be permitted for certain purposes, including refreshing a witness's memory, impeaching a hostile witness, introducing nondisputed material, and helping a witness with impaired faculties.

29. *In re Oliver*, 333 U.S. 257 (1948).

30. *Coy* v. *Iowa*, 487 U.S. 1012, 108 S.Ct. 2798 (1988).

31. *Maryland* v. *Craig*.

32. "The Right to Confront Your Accuser," *The Boston Globe Magazine*, April 7, 1991, pp. 19, 51.

33. *Maryland* v. *Craig,* op. cit.

34. *Idaho* v. *Wright,* No. 89-260 (1990).

35. Rule 29.1 of the *Federal Rules of Criminal Procedure.*

36. See *Johnson* v. *Louisiana,* 406 U.S. 356 (1972), and *Apodaca* v. *Oregon,* 406 U.S. 404 (1972).

37. *Allen* v. *U.S.,* 164 U.S. 492 (1896).

38. See for example, John Baldwin and Michael McConville, "Criminal Juries," in Norval Morris and Michael Tonry, eds., *Crime and Justice* Volume 2 (Chicago: University of Chicago Press, 1980).

39. Amiram Elwork, Bruce D. Sales, and James Alfini, *Making Jury Instructions Understandable* (Charlottesville, VA: The Michie Co., 1982).

40. "Juror Hardship Becomes Critical as McMartin Trail Enters Year 3," *Criminal Justice Newsletter,* May 15, 1989, pp. 6–7.

41. Some states have centralized offices called "Administrative Offices of the Courts," or something similar. Such offices, however, are often primarily data gathering agencies which have little or no authority over the day-to-day functioning of state or local courts.

42. See, for example, Larry Berkson and Susan Carbon, *Court Unification: Its History, Politics, and Implementation* (Washington, D.C.: U.S. Government Printing Office, 1978), and Thomas Henderson et al., *The Significance of Judicial Structure: The Effect of Unification on Trial Court Operators* (Alexandria, VA: Institute for Economic and Policy Studies, 1984).

43. See, for example, Kenneth Carlson et al., *Citizen Court Watching: The Consumer's Perspective* (Cambridge, MA: Abt Associates, 1977).

44. See, for example, Thomas J. Cook and Ronald W. Johnson et al., *Basic Issues in Court Performance* (Washington, D.C.: National Institute of Justice, 1982).

45. See, for example, Sorrel Wildhorn et al., *Indicators of Justice: Measuring the Performance of Prosecutors, Defense, and Court Agencies Involved in Felony Proceedings* (Lexington, MA: Lexington Books, 1977).

CHAPTER 8

SENTENCING

We will not punish a man because he hath offended, but that he may offend no more; nor does punishment ever look to the past, but to the future; for it is not the result of passion, but that the same thing be guarded against in time to come.

— Seneca (B.C. 3–65 A.D.)

The root of revenge is in the weakness of the Soul; the most abject and timorous are the most addicted to it.

— Akhenaton (circa B.C. 1375)

Punishment, that is justice for the unjust.

— Saint Augustine (354–430 A.D.)

KEY CONCEPTS

retribution	general deterrence	presentence report
specific deterrence	incapacitation	rehabilitation
presumptive sentencing	aggravating factors	mitigating factors
victim impact statement	indeterminate sentence	probation
parole	alternative sentencing	

❏ THE PHILOSOPHY OF CRIMINAL SENTENCING

Sentencing is the imposition of a penalty upon a person convicted of a crime. Most sentencing decisions are made by judges, although in some cases, especially where a death sentence is possible, juries may be involved in a special sentencing phase of courtroom proceedings. The sentencing decision is one of the most difficult made by any judge or jury. Not only does it involve the future, and perhaps the very life, of the defendant, but society looks to sentencing to achieve a diversity of goals.

Traditional sentencing options have included imprisonment, fines, probation, and — for very serious offenses — death. Limits on the range of options available to sentencing authorities are generally specified in law. Historically those limits have shifted as understandings of crime and the goals of sentencing have changed. Sentencing philosophies, or the justifications upon which various sentencing strategies are based, are manifestly intertwined with issues of religion, morals, values and emotions. Philosophies that gained ascendancy at a particular point in history were likely to be reflections of more deeply held social values.

The mentality of centuries ago, for example, held that crime was due to sin, and suffering was the culprit's due. Judges were expected to be harsh. Capital punishment, torture, and corporal penalties, served the ends of criminal sentencing.

An emphasis on rehabilitation became more prevalent around the time of the American and French revolutions, brought about, in part, by Enlightenment philosophies. Offenders came to be seen as highly rational beings who, more often than not, intentionally and somewhat carefully chose their course of action. Sentencing philosophies of the period stressed the need for sanctions which outweighed the benefits to be derived from making criminal choices. Severity of punishment became less important than quick and certain penalties. Recent thinking has emphasized the need to limit the potential for future harm by separating offenders from society. Not unknown, however, is the belief that offenders are deserving of punishment, nor has the hope for rehabilitation been entirely abandoned. Modern sentencing practices are influenced by five goals which weave their way through widely disseminated professional and legal models, continuing public calls for sentencing reform, and everyday sentencing practice. The five goals of contemporary sentencing are: (1) retribution, (2) incapacitation, (3) deterrence, (4) rehabilitation, and (5) victim restoration. Each goal represents a sentencing philosophy since it makes assumptions about human nature and holds implications for sentencing practice.

> **Sentence:** The penalty imposed by a court upon a person convicted of a crime.

RETRIBUTION

Retribution is punishment based upon a felt, but often inarticulate, need. To those who seek retribution, crimes cry out for vengeance. Retribution is an ancient goal. Most early societies punished offenders whenever they could catch them.[1] Punishment was swift and immediate — often without the benefit of a hearing - and it was generally extreme. Death and exile were commonly imposed. The Old Testament dictum of "An eye for an eye, a tooth for a tooth," often cited as an ancient justification for retribution, was actually intended to reduce the severity of punishment for relatively minor crimes

In its modern guise, retribution corresponds to the just-desserts model of sentencing. The just-desserts philosophy holds that offenders are responsible for their crimes. It sees punishment as deserved, justified — and even required[2] — by the behavior of the offender. The primary sentencing tool of the just desserts model is imprisonment, although in extreme cases capital punishment may become the ultimate retribution.

INCAPACITATION

The protection of innocent members of society is the primary goal of incapacitation. In olden times mutilation and amputation were sometimes used to prevent offenders from repeating their crimes. Modern incapacitation strategies separate offenders from the community in order to reduce opportunities for further criminality.   Incapacitation is sometimes called the "lock 'em up approach" and forms the basis for the contemporary movement toward prison "warehousing," discussed later in this book.

Incapacitation is used as a justification for imprisonment, just as is retribution. A significant difference between the two perspectives, however, lies in the fact that incapacitation requires only restraint — and not punishment. Hence advocates of the incapacitation philosophy of sentencing are sometimes also active prison reformers, seeking to humanize correctional institutions.   At the forefront of technology, confinement innovations are now offering ways to achieve the goal of incapacitation without the need for imprisonment. Electronic confinement (discussed shortly) and biomedical intervention (such as "chemical castration") may be able to prevent repeat offenses and bring society the protection it seeks through effective sentencing.

DETERRENCE

Deterrence relies upon the use of punishment as an example to convince people that criminal activity is not worthwhile. Its overall goal is crime prevention. When efforts are made to reduce the likelihood of recidivism by convicted offenders we speak of specific deterrence.   General deterrence, on the other hand, strives to influence the future behavior of people not yet arrested, who may be tempted to turn to crime.

Deterrence is one of the more "rational" goals of sentencing.   It is rational because it is an easily articulated goal, and also because the amount of punishment required to deter is amenable to objective investigation. Jeremy Bentham's hedonistic calculus, discussed earlier in this text, laid the groundwork for many later calculations of just how harsh punishments need be to deter effectively.   It is generally agreed today that harsh punishments can virtually eliminate many minor forms of criminality.[3] Few traffic tickets would have to be written, for example, if minor driving offenses were punishable by death. A free society such as our own, of course, is not willing to impose extreme punishments on petty offenders, and even harsh punishments are not demonstrably effective in reducing the incidence of serious crimes such as murder and drug running.

Deterrence is compatible with the goal of incapacitation, since at least *specific* deterrence can be achieved through incapacitating offenders. Hugo Bedau,[4] however, points to significant differences between retribution and deterrence. Retribution is oriented toward the past, says Bedau. It seeks to redress wrongs already committed. Deterrence, in contrast, is a strategy for the future. It aims to prevent new crimes. But as H.L.A. Hart has observed,[5] retribution can be the means through which deterrence is achieved. By serving as an example of what might happen to others, punishment may have an inhibiting effect.

REHABILITATION

Rehabilitation seeks to bring about fundamental changes in offenders and their behavior. As in the case of deterrence, the ultimate goal of rehabilitation is a reduction in the number of criminal offenses. Whereas, however, deterrence depends upon a "fear of the law" and the consequences of violating it, rehabilitation generally works through education and psychological treatment in order to reduce the likelihood of future criminality.

Copyright 1988 by USA Today. Reprinted with permission.
Decisions as to appropriate levels of punishment are central to the sentencing process.

The term "rehabilitation," however, may actually be a misnomer for the kinds of changes that its supporters seek. Rehabilitation literally means to return a person (or thing) to his or her previous condition. Hence, medical rehabilitation programs seek to restore functioning to atrophied limbs, rejuvenate injured organs, and mend shattered minds. In the case of criminal offenders, however, it is unlikely that restoring many to their previous state will result in anything other than a more youthful type of criminality.

In the past, rehabilitation as a sentencing strategy, if it existed at all, was primarily applied to youths. One of the first serious efforts to reform adult offenders was begun by the Pennsylvania Quakers, who initiated the development of the late–eighteenth century penitentiary. The penitentiary, which attempted to combine enforced penance with religious instruction, proved, however, to be something of an aberration. Within a few decades it had been firmly supplanted by a retributive approach to corrections.

It was not until the 1930s that rehabilitation achieved a primary role in the sentencing of adult offenders in the United States. At the time, the psychological world-view of therapists such as Sigmund Freud was entering popular culture. Psychology held out, as never before, the possibility of a structured approach to rehabilitation through thera-peutic intervention. The rehabilitative approach of the mid-1900s became known as the medical model of corrections, since it was built around a prescriptive approach to the treatment of offenders which provided at least the appearance of clinical predictability.

The primacy of the rehabilitative goal in sentencing fell victim to a "nothing works" philosophy in the late 1970s. The nothing works doctrine was based upon studies of recidivism rates which consistently showed that rehabilitation was more an ideal than a reality. With as many as 90% of former convicted offenders returning to lives of crime following release from prison-based treatment programs, public sentiments in favor of incapacitation grew. Although the rehabilitation ideal has clearly suffered in the public arena, some emerging evidence has begun to suggest that effective treatment programs do exist and may even be growing in number.[6]

RESTORATION

Victims or their survivors are frequently traumatized by the victimization experience. Some are killed and others receive lasting physical injuries. For many the world is never the same. The victimized may live in constant fear, reduced in personal vigor, and unable to form trusting relationships. Restoration is a sentencing goal which seeks to make the victim and the community "whole again."

The "healing" of victims involves many facets, arrayed throughout the criminal justice system, ranging from victim assistance programs to legislation supporting victim compensation. Sentencing options which seek to restore the victim have focused primarily on restitution payments which offenders are ordered to make either to their victims, or into a general fund which may then go to reimburse victims for suffering, lost wages, and medical expenses. In support of these goals, the 1984 Federal Comprehensive Crime Control Act specifically requires: "If sentenced to probation, the defendant must also be ordered to pay a fine, make restitution, and/or work in community service."[7]

Texas provides an example of a statewide strategy to utilize restitution as an alternative to prison.[8] The Texas Residential Restitution Program operates community-based centers which house selected nonviolent felony offenders. Residents work at regular jobs in the community, pay for support of their families, make restitution to their victims, and pay for room and board. During nonworking hours they are required to perform community service work.

Some advocates of the restoration philosophy of sentencing point out that court-ordered restitution payments or work programs which benefit the victim can also have the added benefit of rehabilitating the offender. The hope is that such sentences may teach the offender personal responsibility through structured financial obligations, work programs, regularly scheduled payments, and the like.

◻ INDETERMINATE SENTENCING

During most of the twentieth century, the rehabilitative goal held primacy.   Rehabilitation required a close consideration of the personal characteristics of individual offenders in order to define effective treatment strategies.   Hence, judges were permitted wide discretion in choosing from among sentencing options.   Although incapacitation is increasingly becoming the sentencing strategy of choice, many state criminal codes still allow judges to impose fines, probation, or widely varying prison terms, all for the same offense.   These sentencing practices, characterized primarily by vast judicial choice, constitute an indeterminate sentencing model.

Indeterminate sentencing relies heavily upon the discretionary decisions of judges who not only choose among types of sanctions, but also set upper and lower limits on the length of prison stays.   Indeterminate sentences are typically imposed with wording such as: "The defendant shall serve not less than 5, nor more than 25 years in the state's prison, under the supervision of the state department of correction."   Judicial discretion under the indeterminate model also extends to the imposition of concurrent or consecutive sentences, where the offender is convicted on more than one charge.   Consecutive sentences are served one after the other, while concurrent sentences expire simultaneously.

Under the indeterminate sentencing model, the inmate's behavior while incarcerated is the primary determinate of the actual amount of time served.   State parole boards wield great discretion under the model, acting as the final arbiters of the actual sentence served.

Indeterminate sentencing has both an historical and a philosophical basis in the belief that convicted offenders are more likely to participate in their own rehabilitation if they can reduce the amount of time they have to spend in prison.   Inmates on good behavior will be released early, while recalcitrant inmates will remain in prison until the end of their terms. For that reason, parole generally plays a significant role in states which employ the indeterminate sentencing model.

The indeterminate model was also created to take into consideration detailed differences in culpability.   Under the model judges could weigh minute differences among cases, situations and offenders.   All the following could be considered before sentence was passed: (1) whether the offender committed the crime out of a need for money, for the thrill it afforded, out of a desire for revenge, or for the "hell of it," (2) the harm the offender intended, (3) the contribution of the victim to his or her own victimization, (4) the extent of the damages inflicted, (5) the mental state of the offender,   (6) the likelihood of successful rehabilitation, (7) the degree of the offender's cooperation with authorities, and (8) a near-infinity of other individual factors.

A few states employ a partially indeterminate sentencing model. Partially indeterminate sentencing systems allow judges who are imposing prison sentences to specify only the maximum amount of time to be served. Some minimum is generally implied by law, but is not under the control of the sentencing authority. General practice is to set one year as a minimum for all felonies, while a few jurisdictions assume no minimum time at all — making persons sentenced to imprisonment eligible for immediate parole.

PROBLEMS WITH THE INDETERMINATE MODEL

Indeterminate sentencing is still the rule in many jurisdictions. The model, however, has come under increasing fire in recent years for contributing to inequality in sentencing. Critics claim that the indeterminate model allows divergent judicial personalities, and the often too-personal philosophies of judges, to produce an unwarranted gamut of sentencing practices ranging from very lenient to very strict. The "hanging judge," who still exists in some jurisdictions, was one who, more often than not, tended to impose the maximum sentence allowable under law. Worse still, the indeterminate model allows for the possibility that offenders might be sentenced, at least by some judges, more on the basis of social characteristics rather than culpability.

Offenders who face sentencing under the indeterminate model often depend upon the counsel of their attorneys to appear before a judge predicted to be a good sentencing risk. Requests for delays became a commonly used defense strategy in attempts to manipulate the selection of personalities involved in sentencing decisions.

TABLE 8-1
Estimated Time to Be Served in State Prison
Versus Mean Prison Sentence

Offense	Mean Prison Sentence	Estimated Time to Be Served in Prison
Murder	221 months	86 months
Rape	151	66
Robbery	139	57
Aggravated Assault	97	41
Burglary	75	31
Larceny	46	20
Drug		
Trafficking	69	22
Other Felonies	56	24
Average for **All Felonies**	81 months	33 months

Source: Bureau of Justice Statistics, *Felony Sentences in State Courts, 1986*, BJS Bulletin, February 1989.

Another charge leveled against indeterminate sentencing was that it tended to produce dishonesty in sentencing. Because of sentence cutbacks for good behavior, and other reductions available to inmates through involvement in work and study programs, punishments rarely meant what they said. A sentence of five to ten years, for example, might actually see an inmate released in a matter of months after all "gain time" had been calculated. Even today, time served in prison is generally far less than sentences would seem to indicate. Table 8-1 shows recent estimates of time to be served in prison versus actual sentences of felons convicted under state jurisdiction.

Indeterminate sentencing came under increasing fire as studies identified widely disparate sentencing practices. An early New Jersey study[9] of six judges handling similar cases found, for example, that the strictest judge imposed prison sentences on 57.7% of convicted criminal defendants who came before him for sentencing; while another, more lenient judge, ordered such sentences only 33.6% of the time. Sentencing practices of the other four judges fell somewhere between these two extremes. A later experiment,[10] which presented 43 active federal trial judges with 20 criminal case scenarios, resulted in enormously varied decisions. One judge chose a sanction of 3 to 20 years; another, probation to 7½ years. The norm, concluded commentators, was the absence of a norm.[11]

☐ THE RISE OF DETERMINATE SENTENCING

Until the 1970s some form of indeterminate (or partially indeterminate) sentencing was the model employed by all 50 states. Soon, however, calls for equity and proportionality in sentencing, heightened by claims of racial disparity in the sentencing practices[12] of some judges, led many states to move toward closer control over their sentencing systems.

Critics of the indeterminate model called for the recognition of three fundamental sentencing principles: proportionality, equity, and social debt. Proportionality refers to the belief that the severity of sanctions should bear a direct relationship to the seriousness of the crime committed. Equity is based upon a concern with social equality. Equity in sentencing means that similar crimes should be punished with the same degree of severity, regardless of the general social or personal characteristics of offenders. According to the principle of equity, for example, two bank robbers in different parts of the country, who use the same techniques and weapons, with the same degree of implied threat, even though they are tried under separate circumstances, should receive roughly the same kind of sentence. The equity principle needs to be balanced, however, against the notion of social debt. In the case of the bank robbers, the offender who has a prior criminal record can be said to have a higher level of social debt than the one-time robber, where all else is equal. Greater social debt, of course, would suggest a heightened severity of punishment or a greater need for treatment, and so on.

In 1976 Maine became the first state to eliminate old sentencing practices and adopt determinate sentencing. It was quickly followed by other states including Colorado, California, Connecticut, Florida, Illinois, Indiana, Minnesota, New Mexico, North Carolina, and Washington.[13] Colorado, while opting for determining sentencing in 1979, returned to the use of an indeterminate model in 1985. Determinate sentencing states observe a pattern of abolishing parole, eliminating parole boards, and establishing sentencing commissions with the authority to develop and modify sentencing guidelines.

Determinate sentencing depends upon a well-defined penalty hierarchy codified in state law, whereby specified terms of imprisonment are associated with each criminal offense category. Sentencing statutes may, for example, require that assault on a police officer is to be punished by six months in prison. Determinate sentencing is also called presumptive or fixed sentencing since it *presumes* a direct relationship between the offense and the sentence and sets sentences which are fixed by law. Even presumptive sentences, however, often allow judges a certain leeway in the actual sentences they impose.

Presumptive sentencing guidelines in some jurisdictions specify only a range of sentences from which a judge is expected to chose. In California, for example, the presumptive term for a number of crimes is three years, but a judge may select a sentence anywhere between two and four years and still fall within statutory guidelines.

Even states which use a single presumptive sentence for a given offense generally allow for "aggravating" or "mitigating" factors, indicating greater or lesser degrees of culpability, which judges can take into consideration in imposing a sentence somewhat at variance from the presumptive term. Aggravating factors are those which appear to call for a tougher sentence, and may include especially heinous behavior, cruelty, injury to more than one person, and so on. Mitigating factors, or those which indicate that a lesser sentence is called for, are generally similar to legal defenses, although in this case they only reduce criminal responsibility, not eliminate it. Mitigating factors include such things as cooperation with the investigating authority, surrender, good character, and so forth.

A CRITIQUE OF THE DETERMINATE MODEL

Determinate sentencing models, which have sought to address the shortcomings of their predecessors through legislative curtailment of judicial discretion in the sentencing realm, are not without their critics. Detractors charge that determinate sentencing is overly simplistic, based upon a primitive concept of culpability, and incapable of offering hope for rehabilitation and change. For one thing, they say, determinate sentencing has built-in limitations which render it far less capable of judging the blameworthiness of individual offenders. Legislatures simply cannot anticipate all the differences that individual cases can present. Aggravating and mitigating circumstances, while intended to cover most circumstances, will inevitably shortchange some defendants who don't fall neatly into the categories they provide.

A second critique of determinate sentencing is that such a strategy, while it may reduce the discretion of judges substantially, may do nothing to hamper the huge discretionary decision making power of prosecutors.[14] In fact federal sentencing reformers, who have adopted the determinate sentencing model, have specifically decided not to modify the discretionary power of prosecutors, citing the large number of cases which are resolved through plea bargaining. Such a shift in discretionary authority, away from judges and into the hands of prosecutors, may be misplaced.

Another criticism of determinate sentencing questions its fundamental purpose. Advocates of determinate sentencing inevitably cite greater equity in sentencing as the primary benefits of such a model. Reduced to its essence this means that "those who commit the same crime get the same time." Sentencing reformers have thus couched the drive toward determinate sentencing in progressive terms. Others, however, have pointed out that the philosophical underpinnings of the movement may be quite different. Albert Alschuler,[15] for example, suggests that determinate sentencing is a regressive social policy which derives from a weariness among Americans for considering offenders as individuals. Describing this kind of thinking Alschuler writes: "Don't tell us that a robber was retarded. We don't care about his problems. We don't know what to *do* about his problems, and we are no longer interested in listening to a criminal's sob stories. The most important thing about this robber is simply that he *is* a robber."[16] A different line of thought is proposed by

Christopher Link and Neal Shover[17] who found in a study of state-level economic, political, and demographic data that determinate sentencing may ultimately be the result of declining economic conditions and increasing fiscal strain on state governments rather than any particular set of ideals.

A third critique of determinate sentencing centers on its alleged inability to promote effective rehabilitation. Under indeterminate sentencing schemes offenders have the opportunity to act responsibly and thus to participate in their own rehabilitation.[18] Lack of responsible behavior results in denial of parole and extension of the sentence. Determinate sentencing schemes, by virtue of dramatic reductions in good time allowances and parole opportunities, leave little incentive for offenders to participate in educational programs, to take advantage of opportunities for work inside of correctional institutions, to seek treatment, or to contribute in any positive way to their own change.

While these critiques may be valid, they will probably do little to stem the tide toward presumptive sentencing. The rise of determinate sentencing represents the ascendancy of the "just-desserts" perspective over other sentencing goals. In a growing number of jurisdictions, punishment, deterrence, and incapacitation have replaced rehabilitation and restitution as the goals which society seeks to achieve through sentencing practices.

☐ FEDERAL SENTENCING GUIDELINES

In 1984, with passage of The Comprehensive Crime Control Act, the federal government adopted determinate sentencing for nearly all federal offenders.[19] The act established the seven-member U.S. Sentencing Commission, composed of presidential appointees, including three federal judges. Heading the Commission was William W. Wilkins, Jr., U.S. Circuit Judge for the Fourth Circuit. The Commission was charged with the task of creating federal determinate sentencing guidelines. To guide the Commission, Congress specified the purposes of sentencing to include deterring criminals, incapacitating and/or rehabilitating offenders, and providing "just desserts" in punishing criminals. Congress charged the Commission with eliminating sentencing disparities, and reducing confusion in sentencing, and asked for a system which would permit flexibility in the face of mitigating or aggravating elements.

The 1984 Crime Control Act also addressed the issue of honesty in sentencing. Under the old federal system, a sentence of ten years in prison might actually have meant only a few years spent behind bars before the offender was released. On average, good time credits and parole reduced time served to about one-third of actual sentences.[20] While such a reduction in time may have benefited the offender, it often outraged victims who felt betrayed by the sentencing process. The act nearly eliminated good time credits,[21] and targeted 1992 (which was later extended to 1997) as the date for phasing out parole and eliminating the U.S. Parole Commission. The emphasis on honesty in sentencing created, in effect, a sentencing environment of "what you get is what you serve."

FEDERAL GUIDELINE PROVISIONS

Guidelines established by the Commission took effect in November 1987. They immediately became embroiled in appellate battles, many of which focused on the constitutionality of the membership of the Sentencing Commission.[22] The U.S. Supreme Court considered the constitutionality question in 1989. By the time it did, 158 federal district courts had ruled the guidelines unconstitutional, while 116 others had upheld them.[23] The 9th U.S. Circuit Court of Appeals had struck the guidelines down, while the 3rd Circuit Court had found them acceptable. On January 18, 1989, in deciding the case of *Mistretta* v. *U.S.*,[24] the Supreme Court, by a vote of 8 to 1, held that Congress had acted appropriately and that the guidelines developed by the Commission could be applied nationwide.

The federal guidelines specify a sentencing range for each criminal offense, from which judges must choose. If a particular case represents "atypical features" judges are allowed to depart from the guidelines. Departures are generally expected to be made only in the presence of mitigating or aggravating factors, a number of which are specified in the guidelines. Any departure may, however, become the basis for appellate review concerning the reasonableness of the sentence imposed.

Federal sentencing guidelines are built around a table containing 43 rows, each corresponding to one offense level. Penalties associated with each level overlap those of levels above or below in order to discourage unnecessary litigation. A person charged with a crime involving $11,000, for example, upon conviction is unlikely to receive a penalty substantially greater than if the amount involved had been somewhat less than $10,000 — a sharp contrast to the old system. A change of six levels roughly doubles the sentence imposed under the guidelines, regardless of the level at which one starts.

To determine what sentences would be most appropriate for each range, the Commission began by computing the actual sentences being served, on average, under the old system for each type of offense.[25] The Commission also considered relevant federal law, parole guidelines, and the anticipated impact of changes upon federal prison populations. One boundary was set by statute: in creating the Sentencing Commission, Congress had also specified that the degree of discretion available in any one sentencing category could not exceed 25% of the basic penalty for that category or six months, whichever might be greater.

The sentencing table also contains six rows, corresponding to the criminal history category into which an offender falls. Criminal history categories are determined on a point basis. Offenders earn points through previous convictions. Each prior sentence of imprisonment for more than one year and one month counts as three points. Two points are assigned for each prior prison sentence over six months, or if the defendant committed the offense while on probation, parole, or work release. The system also assigns points for other types of previous convictions and for offenses committed less than two years after release from imprisonment. Points are added together in order to determine the criminal history category into which an offender falls. Thirteen points or more are required for the highest category. At each offense level, sentences in the highest criminal history category are generally two to three times as severe as for the lowest category.

Defendants may also move into the highest criminal history category (number VI) by virtue of being designated career offenders.   Under the sentencing guidelines, a defendant is a career offender if: "(1) the defendant was at least eighteen years old at the time of the . . . offense, (2) the . . . offense is a crime of violence or trafficking in a controlled substance, and (3) the defendant has at least two prior felony convictions of either a crime of violence or a controlled substance offense."[26]

PLEA BARGAINING UNDER THE GUIDELINES

Plea bargaining plays a major role in the federal judicial system. Approximately 90% of all federal sentences are the result of guilty pleas,[27] and the large majority of those are the result of plea negotiations.   In the words of Commission Chairman Wilkins, "With respect to plea bargaining, the Commission has proceeded cautiously . . . the Commission did not believe it wise to stand the federal criminal justice system on its head by making too drastic and too sudden a change in these practices."[28]

Although the Commission allowed for the continuation of plea bargaining, it did require that the agreement (1) be fully disclosed in the record of the court (unless there is an overriding and demonstrable reason why it should not) and (2) detail the actual conduct of the offense. Under these requirements defendants will no longer be able to "hide" the actual nature of their offense behind a substitute plea.

The thrust of the new rules concerning plea bargaining is to reduce the veil of secrecy which had heretofore surrounded the process. Information on the decision-making process itself will be available to victims, the media, and the public. Although for now the Commission has assumed a "hands-off" approach to the actual negotiations involved in plea bargaining, it is planning a future review of the process.[29]

Prior to implementation of the new guidelines, 41.4% of all persons convicted of federal crimes received some form of probation.[30] Under the new guidelines, it is predicted that only 18.5% of federal offenders will be able to avoid prison. Similar estimates project that only 13.3% of federal drug offenders will receive probation.   More than 33% of such offenders were released on probation under the old system.

Stiffer penalties under the new sentencing guidelines, combined with the elimination of good time and parole will inevitably contribute to an increase in the number of federal prisoners. In 1987 federal prisons held about 42,000 inmates. By 1997 the federal prison population is expected to increase to as many as 118,000 prisoners.[31] By 2002 the figure may reach 156,000 — an increase of 300% in 15 years.[32]

Analyses of the impact of various factors on the growth of federal prison populations, however, attribute only 4% to 7% of the overall increment to the new guidelines. Career criminal provisions of the 1984 Comprehensive Crime Control Act, considered separately from the guidelines themselves, are expected to add substantially to the increase in federal inmates. The largest addition will most likely be due, however, to the Anti-Drug Abuse Act of 1986, which substantially raises the penalty for many federal drug offenses.

Early implementation studies[33] during the first year the guidelines were operational showed that 82% of sentences handed down by federal judges were within the sentencing parameters established by the guidelines. Nine percent of sentences were less than the guidelines called for, and 3% were greater. During the first year, 5% of sentences imposed by federal judges were reduced because the offender cooperated with authorities.[34]

☐ THE PRESENTENCE INVESTIGATIVE REPORT

Prior to imposing sentence a judge may request information on the background of a convicted defendant. This is especially true in nondeterminate sentencing jurisdictions, where judges retain considerable discretion in selecting sanctions. Traditional wisdom has held that the presence of certain factors in the lives of less serious offenders increase the likelihood of rehabilitation and reduce the need for lengthy prison terms. These indicators include a good job record, satisfactory educational attainment, strong family ties, church attendance, an arrest history of only nonviolent offenses, and psychological stability.

Information about a defendant's background often comes to the judge in the form of a presentence report. The task of preparing presentence reports usually falls to the probation/parole office. Presentence reports take one of three forms: (1) a detailed written report on the defendant's personal and criminal history, including an assessment of present conditions in the defendant's life (often called the "long form"); (2) an abbreviated written report summarizing the type of information most likely to be useful in a sentencing decision (the "short form"); and (3) a verbal report to the court made by the investigating officer based on field notes, but structured according to categories established for the purpose. A presentence report is much like a resume or *vita* except that it focuses on what might be regarded as positive as well as negative life experiences.

Jurisdictions vary in their use of presentence reports and in the form they take. Federal law mandates presentence reports in federal criminal courts and specifies 15 topical areas which each report is to contain. The 1984 federal Determinate Sentencing Act directs report writers to include information on the classification of the offense and of the defendant under the categories established by the statute.

Some states require presentence reports only in felony cases, and others in cases where defendants face the possibility of incarceration for six months. Still others may have no requirement for presentence reports beyond those ordered by a judge. Even so, report writing, rarely anyone's favorite activity, may seriously tax the limited resources of probation agencies.   According to Andrew Klein,[35] during a recent year New York state probation officers wrote 108,408 presentence investigation reports. Most (63,902) were for misdemeanors, but 44,506 reports described the backgrounds of newly convicted felons. In the same year in New York City alone, more than 37,000 presentence investigation reports were completed, averaging 25 reports per probation officer per month.

The length of the completed form is subject to great variation. One survey[36] found that Texas used one of the shortest forms of all — a one-page summary supplemented by other materials which the report writer thought might provide meaningful additional details. Orange County, California, provides an example of the opposite kind and may use the most detailed form of any jurisdiction in the country. The instructions for completing the form consist of a dozen single-spaced pages.[37]

A typical "long form" is divided into ten major informational sections as follows: (1) personal information and identifying data describing the defendant, (2) a chronology of the current offense and circumstances surrounding it, (3) a record of the defendant's previous convictions, if any, (4) home-life and family data, (5) educational background, (6) health history and current state of health, (7) military service, (8) religious preference, (9) financial condition, and (10) sentencing recommendations made by the probation/parole officer completing the report.

A CAREER WITH THE U.S. CUSTOMS SERVICE

Typical Positions. Criminal investigator, special agent, customs inspector, canine enforcement officer, and import specialist. Support positions include intelligence research specialist, computer operator, auditor, customs aide, investigative assistant, and clerk.

Employment Requirements. Applicants must (1) be U.S. citizens, (2) pass an appropriate physical examination, (3) pass a personal background investigation, (4) submit to urinalysis for the presence of controlled substances, (5) have at least three years of work experience, and (6) be under 35 years of age. Appointment at the GS-7 level also requires (1) one year of specialized experience (i.e., "responsible criminal investigative or comparable experience"), (2) a Bachelor's degree with demonstration of superior academic achievement (a 3.0 grade point average in all courses completed at time of application or a 3.5 grade point average for all courses in the applicant's major field of study, or rank in the upper third of the applicant's undergraduate class, or membership in a national honorary scholastic society), or (3) one year of successful graduate study in a related field.

Other Requirements. Applicants must (1) be willing to travel frequently, (2) be able to work overtime, (3) be capable of working under stressful conditions, and (4) be willing to carry weapons and be able to qualify regularly with firearms.

Salary. Starting salary in 1993 was $25,745 for entry-level positions.

Benefits. Benefits include (1) 13 days of sick leave annually, (2) 2½ to 5 weeks of annual paid vacation and 10 paid federal holidays each year, (3) federal health and life insurance, and (4) a comprehensive retirement program.

Direct inquiries to: Office of Human Resources, U.S. Customs Service, 2120 L Street, Room 7402, P.O. Box 7108, Washington, D.C. 20044. Phone: (202) 634-5025.

The data on which a presentence report are based come from a variety of sources. Since the 1960s modern computer-based criminal information clearinghouses, such as the FBI's National Crime Information Center (NCIC), have simplified at least a part of the data gathering process. The NCIC began in 1967 and contains information on wanted persons throughout the United States. Individual jurisdictions also maintain criminal records repositories which are able to provide comprehensive files on the criminal history of persons processed by the justice system. In the late 1970s the federal government encouraged states to develop criminal records repositories utilizing computer technology.[38] The 15 years that followed have been described as "the focus of a data-gathering effort more massive and more coordinated than any other in criminal justice."[39]

Almost all third-party data are subject to ethical and legal considerations. The official records of almost any agency or organization, while they may prove to be an ideal source of information, are often protected by state and federal privacy requirements. In particular, the Federal Privacy Act of 1974[40] may limit records access. Investigators should first check on the legal availability of all records before requesting them, and should receive in writing the defendant's permission to access records. Other public laws, among them the Federal Freedom of Information Act,[41] may make the presentence report itself available to the defendant, although courts and court officers have generally been held to be exempt from the provisions of such statutes.

Sometimes the defendant is a significant source of much of the information which appears in the presentence report. When such is the case, efforts should be made to corroborate the information provided by the defendant. Unconfirmed data will generally be marked on the report as "defendant-supplied data," or simply "unconfirmed."

The final section of a presentence report is usually devoted to recommendations made by the investigating officer. A recommendation may be made in favor of probation, split sentencing, a term of imprisonment, or any other sentencing options available in the jurisdiction. Participation in community service programs may be recommended for probationers, and drug- or substance-abuse programs may be suggested as well. Some authors have observed that a "judge accepts an officer's recommendation in an extremely high percentage of cases."[42] Most judges are willing to accept the report writer's recommendation because they recognize the professionalism of presentence investigators, and because they know that the investigator may well be the supervising officer assigned to the defendant should a community alternative be the sentencing decision.

Presentence reports may be useful sentencing tools. Many officers who prepare them take their responsibilities seriously. A recent study,[43] however, shows a tendency among presentence investigators to satisfy judicial expectations about defendants by tailoring reports to fit the image the defendant projects. Prior criminal record and present offense may provide a kind of shorthand used by investigators to interpret all the other data they gather.[44]

VICTIM IMPACT STATEMENTS

Victim Impact Statements

The growth of a national victim-witness rights movement has been described earlier in this book. One consequence of the movement has been a call for the use of victim impact statements prior to sentencing. A victim impact statement generally takes the form of a written document which describes the losses, suffering, and trauma experienced by the crime victim or the victim's survivors. Judges are expected to consider it in arriving at an appropriate sanction for the offender.

Although the drive to mandate inclusion of victim impact statements in sentencing decisions has gathered much momentum, their final role has yet to be finally decided. The Victim Task Force, commissioned by then-President Reagan shortly after he took office, recommended adoption of a change to the Sixth Amendment of the U.S. Constitution. The Commission specifically recommended adding the words: "Likewise, the victim, in every criminal prosecution shall have the right to be present and to be heard at all critical stages of judicial proceedings."[45] Although such an amendment may be a long way off, significant federal legislation has already occurred. The 1982 Victim and Witness Protection Act[46] requires victim impact statements to be considered at sentencing and places responsibility for their creation on federal probation officers.

Some states have gone the federal government one better. In 1984 the state of California, for example, passed legislation[47] to allow victims a right to attend and participate in sentencing and parole hearings. Approximately 20 states now have laws mandating citizen involvement in sentencing. Where written victim impact statements are not available, courts may invite the victim to testify directly at sentencing.

The case of actress Theresa Saldana is representative of that of the many victims who feel they need more say in sentencing and parole decisions. Saldana, star of such movies as *Raging Bull* and *I Want to Hold Your Hand*, was attacked outside her apartment by a crazed Scottish drifter in 1982. She was stabbed ten times and may have been saved only by the fact that the knife her attacker was wielding bent from the force of the blows. Although seriously injured, she recovered. The man who attacked her, Arthur Jackson, had a long history of psychiatric problems and claimed to be on a divine mission to unite with Ms. Saldana in heaven. Although imprisoned for the attack, Jackson continued to write his victim, promising that when he got out he would finish the job. California prison authorities claimed they were powerless to stop his letters.

In 1984, under California's new victim right's statute, Ms. Saldana testified before a resentencing body considering Jackson's case. "I will never forget the searing, ghastly pain, the grotesque and devastating experience of this person nearly butchering me to death, or the bone-chilling sight of my own blood splattered everywhere,"[48] she told the examiners. Her testimony resulted in Jackson's release being delayed until June 1989. As Jackson's release date arrived, Ms. Saldana told reporters: "It is just unbelievable that he is getting out. I feel like I am in a nightmare. I really feel my rights are being overlooked. Why is it life, liberty and the pursuit of happiness [are] being taken from me?"[49] There is little information to date on what changes, if any, the appearance of victims at sentencing is having on the criminal justice system. At least one study, however, found that very few victims are taking advantage of their new-found opportunities. Fewer than 3% of California victims chose to appear or testify at sentencing hearings after that state's new victim rights law was enacted.[50]

In 1987 the legality of victim impact statements was called into question by the U.S. Supreme Court case of *Booth* v. *Maryland*.[51] The case involved Irvin Bronstein, age 78, and his wife Rose, 75, who were robbed and brutally murdered in their home in Baltimore, Maryland, in 1983. The killers were John Booth and Willie Reid, acquaintances of the Bronstein's, caught stealing to support heroin habits. The bodies were discovered two days later by a son. The murder had occurred at the time a family wedding was scheduled.

After being convicted of murder, Booth decided to allow the jury (rather than the judge) to set his sentence. The jury considered a victim impact statement which was part of a presentence report prepared by probation officers — as required by state law. The victim impact statement used in the case was a powerful one, describing the wholesome personal qualities of the Bronsteins and the emotional suffering experienced by their children as a result of the murder. After receiving a death sentence, Booth appealed to the U.S. Supreme Court. The Court overturned his sentence, reasoning that victim impact statements, at least in capital cases, violate the Eighth Amendment ban on cruel and unusual punishments. In a close (5 to 4) decision, the majority held that information in victim impact statements leads to the risk that the death penalty might be imposed in an arbitrary and capricious manner.

In a complete about-face, affected in no small part by the gathering conservative majority among its justices, the Supreme Court held in the 1991 case of *Payne* v. *Tennessee*[52] that the *Booth* ruling had been based upon "a misreading of precedent."[53] The *Payne* case began with a 1987 double murder, in which a 28-year-old mother and her 2-

year-old daughter were stabbed to death in Millington, Tennessee.[54] A second child, 3-year-old Nicholas Christopher, himself severely wounded in the incident, witnessed the deaths of his mother and young sister. In a trial following the killings, the prosecution claimed that Pervis Tyrone Payne, a 20-year-old retarded man, had killed the mother and child after the woman resisted his sexual advances. Payne was convicted of both murders. At the sentencing phase of the trial, Mary Zvolanek, Nicholas's grandmother, testified that the boy continued to cry out daily for his dead sister. Following *Booth*, Payne's conviction was upheld by the Tennessee Supreme Court in an opinion which then-Justice Thurgood Marshall said did little to disguise the Tennessee court's contempt for the precedent set by *Booth*.

This time, however, the Supreme Court agreed with the Tennessee justices, holding that "[v]ictim impact evidence is simply another form or method of informing the sentencing authority about the specific harm caused by the crime in question, evidence of a general type long considered by sentencing authorities." As Chief Justice Rehnquist wrote for the majority, "[c]ourts have always taken into consideration the harm done by the defendant in imposing sentence . . ." In a concurring opinion, Justice Antonin Scalia held that "*Booth* significantly harms our criminal justice system . . ." and had been decided with "plainly inadequate rational support." Given the seemingly firm authority with which the Court's conservative majority now speaks, it is likely that the *Payne* decision will remain in place for a long time to come.

☐ TRADITIONAL SENTENCING OPTIONS

Sentencing is fundamentally a risk management strategy designed to protect the public while serving the ends of rehabilitation, deterrence, retribution, and restoration. Because the goals of sentencing are difficult to agree on, so are sanctions. Lengthy prison terms do little for rehabilitation, while community release programs can hardly protect the innocent from offenders bent on continuing criminality.

Assorted sentencing philosophies continue to permeate state-level judicial systems. Each state has its own sentencing laws, and frequent revisions of those statutes are not uncommon. Because of huge variations from one state to another in the laws and procedures which control the imposition of criminal sanctions, sentencing has been called "the most diversified part of the Nation's criminal justice process."[55] There is at least one common ground, however. It can be found in the four traditional sanctions which continue to dominate the thinking of most legislators and judges. The four traditional sanctions are:

- ♦   Incarceration
- ♦   Fines
- ♦   Probation
- ♦   Death

In the case of indeterminate sentencing, the first three options are widely available to judges. The option selected generally depends upon the severity of the offense and the judge's best guess as the likelihood of future criminal involvement on the part of the defendant. Sometimes two or more options are combined, as when an offender might be fined and sentenced to prison, or placed on probation and fined in support of restitution payments.

Jurisdictions which operate under presumptive sentencing guidelines generally limit the judge's choice to only one option, and often specify the extent to which that option can be applied. Dollar amounts of fines, for example, are rigidly set, and prison terms are specified for each type of offense. The death penalty, remains an option in a fair number of jurisdictions, but only for a highly select group of offenders.

FINES

The fine is one of the oldest forms of punishment, predating even the Code of Hammurabi.[56] Until recently, however, the use of fines as criminal sanctions suffered from built-in inequities and a widespread failure to collect them. Inequities arose when offenders with vastly different financial resources were fined similar amounts. A fine of $100, for example, can place a painful economic burden upon a poor defendant, but is only laughable when imposed on a wealthy offender.

Today fines are once again receiving attention as serious sentencing alternatives. One reason for the renewed interest is the stress placed upon state resources by burgeoning prison populations. The extensive imposition of fines not only results in less crowded prisons, but can contribute to state and local coffers and lower the tax burden of law-abiding citizens. Other advantages of the use of fines as criminal sanctions include:

- ◆ Fines can deprive offenders of the proceeds of criminal activity.

- ◆ Fines can promote rehabilitation by enforcing economic responsibility.

- ◆ Fines can be collected by existing criminal justice agencies, and are relatively inexpensive to administer.

- ◆ Fines can be made proportionate to both the severity of the offense and the ability of the offender to pay.

A recent National Institute of Justice (NIJ) survey found that an average of 86% of convicted defendants in courts of limited jurisdiction receive fines as sentences, some in combination with another penalty.[57] Fines are also experiencing widespread use in courts of general jurisdiction, where the NIJ study found judges imposing fines in 42% of all cases which came before them for sentencing. Some studies estimate that over $1 billion in fines are collected nationwide each year.[58]

Fines are often imposed for relatively minor law violations such as driving while intoxicated, reckless driving, disturbing the peace, disorderly conduct, public drunkenness, and vandalism. Judges in many courts, however, report the use of fines for relatively serious violations of the law including assault, auto theft, embezzlement, fraud, and the sale and possession of various controlled substances. Fines are much more likely to be imposed,

however, where the offender has both a clean record and the ability to pay.[59]
     Opposition to the use of fines is based upon the following arguments:

- ◆   Fines may result in the release of convicted offenders into the community but do not impose stringent controls on their behavior.

- ◆   Fines are a relatively mild form of punishment, and are not consistent with "just desserts" philosophy.

- ◆   Fines discriminate against the poor and favor the wealthy.

- ◆   Indigent offenders are especially subject to discrimination since they entirely lack the financial resources with which to pay fines.

- ◆   Fines are difficult to collect.

     A number of these objections can be answered by procedures which make available to judges complete financial information on defendants. Studies have found, however, that courts of limited jurisdiction, which are the most likely to impose fines, are also the least likely to have adequate information on offenders' economic status.[60]   Perhaps as a consequence, judges themselves are often reluctant to impose fines. Two of the most widely cited objections by judges to the use of fines are (1) fines allow more affluent offenders to "buy their way out," and (2) poor offenders cannot pay fines.[61]

     A solution to both objections can be found in the Scandinavian system of day fines. The day-fine system is based on the idea that fines should be proportionate to the severity of the offense, but also need to take into account the financial resources of the offender. Day fines are computed by first assessing the seriousness of the offense, the defendant's degree of culpability, and his or her prior record as measured in "days." The use of days as a benchmark of seriousness is related to the fact that, without fines, the offender could be sentenced to a number of days (or months or years) in jail or prison. The number of days an offender is assessed is then multiplied by the daily wages that person earns. Hence, if two persons were sentenced to a five-day fine, but one earned only $20 per day and the other $200 per day, the first would pay a $100 fine and the second a $1,000 fine.

PROBATION

     Probation is "a sentence served while under supervision in the community."[62] Like other sentencing options, probation is a court-ordered sanction. Its goal is to allow for some degree of control over criminal offenders while employing available community programs in the service of rehabilitation. Although probation can be directly imposed, most probationers are technically sentenced to confinement, but have their sentence suspended and are remanded into the custody of an officer of the court — the probation officer.
     Probation has a diversity of historical roots. By the 1300s English courts had

established the practice of "binding over for good behavior,"[63] in which offenders could be entrusted into the custody of willing citizens. John Augustus, however (1784 — 1859), is generally recognized as the world's first probation officer. Augustus, a Boston shoemaker, attended sessions of criminal court in the 1850s and would offer to take carefully selected offenders into his home as an alternative to imprisonment.[64] At first, he supervised only drunkards, but by 1857 Augustus was accepting many kinds of offenders and devoting all his time to the service of the court.[65] Augustus died in 1859, having bailed out more than 2,000 convicts in his lifetime. In 1878 the Massachusetts legislature enacted a statute which authorized the city of Boston to hire a salaried probation officer. Missouri (1897) followed suit, along with Vermont (1898) and Rhode Island (1899).[66] Before the end of the nineteenth century, probation had become an accepted and widely used form of community-based supervision. By 1925 all 48 states had adopted probation legislation. In the same year the National Probation Act enabled federal district court judges to appoint paid probation officers and impose probationary terms.[67]

Today, probation is the most common form of criminal sentencing used in the United States. Nearly 65% of all persons under correctional supervision in the United States during 1992 were on probation. The number of persons supervised yearly on probation is increasing at almost twice the rate of imprisonment.[68] This observation has caused some writers to call probation crowding an "immediate threat to the criminal justice process and to community protection."[69]

> **Probation:** The conditional freedom granted by a judicial officer to an alleged or adjudged adult or juvenile offender, as long as the person meets certain conditions of behavior.

Probation Conditions

Those sentenced to probation must agree to abide by court-mandated conditions of probation. Such conditions are of two types: general and specific. General conditions apply to all probationers in a given jurisdiction and usually include requirements that the probationer "obey all laws," "maintain employment," "remain within the jurisdiction of the court," "possess no firearm," "allow the probation officer to visit at home or at work," and so forth. Many probationers are also required to pay a fine to the court, usually in a series of installments. Monthly payments are designed to reimburse victims for damages and to pay lawyer's fees and others costs of court.

Special conditions may be mandated by a judge who feels that the probationary client is in need of particular guidance or control. A number of special conditions are routinely imposed upon sizable subcategories of probationers. Special conditions may be tailored specifically to individual probationers. Individualized conditions may prohibit a person from associating with named others (a co-defendant, for example), they may require that the probationer be at home during the hours of darkness, or they may demand that a particular treatment program be completed within a set time period.

WHAT IS PAROLE?

Parole is the supervised early release of inmates from correctional confinement. Parolees have already served a part of their sentence in prison, being released upon a determination by a paroling authority (usually called a parole board or parole commission) that they are ready for a safe return to community life. While probation is a sentencing strategy, parole is a correctional strategy whose primary purpose is to return offenders gradually to productive lives. Parole, by making early release possible, can also act as a stimulus of positive behavioral change.

The use of parole in this country began with the Elmira Reformatory in 1876. The indeterminate sentence, upon which the reformatory philosophy depended, was made possible by an innovative New York law following the call of leading correctional innovators. Parole was a much-heralded tool of nineteenth century corrections, whose advocates had been looking for a behavioral incentive to induce reformation among youthful offenders. Parole, through its promise of earned early release, seemed the ideal innovation.

> **Parole:** The status of an offender conditionally released from a prison by discretion of a paroling authority prior to expiration of sentence, required to observe conditions of parole, and placed under the supervision of a parole agency.

At year-end 1990, only 456,797 people were on parole in the United States out of a total correctional population of over 3.7 million adults.[70] A growing reluctance to use parole seems due to the expanding realization that today's correctional routines have been generally ineffective at producing any substantial reformation among many offenders prior to their release back into the community. The abandonment of the rehabilitation goal, combined with a return to determinate sentencing in many jurisdictions, including the federal judicial system, has substantially reduced the amount of time the average correctional client spends on parole. Where parole supervision might have involved a five-year period only a decade ago, modern parole is often quite brief, and may extend for 90 days or less. Similarly, the power of parole boards is declining. The percentage of release decisions made by parole boards fell from 72% of all releases in 1977, to 43% in 1985.[71]

Parole Conditions

In those jurisdictions which retain parole, the conditions of parole remain very similar to the conditions agreed to by probationers. The successful and continued employment of parolees is one of the major concerns of parole boards and their officers. Working offenders can pay fines and penalties. A provision for making restitution payments is often included as a condition of parole, with the names and addresses of recipients clearly specified by the paroling authority.

Special parole conditions may require the parolee to pay a parole supervision fee (often totaling about $15–25) every month, a requirement now being routinely imposed in some jurisdictions. A relatively new innovation, parole supervision fees shift some of the expenses of community corrections to the offender.

THE EXTENT OF PROBATION AND PAROLE

Probation is the most commonly used alternative to imprisonment. Between 60% and 80% of all persons found guilty of crimes are sentenced to some form of probation.[72] Even serious offenders stand about a 1-in-4 chance of receiving a probationary term. A Rand Corporation study[73] of 28 jurisdictions found that 8% of people convicted of homicide were placed on probation, as were 16% of convicted rapists. Thirteen percent of convicted robbers and 25% of burglars were similarly sentenced to probation rather than active prison time.

Over 450,000 people were on parole throughout the United States at the end of 1991. States vary considerably in the use they make of parole, influenced as they are by the legislative requirements of sentencing schemes. For example, in 1990 Alaska, a determinate sentencing state, reported 533 people under supervised parole, and North Dakota only 139, while Texas had a parole population in excess of 91,000, and California officials were busy supervising more than 57,000 persons.[74] The difference in rate of parole usage is even greater. Of the entire population of Texas, approximately 1 out of every 250 people were on parole. In Connecticut only 1 of about 5,000 people in the state were on parole.

Most inmates who are freed from prison are paroled (about 75%) or granted some other form of conditional release (about 5.5%).[75] Discretionary parole refers to release decisions made by a parole board. Mandatory release describes discharge from prison at a time fixed by sentencing statutes. Some states operating under determinate sentencing guidelines require that inmates serve a short period of time, such as 90 days, on reentry parole — a form of mandatory release. Mandatory releases have increased fivefold - from 6% of all releases in 1977 to over 31% today.[76] Mandatory sentencing schemes have changed the face of parole in America, resulting in a dramatic reduction of the average time spent under postprison supervision, while having little impact upon the number of released inmates who experience some form of parole.

Statistics from the National Corrections Reporting Program show that the average time served in prison for individuals who are later paroled is about 17 months.[77] As measured by the program, average time served included jail time credited toward the offender's prison sentence. The study found that time served in confinement was about 45% of the original court-ordered sentence. The more serious the offense, the longer the time served in prison prior to parole. Murderers, for example, served an average of 78 months behind bars; rapists, 44 months; robbers, 30 months; burglars, 17 months; and drug traffickers, 16 months.[78]

Females under parole supervision, although far fewer in number than males, are more likely to be successful than male parolees. Studies have found about 22% of men returned to custody for a parole violation versus 14% of women.[79] However, men released from custody have generally served longer periods in confinement than women for the same types of offenses.[80]

At the beginning of 1990 a total of 2,520,479 adults were reportedly[81] on probation across the nation — making probation the correctional choice for the majority of offenders. As with parole, individual states made greater or lesser use of probation. North Dakota authorities, with the smallest probationary population, supervised only 1,652 people, while Texas and California both reported almost 300,000 persons each on probation. Over the decade 1980–1990, the probation population increased by 126%, while the number of individuals on parole increased by 107%.

PROBATION AND PAROLE: THE LEGAL ENVIRONMENT

Nine Supreme Court decisions provide a legal framework for probation and parole supervision. Among recent cases, that of *Griffin* v. *Wisconsin*[82] (1987) may be the most significant. In *Griffin* the U.S. Supreme Court ruled that probation officers may conduct searches of a probationer's residence without need for either a search warrant or probable cause. According to the Court, "[a] probationer's home, like anyone else's, is protected by the Fourth Amendment's requirement that searches be reasonable." However, "[a] State's operation of a probation system . . . presents 'special needs' beyond normal law enforcement that may justify departures from the usual warrant and probable cause requirements." Probation, the Court concluded, is similar to imprisonment because it is a "form of criminal sanction imposed upon an offender after a determination of guilt."

Other cases focus on the conduct of revocation hearings. Revocation of probation or parole may be requested by the supervising officer if a client has allegedly violated the conditions of community release or has committed a new crime. Revocation hearings may result in an order that a probationer's suspended sentence be made "active" or that a parolee return to prison to complete their sentence in confinement. In a 1935 decision (*Escoe* v. *Zerbst*),[83] which has since been greatly modified, the Supreme Court held that probation "comes as an act of grace to one convicted of a crime" and that the revocation of probation without hearing or notice to the probationer was acceptable practice.

By 1967, however, the case of *Mempa* v. *Rhay*[84] found the Court changing direction as it declared that both notice and a hearing were required, along with the opportunity for representation by counsel before a prison sentence, which had been deferred[85] pending probation, could be imposed. Jerry Mempa had been convicted of riding in a stolen car at age 17 in 1959 and sentenced to prison, but his sentence was deferred and he was placed on probation. A few months later he was accused of burglary. A hearing was held, and Mempa admitted his involvement in the burglary. An active prison sentence was then imposed.

At the hearing Mempa had not been offered the chance to have a lawyer represent him nor was he given the chance to present any evidence or testimony in his own defense. In response to a writ of *habeas corpus* filed by Mempa's attorneys, the Supreme Court ruled that probationers are entitled to the representation of counsel in a revocation hearing.

Two of the most widely cited cases affecting parolees and probationers are *Morrissey* v. *Brewer* (1972)[86] and *Gagnon* v. *Scarpelli* (1973).[87] The Supreme Court decided *Morrissey* in 1972, declaring the need for procedural safeguards in revocation hearings involving *parolees*. The *Morrissey* case began with John J. Morrissey and G. Donald Booher, two Iowa convicts. Morrissey had pled guilty in 1967 to a bad-check charge and was sentenced to not more than seven years in prison. He was paroled a year later, but rearrested within seven months for obtaining credit and buying a car under an assumed name, for failing to inform his parole officer of changes in his address, and for giving false information to the police.　Booher had also been convicted of forgery in 1966, was sentenced to a maximum of ten years, and was paroled in 1968.　In 1969 a report alleging violation of the conditions of parole was filed by Booher's parole officer, claiming that Booher had obtained a driver's license using a fictitious identify, operated a motor vehicle without permission, and had improperly left the jurisdiction of the parole authority. Both Morrissey and Booher had their parole revoked after an administrative review of violation reports written by parole officers.　In ruling for the petitioners, the Court established procedural requirements pertaining to parole revocation proceedings.

After *Morrissey*, revocation proceedings would require　that (1) written notice specifying the alleged violation be given to the parolee; (2) evidence of the violation be disclosed; (3) a neutral and detached body constitute the hearing authority; (4) the parolee should have the chance to appear and offer a defense, including testimony, documents, and witnesses; (5) the parolee has the right to cross-examine witnesses; and (6) a written statement be provided to the parolee at the conclusion of the hearing which includes the decision of the hearing body, the testimony considered, and reasons for revoking parole if such occurs.[88]

In 1973 the Court extended the procedural safeguards of *Morrissey* to *probationers* in *Gagnon* v. *Scarpelli* (1973).　John Gagnon had pled guilty to armed robbery in Wisconsin and was sentenced to 15 years in prison.　His sentence was suspended, and the judge ordered him to serve a 7-year probationary term.　One month later, and only a day after having been transferred to the supervision of the Cook County, Illinois, Adult Probation Department, Gagnon was arrested by police in the course of a burglary.　He was advised of his rights, but confessed to officers that he was in the process of stealing money and property when discovered.　His probation was revoked without a hearing.　Citing its own decision a year earlier in *Morrissey* v. *Brewer*, the Supreme Court ruled that probationers, because they faced a substantial loss of liberty, were entitled to two hearings — the first, a preliminary hearing, to determine whether there is "probable cause to believe that he has committed a violation of his parole" — and the second, "a somewhat more comprehensive hearing prior to the making of the final revocation decision." The Court also ruled that probation revocation hearings were to be held "under the conditions specified in *Morrissey* v. *Brewer*."

A separate question dealt with by the Court centered on the indigent status of petitioner Gagnon.　While being careful to emphasize the narrowness of the particulars in this case, the Court added to the protections granted under *Morrissey* v. *Brewer*, ruling that probationers have the right to a lawyer, even if indigent, provided they claimed that either (1) they had not committed the alleged violation or (2) had substantial mitigating evidence to explain their violation.　In *Gagnon* and later cases,　however, the Court reasserted that probation and parole revocation hearings were not a stage in the criminal prosecution process, but a simple adjunct to it, even though they might result in substantial loss of liberty.　The difference is a crucial one, for it permits hearing boards and judicial review officers to function, at least to some degree, outside of the adversarial context of the trial court and with lessened attention to the rights of the criminally accused guaranteed by the Bill of Rights.

A more recent case, *Greenholtz* v. *Nebraska* (1979),[89] established that parole boards do not have to specify the evidence used in deciding to deny parole.　The *Greenholtz* case focused on a Nebraska statute which required that inmates denied parole be provided with reasons for the denial. The Court held that reasons for parole denial might be provided in the interest of helping inmates prepare themselves for future review, but that to require the disclosure of evidence used in the review hearing would turn the process into an adversarial proceeding.

The 1983 Supreme Court case of *Bearden* v. *Georgia*[90] established that a defendant's probation could not be revoked for failure to pay a fine and make restitution if it could not be shown that the defendant was responsible for the failure. The Court also held that alternative forms of punishment must be considered by the hearing authority and be shown to be inadequate before the defendant can be incarcerated. Bearden had pled guilty to burglary and had been sentenced to three years' probation. One of the conditions of his probation required that he pay a fine of $250 and make restitution payments totaling $500. Bearden successfully made the first two payments, but then lost his job. His probation was revoked and he was imprisoned. The Supreme Court decision stated that "if the State determines a fine or restitution to be the appropriate and adequate penalty for the crime, it may not thereafter imprison a person solely because he lacked the resources to pay it."[91] The Court held that if a defendant lacks the capacity to pay a fine or make restitution, then the hearing authority must consider any viable alternatives to incarceration prior to imposing a term of imprisonment.

In another ruling affecting restitution, *Kelly* v. *Robinson* (1986),[92] the Court held that a restitution order cannot be vacated by a filing of bankruptcy. In the *Kelly* case, a woman convicted of illegally receiving welfare benefits was ordered to make restitution in the amount of $100 per month. Immediately following the sentence the defendant filed for bankruptcy and listed the court-ordered restitution payment as a debt from which she sought relief. The bankruptcy court discharged the debt, and a series of appeals resulted in the U.S. Supreme Court granting *certiorari*, and eventually holding that fines and other financial penalties ordered by criminal courts are not capable of being voided by bankruptcy proceedings.

Incriminating statements made by a probationer to a probation officer may be used as evidence if the probationer did not specifically claim a right against self-incrimination according to *Minnesota* v. *Murphy* (1984).[93] Marshall Murphy was sentenced to three years probation in 1980 on a charge of "false imprisonment" stemming from an alleged attempted sexual attack. One condition of his probation required him to be entirely truthful with his probation officer "in all matters." Some time later Murphy admitted to his probation officer that he had confessed to a rape and murder in conversations with a counselor. He was later convicted of first-degree murder, partially on the basis of the statements made to his probation officer. Upon appeal, Murphy's lawyers claimed that their client should have been advised of his right against self-incrimination during his conversation with the parole officer. Although the Minnesota Supreme Court agreed, the U.S. Supreme Court found for the state, saying that the burden of invoking the Fifth Amendment privilege against self-incrimination in this case lay with the probationer.

An emerging legal issue today surrounds the potential liability of probation officers, and parole boards and their representatives, for the criminal actions of offenders under their supervision, or who they have released. Some courts have held that officers are generally immune from suit because they are performing a judicial function on behalf of the state.[94]

Other courts, however, have indicated that parole board members who did not carefully consider mandated criteria for judging parole eligibility could be liable for injurious actions committed by parolees.[95]   In general, however, most experts agree that parole board members cannot be successfully sued unless release decisions are made in a grossly negligent or wantonly reckless manner.[96]   Discretionary decisions of individual probation and parole officers which result in harm to members of the public, however, may be more actionable under civil law, especially where their decisions were not reviewed by judicial authority.[97]

In a case which is unresolved as of this writing, a 15-year-old Oakland, California, girl brought suit in July 1991 against the California Department of Corrections, the California Parole Board, and Alameda County claiming negligence in the release of a man who raped her when she was 9 years old. The man, released from prison after serving 6 years of a 12-year sentence for the original rape, allegedly kidnapped and attacked the same girl again almost immediately after he was set free. In commenting on the case, the girl's attorney, Melvin Belli, said[98] "It's utterly inexcusable and intolerable in a civilized society that a Department of Corrections could have been so negligent to have let this dangerous man out. Their failure to protect that young girl and notify her or her family of his impending release, after he had violated her before, displays utter incompetence on their part." Parole officials said the family had never made a request to be notified of the offender's release.

THE FEDERAL PROBATION SYSTEM

The Federal Probation System is only a few decades old.[99]   In 1916 the U.S. Supreme Court in the *Killets* case[100] ruled that federal judges did not have the authority to suspend sentences and order probation.   After a vigorous campaign by the National Probation Association, Congress finally passed the National Probation Act in 1925, authorizing the use of probation in federal courts. The bill came just in time to save a burgeoning federal prison system from serious overcrowding. The Mann Act, prohibition legislation, and the growth of organized crime had all led to increased arrests and a dramatic growth of federal probationers in the early years of the system.

Although the 1925 act authorized one probation officer per federal judge, it allocated only $25,000 for officers' salaries. As a consequence, only eight officers were hired to serve 132 judges, and the system came to rely heavily upon voluntary probation officers. Some sources indicate that as many as 40,000 probationers were under the supervision of volunteers at the peak of the system.[101]   By 1930, however, Congress provided adequate funding, and a corps of salaried professionals began to provide probation services to the U.S. courts.

In recent years the work of federal probation officers has been dramatically affected by new rules of federal procedure. Presentence investigations have been especially affected. Revised Rule 32 of the Federal Criminal Rules of Procedure, for example, now mandates that federal probation officers who prepare presentence reports must[102] (1) evaluate the evidence in support of facts, (2) resolve certain disputes between the prosecutor and defense attorney, (3) testify when needed to provide evidence in support of the administrative application of sentencing guidelines, and (4) utilize an addendum to the report which, among other things, demonstrates that the report has been disclosed to the defense attorney, defendant, and government counsel.

Some authors have argued that these new requirements demand previously unprecedented skills from probation officers. Officers must now be capable of drawing objective conclusions based upon the facts they observe, and they must be able to make "independent judgments in the body of the report regarding which sets of facts by various observers the court should rely upon in imposing sentence."[103] They must also be effective witnesses in court during the trial phase of criminal proceedings. While in the past officers have often been called upon to provide testimony during revocation hearings, the informational role now mandated throughout the trial itself is new.

☐ THE MOVE TOWARD INNOVATIVE OPTIONS IN SENTENCING

Significant new options in sentencing have become available to judges in innovative jurisdictions over the past few decades. Impetus toward the widening of sentencing alternatives is being provided by a number of citizen groups and special interest organizations. One organization of special note is the Washington, D.C.—based Sentencing Project. The Sentencing Project was formed in 1986[104] through support from foundation grants.[105] It is dedicated to promoting a greater use of alternatives to incarceration, and provides technical assistance to public defenders, court officials, and other community organizations.

The Sentencing Project and associated groups have contributed to the development of over 100 alternative sentencing service organizations. Most alternative sentencing services work in conjunction with defense attorneys to develop written sentencing plans. Such plans are basically well-considered citizen suggestions as to what appropriate sentencing should entail. Plans are often quite detailed and may include letters of agreement from employers, family members, the defendant, and even victims. Sentencing plans may be used in plea bargaining sessions, or presented to judges following trial and conviction. The basic philosophy behind defense-based alternative sentencing programs is quite simple: where well-planned alternatives to imprisonment can be offered to judges, the likelihood of a prison sentence can be reduced. An early analysis of alternative sentencing plans such as those sponsored by the Sentencing Project show that they are accepted by judges in up to 80% of the cases in which they are recommended and that as many as two-thirds of offenders who receive alternative sentences successfully complete them.[106]

THE NEW OPTIONS

Innovative sentencing alternatives are also called intermediate sanctions. They include shock probation, split sentencing, shock parole, intensive supervision, shock incarceration, and home confinement. Intermediate sanctions have three distinct advantages:[107] (1) they are less expensive to operate on a per offender basis than imprisonment; (2) they are "socially cost-effective," because they keep the offender in the community, thus avoiding both the breakup of the family and the stigmatization which accompanies imprisonment; and (3) they provide flexibility in terms of resources, time of involvement, and place of service. Some of these new options are described in the paragraphs that follow.

Split Sentencing

In jurisdictions where split sentencing is an option, judges may impose a combination of a brief period of imprisonment and probation. Defendants sentenced under split sentencing are often ordered to serve time in a local jail rather than a long-term confinement facility. "Ninety days in jail, together with two years of supervised probation" would be a typical split sentence.

Shock Probation/Shock Parole

Shock probation bears a considerable resemblance to split sentencing. Again, the offender serves a relatively short period of time in custody (usually in a prison rather than jail) and is released on probation by court order. The difference is that shock probation clients must apply for probationary release from confinement, and cannot be certain of the judge's decision. Shock probation is, in effect, a resentencing decision made by the court. Probation is only a statutory possibility, and often little more than a vague hope of the offender as imprisonment begins. If probationary release is ordered, it may well come as a "shock" to the offender who, facing a sudden reprieve, may forswear future criminal involvement. Shock probation was first begun in Ohio in 1965[108] and is used today in about half of the United States.[109]

New Jersey runs a model modern shock probation program which is administered by a specially appointed Screening Board composed of correctional officials and members of the public. The New Jersey program has served as an example to many other states. It has a stringent set of selection criteria which allow only inmates serving sentences for nonviolent crimes to apply to the Screening Board for release.[110] Inmates must have served at least 30 days prior to making application. Those who have served over 60 days are ineligible. Offenders are required to submit a personal plan describing anticipated activities upon release. The plan must include descriptions of the offender's problems, future plans, community resources, and people who can be relied upon to provide assistance. Part of the plan involves a community sponsor with whom the inmate must reside for a fixed period of time (usually a few months) following release. The New Jersey program is especially strict because it does not grant outright release, but rather allows only a 90-day initial period of freedom. If the inmate successfully completes the 90-day period, continued release may be requested.

Shock probation lowers the cost of confinement, maintains community and family ties, and may be an effective rehabilitative tool.[111] Similar to shock probation is shock parole. Whereas shock probation is ordered by judicial authority, shock parole is an administrative decision made by a paroling authority. Parole commissions or their representatives may order an inmate's early release, hoping that brief exposure to prison may have reoriented the offender's life in a positive direction.

Shock Incarceration

Shock incarceration is the newest of the alternative sanctions discussed here. Shock incarceration, designed primarily for young, first offenders, utilizes military-style "boot camp" prison settings to provide a highly regimented program involving strict discipline, physical training, and hard labor. Shock incarceration programs are of short duration, lasting for only 90–180 days. Offenders who successfully complete these programs are generally placed under community supervision. Program "failures" may be moved into the general prison population for longer terms of confinement.

The first shock incarceration program began in Georgia in 1983.[112] Since then, other programs have opened in Alabama, Arkansas, Arizona, Florida, Louisiana, Maryland, Michigan, Mississippi, New Hampshire, New York, Oklahoma, South Carolina, and Texas.[113] New York's program is the largest, with a capacity for 1,602 participants, while Tennessee's program can handle only 42.[114] There are other substantial differences between the states. About half provide for voluntary entry into their shock incarceration programs. A few allow inmates to decide when and whether they want to quit. Although most states allow judges to place offenders in such programs, some delegate that authority to corrections officials. Two, Louisiana and Texas, authorize judges and corrections personnel joint authority in the decision-making process.[115]

The few studies of shock incarceration programs which have been done appear to indicate that the programs are having a rehabilitative effect.[116] Participating offenders tend to report positive feelings about the programs and about their ability to modify their law-violating behavior.[117]

Mixed Sentencing and Community Service

Mixed sentences require that offenders serve weekends in jail while undergoing probation supervision during the week. Other types of mixed sentencing require participation in treatment or community service programs while a person is on probation. Community service programs began in Minnesota in 1972 with the Minnesota Restitution Program,[118] which gave property offenders the opportunity to work and turn over part of their pay as restitution to their victims. Courts throughout the nations quickly adopted the idea and began to build restitution orders into suspended sentence agreements.

Community service is more an adjunct to, rather than a type of, correctional sentence. Community service is compatible with most other forms of innovation in probation and parole, except, perhaps, for home confinement. Even there, however, offenders could be sentenced to community service activities which might be performed in the home or at a job site during the hours they are permitted to be away from their homes. Washing police cars, cleaning school buses, refurbishing public facilities, and assisting in local government offices are typical forms of community service. Some authors have linked the development of community service sentences to the notion that work and service to others are good for the spirit.[119] Community service participants are usually minor criminals, drunk drivers, and youthful offenders.

One problem with community service sentences is that authorities rarely agree on what they are supposed to accomplish. Most people admit that offenders who work in the community are able to reduce the costs of their own supervision. There is little agreement, however, over whether such sentences reduce recidivism, provide a deterrent, or act to rehabilitate offenders.

Intensive Supervision

Intensive probation supervision (IPS) has been described as the "strictest form of probation for adults in the United States."[120]   In 1982 Georgia became one of the first states to   implement intensive probation supervision.   The Georgia program involves a minimum of five face-to-face contacts between the probationer and supervising officer per week, mandatory curfew, required employment, a weekly check of local arrest records, routine and unannounced alcohol and drug testing, automatic notification of arrest via the State Crime Information Network, and 132 hours of community service.[121]   Caseloads of probation officers involved in IPS are much lower than the national average.   Georgia officers work as a team with one probation officer and two surveillance officers supervising around 40 probationers.[122]   IPS is designed to achieve control in a community setting over offenders who would otherwise have gone to prison.

North Carolina's Intensive Supervision Program follows the model of the Georgia program and adds a mandatory "prison awareness visit" within the first three months of supervision.   North Carolina selects candidates for the Intensive Supervision Program on the basis of six factors: (1) the level of risk the offender is deemed to represent to the community; (2) assessment of the candidate's potential to respond to the program; (3) existing community attitudes towards the offender; (4) the nature and extent of known substance abuse; (5) the presence or absence of favorable community conditions, such as positive family ties, the possibility of continuing meaningful employment, constructive leisure-time activities, and   adequate residence; and (6) the availability of community resources relevant to the needs of the case (such as drug treatment services, mental health programs, vocational training facilities, and volunteer services).[123]

Some states have extended intensive supervision to parolees, allowing the early release of persons who would otherwise serve lengthy prison terms.   The North Carolina program, for example, contained 1,522 probationers and 260 parolees under intensive supervision during 1987 and reported a failure (revocation) rate of 15.2%.[124]

Home Confinement

Home confinement is also referred to as house arrest.   It has been defined as "a sentence imposed by the court in which offenders are legally ordered to remain confined in their own residences."[125]   They may leave only for medical emergencies, employment, and to purchase household essentials.   House arrest has been cited as offering a valuable alternative to prison for offenders with special needs. Pregnant women, geriatric convicts, offenders with special handicaps, seriously or terminally ill offenders, and the mentally retarded might all be better supervised through home confinement than traditional incarceration.

Florida's Community Control Program, authorized by the state's Correctional Reform Act of 1983, is the most ambitious home confinement program in the country.[126] On any given day in Florida as many as 5,000 offenders are restricted to their homes and supervised by community control officers who visit unannounced. Candidates for the program are required to agree to specific conditions, including (1) restitution, (2) family support payments, and (3) supervisory fees (around $50 per month).   They are also obligated to fill out daily logs about their activities.

Community control officers are required to maintain a minimum of 20 contacts per month with each offender. Additional discussions are held with neighbors, spouses, friends, landlords, employers, and others in order to allow the earliest possible detection of program violations or renewed criminality.

Florida's most serious home confinement offenders are monitored via a computerized system of electronic bracelets (or anklets). Random telephone calls require the offender to insert a computer chip worn in a band into a specially installed modem in the home, verifying the subject's presence. More modern units make it possible to record the time a supervised person entered or left the home, whether the phone line or equipment had been tampered with, and to send or receive messages.[127]   Electronic monitoring of offenders has undergone dramatic growth both in Florida and across the nation. A survey by the National Institute of Justice[128] showed only 826 offenders being monitored electronically in mid-1987, while by 1989 the number had grown to around 6,500. By the start of 1990, industry sources reported having shipped over 15,000 monitoring devices.

House arrest is viewed by many states as a cost-effective response to the rising expense of imprisonment. Estimates show that traditional home confinement programs cost about $1,500 to $7,000 per offender per year, while electronic monitoring increases the costs by at least $1,000.[129]   Advocates of house arrest argue that it is also socially cost effective,[130] as it provides no opportunity for the kinds of negative socialization which occurs in prison. Opponents have pointed out that house arrest may endanger the public, that it may be illegal[131] and that it may be little or no punishment. In 1988 John Zaccaro, Jr., the son of former vice presidential candidate Geraldine Ferraro, was sentenced to four months of house arrest for selling cocaine. His $1,500-a-month luxury apartment, with maid service, cable TV, and many other expensive amenities, was in a building designed for expense-account businesspeople on short assignments to the Burlington, Vermont, area. Zaccaro's prosecutor observed, "This guy is a drug felon and he's living in conditions that 99.9% of the people of Vermont couldn't afford."[132]

THE FUTURE OF PROBATION AND PAROLE

Parole has been widely criticized in recent years. Citizen groups claim that it unfairly reduces prison sentences imposed on serious offenders. Officials say that parole gives a false impression of the realities of criminal punishment. Academicians allege that parole programs can provide no assurance against continued criminal victimization. Media attacks upon parole have centered on recidivism and have highlighted the so-called "revolving door" of prisons as representative of the failure of parole.

In the late 1980s the case of Larry Singleton came to represent all that is wrong with parole. Singleton was convicted of raping 15-year-old Mary Vincent, then hacking off her arms, and leaving her for dead on a hillside.[133] When an apparently unrepentant[134] Singleton was paroled after eight years in prison, public outcry was tremendous. Communities banded together to deny him residence, and he had to be paroled to the grounds of San Quentin prison.

Official attacks upon parole have come from some powerful corners. Senator Edward Kennedy has called for the abolition of parole, as did former Attorney General

Griffin Bell and former U.S. Bureau of Prisons Director Norman Carlson.[135] Prisoners have also challenged the fairness of parole, saying it is sometimes arbitrarily granted and creates an undue amount of uncertainly and frustration in the lives of inmates. Parolees have complained about the unpredictable nature of the parole experience, citing their powerlessness in the parole contract. Against the pressure of official attacks and cases like that of Singleton, parole advocates struggle to clarify and communicate their own value in the correctional process.

Probation, although it has generally fared better than parole, is not without its critics. The primary purpose of probation has always been rehabilitation. Probation is a powerful rehabilitative tool because, at least in theory, it allows the resources of a community to be brought to bear in a focused rehabilitative effort. Unfortunately for advocates of probation, however, the rehabilitative ideal holds far less significance today than it has in the past. The contemporary demand for "just desserts" has eclipsed the rehabilitative ideal and appears to have reduced the tolerance society as a whole feels for even relatively minor offenders. Added to that is the fact that the image of probation has not benefited from its all-too-frequent and inappropriate use with repeat or relatively serious offenders. Probation advocates themselves have been forced to admit that it is not a very powerful deterrent because it is far less punishing than a term of imprisonment.

Other arguments in support of probation have been weakened because some of the positive contributions probation had to offer are now being made available from other sources. Victims' compensation programs, for example, have taken the place of direct restitution payments to victims by probationers.

Probation will probably always remain a viable sentencing option if only because there will always be minor offenders for whom imprisonment is hard to justify. The return to determinate sentencing, however, cited earlier in this book is a clear indication that parole, as it has existed for the last half century, is in for serious restructuring and may not survive in a recognizable form. The overcrowded conditions of our nation's prisons, however, will probably work to continue at least a limited use of parole. Even states which have adopted determinate sentencing statutes still depend upon a brief parole experience to successfully meet the basic needs faced by ex-offenders of finding housing, employment, and social services.

The movement toward determinate sentencing, generally seen as the deathknell of parole programs, may in fact eliminate two of the most often-cited shortcoming of parole, while allowing at least limited forms of parole to continue. Where determinate sentencing laws coexist with parole programs, release on parole is no longer the result of potentially arbitrary decisions made by parole boards staffed with nonexpert political appointees. Second, because determinate sentencing laws specify parole release dates and the precise period of parole supervision which an inmate can anticipate serving, they eliminate the unpredictability complained of by parolees themselves.

☐ DEATH: THE ULTIMATE SANCTION

Capital punishment has a long and gruesome history. As times changed so did accepted methods of execution. Under the Davidic monarchy, biblical Israel institutionalized the practice of stoning convicts to death.[136]   The entire community where the crime occurred had the opportunity to participate in dispatching the offender. As an apparent aid to deterrence, the convict's deceased body could be impaled on a post at the gates of the city, or otherwise exposed to the elements for a period of time.[137]

Athenian society, around 200 B.C., was progressive by the standards of its day. The ancient Greeks restricted the use of capital punishment and limited the suffering of the condemned through the use of poison derived from the hemlock tree. Socrates, the famous Greek orator, accused of being a political subversive, died this way.

The Romans were far less sensitive. Beheading was the form capital punishment most often took in ancient Rome, although the law provided that arsonists should be burned and false witnesses thrown from a high rock.[138] Suspected witches were clubbed to death, and slaves were ignominiously strangled. Even more brutal sanctions, including drawing and quartering and throwing to the lions, were used on rabble rousers, Christians, and other social outcasts.

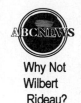

Why Not Wilbert Rideau?

After the fall of the Roman Empire Europe was plunged into the Dark Ages, a period of superstition marked by widespread illiteracy and political turmoil. The Dark Ages lasted from 426 A.D. until the early thirteenth century. During the Dark Ages, executions were institutionalized through the use of ordeals designed to both judge and punish. Suspects were submerged in cold water, dumped in boiling oil, crushed under huge stones, forced to do battle with professional soldiers, or thrown into bonfires. Theological arguments prevalent at the time held that innocents, protected by God and heavenly forces, would emerge from any ordeal unscathed, while guilty parties would perish. Trial by ordeal was eliminated through a decree of the Fourth Lateran Council of 1215, under the direction of Pope Innocent III, after later evidence proved that many who died in ordeals could not have committed the crimes of which they were accused.[139]

Following the Fourth Lateran Council, trials, much as we know them today, became the basis for judging guilt or innocence. The death penalty remained in widespread use. As recently as a century and a half ago, 160 crimes were punishable in England by death.[140] The young received no special privilege. In 1801 a child of 13 was hanged at Tyburn, England, for stealing a spoon.[141]

Sophisticated techniques of execution were in use by the nineteenth century. One engine of death was the guillotine, invented in France around the time of the French Revolution. The guillotine was described by its creator, Dr. Joseph-Ignace Guillotin, as "a cool breath on the back of the neck"[142] and found widespread use in eliminating opponents of the revolution.

In America hanging became the preferred mode of execution. It was especially popular on the frontier, since it required little by way of special materials and was a relatively efficient means of dispatch. By the early 1900s electrocution had replaced hanging as the preferred form of capital punishment in America. The appeal of electrocution was that it stopped the heart without visible signs of gross bodily trauma.

EXECUTIONS: THE GRIM FACTS

The twentieth century has seen a constant decline in the number of persons legally executed in the United States. Accurate statistics on the number of persons legally executed began to be collected around 1930. Between 1930 and 1967, when the U.S. Supreme Court ordered a stay of pending executions, nearly 3,800 persons were put to death. The years 1935 and 1936 were peak years, with nearly 200 legal killings each year. Executions declined substantially every year thereafter. Between 1967 and 1977 a de facto moratorium existed, with no executions carried out in any U.S. jurisdiction. From 1977 through to the end of 1991, a total of 157 executions were carried out by 16 states.

Today, 36 of the 50 states and the federal government retain capital punishment laws. All 36 permit execution for first-degree murder; while treason, kidnapping, the murder of a police or correctional officer, and murder while under a life sentence are punishable by death in selected jurisdictions.[143] However, of the 2,482 persons under sentence of death throughout the United States at year-end 1991,[144] all but 1 had been convicted of murder. The 1 exception involved a conviction for the rape of a child. Ninety-nine percent of death row inmates were male; 57% were white. Two-thirds had other felony convictions, and more than 10% had prior homicide convictions. A third of those awaiting execution were under sentence for another crime when the capital offense was committed.[145]

Copyright 1991 by USA Today. Reprinted with permission.
In an effort to acquire greater freedom of information, some television stations have gone to court, seeking to televise executions.

Methods of imposing death vary by state. The majority of death penalty states authorize execution through lethal injection. Electrocution is the second most common means of dispatch, while hanging, the gas chamber, and firing squads have survived, at least as options available to the condemned, in a few states.

OPPOSITION TO DEATH

Considerable debate surrounds the contemporary use of capital punishment. One serious difficulty centers on the fact that automatic review of all death sentences by appellate courts and constant legal maneuvering by defense counsel, often lead to a dramatic delay between the time sentence is passed and the time it is carried out. Such lengthy delays, compounded with uncertainty over whether a sentence will *ever* be finally imposed, directly contravene the generally accepted notion that punishment should be swift and certain.

Delays in the imposition of capital sanctions have been the source of much anguish for condemned prisoners as well as for victims and the family members of both. In a 1989 speech before the American Bar Association, Chief Justice William H. Rehnquist called for reforms of the current federal *habeas corpus* system, which allows condemned prisoners constant opportunities for appeal. In the words of Rehnquist, "The capital defendant does not need to prevail on the merits in order to accomplish his purpose; he wins temporary victories by postponing a final adjudication."[146]

The first recorded attempt to abolish the death penalty in the United States occurred at the home of Benjamin Franklin in 1787.[147] At a meeting on March 9 of that year, Dr. Benjamin Rush, a signer of the Declaration of Independence and leading medical pioneer, read a paper against capital punishment to a small but influential audience. Although his immediate efforts came to naught, his arguments laid the groundwork for many debates which followed. Michigan, widely regarded as the first abolitionist state, joined the Union in 1847 without a death penalty.   A number of other states, including New York, Massachusetts, West Virginia, Wisconsin, Minnesota, Alaska, and Hawaii have since spurned death as a possible sanction for criminal acts.   Many Western European countries have also rejected the death penalty. It remains, however, a viable sentencing option in 36 of the states and all federal jurisdictions. As a consequence, arguments continue to rage over its value.

Today, four main abolitionist rationales are heard. They are: (1) the death penalty can and has been inflicted on innocent people; (2) evidence has shown that the death penalty is not an effective deterrent; (3) the imposition of the death penalty is, by the nature of our legal system, completely arbitrary and even discriminatory; and (4) human life is sacred, and killing at the hands of the state is not a righteous act, but rather one which is on the same moral level as the crimes committed by the condemned.

The first three abolitionist claims are pragmatic; that is, they are subject to at least limited measurability and therefore some degree of verifiability. The last claim is primarily philosophical and therefore not amenable to scientific investigation.

While some evidence does exist that a few innocent people have been executed, most research by far has centered on examining the deterrent effect of the death penalty. During the 1970s and 1980s[148] the deterrent effect of the death penalty became a favorite subject for debate in academic circles. Studies[149] of states which had eliminated the death penalty failed to show any increase in homicide rates. Similar studies[150] of neighboring states, in which jurisdictions retaining capital punishment were compared with those which had abandoned it, also failed to demonstrate any significant differences. Although death penalty advocates remain numerous, few any longer argue for the penalty based on its deterrent effects. Deterrent studies continue, however.   In 1988, for example, a comprehensive review[151] of capital punishment in Texas, which correlated executions since 1930 with homicide rates, failed again to find any support for the use of death as a deterrent. The study was especially significant because Texas has been very active in the capital punishment arena, executing 317 persons between 1930 and 1986.[152]

The abolitionist claim that the death penalty is discriminatory is harder to investigate. While there may be past evidence that blacks and other minorities in the United States have been disproportionately sentenced to death,[153] the present evidence is not so clear. At first glance, disproportionality seems apparent: 65 of the 143 prisoners executed between January 1977 and December 1990 were black or Hispanic, and around 80% of those had been convicted of killing whites. For an accurate appraisal to be made, however, any claims of disproportionality must go beyond simple comparisons with racial representation in the larger population and must somehow measure both frequency and seriousness of capital crimes between and within racial groups. Following that line of reasoning, the Supreme

Court, in the 1987 case of *McCleskey* v. *Kemp*[154] held that a simple showing of racial discrepancies in the application of the death penalty do not constitute a Constitutional violation.

JUSTIFICATIONS FOR DEATH

Justifications for the death penalty are collectively referred to as the retentionist position. Retentionist arguments are three in number. They are (1) revenge, (2) protection, and (3) just desserts. Those who justify capital punishment as revenge, attempt to appeal to the visceral feeling that survivors, victims, and the state are entitled to "closure." Only after execution of the criminal perpetrator, they say, can the psychological and social wounds engendered by the offense begin to heal.

The just desserts argument is slightly different. It makes the simple and straightforward claim that some people deserve to die for what they have done. Death is justly deserved; anything less cannot suffice as a sanction for the most heinous crimes. As Justice Potter Stewart once wrote: "the decision that capital punishment may be the appropriate sanction in extreme cases is an expression of the community's belief that certain crimes are themselves so grievous an affront to humanity that the only adequate response may be the penalty of death."[155]

The third retentionist claim, that of protection, asserts that offenders, once executed, can commit no further crimes. Clearly the least emotional of the retentionist claims, the protectionist argument may also be the weakest, since societal interests in protection can also be met in other ways such as incarceration. In addition, various studies have shown that there is little likelihood of repeat offenses among people convicted of murder and later released.[156] One reason for such observations, however, may be that murderers generally serve lengthy prison sentences prior to release and may have lost whatever youthful propensity for criminality they previously possessed.

THE FUTURE OF THE DEATH PENALTY

Because of the nature of the positions both advocate, there is little common ground even for discussion between retentionists and abolitionists. Foes of the death penalty hope that its demonstrated lack of deterrent capacity will convince others that capital punishment should be abandoned. Their approach, based as it is upon statistical evidence, appears on the surface to be quite rational. However, it is doubtful that many capital punishments opponents could be persuaded to support the death penalty even if statistics showed it to be a deterrent. Likewise, the tactics of death penalty supporters are equally instinctive. Retentionists could probably not be swayed by statistical studies of deterrence, no matter what they show, since their support is bound up with emotional calls for retribution.

The future of the death penalty rests primarily on legislative authority. Short of renewed Supreme Court intervention, the future of capital punishment may depend more upon popular opinion than it does on arguments pro or con. Elected legislators, because the careers of their members lie in the hands of their constituency, are likely to follow the public mandate. Hence, it may be that studies of public attitudes toward the death penalty may have the greatest utility in predicting the sanction's future.

National opinion polls conducted by the Gallup and Harris organizations detail massive support for capital punishment as far back as 1936, but show a gradual decline in backing until 1966, when a resurgence in support began.[157] The proportion of the American public which today endorses the death penalty in national polls is at an all-time high since record keeping began, surpassing even the support of 1936.[158] When asked if they would still favor the death penalty if evidence showed conclusively that it did not deter criminals, a slim majority of Americans still say "yes."[159]

Demographic differences account for a considerable degree of variation in public opinion polls. Robert Bohm, for example, analyzing differences among respondents in nearly two dozen polls reports that:[160] (1) "[i]n all 21 polls, the percentage of whites who favor the death penalty is greater than the percentage of blacks, while the percentage of blacks opposed and undecided is greater than the percentage of whites. . . ," (2) "[i]n every year for which there are data, people in the top income or socioeconomic category have been more likely to support the death penalty and less likely to oppose it than people in the bottom category . . . ," (3) "[i]n all 21 polls, the percentage of males who favor the death penalty exceeds the percentage of females, and the percentage of females opposed to the death penalty exceeds the percentage of males . . . ," (4) " . . . Democrats have shown the greatest opposition and the least support for the death penalty; Independents are less opposed and more supportive; and Republicans are least opposed and most supportive . . ," and (3) " . . . the South, surprisingly, has been the region least likely to support and most likely to oppose the death penalty . . ." Other variables, such as age, religion, occupation, and city size, show less clear-cut relationships to self-avowed attitudes toward the death penalty.[161]

Some contemporary studies,[162] however, have purported to show that support for capital punishment may be a relatively abstract form of endorsement. According to Frank P. Williams and Dennis Longmire, "A majority of citizens assert support for the general concept of the death penalty but their willingness to advocate execution as an acceptable sanction decreases as they are asked about its use in specific instances."[163] Even so, few legislators are apt to examine closely the results of polls which show such strong public leanings.

Changes in public opinion could conceivably come quickly, however. Citing the First Amendment to the U.S Constitution, California television station KQED filed suit in 1990 in U.S. District Court in San Francisco, asking that it be allowed to provide broadcast coverage of executions. The lawsuit claimed that the current state policy, of barring cameras at executions, "impedes effective reporting of executions which are events of major public and political significance."[164] Although the station's claims were denied by the court in a 1991 opinion, the station is considering an appeal.

THE COURTS AND DEATH

The U.S. Supreme Court has served as a constant sounding board for issues surrounding the death penalty. One of the Court's earliest cases in this area was *Wilkerson* v. *Utah* (1878),[165] which questioned shooting as a method of execution and raised Eighth Amendment claims that firing squads constituted a form of cruel and unusual punishment. The Court disagreed, however, contrasting the relatively civilized nature of firing squads with the various forms of torture often associated with capital punishment around the time the Bill of Rights was written.

In similar fashion, electrocution was supported as a permissible form of execution in *In re Kemmler* (1890).[166]   In *Kemmler* the Court defined cruel and unusual methods of execution as follows: "Punishments are cruel when they involve torture or a lingering death; but the punishment of death is not cruel, within the meaning of that word as used in the Constitution. It implies there something inhuman and barbarous, something more than the mere extinguishing of life."[167]   Almost 60 years later, the Court ruled that a second attempt at the electrocution of a convicted person did not violate the Eighth Amendment.[168] The Court reasoned that the initial failure was the consequence of accident or unforeseen circumstances, and not the result of an effort on the part of executioners to be intentionally cruel.

It was not until 1972, however, in the landmark case of *Furman* v. *Georgia*[169] that the Court recognized "evolving standards of decency"[170] which might necessitate a reconsideration of eighth amendment guarantees. In a 5 to 4 ruling the *Furman* decision invalidated Georgia's death penalty statute on the basis that it allowed a jury's unguided discretion in the imposition of a capital sentence. The majority of justices concluded that the Georgia statute, which permitted a jury to decide simultaneously issues of guilt or innocence while it weighed sentencing options, allowed for an arbitrary and capricious application of the death penalty.

Many other states, with statutes similar to Georgia's were affected by the *Furman* ruling, but moved quickly to modify their procedures. What evolved was a two-step procedure to be used in capital cases. During the first, or trial phase, the guilt or innocence of the defendant was decided. If conviction resulted, then a second, or sentencing, stage was initiated during which separate arguments were made as to the appropriateness of death or other sanctions.

The two-step trial procedure was specifically approved by the Court in *Gregg* v. *Georgia* (1976).[171]   In *Gregg* the Court upheld the two-stage procedural requirements of Georgia's new capital punishment law as necessary for ensuring the separation of the highly personal information needed in a sentencing decision, from the kinds of information reasonably permissible in a jury trial where issues of guilt or innocence alone are being decided.   In the opinion written for the majority, the Court for the first time recognized the significance of public opinion in deciding upon the legitimacy of questionable sanctions.[172] Its opinion cited the strong showing of public support for the death penalty following *Furman* to mean that death was still a socially and culturally acceptable penalty.

Post-*Gregg* decisions set limits upon the use of death as a penalty for all but the most severe crimes. In 1977, in the case of *Coker* v. *Georgia*,[173]   the Court struck down a Georgia law imposing the death penalty for the rape of an adult woman. The Court concluded that capital punishment under such circumstances would be "grossly disproportionate" to the crime. Somewhat later, in *Woodson* v. *North Carolina*[174] a law requiring mandatory application of the death penalty for specific crimes was overturned.

In two 1990 rulings, *Blystone* v. *Pennsylvania* and *Boyde* v. *California*, the Court upheld state statutes which had been interpreted to dictate that death penalties must be imposed where juries find a lack of mitigating factors capable of offsetting obvious aggravating circumstances. Similarly, in the 1990 case of R. Gene Simmons, an Arkansas mass murderer convicted of killing 16 relatives during a 1987 shooting rampage, the Court granted inmates under sentence of death the right to waive appeals. Prior to the *Simmons* case, any interested party could file a brief on behalf of condemned persons — with or without their consent.

Today, an average of 7 years and 11 months[175] passes between the time a sentence of death is imposed and it is carried out. In a strong move to reduce delays in the conduct of executions, the U.S. Supreme Court, in the case of *McCleskey* v. *Zandt* (1991),[176] limited the numbers of appeals a condemned person may lodge with the courts. Saying that repeated filings for the sole purpose of delay promotes "disrespect for the finality of convictions," and "disparages the entire criminal justice system," the Court established a two-pronged criteria for future appeals. According to *McCleskey*, in any petition, beyond the first, filed with a federal court, capital defendants must demonstrate (1) good cause why the claim now being made was not included in the first filing and (2) how the absence of that claim may have harmed the petitioner's ability to mount an effective defense. Two months later, the Court reinforced *McCleskey*, when it ruled, in *Coleman* v. *Thompson*,[177] that state prisoners could not cite "procedural default," such as a defense attorney's failure to meet a state's filing deadline for appeals, as the basis for an appeal to federal court.

Observers noted that the Court's spate of decisions limiting the opportunity of convicted offenders to appeal, would swiftly and dramatically increase the rate of executions across the nation. Shortly thereafter, Florida death row inmate Bobby Marion Francis became the first person put to death in the post-*McCleskey* period. Francis had been convicted of the 1975 torture death of a drug informant, Titus R. Walters. In an attempt to kill Walters, Francis injected him with Drano and battery acid, then shot him twice in the head. Still conscious, Walters was finally shot through the heart. Francis died in Florida's electric chair on June 25, 1991 at 7:07 A.M. — 16 years after torturing and killing Walters.

☐ SUMMARY

The just-desserts model, with its emphasis on retribution and revenge, is today the ascendant sentencing philosophy in the United States. Many citizens, however, still expect sentencing practices to provide for the general goals of deterrence, rehabilitation, incapacitation, and restitution. This ambivalence toward the purpose of sentencing reflects a more basic cultural uncertainty regarding the root causes of crime and the goals of the criminal justice system.

Determinate sentencing is the child of the just-desserts philosophy. The determinate sentencing model, while apparently associated with a reduction in biased and inequitable sentencing practices, may not be the panacea it once seemed. Inequitable practices under the indeterminate model may never have been as widespread as opponents of the model claimed them to be. Worse still, the determinate sentencing model may not reduce sentencing discretion, but simply move it out of the hands of judges and into the ever-widening sphere of plea bargaining. Doubly unfortunate, determinate sentencing, by its de-emphasis of parole, weakens incentives among the correctional population for positive change, and tends to swell prison populations until they're overflowing.

DISCUSSION QUESTIONS

1. Outline the various sentencing rationales discussed in this chapter. Which of these rationales do you find most acceptable as the goal of sentencing? How might the acceptability of the choice you make vary with type of offense? Can you envision any other circumstances which might make your choice less acceptable?

2. In your opinion, is the return to "just desserts" consistent with the determinate sentencing model?

3. Trace the differences between determinate and indeterminate sentencing. Which model holds the best long-term promise for crime reduction? Why?

4. What is a victim impact statement? Do you think victim impact statements should be admissible at the sentencing stage of criminal trials? If so, what material should they contain? What material should not be permitted in such reports? How could the information in victim impact statements be best verified?

5. Probation is a sentence served while under supervision in the community. Do you believe that a person who commits a crime should be allowed to serve all or part of their sentence in the community? If so, what conditions would you impose on the offender?

6. Do you think home confinement is a good idea? What do you think is the future of home confinement? In your opinion, does it discriminate against certain kinds of offenders? How might it be improved?

NOTES

1. For a good survey of early practices see Herbert A. Johnson, *History of Criminal Justice* (Cincinnati, OH: Anderson, 1988).

2. The requirement for punishment is supported by the belief that social order (and the laws which represent it) could not exist for long if transgressions went unsanctioned.

3. For a thorough review of the literature on deterrence, see Raymond Paternoster, "The Deterrent Effect of the Perceived Certainty and Severity of Punishment: A Review of the Evidence and Issues," *Justice Quarterly,* Volume 4, no. 2 (June 1987), pp. 174–217.

4. Hugo Adam Bedau, "Retributivism and the Theory of Punishment," *Journal of Philosophy*, Vol. 75 (November 1978), pp. 601-620.

5. H. L. A. Hart, *Punishment and Responsibility: Essays in the Philosophy of Law* (Oxford: Clarendon Press, 1968).

6. Paul Gendreau and Robert R. Ross, "Revivification of Rehabilitation: Evidence from the 1980s," *Justice*

Quarterly Vol. 4, no. 3 (September 1987), pp. 349–408.

7. 18 U.S.C. 3563 (a) (2).

8. See Joan Petersilia, *Expanding Options for Criminal Sentencing* (Santa Monica, CA: The Rand Corporation, 1987).

9. Frederick J. Gaudet, "Individual Differences in the Sentencing Tendencies of Judges," No. 230, *Archives of Psychology (New York: Columbia University Press, 1933).*

10. Patridge and Eldridge, *The Second Circuit Sentencing Study: A Report to the Judges of the Second Circuit,* 1974.

11. Michael H. Tonry and Norval Morris, *Sentencing Reform in America,* in Gordon Hawkins and Franklin E. Zimring, eds., *The Pursuit of Criminal Justice* (Chicago: University of Chicago Press, 1984), pp. 249–266.

12. For a thorough consideration of alleged disparities, see G. Kleck, "Racial Discrimination in Criminal Sentencing: A Critical Evaluation of the Evidence with Additional Evidence on the Death Penalty," *American Sociological Review,* No. 46 (1981), pp. 783–805, and G. Kleck, "Life Support for Ailing Hypotheses: Modes of Summarizing the Evidence for Racial Discrimination in Sentencing," *Law and Human Behavior,* No. 9 (1985), pp. 271–285.

13. Bureau of Justice Statistics, *Report to the Nation on Crime and Justice,* 2nd ed. (Washington, D.C.: U.S. Department of Justice, 1988), p. 91.

14. For an early statement of this problem, see Franklin E. Zimring, "Making the Punishment Fit the Crime: A Consumer's Guide to Sentencing Reform," in Gordon Hawkins and Franklin Zimring, eds., *The Pursuit of Criminal Justice* (Chicago: University of Chicago Press, 1984), pp. 267–275.

15. Albert W. Alschuler, "Sentencing Reform and Prosecutorial Power: A Critique of Recent Proposals for 'Fixed' and 'Presumptive' Sentencing," in Sheldon L. Messinger and Egon Bittner, *Criminology Review Yearbook,* Volume 1 (Beverly Hills, CA: Sage, 1979), pp. 416–445.

16. Ibid., p. 422.

17. Christopher T. Link and Neal Shover, "The Origins of Criminal Sentencing Reforms," *Justice Quarterly,* Vol. 3, no. 3 (September 1986), pp. 329–342.

18. For a good discussion of such issues see Hans Toch, "Rewarding Convicted Offenders," *Federal Probation,* June 1988, pp. 42–48.

19. As discussed later in this chapter, federal sentencing guidelines did not become effective until 1987 and still had to meet many court challenges.

20. U.S. Sentencing Commission, *Federal Sentencing Guidelines Manual,* (Washington, D.C.: U.S. Government Printing Office, 1987), p. 2.

21. A maximum of 54 days per year of good time credit can still be earned.

22. Litigants claimed that Congress had violated constitutional guarantees of a separation of powers by including three judges on the Commission.

23. "Supreme Court Upholds Federal Sentencing Reforms," *Criminal Justice Newsletter*, Vol. 20, no. 3 (February 1, 1989), p. 1.

24. *Mistretta* v. *U.S.*, No. 87-7028, 1989.

25. *Guidelines*, p. 10.

26. Ibid., p. 207.

27. Ibid., p. 8.

28. "Sentencing Commission Chairman Wilkins Answers Questions on the Guidelines," *NIJ Research in Action* (September 1987), p. 7.

29. *Guidelines*, p. 8.

30. Michael K. Block and William M. Rhodes, *The Impact of the Federal Sentencing Guidelines*, an NIJ Research in Action Report (Washington, D.C.: National Institute of Justice, 1987), p. 1.

31. Ibid.

32. These figures represent a "high-growth scenario." Low growth scenarios place the 1997 figure at 92,000 and the 2002 population at 105,000 inmates (see Block and Rhodes, *The Impact of the Federal Sentencing Guidelines*) — still a very substantial increase.

33. "Sentencing Rules," *U.S.A. Today*, June 28, 1989, p. 3a.

34. Ibid.

35. Andrew Klein, *Alternative Sentencing: A Practitioner's Guide* (Cincinnati, OH: Anderson, 1988).

36. Ibid., p. 23.

37. Ibid.

38. National Criminal Justice Information and Statistics Service, *Privacy and Security Planning Instructions* (Washington, D.C.: U.S. Government Printing Office, 1976).

39. U.S. Department of Justice, *State Criminal Records Repositories*, a BJS Technical Report, 1985.

40. Privacy Act of 1974, 5, U.S.C.A. section 522a, 88 Statute 1897, Public Law 93-579 (December 31, 1974).

41. Freedom of Information Act, 5 U.S.C. 522 and amendments. The status of Presentence Investigative Reports has not yet been clarified under this Act to the satisfaction of all legal scholars, although generally state and federal courts are thought to be exempt from the provisions of the Act.

42. Alexander B. Smith and Louis Berlin, *Introduction to Probation and Parole* (St. Paul, MN: West, 1976), p. 75.

43. John Rosecrance, "Maintaining the Myth of Individualized Justice: Probation Presentence Reports,"

Justice Quarterly Vol. 5, no. 2 (June 1988), pp. 237–256.

44. Ibid.

45. President's Task Force on Victims of Crime, *Final Report* (Washington, D.C.: U.S. Government Printing Office, 1982).

46. Public Law 97-291.

47. Proposition 8, *California's Victims' Bill of Rights.*

48. "Crazed Fan's Deadly 'Mission' Threat Terrified Actress," *The Fayetteville Times*, June 8, 1989, p. 11D.

49. Ibid.

50. Edwin Villmoare and Virginia V. Neto, "Victim Appearances at Sentencing Under California's Victim's Bill of Rights," NIJ *Research in Brief*, August 1987.

51. *Booth* v. *Maryland*, 107 S. Ct. 2529 (1987).

52. *Payne* v. *Tennessee*, No. 90-5721 (1991).

53. "Supreme Court Closes Term with Major Criminal Justice Rulings," *Criminal Justice Newsletter*, (July 1, 1991), Vol. 22, no. 13, p. 2.

54. See, "What Say Should Victims Have?" *Time*, May 27, 1991, p. 61.

55. Bureau of Justice Statistics (BJS), *Report to the Nation on Crime and Justice*, 2nd ed. (Washington, D.C., 1988: U.S. Government Printing Office), p. 90.

56. Sally T. Hillsman, Barry Mahoney, George F. Cole, and Bernard Auchter, "Fines as Criminal Sanctions," NIJ *Research in Brief*, September 1987, p. 1.

57. Ibid., p. 2.

58. Sally T. Hillsman, Joyce L. Sichel, and Barry Mahoney, *Fines in Sentencing* (New York: Vera Institute of Justice, 1983).

59. Ibid., p. 2.

60. Hillsman, Mahoney, Cole, and Auchter, "Fines as Criminal Sanctions," p. 4.

61. Ibid.

62. The President's Commission on Law Enforcement and Administration of Justice, *The Challenge of Crime in a Free Society* (Washington, D.C.: U.S. Government Printing Office, 1967), p. 166.

63. Alexander B. Smith and Louis Berlin, *Introduction to Probation and Parole* (St. Paul, MN: West, 1976), p. 75.

64. *John Augustus, First Probation Officer* (Montclair, NJ: Patterson-Smith, 1972).

65. Smith and Berlin, *Introduction to Probation and Parole*, p. 77.

66. Ibid., p. 80.

67. George G. Killinger, Hazel B. Kerper, and Paul F. Cromwell, Jr., *Probation and Parole in the Criminal Justice System* (St. Paul, MN: West, 1976), p. 25.

68. James M. Byrne, "Probation," a National Institute of Justice Crime File Series Study Guide (Washington, D.C.: U.S. Department of Justice, 1988), p. 1.

69. Ibid.

70. Bureau of Justice Statistics, *Probation and Parole, 1990* (Washington, D.C.: U.S. Department of Justice, 1991).

71. BJS, *Report to the Nation on Crime and Justice*, p. 105.

72. Joan Petersilia, Susan Turner, James Kahan, and Joyce Peterson, *Granting Felons Probation: Public Risks and Alternatives* (Santa Monica, CA: The Rand Corporation, 1985).

73. Ibid.

74. Bureau of Justice Statistics (BJS), *Probation and Parole in the United States, 1989* (Washington, D.C.: U.S. Government Printing Office, 1990).

75. Stephanie Minor-Harper and Christopher A. Innes, *Time Served in Prison and on Parole, 1984*, a BJS Special Report. 1987.

76. Ibid.

77. Ibid.

78. Ibid.

79. Ibid., p. 6.

80. Ibid., p. 4.

81. BJS, *Probation and Parole, 1989*.

82. *Griffin* v. *Wisconsin*, 483 U.S. 868, 107 S.Ct. 3164 (1987).

83. *Escoe* v. *Zerbst*, 295 U.S. 490 (1935).

84. *Mempa* v. *Rhay*, 389 U.S. 128 (1967).

85. A deferred sentence involves postponement of the sentencing decision, which may be made at a later time, following an automatic review of the defendant's behavior in the interim. A suspended sentence requires no review unless the probationer violates the law or conditions of probation. Both may result in imprisonment.

86. *Morrissey* v. *Brewer*, 408 U.S. 471 (1972).

87. *Gagnon* v. *Scarpelli*, 411 US 778 (1973).

88. Smith and Berlin, *Introduction to Probation and Parole*, p. 143.

89. *Greenholtz* v. *Inmate of Nebraska Penal and Correctional Complex*, 442 U.S. 1 (1979).

90. *Bearden* v. *Georgia*, 461 U.S. 660, 103 S.Ct. 2064, 76 L.Ed. 2d 221 (1983).

91. Ibid.

92. *Kelly* v. *Robinson*, U.S., 107 S.Ct. 353, 93 L.Ed. 2d 216.

93. *Minnesota* v. *Murphy*, U.S., 104 S.Ct. 1136, 79 L.Ed. 2d 409 (1984).

94. *Harlow* v. *Clatterbuick*, 30 CLr. 2364 (VA S.Ct. 1986); *Santangelo* v. *State*, 426 N.Y.S. 2d. 931 (1980); *Welch* v. *State*, 424 N.Y.S. 2d. 774 (1980); and *Thompson* v. *County of Alameda*, 614 P. 2d. 728 (1980).

95. *Tarter* v. *State of New York*, 38 CLr. 2364 (NY S.Ct. 1986); *Grimm* v. *Arizona Board of Pardons and Paroles*, 115 Arizona 260, 564 P. 2d. 1227 (1977); and *Payton* v. *United States*, 636 F. 2d. 132 (5th Cir.).

96. Rolando V. del Carmen, *Potential Liabilities of Probation and Parole Officers* (Cincinnati, OH: Anderson, 1986), p. 89.

97. See, for example, *Semler* v. *Psychiatric Institute*, 538 F. 2d 121 (4th Cir. 1976).

98. "Girl Sues County, State for Attack by Parolee," *The Fayetteville Observer*, July 7, 1991, p. 5A.

99. This section owes much to Sanford Bates, "The Establishment and Early Years of the Federal Probation System," *Federal Probation* (June 1987), pp. 4–9.

100. *Ex parte United States*, 242 U.S. 27.

101. Bates, "The Establishment and Early Years of the Federal Probation System," p. 6.

102. As summarized by Susan Krup Grunin and Jud Watkins, "The Investigative Role of the United States Probation Officer Under Sentencing Guidelines," *Federal Probation* (December 1987), pp. 43–49.

103. Ibid., p. 46.

104. Although now an independent nonprofit corporation, The Sentencing Project has its roots in a 1981 project of the National Legal Aid and Defender Association.

105. The Sentencing Project, *1989 National Directory of Felony Sentencing Services* (Washington, D.C.: The Sentencing Project, 1989).

106. The Sentencing Project, *Changing the Terms of Sentencing: Defense Counsel and Alternative Sentencing Services* (Washington, D.C.: The Sentencing Project, no date).

107. Joan Petersilia, *Expanding Options for Criminal Sentencing* (Santa Monica, CA: The Rand Corporation, 1987).

108. *Ohio Revised Code*, 2946.06.1, July 1965.

109. Lawrence Greenfield, *Probation and Parole 1984* (Washington, D.C.: U.S. Government Printing Office, 1986).

110. For a complete description of this program see Petersilia, *Expanding Options for Criminal Sentencing*.

111. Harry Allen, Chris Eskridge, Edward Latessa, and Gennaro Vito, *Probation and Parole in America* (New York: The Free Press, 1985), p. 88.

112. Doris Layton MacKenzie and Deanna Bellew Ballow, "Shock Incarceration Programs in State Correctional Jurisdictions–An Update," *NIJ Report*, (May/June 1989), pp. 9 - 10.

113. "Boot Camp Prisons Grow in Scope and Number," *NIJ Reports* (Nov./Dec. 1990), p. 6.

114. Ibid.

115. Ibid.

116. For an excellent analysis of shock incarceration programs see Jerald C. Burns, "A Comparative Evaluation of the Alabama Department of Corrections' Boot Camp Program," paper presented at the annual meeting of the Academy of Criminal Justice Sciences, Nashville, TN, March 1991, and Jerald C. Burns "A Survey of State Correctional Boot Camp Programs: A Preliminary Analysis," unpublished manuscript.

117. Dale G. Parent, "Incarceration: An Overview of Existing Programs," an *NIJ Issues and Practices Report*, June 1989.

118. Douglas C. McDonald, "Restitution and Community Service," an *NIJ Crime File Study Guide*, 1988.

119. Richard J. Maher and Henry E. Dufour, "Experimenting with Community Service: A Punitive Alternative to Imprisonment." *Federal Probation* (September 1987), pp. 22–27.

120. James P. Levine et al., *Criminal Justice in America: Law in Action* (New York: John Wiley and Sons, 1986), p. 549.

121. Billie S. Erwin and Lawrence A. Bennett, "New Dimensions in Probation: Georgia's Experience with Intensive Probation Supervision (IPS)," *NIJ Research in Brief* (Washington, D.C.: U.S. Government Printing Office, 1987).

122. Ibid., p. 2.

123. North Carolina Department of Correction, *Intensive Supervision Manual* (Raleigh, NC: Division of Adult Probation and Parole, 1988). pp. 3–5.

124. "An Overview of the Intensive Supervision Program," *N.C. Division of Adult Probation and Parole* (memo), April 7, 1988.

125. Joan Petersilia, "House Arrest," *NIJ Crime File Study Guide* (Washington, D.C.: U.S. Government Printing Office, 1988).

126. Ibid.

127. Ibid.

128. Marc Renzema and David T. Skelton, *The Use of Electronic Monitoring by Criminal Justice Agencies 1989,* NIJ grant number OJP-89-M-309 (Washington, D.C.: National Institute of Justice, 1990).

129. Ibid.

130. BI Home Escort, *Electronic Monitoring System* (advertising brochure), BI Incorporated, Boulder, Colorado (no date).

131. For additional information on the legal issues surrounding electronic home confinement see Bonnie Berry, "Electronic Jails: A New Criminal Justice Concern," *Justice Quarterly,* Vol. 2, no. 1 (1985), pp. 1–22, and J. Robert Lilly, Richard A. Ball, and W. Robert Lotz, Jr., "Electronic Jail Revisited," *Justice Quarterly,* Vol. 3, no. 3 (September 1986), pp. 353–361.

132. "Zaccaro Serving Sentence in Luxury Apartment," *The Fayetteville Observer,* August 15, 1988, p. 10A.

133. "A Victim's Life Sentence," *People Magazine* April 25, 1988.

134. Ibid., p. 40.

135. James A. Inciardi, *Criminal Justice,* 2nd ed. (New York: Harcourt, 1987), p. 664.

136. Herbert A. Johnson, *History of Criminal Justice* (Cincinnati, OH: Anderson, 1988), pp. 30–31.

137. Ibid., p. 31.

138. Ibid., p. 36.

139. Ibid., p. 51.

140. Arthur Koestler, *Reflections on Hanging* (New York: Macmillan, 1957), p. xi.

141. Ibid., p. 15.

142. Merle Severy, "The Great Revolution," *National Geographic* (July 1989), p. 20.

143. U.S. Department of Justice, *Capital Punishment, 1990* (Washington, D.C.: Bureau of Justice Statistics, 1991).

144. Bureau of Justice Statistics, *National Update* (Washington, D.C.: The Bureau, January 1993).

145. Bureau of Justice Statistics (BJS), *BJS Data Report, 1988* (Washington, D.C.: U.S. Government Printing Office, 1989), p. 67.

146. "Chief Justice Calls for Limits on Death Row Habeas Appeals," *Criminal Justice Newsletter*, Vol. 20, no. 4 (February 15, 1989), pp. 6–7.

147. Koestler, *Reflections on Hangings*, p. xii.

148.   A few studies include S. Decker and C. Kohfeld, "A Deterrence Study of the Death Penalty in Illinois: 1933–1980," *Journal of Criminal Justice*, Vol. 12, no. 4 (1984), pp. 367–379; and S. Decker and C. Kohfeld, "An Empirical Analysis of the Effect of the Death Penalty in Missouri," *Journal of Crime and Justice*, Vol. 10, no. 1 (1987), pp. 23–46.

149.   See especially the work of W. C. Bailey, "Deterrence and the Death Penalty for Murders in Utah: A Time Series Analysis," *Journal of Contemporary Law*, Vol. 5, no. 1 (1978), pp. 1–20, "An Analysis of the Deterrent Effect of the Death Penalty for Murder in California," *Southern California Law Review*, Vol. 52, no. 3 (1979), pp. 743–764.

150.   B. E. Forst, "The Deterrent Effect of Capital Punishment: A Cross-State Analysis of the 1960's," *Minnesota Law Review*, Vol. 61 (1977), pp. 743–767.

151.   Scott H. Decker and Carol W. Kohfeld, "Capital Punishment and Executions in the Lone Star State: A Deterrence Study," *Criminal Justice Research Bulletin*, (Huntsville, TX: Sam Houston State University), Vol. 3, no. 12 (1988).

152.   Ibid.

153.   As some of the material presented before the U.S. Supreme Court in the case of *Furman* v. *Georgia* (408 U.S. 238, 1972) suggested.

154.   *McCleskey* v. *Kemp*, 1987.

155.   Justice Stewart, as quoted in *USA Today*, April 27, 1989, p. 12A.

156.   Koestler, pp. 147–148, and Gennaro F. Vito and Deborad G. Wilson, "Back from the Dead: Tracking the Progress of Kentucky's Furman-Commuted Death Row Population," *Justice Quarterly*, Vol. 5, no. 1 (1988), pp. 101–111.

157. P. Harris, "Over-Simplification and Error in Public Opinion Surveys on Capital Punishment," *Justice Quarterly* (1986), pp. 429–55.

158. Ibid.

159.   James O. Finckenauer, "Public Support for the Death Penalty: Retribution as Just Desserts or Retribution as Revenge?" *Justice Quarterly*, Vol. 5, no. 1 (March 1988), p. 83.

160.   Robert M. Bohm, *The Death Penalty in America: Current Research* (Cincinnati, OH: Anderson, 1991), pp. 119–127.

161.   Ibid., p. 135.

162.   Frank P. Williams III, Dennis R. Longmire, and David B. Gulick, "The Public and the Death Penalty: Opinion as an   Artifact of Question Type," *Criminal Justice Research Bulletin* (Huntsville, TX: Sam Houston State University), Vol. 3, no. 8 (1988).

163.   Ibid., p. 4.

164.   *Criminal Justice Newsletter*, Vol. 21, no. 23 (December 3, 1990), p. 1.

165.   *Wilkerson* v. *Utah* 99 U.S. 130 (1878).

166. *In re Kemmler*, 136 U.S. 436 (1890).

167. Ibid., at 447.

168. *Louisiana ex rel. Francis* v. *Resweber*, 329 U.S. 459 (1947).

169. *Furman* v. *Georgia*, 408 U.S. 238 (1972).

170. A position first ascribed to in *Trop* v. *Dulles*, 356 U.S. 86 (1958).

171. *Gregg* v. *Georgia*, 428 U.S. 153 (1976).

172.   Ibid., at 173.

173. *Coker* v. *Georgia*, 433 U.S. 584 (1977).

174. *Woodson* v. *North Carolina*, 428 U.S. 280 (1976).

175. Lawrence A. Greenfeld, *Capital Punishment, 1989* (Washington, D.C.: Bureau of Justice Statistics, 1990), p. 1.

176. *McCleskey* v. *Zandt*, No. 89-7024 (1991).

177. *Coleman* v. *Thompson*, No. 89-7662 (1991).

INDIVIDUAL RIGHTS VERSUS SOCIAL CONCERNS
✪ The Rights of the Imprisoned ✪

Common law, constitutional, and humanitarian rights of the imprisoned:

A Right Against Cruel or Unusual Punishment
A Right to Religious Freedom While Imprisoned
A Right to Freedom of Speech
A Right to Legal Assistance
A Right to Sanitary and Healthy Conditions
A Right to Protection From Physical Harm
A Right Against Corporeal Punishments
A Right to Due Process Prior to Denial of Privileges

The individual rights listed must be effectively balanced against these community concerns:

Secure Prisons
Control over Inmates
The Prevention of Escape
Punishment of the Guilty
The Reduction of Recidivism
Affordable Prisons

How does our system of justice work toward balance?

PART 4
Corrections in America

Eye for eye, tooth for tooth, hand for hand, foot for foot.
— *Exodus* 21:24 (B.C. circa 1200)

The work of eradicating crimes is not by making punishment familiar, but formidable.
— *Oliver Goldsmith* (1728–1774)

Justice delayed, is justice denied.
— *William Gladstone* (1809–1898)

CHAPTER 9

PRISONS and JAILS

To put people behind walls and bars and do little or nothing to change them is to win a battle but lose a war. It is wrong. It is expensive. It is stupid.

— Former U.S. Supreme Court
Chief Justice Warren E. Burger[1]

KEY CONCEPTS

lex talionis	prison	overcrowding
early release	jail	direct supervision
maximum custody	count	minimum security
accreditation	Federal Bureau of Prisons	prison capacity

□ EARLY PUNISHMENTS

To the popular mind, prisons stand as bastions of criminal punishment. Because they are so much with us, however, we tend to forget that prisons, as correctional institutions, are relatively new. Prior to the emergence of imprisonment, convicted offenders were subjected to fines, physical punishment, or death. Corporal punishments were the most common, and generally fit the doctrine of *lex talionis* (the law of retaliation). Under *lex talionis* the convicted offender was sentenced to a punishment which most closely approximated the original injury. Also called "an eye for an eye, a tooth for a tooth," this early rule of retaliation generally duplicated the offense, with the offender as the substitute victim. If a person blinded another, they were blinded in return. Murderers were themselves killed, with the form of execution sometimes being tailored to approximate the method they had used.

The whipping post at New Castle, Delaware, circa 1810.
Courtesy of the Library of Congress

☐ OVERCROWDING

Throughout the 1960s and 1970s convicted offenders were increasingly sentenced to prison. Over the past 30 years the American prison population has grown dramatically (see Figure 9-1), and prisons everywhere have become notoriously overcrowded. In February 1990, in a startling example of just how bad crowding is, Hampden County, Massachusetts, Sheriff Michael Ashe, supported by 30 deputies commandeered a national guard armory for use as a jail. Sheriff Ashe claimed a 17th-century state law gave him the authority to seize public property "when there is imminent danger of a breach of peace." Ashe cited the "collapse of the criminal justice system" as having led to a loss of "the ability to implement sentences," especially those requiring imprisonment.[2]

> **Prison:** A state or federal confinement facility having custodial authority over adults sentenced to confinement.

A survey of 1,400 criminal justice officials across the country conducted in the 1980's by the National Institute of Justice identified crowding in prisons and jails as the most serious problem facing the criminal justice system today.[3] Between 1980 and 1990 state and federal prison populations more than doubled.[4] In four states — California, New Hampshire, Alaska, and New Jersey — prison populations tripled, with California experiencing the largest increase (from 23,264 inmates in 1980 to 97,309 by 1990).[5] By 1990, federal prisons had become as much as 73% overcrowded,[6] and a major program of expansion had been implemented.

Building programs in most jurisdictions, however, have not been able to keep pace with burgeoning populations. During 1988 increased incarceration rates translated into a nationwide need for 800 additional prison beds per week.[7] During the first half of 1989, the fastest growth in U.S. incarceration ever recorded occurred, necessitating 1,800 additional prison beds per week.[8] The American Correctional Association estimates that prison populations will soon grow to a total of more than 1 million persons under confinement throughout the country in 1994.[9]

In 1990 institutions in 38 states and the District of Columbia were operating under court orders to alleviate crowded conditions.[10] Entire prisons systems in nine jurisdictions had come under court control. These jurisdictions were Alaska, Florida, Kansas, Louisiana, Mississippi, Nevada, Rhode Island, South Carolina, and Texas.[11] Figure 9-2 depicts overcrowding in state and federal prison systems through a comparison of present inmate populations with the original design capacity of existing facilities. Even so, incarceration rates vary dramatically from one state to another.

Some states have dealt with overcrowded facilities by constructing "temporary" tent cities within prison yards. Others have moved more beds into already packed dormitories, often stacking prisoners three high in triple bunk beds. A few states have declared a policy of early release for less dangerous inmates and instituted mandatory diversion programs for first time nonviolent offenders. Others use sentence rollbacks to reduce the sentences of selected inmates by a fixed amount, usually 90 days. Early parole is employed by eight states to reduce overcrowded conditions.[12]   In 1985 18,617 persons were freed from state prisons prior to their anticipated release dates because of overcrowding. In 1987 Steven R. Schlesinger, director of the Bureau of Justice Statistics, pointed out that prison overcrowding has dramatically reduced the average time served even for serious offenses. Citing 1933 as a base year, Schlesinger pointed to the fact that robbers now spend about seven months less in prison than they did in 1933 (32 months in 1933), violent assaults results in 2 months less time (17 months versus 15), and larceny now means a 10 month prison sentence compared to 16 months in 1933.[13] Almost all states have shifted some of the correctional burden to local jails, with jails now housing over 10,000 sentenced inmates because of overcrowding at long-term institutions.[14]

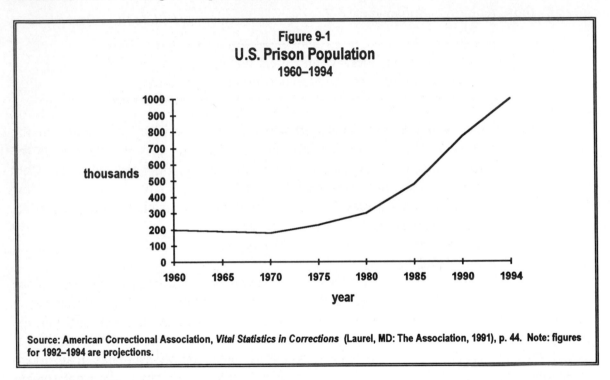

Figure 9-1
U.S. Prison Population
1960–1994

Source: American Correctional Association, *Vital Statistics in Corrections* (Laurel, MD: The Association, 1991), p. 44. Note: figures for 1992–1994 are projections.

NEW PRISON CONSTRUCTION

Diversion, early release, and a number of practices cited earlier provide techniques for alleviating overcrowding. Another approach is to increase prison populations via the construction of new prison facilities. Prison construction is very expensive, with costs averaging between $50,000 and $75,000 per bed.[15]   To assist states in the efficient expansion of prison facilities, the National Criminal Justice Reference Service began a Construction Information Exchange in the mid-1980s.   The Exchange functions to disseminate information on innovative construction techniques to states throughout the nation.   Since its implementation, the Exchange has issued a number of "construction bulletins" highlighting programs such as Florida's use of prefabricated modular concrete cells, California's precast and "tilt-up" construction innovations, and South Carolina's use of inmate labor in new prison construction.[16] To prevent escapes while saving money, many new prisons are built with fences reinforced with detection devices in place of the traditional high wall. Electronic perimeter detection devices include video motion sensors, infrared detectors, microwave sensors, and seismic sensors and are now being installed in new and existing prisons in record numbers. Some critics of the devices argue that they produce too many false alarms, and have not been adequately tested under rigorous conditions.[17]

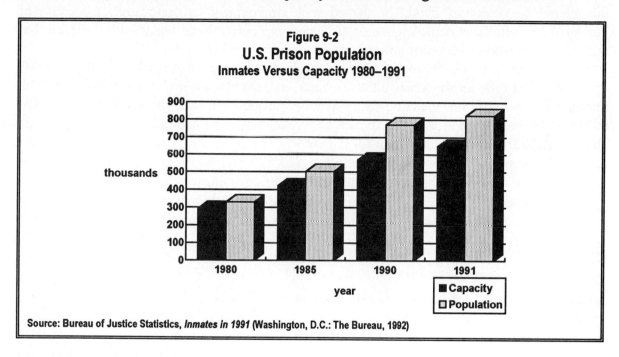

Figure 9-2
U.S. Prison Population
Inmates Versus Capacity 1980–1991

Source: Bureau of Justice Statistics, *Inmates in 1991* (Washington, D.C.: The Bureau, 1992)

☐ PRISONS TODAY

Today there are approximately 900 state and 70 federal prisons in operation across the country. As of July 1992 they held 855,958 inmates,[18] 97% of whom were housed in traditional confinement facilities, with the remaining 3% held in community-based institutions.[19] Six percent of those imprisoned were women.

The size of prison facilities varies greatly. One out of every four state institutions is a large, maximum security prison, with a population approaching 1,000 inmates. A few exceed that figure, but the typical state prison is small, with an inmate population of less than 500, while community-based facilities average around 50 residents.

Most people sentenced to state prisons have been convicted of burglary (21.2%), while robbery (13.3%) and drug crimes (13.2%) are the next most common offenses for which "active" sentences are imposed. Studies show that larceny (10.1%) accounts for the fourth largest group of imprisoned offenders, with only 6.2% of prison admissions occurring for the offense of murder and 2.7% for rape. Overall, one-third of prisoners entering correctional facilities are there for a violent crime.[20] The inmate population in general suffers from a low level of formal education, comes from a socially disadvantaged background, and lacks significant vocational skills.[21] Most adult inmates have served some time in juvenile correctional facilities.[22]

In a recent year, approximately 352,000 staff members were employed in corrections,[23] with the majority performing direct custodial tasks in state institutions. Females accounted for 17% of all correctional officers in 1990, with the proportion of women officers increasing at around 19% per year.[24] In an effort to encourage the increased employment of women in corrections, the American Correctional Association has formally adopted a statement[25] to that effect. The statement reads: "Women have a right to equal employment. No person who is qualified for a particular position/assignment or for job-related opportunities should be denied such employment or opportunities because of gender." The official statement goes on to encourage correctional agencies to "ensure that recruitment, selection, and promotion opportunities are open to women."

According to a 1991 report by the American Correctional Association (ACA), 70% of correctional officers are white, 22% are black, and slightly over 5% are Hispanic.[26] The inmate/custody staff ratio in state prisons averages around 4.1 to 1. Incarceration costs the states an average of $11,302 per inmate per year, while the federal government spends about $13,162 to house one inmate for a year.[27] The ACA reports[28] that in 1991, entry-level correctional officers were paid between $13,520 and $33,996, depending upon the state in which they were hired. Salaries for systems administrators in adult correctional systems were as high $131,731 (South Carolina), with institutional superintendents earning in the range of $26,436–93,693 during 1991.

☐ JAILS

Jails are short-term confinement facilities which were originally intended to hold suspects following arrest and pending trial. Today, jails also house convicted misdemeanants serving relatively short sentences and felony offenders awaiting transportation to long-term confinement facilities. Numerically, 52% of jail inmates are pretrial detainees or are defendants involved in some stage of the trial process.[29] Ten percent of all jail inmates are being held for drunken driving, and driving under the influence is the most common charge for jailed persons 45 years of age or older.[30] Bond has been set by the court, although not yet posted, for almost nine out of ten jail inmates.[31] Significantly, the fastest-growing sector of the jail population consists of sentenced offenders serving time in local jails because overcrowded prisons cannot accept them.

> **Jail:** A short-term confinement facility originally intended to hold prisoners awaiting trial or awaiting transfer to a long-term facility following conviction.

More than 3,300 jails are in operation throughout the United States today, staffed by approximately 92,600 correctional workers. Overall, the jail budget is huge, and facilities overflowing. Some $3.5 billion was spent to operate the nation's jails in 1988, with another $1.2 billion earmarked in the same year for the maintenance of existing structures and for new jail construction. Approximately 8.6 million people are admitted to the nation's jails each year.[32] Some stay for as little as one day, while others serve extended periods of jail time. Most jails are small. Two out of three were built to house 50 or fewer inmates. Most people who spend time in jail, however, do so in larger institutions.[33] Eighty-one percent of the nation's jail population are housed in the jails of 508 large jurisdictions.[34] Due to overcrowding, 134 of these jurisdictions were laboring under court order to reduce populations or improve the conditions of confinement.[35] Although there are many small and medium-sized jails across the country, a handful of "megajails" house thousands of inmates. The largest such facilities can be found in New York City's Riker's Island (with an average daily population of around 12,000 inmates, Los Angeles County's Men's Central Jail (7,679 inmates), the Cook County jail in Chicago (5,700 inmates), Houston's Harris County Downtown Central Jail (6,100 inmates),[36] the New Orleans Parish Prison System (3,530 inmates), and Los Angeles County's Pitchess Honor Ranch (3,254 inmates). The largest employer among these huge jails is the Cook County facility, with over 1,200 personnel on its payroll.

Jails are busy places, as Figure 9-3 shows. In 1991 there were over 20 million jail admissions and releases throughout the nation, while the daily jail population averaged around 422,609 people, of whom 2,140 were juveniles.[37] Most people processed through the country's jails are white (51%) male (91%). On average, approximately $10,500 is spent yearly to house one jail inmate.

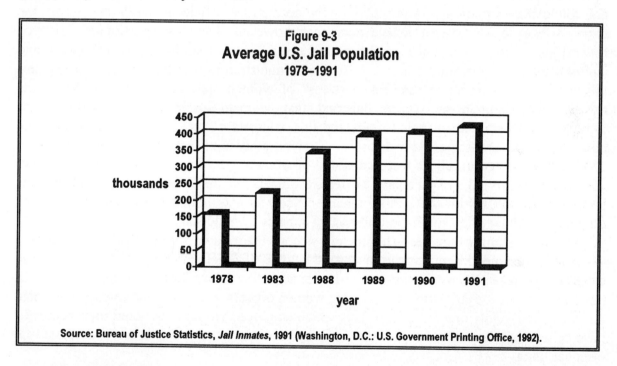

Figure 9-3
Average U.S. Jail Population
1978–1991

Source: Bureau of Justice Statistics, *Jail Inmates*, 1991 (Washington, D.C.: U.S. Government Printing Office, 1992).

WOMEN AND JAIL

Although women comprise only 9.3% of the country's jail population, they are "virtually the largest growth group in jails nationwide."[38] Jailed women face a number of special problems. Only 25.7% of the nation's jails report having a classification system specifically designed to evaluate female inmates,[39] and although "a large proportion of jurisdictions" report plans "to build facilities geared to the female offender,"[40] not all jurisdictions today even provide separate housing areas for female inmates. Educational levels are very low among jailed women, and fewer than half are high school graduates.[41] Pregnancy is another problem. Nationally 4% of female inmates are pregnant at the time they come to jail,[42] but as much as 10% of the female population of urban jails is reported to be pregnant on any given day.[43] As a consequence, a few hundred children are born in jails each year. Jailed mothers are not only separated from their children, they may have to pay for their support.   Twelve percent of all jails in one study group reported requiring employed female inmates to contribute to the support of their dependent children.

Drug abuse is another significant source of difficulty for jailed women.   Over 30% of women who are admitted to jail have a substance abuse problem at the time of admission, and in some parts of the country that figure may be as high as 70%.[44]   Adding to the problem is the fact that substantive medical programs for female inmates, such as obstetrics and gynecological care, are often lacking.   In planning medical services for female inmates into the next century, some writers have advised jail administrators to expect to see an increasingly common kind of inmate: "[a]n opiate-addicted female who is pregnant with no prior prenatal care having one or more sexually transmitted diseases, and fitting a high-risk category for AIDS (prostitution, IV drug use)."[45]

Female inmates are only half of the story.   Women working in corrections are the other.   In a 1991 study[46] Linda Zupan, one of the new generation of outstanding jail scholars, found that women comprised 22% of the correctional officer force in jails across the nation.   The deployment of female personnel, however, was disproportionately skewed toward jobs in the lower ranks.   Although 60% of all support staff (secretaries, cooks, and janitors) were women, only 1 in every 10 chief administrators was female.   Zupan explains this pattern by pointing to the "token status" of women staff members in some of the nation's jails.[47]   Even so, Zupan did find that women correctional employees were significantly committed to their careers and that attitudes of male workers toward female coworkers in jails were generally positive.   Zupan's study uncovered 626 jails in which over 50% of the correction officer force consisted of women.   On the opposite side of the coin, 954 of the nation's 3,316 jails have no female officers.[48]   As Zupan notes, "[a]n obvious problem associated with the lack of female officers in jails housing females concerns the potential for abuse and exploitation of women inmates by male staff."[49]

Jails which do hire women generally accord them equal footing with male staffers. Although cross-gender privacy is a potential area of legal liability, few jails limit the supervisory areas which may be visited by female officers working in male facilities.   In three quarters of the jails studied by Zupan, women officers were assigned to supervise male housing areas.   Only one out of four jails which employed women restricted their access to unscreened shower and toilet facilities used by men and/or to other areas such as sexual offender units.

CROWDING IN JAILS

Jails have been called the "shame of the criminal justice system." Many are old, overcrowded, poorly funded, scantily staffed by underpaid and poorly trained employees, and given low priority in local budgets.   Court-ordered caps on jail populations are increasingly common. Recently, for example, the Harris County Jail in Houston, Texas, was forced to release 250 inmates after missing a deadline for reducing its resident population to 6,100 people.[50]   A nationwide survey, published by the Bureau of Justice Statistics in 1991, found that 46% of all jails were built more than 25 years ago, and of that percentage, over half were more than 50 years old.[51]

Jail populations are growing by 28% yearly nationwide and, while new jail construction has been increasing overall capacity by around 15% per year, overcrowded jails have become a critical issue throughout the justice system.[52]   A 1983 national census revealed that jails were operating at only 85% of their rated capacity.[53]   By 1992, however, the nation's jails were running at 110% of capacity, and new jails could be found on drawing boards and under construction across the country. With square footage per inmate averaging only 58.3[54] in jails today, managers now cite crowding and staff shortages as the two most critical problems facing jails.[55]

The root cause of jail overcrowding can be found in a growing crime rate combined with a punitive public attitude which has heavily influenced correctional practice.   In addition, prison overcrowding in recent years has forced many states to begin using jails instead of prisons for the confinement of convicted felons, exacerbating the crowding of jails still further. In 1992, 40% of local jails held inmates because of crowding in state prisons.   Another problem arises from the sentencing of individuals who are unable to make restitution, alimony, or childcare payments to jail time — a practice which has made the local lockup at least partially a debtor's prison.   Symptomatic of problems brought on by overcrowding, the National Center on Institutions and Alternatives reported 401 suicides in jails across the nation during a recent year.[56] Suicide, in fact, accounts for the largest proportion of all jail deaths among both male and female inmates.

Copyright 1989 by USA Today. Reprinted with permission.
Given the rise in crime throughout the country, personal security has become a major issue.

Although   the   societal underpinnings of overcrowding are difficult to assess, some causes of jail crowding which can be immediately addressed include the following:[57]

♦ The inability of jail inmates to make bond due to bonds (wo)men
    practices and lack of funding sources for indigent defendants

♦ Unnecessary delays between arrest and final case disposition

♦ Unnecessarily limited access to vital information about defendants
    which could be useful in facilitating court-ordered pretrial release

♦ The limited ability of the criminal justice system to handle cases
    expeditiously due to a lack of needed resources (judges, assistant

prosecuting attorneys, etc.)

♦ Inappropriate attorney delays in moving cases through court (motions to delay cases as part of an attorney's strategy, etc.)

♦ Unproductive statutes requiring that specified nonviolent offenders be jailed (including those requiring mandatory pretrial jailing of DWIs, minor drug offenders, second offense shoplifting, etc.)

Some innovative jurisdictions have already substantially reduced jail crowding. San Diego, California, for example, uses a privately operated detoxification reception program in order to divert many inebriates from the proverbial "drunk tank."[58] Officials in Galveston County, Texas, routinely divert mentally ill arrestees directly to a mental health facility.[59] Some areas use pretrial services and magistrates offices which are open 24 hours a day for the purpose of setting bail, making release possible.

DIRECT SUPERVISION JAILS

Some authors have suggested that the dilemmas found in many jails today stem from "mismanagement, lack of fiscal support, heterogeneous inmate populations, overuse and misuse of detention, overemphasis on custodial goals, and political and public apathy."[60] Others propose that environmental and organizational elements inherent in traditional jail architecture and staffing have given rise to today's difficulties.[61] Traditional jails, say these observers, were built upon the assumption that inmates are inherently violent and potentially destructive. Hence, most of today's jails were constructed in such a way as to maximize custodial control over inmates — via the use of thick walls, bars, and other architectural barriers to the free movement of inmates. Such institutions, however, have the adverse affect of limiting the visibility and access of correctional personnel to many confinement areas. As a consequence, they tend to encourage just the kinds of inmate behavior that jails were meant to control. Inefficient hallway patrols and expensive video technology have provided temporary patches, intended to overcome the limits that old jail architecture places on supervisory activities.

In an effort to solve many of the problems which have dogged jails in the past, a new jail management strategy emerged during the 1980s. Called direct supervision, this contemporary approach "joins podular/unit architecture with a participative, proactive management philosophy."[62] Often built in a system of "pods," or modular self-contained housing areas linked to one another, direct supervision jails eliminate the old physical barriers which separated staff and inmates. Gone are bars and isolated secure observation areas for officers. They are replaced by an open environment, in which inmates and correctional personnel mingle with relative freedom. In a growing number of such "new-generation" jails, large reinforced Plexiglas® panels have supplanted walls, and serve to separate activity areas, such as classrooms and dining halls, from one another. Soft furniture is often found throughout these institution, and individual rooms take the place of cells, allowing inmates at least a modicum of personal privacy. In today's direct supervision jails 16 to 46 inmates typically live in one pod, with correctional staffers present among the inmate population on an around-the-clock basis.

The first direct supervision jail opened in the 1970s in Contra Costa County, California. This 386-bed facility became a model for the nation, and other new-generation jails soon commenced operations in Las Vegas; Portland; Reno; New York City; Bucks County, Pennsylvania; Vancouver, British Columbia; and Miami.

Direct supervision jails have been touted for their tendency to reduce inmate dissatisfaction, and for their ability to deter rape and violence among the inmate population. By eliminating architectural barriers to staff/inmate interaction, direct supervision facilities are said to place officers back in control of institutions. While these innovative facilities are still too new to assess fully, a number of studies have already demonstrated their success at reducing the likelihood of inmate victimization. One such study[63] found that traditional facilities averaged nearly 15 times as many aggravated assaults (between inmates) as did direct supervision jails. Similarly, homicide, sexual assault, jail rape, suicide, and escape have all been found to occur far less frequently in direct supervision facilities than in traditional institutions.[64] Staff members working in direct supervision jails report being happier and less stressed than in old-style facilities.[65] Significantly, new-generation jails appear to substantially reduce the number of lawsuits brought by inmates and lower the incidence of adverse court-ordered judgments against jail administrators.

Direct supervision jails are not without their problems. Some authors[66] have recognized that new-generation jails are too frequently run by old-style managers and that correctional personnel sometimes lack the training needed to make the transition to the new style of supervision. Others[67] have suggested that managers of direct supervision jails, especially those at the midlevel, could benefit from clearer job descriptions and additional training. In the words of one Canadian advocate of direct supervision,[68] "training becomes particularly critical in direct supervision jails where relationships are more immediate and are more complex." Finally, recommendations have arisen from those tasked with hiring[69] that potential new staff members should be psychologically screened and that intensive use be made of preemployment interviews, to determine the suitability of applicants for correctional officer positions in direction supervision jails.

JAILS AND THE FUTURE

In contrast to more visible issues confronting the justice system, such as the death penalty, gun control, the war on drugs, and big-city gangs, jails have received relatively little attention from the media and have generally escaped close public scrutiny. National efforts, however, to improve the quality of jail life are under way. Some changes involve programmatic additions. A recent American Jail Association study of drug treatment programs in jails, for example, found that "a small fraction (perhaps fewer than 10%) of inmates needing drug treatment actually receive these services."[70] Follow-up efforts were aimed at developing standards to guide jails administrators in increasing the availability of drug treatment services to inmates.

Jail industries are another growing programmatic area. The best of them serve the community while training inmates in marketable skills.[71] In an exemplary effort to humanize its megajails,[72] for example, the Los Angeles County Sheriff's Department recently opened an inmate telephone answering service. Many calls are received by the Sheriff's Department daily, requesting information about a significant number of the county's 22,000 jail inmates. These requests for public information were becoming increasingly difficult to handle by the growing fiscal constraints facing local government. To handle the huge number of calls effectively without tying up sworn law enforcement personnel, the department began using inmates specially trained to handle incoming calls. Eighty inmates were assigned to the project, with groups of different sizes covering shifts throughout the day. Each inmate staffer went through a program designed to provide coaching in proper telephone procedures and to teach each operator how to run computer terminals containing routine data on the department's inmates. The new system is now fully in place and handles 4,000 telephone inquires a day. The time needed to answer a call and provide information has dropped from 30 minutes under the old system to a remarkable 10 seconds today.

One final element in the unfolding saga of jail development should be mentioned: the emergence of state jail standards. Thirty-two states have set standards for municipal and county jails.[73] In 25 states those standards are mandatory. The purpose of jail standards is to identify some basic minimum level of conditions necessary for inmate health and safety. On a national level, the Commission on Accreditation for Corrections, operated jointly by the American Correctional Association and the federal government, has developed its own set of jail standards,[74] as has the National Sheriff's Association. Both sets of standards are designed to ensure a minimal level of comfort and safety in local lockups. Increased standards, though, are costly. Local jurisdictions, already hard pressed to meet other budgetary demands, will probably be slow to upgrade their jails to meet such external guidelines, unless forced to. Ken Kerle, in a study[75] of 61 jails which was designed to test compliance with National Sheriff's Association guidelines, discovered that in many standards areas — especially those of tool control, armory planning, community resources, release preparation, and riot planning — the majority of jails were sorely out of compliance. Lack of a written plan was the most commonly cited reason for failing to meet the standards.

In what may be one of the best set of recommendations designed to foster the development of jails which can serve into the next century, Joel A. Thompson and G. Larry Mays[76] suggest that: (1) states should provide financial aid and/or incentives to local governments for jail construction and renovation; (2) mandatory jail standards must be developed by all states; (3) mandatory jail inspections should become commonplace in the enforcement of standards; (4) citizens should be educated as to the function and significance of jails in an effort to increase the public's willingness to fund new jail construction; (5) all jails need to have written policies and procedures to serve as training tools and as a basis for a defense against lawsuits; and (6) "[c]ommunities should explore alternatives to incarceration [because] many jail detainees are not threats to society and should not occupy scarce and expensive cell space."

SECURITY LEVELS

Maximum custody prisons are the institutions most often portrayed in movies and on television. They tend to be massive old prisons with large inmate populations. Some, like Central Prison in Raleigh, North Carolina, are much newer and incorporate advances in prison architecture to provide tight security without sacrificing building aesthetics.

Maximum custody prisons tend to locate cells and other inmate living facilities at the center of the institution and place a variety of barriers between the living area and the institution's outer perimeter. Maximum custody is actually a level of security characterized by high fences, thick walls, secure cells, gun towers, and armed prison guards. Technological innovations such as electric perimeters, laser motion detectors, electronic and pneumatic locking systems, metal detectors, X-ray machines, television surveillance, radio communications, and computer information systems, are frequently used today to reinforce the more traditional maximum security strategies. These new technologies have helped to lower the cost of new prison construction, although some argue that prison electronic detection devices may be relied upon too heavily and have not yet been adequately tested.[77] Death row inmates are all maximum security prisoners, although the level of security on death row exceeds even that experienced by most prisoners held in maximum custody. Prisoners on death row must spend much of the day in single cells and are often only permitted a brief shower once a week under close supervision.

Most states today have one large centrally located maximum security institution. Some of these prisons combine more than one custody level and may be both maximum and medium security facilities. Medium security is a custody level which bears many resemblances to maximum security. Medium security prisoners are generally permitted more freedom to associate with one another, and are able to frequent the prison yard, exercise room, library, and shower and bathroom facilities under less intense supervision than their maximum security counterparts. An important security tool in medium security prisons is the count, which is literally a headcount of inmates taken at regular intervals. Counts may be taken four times a day and usually require inmates to report to designated areas to be counted. Until the count has been "cleared," all other inmate activity must cease. Medium security prisons tend to be smaller than maximum security institutions and often have barbed-wire–topped chain-link fences in place of the more secure stone or concrete block walls found in many of the older maximum security facilities. Cells and living quarters tend to have more windows and are often located closer to the perimeter of the institution than is the case in maximum security. Dormitory-style housing, where prisoners live together in wardlike arrangements, may be employed in medium security facilities. Medium security facilities generally have a greater number of prison programs and opportunities for inmates to participate in recreational and other programs than do maximum custody facilities.

Minimum security institutions do not fit the stereotypical conception of prisons. Minimum security inmates are generally housed in dormitory-like settings and are free to walk the yard and visit most of the prison facilities. Some newer prisons provide minimum security inmates with private rooms which they can decorate (within limits) according to their tastes. Inmates usually have free access to a "canteen" which sells personal products like cigarettes, toothpaste, and candy bars. Minimum security inmates often wear uniforms of a different color from that for inmates in higher custody levels, and in some institutions may wear civilian clothes. They work under only general supervision and usually have access to recreational, educational, and skills training programs on the prison grounds. Guards are unarmed, gun towers do not exist, and fences, if they are present at all, are usually low and sometimes even unlocked. Many minimum security prisoners participate in some sort of work or study release program, and some have extensive visitation and furlough privileges.   Counts may still be taken, although most minimum security institutions keep track of inmates through daily administrative work schedules.   The primary "force" holding inmates in minimum security institutions is their own restraint.   Inmates live with the knowledge that minimum security institutions are one step removed from close correctional supervision and that any failure on their part to meet the expectations of administrators will result in their being transferred into more secure institutions and will probably delay their release. Inmates returning from assignments in the community may be frisked for contraband, but body cavity searches are rare in minimum custody, being reserved primarily for inmates suggested of smuggling.

Upon entry into the prison system most states assign prisoners to initial custody levels based upon their perceived dangerousness, escape risk, and type of offense. Some inmates may enter the system at the medium (or even minimum) custody level.   Inmates move through custody levels according to the progress they are judged to have made in self-control and demonstrated responsibility. Serious, violent criminals, who begin their prison careers with lengthy sentences in maximum custody have the opportunity in most states to work their way up to minimum security, although the process usually takes a number of years.   Those who "mess up" and represent continuous disciplinary problems are returned to closer custody levels. Minimum security prisons, as a result, house inmates convicted of all types of criminal offenses.

The typical American prison today is medium or minimum custody. Some states have as many as 80 or 90 small institutions, which may originally have been located in every county to serve the needs of public works and highway maintenance.   Medium and minimum security institutions house the bulk of the country's prison population and offer a number of programs and services designed to assist with the rehabilitation of offenders, and to create the conditions necessary for a successful reentry of the inmate into society. Most prisons offer at least limited programs in the following areas:[78]

Psychiatric Services	Counseling
Academic Education	Recreation
Vocational Education	Library Services
Substance-Abuse Treatment	Religious Programs
Health Care	Industrial and Agricultural Services

☐ THE FEDERAL PRISON SYSTEM

In 1895 the federal government opened a prison at Leavenworth, Kansas, for civilians convicted of violating federal law. Leavenworth had been a military prison, and control over the facility was transferred from the Department of the Army to the Department of Justice. By 1906 the Leavenworth facility had been expanded to a 1,200-man capacity and another prison — in Atlanta, Georgia — had been built.   McNeil Island Prison in Washington State was functioning by the early 1900s. The first federal prison for women opened in 1927 in Alderson, West Virginia. With increasing complexity in the federal criminal code, the number of federal prisoners grew.[79]

On May 14, 1930 the Federal Bureau of Prisons was created under the direction of

Sanford Bates. The Bureau inherited a system which was dramatically overcrowded. Many federal prisoners were among the most notorious criminals in the nation, and ideals of humane treatment and rehabilitation were all but lacking in the facilities of the 1930s. Director Bates began a program of improvements to relieve overcrowding and to increase the treatment capacity of the system. In 1933 the Medical Center for Federal Prisoners opened in Springfield, Missouri, with a capacity of around 1,000 inmates. Alcatraz Island began operations in 1934.

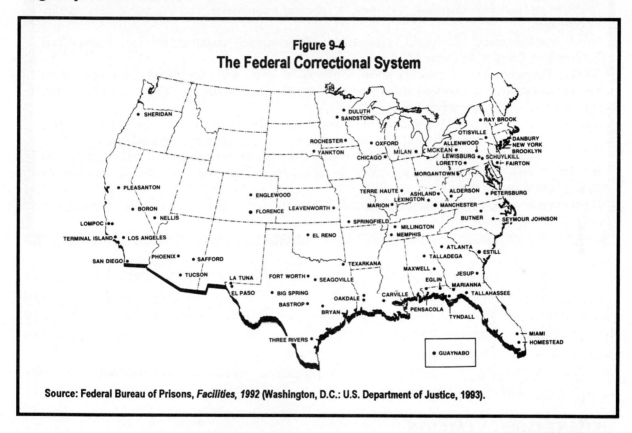

Figure 9-4
The Federal Correctional System

Source: Federal Bureau of Prisons, *Facilities, 1992* (Washington, D.C.: U.S. Department of Justice, 1993).

By the 1960s the federal prison system classified its institutions according to six security levels. The most severe security risks were housed in maximum custody facilities called "United States Penitentiaries." All such penitentiaries were designed to house adult male offenders. Among those functioning today, the facilities in Atlanta, Georgia; Lewisburg, Pennsylvania; Terre Haute, Indiana; and Leavenworth, Kansas, are probably the best known maximum security federal institutions. Medium security prisons were called "Federal Correctional Institutions" and generally house inmates with shorter sentences and those who were judged to represent smaller security risks. Terminal Island, California; Lompoc, California; and Seagoville, Texas, are well-known sites of a few such prisons. Minimum custody prisoners were held at the Allenwood facility in Montgomery, Pennsylvania; Eglin Air Force Base, Florida; and Maxwell Air Force Base, Alabama. Other minimum custody facilities held juveniles, such as those at Pleasanton, California; Englewood, Colorado; and Ashland, Kentucky. A number of "Community Treatment Centers," operated in large cities across the nation, complemented the Bureau's prisons.

A CAREER WITH THE FEDERAL BUREAU OF PRISONS

Typical Positions. Psychologists, physicians, nurses, chaplains, correctional treatment specialists, safety specialists, teachers, program officers, vocational instructors, correctional officers, and others.

Employment Requirements. Applicants must (1) be U.S. citizens, (2) be less than 35 years of age (although for some hard-to-fill positions an age waiver may be granted), (3) successfully complete an employee interview, (4) pass a physical examination, and (5) pass a field security investigation.

Other Requirements. Successful completion of in-service training at the Federal Law Enforcement Training Academy at Glynco, Georgia.

Salary. Correctional officers are appointed at the GS-6 level, with entry-level salaries set around $23,850 in mid-1993. A correctional officer may be advanced to the next higher grade level after six months of satisfactory service.

Benefits. Benefits include (1) participation in the Federal Employees' Retirement System, (2) paid annual leave, (3) paid sick leave, (4) low-cost health and life insurance, and (5) paid holidays. Other benefits naturally accrue from what the Bureau describes as "strong internal merit promotion practices" and "unlimited opportunities for advancement in one of the fastest-growing government agencies."

Direct inquiries to: Federal Bureau of Prisons, Room 400, 320 First Street, N.W., Washington, D.C. 20534. Phone: (202) 514-2000.

The federal system today is substantially unchanged (see Figure 9-4). Approximately 70 federal prisons are in operation, with one of the most recent additions to the system — the Federal Correctional Institution at Butner, North Carolina — designed to house suicidal and acutely psychotic offenders. A new grading system classifies facilities according to six security levels, and custodial terms such as "maximum" and "minimum" are avoided. Crowding in federal prisons is pervasive, where the warehousing mentality prevails, as it does in state institutions.

RECENT IMPROVEMENTS

In the midst of frequent lawsuits, court ordered changes in prison administration, and overcrowded conditions, outstanding prison facilities are being recognized through the American Correctional Association's program of accreditation. The ACA Commission on Accreditation has developed a set of standards which correctional institutions can use in self-evaluation. Those which meet the standards can apply for accreditation under the program. Unfortunately, accreditation of prisons has few "teeth." Although unaccredited universities would not long be in business, few prisoners can choose the institution they want to be housed in.

Another avenue toward improvement of the nation's prisons can be found in the National Academy of Corrections, the training arm of the National Institute of Corrections. The Academy, located in Boulder, Colorado, offers seminars and training sessions for state and local correctional managers, trainers, personnel directors, sheriffs, and state legislators.[80] Issues covered include strategies to control overcrowding, community corrections program management, prison programs, gangs and disturbances, security, and public and media relations, as well as many other topics.[81]

□ SUMMARY

Modern prisons are the result of historical efforts to humanize the treatment of offenders. "Doing time for crime" has become society's answer to the corporeal punishments of centuries past. Even so, questions remain about the conditions of imprisonment in contemporary prisons and jails, and modern corrections is far from a panacea. The security orientation of correctional staff and administration leaves little room for capable treatment programs. Existing prisons are overcrowded and new ones are expensive An end to crowding is nowhere in sight. Studies demonstrating the likelihood of recidivism among prior correctional clients have called the whole correctional process into question, and the modern practice of "warehousing" seems more a strategy of frustration than one of hope. Prisons today exist in a kind of limbo. Emphasis is on reducing the costs and the pains of incarceration. Uncertainties about the usefulness of treatment have left few officials confident of their ability to rehabilitate offenders. The return of prison industries, the interest in efficient technologies of effective imprisonment, and court mandated reforms are all signs that society has given up any hope of large scale reformation among inmate populations.

DISCUSSION QUESTIONS

1. What solutions do you see to the present overcrowded conditions of prisons today?

2. What is the difference between jails and prisons? How are these differences beginning to blur? Do you think correctional administrators should strive to maintain traditional differences? Why or why not?

3. What are direct supervision jails? How do they differ from traditional jails? Do you think direct supervision jails are really an improvement over traditional jails? Why or why not?

4. How would you deal with overcrowding in our nations jails and prisons? What long-term solutions to overcrowding do you foresee?

NOTES

1. As cited in the National Conference on Prison Industries, *Discussions and Recommendations* (Washington, D.C.: U.S. Government Printing Office, 1986), p. 23.

2. "A Sheriff Takes Over an Armory to Ease Jail Crowding Crisis," *Criminal Justice Newsletter*, Vol. 21, no. 5 (March 1, 1990), p. 5.

3.   Bureau of Justice Statistics (BJS), *Prisoners in 1987* (Washington, DC: The Bureau, 1988).

4.   Bureau of Justice Statistics (BJS), *Prisoners in 1990* (Washington, D.C.: The Bureau, 1991).

5.   Ibid.

6.   Wade B. Houck, "Acquiring New Prison Sites: The Federal Experience," *NIJ Construction Bulletin*, December 1987.

7.   Bureau of Justice Statistics, *Prisoners in 1988* (Washington, D.C.: The Bureau, 1989).

8.   Ibid.

9.   American Correctional Association (ACA), *Vital Statistics in Corrections* (Laurel, MD: The Association, 1991), p. 44.

10.   "37 States Operating Prisons Under Court Orders, Study Finds," *Criminal Justice Newsletter*, Vol. 20, no. 1 (January 3, 1989), p. 4.

11.   ACA, *Vital Statistics in Corrections*, p. 52.

12.   BJS, *Prisoners in 1987*.

13.   Steven R. Schlesinger, "Prison Crowding in the United States: The Data," *Criminal Justice Research Bulletin* (Huntsville, TX: Sam Houston State University), Vol. 3, no. 1 (1987).

14.   U.S. Department of Justice, *Annual Report—Fiscal 1987* (Washington, D.C.: U.S. Government Printing Office), p. 60.

15.   Alfred Blumstein, "Prison Crowding," NIJ Crime File Study Guide (date unknown), p. 2.

16.   Stephen Carter and Ann C. Humphries, "Inmates Build Prisons in South Carolina," *NIJ Construction Bulletin* (December 1987).

17.   George and Camille Camp, "Stopping Escapes: Perimeter Security," *NIJ Construction Bulletin* (August 1987).

18.   Bureau of Justice Statistics (BJS), *National Update* (Washington, D.C.: The Bureau, January 1993).

19.   Gloria A. Grizzle et al., "Measuring Corrections Performance," NIJ grant number 78-NI-AX-0130, 1990, p. 31.

20.   Bureau of Justice Statistics (BJS), *National Corrections Reporting Program, 1985* (Washington, D.C.: The Bureau, December 1990), p. 14.

21.   Ibid., p. 54.

22.   Ibid.

23.   Katherine M. Jamieson and Timothy J. Flanagan, eds., *Sourcebook of Criminal Justice Statistics– 1988* (Washington, D.C.: United States Government Printing Office, 1989).   State corrections employees only.

24. American Correctional Association (ACA), "Correctional Officers in Adult Systems," *Vital Statistics in Corrections* (Laurel, MD: The Association, 1991), p. 30.

25. Ibid., p. 73.

26. Ibid., p. 30. Note: "Other" minorities round out the percentages to a total of 100%.

27. U.S. Department of Justice, *Report to the Nation on Crime and Justice*, 2nd ed. (Washington, D.C.: U.S. Government Printing Office, 1988), p. 123.

28. Ibid., p. 11.

29. U.S. Department of Justice, Bureau of Justice Statistics (BJS), *BJS Data Report, 1988* (Washington, D.C.: U.S. Government Printing Office, April 1989), p. 62.

30. Ibid., p. 19.

31. Ibid., p. 63.

32. U.S. Department of Justice, Bureau of Justice Statistics (BJS), *Jail Inmates, 1987* (Washington, D.C.: The Department, December, 1988), p. 2.

33. U.S. Department of Justice, *Report to the Nation on Crime and Justice*, p. 106.

34. BJS, *BJS Data Report 1988*, p. 61.

35. BJS, *Jail Inmates, 1989*, p. 2.

36. "Jail Overcrowding in Houston Results in Release of Inmates," *Criminal Justice Newsletter,* Vol 21., no. 20 (October 15, 1990), p. 5.

37. Bureau of Justice Statistics (BJS), *National Update* (Washington, D.C.: U.S. Government Printing Office, 1992), p. 11.

38. William Reginald Mills and Heather Barrett, "Meeting the Special Challenge of Providing Health Care to Women Inmates in the '90's," *American Jails,* Vol. 4, no. 3 (September/October 1990), p. 55.

39. American Correctional Association (ACA), *The Female Offender: What Does the Future Hold?* (Washington, D.C.: St. Mary's Press, 1990), p. 14.

40. Ibid., p. 21.

41. Ibid., p. 21.

42. ACA, "Correctional Officers in Adult Systems."

43. Mills and Barrett, "Meeting the Special Challenge," p. 55.

44. Ibid.

45. Ibid.

46. Linda L. Zupan, "Women Corrections Officers in the Nation's Largest Jails," *American Jails* (January/February 1991), pp. 59–62.

47. Ibid., p. 11.

48. Linda L. Zupan, "Women Correction Officers in Local Jails," paper presented at the annual meeting of the Academy of Criminal Justice Sciences, Nashville, TN, March 1991.

49. Ibid., p. 6.

50. "Jail Overcrowding in Houston Results in Release of Inmates," p. 5.

51. Bureau of Justice Statistics (BJS), *Census of Local Jails, 1988* (Washington, D.C.: The Bureau, 1991), p. 31.

52. Jameson and Flanagan, *Sourcebook of Criminal Justice Statistics, 1988.*

53. Ibid.

54. BJS, *Census of Local Jails, 1988*, p. 15.

55. Randall Guynes, *Nation's Jail Managers Assess Their Problems* (Washington, D.C.: National Institute of Justice, 1988).

56. Lindsay M. Hayes and Joseph R. Rowan, *National Study of Jail Suicides: Seven Years Later* (Alexandria, VA: National Center on Institutions and Alternatives, 1988), p. 11.

57. As identified in George P. Wilson and Harvey L. McMurray, *System Assessment of Jail Overcrowding Assumptions,* paper presented at the annual meeting of the Academy of Criminal Justice Sciences, Nashville, TN, March 1991.

58. Andy Hall, *Systemwide Strategies to Alleviate Jail Crowding* (Washington, D.C.: National Institute of Justice, 1987).

59. Ibid.

60. Linda L. Zupan and Ben A. Menke, "The New Generation Jail: An Overview," in Joel A. Thompson and G. Larry Mays, *American Jails: Public Policy Issues* (Chicago: Nelson-Hall, 1991), p. 180.

61. Ibid.

62. Herbert R. Sigurdson, Billy Wayson, and Gail Funke, "Empowering Middle Managers of Direct Supervision Jails," *American Jails* (Winter 1990), p. 52.

63. National Institute of Corrections, *New Generation Jails* (Boulder, CO: The Institute, 1983).

64. H. Sigurdson, *The Manhattan House of Detention: A Study of Podular Direct Supervision* (Washington, D.C.: National Institute of Corrections, 1985).

65. See, for example, Linda L. Zupan, *Jails: Reform and the New Generation Philosophy* (Cincinnati, OH:

Anderson, 1991), pp. 133–150.

66. Jerry W. Fuqua, "New Generation Jails: Old Generation Management," *American Jails* (March/April 1991), p. 80–83.

67. Sigurdson, Wayson, and Funke, "Empowering Middle Managers."

68. Duncan J. McCulloch and Time Stiles, "Technology and the Direct Supervision Jail," *American Jails* (Winter 1990), pp. 97–102.

69. Susan W. McCampbell, "Direct Supervision: Looking for the Right People," *American Jails* (November/December 1990), pp. 68–69.

70. Robert L. May II, Roger H. Peters, and William D. Kearns, "The Extent of Drug Treatment Programs in Jails: A Summary Report," *American Jails* (September/October 1990), pp. 32–34.

71. See, for example, John W. Dietler, "Jail Industries: The Best Thing That Can Happen to a Sheriff," *American Jails* (July/August 1990), pp. 80–83.

72. Robert Osborne, "Los Angeles County Sheriff Opens New Inmate Answering Service," *American Jails,* (July/August 1990), pp. 61–62.

73. Tom Rosazza, "Jail Standards: Focus on Change," *American Jails* (November/December 1990), pp. 84–87.

74. American Correctional Association, *Manual of Standards for Adult Local Detention Facilities* (College Park, MD: The Association, 1991).

75. Ken Kerle, "National Sheriff's Association Jail Audit Review," *American Jails* (Spring 1987), pp. 13–21.

76. Joel A. Thompson and G. Larry Mays, "Paying the Piper but Changing the Tune: Policy Changes and Initiatives for the American Jail," in Joel A. Thompson and G. Larry Mays, *American Jails: Public Policy Issues* (Chicago: Nelson Hall, 1991), pp. 240–246.

77. Camp and Camp, "Stopping Escapes: Perimeter Security."

78. Adapted from Grizzle, et al., "Measuring Corrections Performance," p. 31.

79. Ibid.

80. National Institute of Corrections, "National Academy of Corrections: Outreach Training Programs" (July 1987).

81. National Institute of Corrections, "Correctional Training Programs" (July 1987).

CHAPTER 10

PRISON LIFE

We must remember always that the doors of prisons swing both ways.
— Mary Belle Harris
First Federal Woman Warden[1]

KEY CONCEPTS

total institutions	prison subculture	prisonization
argot	prisoner unions	grievance
hands-off doctrine	civil death	inmate families

☐ THE REALITIES OF PRISON LIFE

For the first 150 years of their existence prisons and prison life could be described by the phrase "out of sight, out of mind." Very few citizens cared about prison conditions, and those unfortunate enough to be locked away were regarded as lost to the world. By the mid-1900s such attitudes had begun to change. Concerned citizens began to offer their services to prison administrations, neighborhoods began accepting work release prisoners and half-way houses, and social scientists initiated a serious study of prison life. Hans Reimer, then-Chairman of the Department of Sociology at Indiana University, set the tone for studies of prison life in 1935 when he voluntarily served three months in prison as an incognito participant observer.[2] Reimer reported the results of his studies to the American Prison Association, stimulating many other, albeit less spectacular, efforts to examine prison life. Other early studies include Donald Clemmer's *The Prison Community* (1940),[3] Gresham M. Sykes's *The Society of Captives: A Study of a Maximum Security Prison* (1958),[4] Richard A. Cloward and Donald R. Cressey's *Theoretical Studies in Social Organization of the Prison* (1960), and Donald R. Cressey's *The Prison: Studies in Institutional Organization and Change* (1961).[5]

These studies and others focused primarily on maximum security prisons for men. They treated correctional institutions as formal or complex organizations and employed the analytical techniques of organizational sociology, industrial psychology, and administrative science.[6] As modern writers on prisons have observed: "[t]he prison was compared to a primitive society, isolated from the outside world, functionally integrated by a delicate system of mechanisms, which kept it precariously balanced between anarchy and accommodation."[7]

TOTAL INSTITUTIONS

Another approach to the study of prison life was developed by Erving Goffman who coined the term "total institutions" in a 1961 study of prisons and mental hospitals.[8] Goffman described total institutions as places where the same people work, play, eat, sleep, and recreate together on a daily basis. Such places include prisons, concentration camps, mental hospitals, seminaries, and other facilities in which residents are cut off from the larger society either forcibly or willingly. Total institutions are small societies. They evolve their own distinctive styles of life and place pressures on residents to fulfill rigidly proscribed behavioral roles.

> **Total Institutions:** Enclosed facilities, generally separated from society both physically and socially, where the inhabitants share all aspects of their lives on a daily basis.

The
Warden

PRISON SUBCULTURES

Two social realities coexist in prison settings. One is the official structure of rules and procedures put in place by the wider society and enforced by prison staff. The other is the far less formal, but decidedly more powerful inmate world. The inmate world, best described by its pervasive immediacy in the lives of inmates, is also called the prison subculture. The realities of prison life — a large and often densely packed inmate population which must look to the prison environment for all of its needs — mean that such subcultures are not easily subject to the control of prison authorities.

Prison subcultures develop independently of the plans of prison administrators, and inmates entering prison discover a social world not mentioned in the handbooks prepared by the staff. Inmate concerns, values, roles, and even language weave a web of social reality in which new inmates must participate. Those who try to remain aloof soon find themselves subjected to dangerous ostracism and may even be suspected of being in league with the prison administration.

The socialization of new inmates into the prison subculture has been described as a process of prisonization.[9] Prisonization refers to the learning of convict values and attitudes. When the process is complete inmates have become "cons." The values of the inmate social system are embodied in a code whose violations can produce sanctions ranging from ostracism and avoidance to physical violence and homicide.[10] Sykes and Messinger[11] recognize five elements of the prison code:

♦ Don't interfere with the interests of other inmates. Never rat on a con.

♦ Don't lose your head. Play it cool and do your own time.

♦ Don't exploit inmates. Don't steal. Don't break your word. Be right.

♦ Don't whine. Be a man.

♦ Don't be a sucker. Don't trust the officers or staff.

Distant prisons share aspects of a common inmate culture,[12] and prisonwise inmates entering a facility far from their home will already know the ropes. Prison argot, or language, provides one example of how widespread prison subculture can be. The terms used to describe inmate roles in one institution are generally understood in others. The word "rat," for example, is prison slang for an informer. Popularized by crime movies of the 1950's, the term "rat" is understood today by members of the wider society. Other words common to prison argot are shown in the accompanying box.

The concept of prisonization was closely examined by Stanton Wheeler in a study of the Washington State Reformatory.[13] Wheeler found that the degree of prisonization experienced by inmates tends to vary over time. He described changing levels of inmate commitment to prison norms and values by way of a "U-shaped" curve. When an inmate first enters prison, Wheeler said, the conventional values of outside society are of paramount importance. As time passes the life-style of the prison is adopted. However, within the half-year prior to release, most inmates begin to demonstrate a renewed appreciation for conventional values.

Prison Argot
The Language of Confinement

Writers who have studied prison life often comment on the use by prisoners of a special language or *argot*. This language generally refers to the roles assigned by prison culture to types of inmates as well as to prison activities. This box lists words identified in past studies by various authors. The first group of words are characteristic of male prisons, while the last few have been used in prisons for women.

Rat: an inmate who squeals (provides information about other inmates to the prison administration).
Gorilla: the inmate who uses force to take what he wants from others.
Merchant (or peddler): one who sells when he should give.
Fish: the newly arrived inmate.
Wolf: the male inmate who assumes the aggressive masculine role during homosexual relations.
Punk: the male inmate who is forced into a submissive or feminine role during homosexual relations.
Fag: the male inmate who is believed to be a "natural" or "born" homosexual.
Lemon Squeezer: the inmate who has an unattractive "girlfriend."
Screw: Guard.
Stud Broad (or Daddy): the female inmate who assumes the role of a male during lesbian relations.
Femme (or Mommy): the female inmate who plays the female role during lesbian relations.
Cherry (or Cherrie): the female inmate who has not yet been introduced to lesbian activities.
Fay Broad: a white female inmate.

Sources: Gresham Sykes, *The Society of Captives* (Princeton, NJ: Princeton University Press, 1958); Rose Giallombardo, *Society of Women: A Study of A Woman's Prison* (New York: John Wiley and Sons, 1966); and; Richard A. Cloward et al., *Theoretical Studies in Social Organization of the Prison* (New York: Social Science Research Council, 1960).

Some criminologists have suggested that inmate codes are simply a reflection of general criminal values. If so, they are brought to the institution rather than created there. Either way, the power and pervasiveness of the inmate code require convicts to conform to the world view held by the majority of prisoners.

THE FUNCTION OF PRISON SOCIETY

Why do prison societies exist? Human beings are by nature social beings. All around the world people live in groups and create a culture suited to their needs. Rarely, however, does the intensity of human interaction approach the level found in prisons. The prisons of today are crowded places where inmates can find no retreat from the constant demands of staff and the pressures brought by fellow prisoners. Even solitary confinement occurs within the context of prison rules and inmate expectations. In *The Society of Captives,* Gresham Sykes described the "pains of imprisonment."[14]

The pains of imprisonment — the result of deprivations and frustrations forced upon inmates by the rigors of confinement — form the nexus of a deprivation model of prison culture. Sykes grouped them into five areas. They include deprivations of (1) liberty, (2) goods and services, (3) heterosexual relationships, (4) autonomy, and (5) personal security. Prison subculture, according to Sykes, is an adaptation to such deprivations.

In contrast to the deprivation model, the importation model of prison culture suggests that inmates bring with them values, roles, and behavior patterns from the outside world. Such external values, second nature as they are to career offenders, depend substantially upon the criminal world view. Upon confinement, these external elements shape the inmate social world. Social structure is a term that refers to accepted social arrangements. Donald Clemmer's early study of the prison recognized nine structural dimensions in inmate society. He said that prison society could be described in terms of:[15]

1. The prisoner-staff dichotomy.
2. The three general classes of prisoners.
3. Work gangs and cellhouse groups.
4. Racial groups.
5. Type of offense.
6. The power of inmate "politicians."
7. Degree of sexual abnormality.
8. The record of repeat offenses.
9. Personality differences due to preprison socialization.

Clemmer's nine structural dimensions are probably still descriptive of prison life today. When applied in individual situations, they designate an inmate's position in the prison "pecking order," and create expectations of the appropriate role for that person. Prison roles serve to satisfy the needs of inmates for power, sexual performance, material possessions, individuality, and personal pleasure. For example, inmate leaders, sometimes referred to as "real men" or "toughs" by prisoners in early studies, offer protection to those who live by the rules. They also provide for a redistribution of wealth inside of prison and see to it that the rules of the complex prison-derived economic system — based on barter, gambling, and sexual favors — are observed.

The Evolution of Subcultures

By the time John Irwin was about to complete his now famous study of *The Felon* (1970), he expressed the worry that his book was already obsolete.[16] *The Felon*, for all its insights into prison subculture, follows in the descriptive tradition of works by Clemmer and Reimer. Irwin recognized that by 1970 prison subcultures had begun to reflect cultural changes sweeping America. A decade later some authors were able to write: "It was no longer meaningful to speak of a single inmate culture or even subculture. By the time we began our field research . . . it was clear that the unified, oppositional convict culture, found in the sociological literature on prisons, no longer existed."[17]

Stastny and Tyrnauer, describing prison life at Washington State Penitentiary in 1982, discovered four clearly distinguishable subcultures: (1) official, (2) traditional, (3) reform, and (4) revolutionary. Official culture was promoted by the staff and by administrative rules of the institution. Enthusiastic participants in official culture were mostly officers and other staff members, although inmates were also well aware of the normative expectations official culture imposed on them.   Official culture impacted the lives of inmates primarily through the creation of a prisoner hierarchy based on sentence length, prison jobs, and the "perks" which cooperation with the dictates of official culture could produce.   Traditional prison culture, as described by Clemmer and Sykes, still existed, but its participants spent much of their time lamenting the decline of the convict code among younger prisoners. Reform culture was unique at Washington State Penitentiary. It was the result of a brief experiment with inmate self-government during the early 1970s. Elements of prison life which evolved during the experimental period sometimes survived the termination of self-government and were eventually institutionalized in what Stastny and Tyrnauer call reform culture.   Such elements included inmate participation in civic-style clubs, citizen involvement in the daily activities of the prison, banquets, and inmate speaking tours. Revolutionary culture built on the radical political rhetoric of the disenfranchised and found a ready audience among minority prisoners who saw themselves as victims of society's basic unfairness. Although they did not participate in it, revolutionary inmates understood traditional prison culture and generally avoided running afoul of its rules.

HOMOSEXUALITY IN PRISON

Sykes's early study of prison argot found many words describing homosexual activity. Among them were the terms "wolf," "punk," and "fag." Wolves were aggressive men who assumed the masculine role in homosexual relations. Punks were forced into submitting to the female role, often by wolves. Fags described a special category of men who had a natural proclivity toward homosexual activity. While both wolves and punks were fiercely committed to their heterosexual identity and participated in homosexuality only because of prison conditions, fags generally engaged in homosexual life-styles before their entry into prison.

Prison homosexuality depends to a considerable degree upon the naïveté of young inmates experiencing prison for the first time. Older prisoners looking for homosexual liaisons may ingratiate themselves with new arrivals by offering cigarettes, money, drugs, food, or protection.   At some future time these "loans" will be "called in," with payoffs demanded in sexual favors. Because the inmate code requires the repayment of favors, the fish who tries to resist may quickly find himself face to face with the brute force of inmate society.

Prison rape represents a special category of homosexual behavior behind bars. Estimates of the incidence of rape in prison vary. One study found 4.7% of inmates in the Philadelphia prison system willing to report sexual assaults.[18]   Most studies find that black inmates are far more likely to commit rape in prison than are whites.[19] Victims of rape, on the other hand, are more likely to be white. This difference seems to hold even in prisons where there is considerable variation in the proportion of black and white inmates.[20]

Lee Bowker, summarizing studies of sexual violence in prison,[21] provides the following observations:

♦ Most sexual aggressors do not consider themselves to be homosexuals.
♦ Sexual release is not the primary motivation for sexual attack.

♦ Many aggressors must continue to participate in gang rapes in order to avoid becoming victims themselves.
♦ The aggressors have themselves suffered much damage to their masculinity in the past.

As in cases of heterosexual rape, sexual assaults in prison are likely to leave psychological scars long after the physical event is over.[22]   The victims of prison rape live in fear, may feel constantly threatened, and can turn to self-destructive activities.[23]   At the very least victims question their masculinity and undergo a personal devaluation.   In some cases victims of prison sexual attacks turn to violence.   Frustrations, long bottled up through abuse and fear, may explode and turn the would-be rapist into a victim of prison homicide.

❑ THE STAFF WORLD

The flip side of inmate society can be found in the world of the correctional officer. Prison staff members bring diverse values and a variety of personality types to the institution. Staff roles encompass those of warden, psychologist, counselor, area supervisor, program director, instructor, guard, and in some large prisons, physician and therapist. Correctional officers, generally seen as at the bottom of the staff hierarchy, may be divided into cellblock and tower officers, while some are regularly assigned to administrative offices where they perform clerical tasks.

Lucien Lombardo has described the process by which officers are socialized into the prison work world.[24]   Lombardo interviewed 359 correctional personnel at New York's Auburn prison and found that rookie officers had to quickly abandon preconceptions of both inmates and other staff members.   According to Lombardo new officers learn that inmates are not the "monsters" much of the public makes them out to be.   On the other hand, the disappointment the rookie finds in the experienced worker comes from the realization that ideals of professionalism, often stressed during early training, are rarely translated into reality.   The pressures of the institutional work environment, however, soon force most correctional personnel to adopt a united front in relating to inmates.

One of the leading formative influences on staff culture is the potential threat posed by inmates.   Inmates far outnumber correctional personnel in any institution, and the hostility they feel for officers is only barely hidden even at the best of times.   Correctional personnel know that however friendly inmates may appear, a sudden change in institutional climate — as can happen in anything from simple disturbances on the yard to full-blown riots — can quickly and violently unmask deep-rooted feelings of mistrust and hatred.

CUSTODY AND CONTROL — STILL PRIMARY TODAY

As in years past, custody and control are still the two paramount concerns of prison staffers today.   Custody is what society expects of correctional staff.   It is the basic prerequisite of successful job performance. Custody is necessary before any other correctional activities, such as instruction or counseling, can be undertaken.

Control, the other major staff concern, ensures order, and an orderly prison is thought to be safe and secure. In routine daily activities, control over almost all aspects of inmate behavior becomes paramount in the minds of most correctional officers. It is the twin interests of custody and control that lead to institutionalized procedures for ensuring security in most facilities. The use of strict rules; body and cell searches; counts; unannounced shakedowns; the control of dangerous items, materials, and contraband; and the extensive use of bars, locks, fencing, cameras, and alarms all support the human vigilance of the officers in maintaining security.

TESTING AND TRAINING OF CORRECTIONAL OFFICERS

Expectations of correctional officers have never been high. Prison staffers are generally accorded low status in occupational surveys. Guard jobs require minimal formal education and hold few opportunities for professional growth and advancement. They are low paying, frustrating, and often boring. Growing problems in our nation's prisons, including emerging issues of legal liability, however, require a well-trained and adequately equipped professional guard force. As correctional personnel become more and more proficient, the old concept of "guard" is becoming supplanted by that of a professional correctional "officer."

The professionalization of corrections is on the rise, having been led by states like California.

A few states and some large-city correctional systems make efforts to eliminate individuals with potentially harmful personalities from correctional officer applicant pools. New York, New Jersey, Ohio, Pennsylvania, and Rhode Island all use some form of psychological screening in assessing candidates for prison jobs.[25]

Although only a few states utilize psychological screening, all make use of training programs intended to prepare successful applicants for prison work. New York, for example, requires trainees to complete six weeks of classroom-based instruction, followed by another six weeks of on-the-job training. New York's 244-hour correctional officer curriculum is supplemented with 40 hours of rifle range practice. Training days begin around 5 A.M. with a mile run and conclude after dark with study halls for students who need extra help. To keep pace with rising inmate populations, the state has often had to run a number of simultaneous training academies.[26]

On the federal level a new model for correctional careers confronts many of the problems of correctional staffing head on. The Federal Bureau of Prisons' Career Development Model stands as an example of what state departments of correction can do in the area of staff training and development. The model establishes five sequential phases for the development of career correctional officers:[27] (1) Phase I, Career Assessment; (2) Phase II, Career Path Development; (3) Phase III, Career Enhancement and Management Development; (4) Phase IV, Advanced Management Development; and (5) Phase V, Senior Executive Service Development. Using a psychological personality inventory, the model seeks to identify the skills, abilities, and interests of officers and matches them with career opportunities in the federal correctional system. The new federal model builds upon the large number and diverse types of federal institutions which allow personnel a wide choice in the conditions of employment. Such a situation may not be possible to duplicate in state correctional systems. Small institutions often have few opportunities for added responsibility, and state systems offer neither the geographical nor the programmatic diversity of the federal Bureau of Prisons.

☐ WOMEN IN PRISON

Nearly 47,000 women were imprisoned in state and federal correctional institutions throughout the United States at the start of 1992.[28] California had the largest number of female prisoners (6,302), exceeding even the federal government (5,654).[29] Figure 10-1 provides a breakdown of the total American prison population by gender. Most women inmates were housed in centralized state facilities known as "women's prisons," which are dedicated exclusively to the holding of female felons. Many states, however, particularly those with small populations, continue to keep women prisoners in special wings of what are otherwise institutions for men.

While there are still far more men imprisoned across the nation than women (approximately 17 men for every woman), the number of female inmates is rising quickly — faster, in fact, than the proportion of male inmates.[30] The number of female inmates nearly tripled during the 1980s, and women now account for 6% of all imprisoned persons. Only a decade ago — in 1984 — women comprised only slightly more than 4% of the nation's overall prison population.

Women's prisons are overcrowded, which individual cases demonstrate. The California Institution for Women at Frontera, for example, was originally designed to hold 1,011 inmates. As of this writing it holds more than 2,500 women. At Bedford Hills Correctional Facility in Westchester County, New York, double-bunking is the rule, and conditions there are so crowded that inmates barely have the room necessary to turn around in their living quarters. Even well-managed prisons with nice facades can have problems. One study of a pleasant-appearing women's prison in New York concluded that it was a place of "intense hostility, frustrations and anger."[31]

Professionals working with imprisoned women, attribute the rise in female prison populations largely to drugs. Figure 10-2 shows, in relative graphics, the proportion of men and women imprisoned for various kinds of offenses. While the figure shows that approximately 17% of all women in prison are there explicitly for drug offenses, other estimates say that the impact of drugs on the imprisonment of women is far greater than a simple reading of the figure indicates. Warden Robert Brennan, of New York City's Rose M. Singer jail for women, estimates that drugs — either directly or indirectly — account for the imprisonment of around 95% of the inmates there. In fact, incarcerated women most frequently list (1) trying to pay for drugs, (2) attempts to relieve economic pressures, and (3) poor judgment as the reasons for their arrest.[32] Drug-related offenses committed by women include larceny, burglary, fraud, prostitution, embezzlement, and robbery, as well as other crimes stimulated by the desire for drugs.

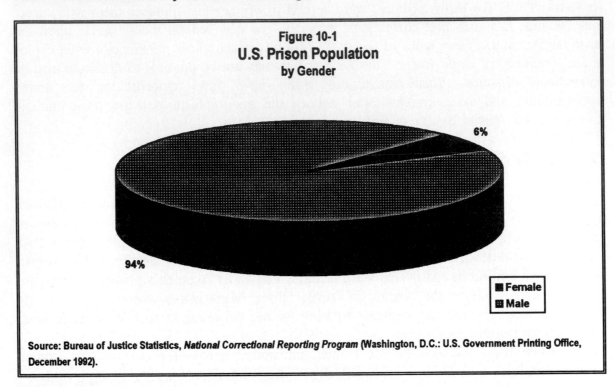

Figure 10-1
U.S. Prison Population
by Gender

6%

94%

☐ Female
☐ Male

Source: Bureau of Justice Statistics, *National Correctional Reporting Program* (Washington, D.C.: U.S. Government Printing Office, December 1992).

Another reason for the rapid growth in the number of women behind bars may be the demise, over the last decade or two, of the "chivalry factor." The chivalry factor, so called because it was based upon an archaic cultural perspective which depicted women as helpless or childlike in their social roles relative to men, allegedly lessened the responsibility of female offenders in the eyes of some male judges and prosecutors, resulting in fewer active prison sentences for women involved in criminal activity. Recent studies show that the chivalry factor is now primarily of historical interest. In jurisdictions examined, the gender of convicted offenders no longer affects sentencing practices except insofar as it may be tied to other social variables. B. Keith Crew,[33] for example, in a comprehensive study of gender differences in sentencing observes, "[a] woman does not automatically receive leniency because of her status of wife or mother, but she may receive leniency if those statuses become part of the official explanation of her criminal behavior (e.g., she was stealing to feed her children; an abusive husband forced her to commit a crime)."

Although there may be no one "typical" prison for women, and no perfectly "average" female inmate, the American Correctional Association's 1990 report by the Task Force on the Female Offender found that women inmates and the institutions which house them could be generally described as follows:[34]

◆ "Most prisons for women are located in towns of less than 5,000 inhabitants."

♦ "A significant number of facilities were not designed for the housing of females."

♦ "The number of female offenders being sent to prison is on the rise."

♦ "Most facilities housing female inmates also house males."

♦ Not many facilities for women have classification programs designed for the female offender.

♦ "Very few major disturbances or escapes are reported among female inmates."

♦ Substance abuse among female inmates is very high.

♦ "Very few work assignments are available to female inmates."

♦ "The number of female inmates without a high school education is very high."

Statistics[35] show that the average age of female inmates is 29–30, most are black or Hispanic (57%), most come from single parent or broken homes, and 50% have other family members who are incarcerated. The typical female inmate is a high school dropout (50%), who left school either because she was bored or because of pregnancy (34%). She has been arrested an average of two to nine times (55%) and run away from home between one and three times (65%). Thirty-nine percent report using drugs to make them feel better emotionally, while 28% have attempted suicide at least once. Sixty-two percent were single parents with one to three children prior to incarceration, and many have been physically and/or sexually abused.[36]

Eighty percent of women entering prison are mothers, and 85% of those women retain custody of their children at the time of prison admission. One out of every four women entering prison has either recently given birth or is pregnant. Critics charge that women inmates face a prison system designed for male inmates and run by men. Hence, pregnant inmates, many of whom are drug users, malnourished, or sick, often receive little prenatal care, a situation which risks additional complications. Separation from their children is a significant deprivation facing incarcerated mothers. Although husbands and/or boyfriends may assume responsibility for the children of imprisoned spouses/girlfriends, such an outcome is the exception to the rule. Eventually, a large proportion of children are released by their imprisoned mothers into foster care or put up for adoption.

Some states do offer parenting classes for women inmates with children. In a national survey[37] of prisons for women, 36 states responded with information about parenting programs which deal with care-taking, reducing violence toward children, visitation problems, and related issues. Some offer facilities as diverse as play areas complete with toys, while others attempt to alleviate difficulties attending mother/child visits. The typical program studied lasts from four to nine weeks and provides for a meeting time of two hours per week. Twenty-five inmates participate in an average parenting program at any given time.

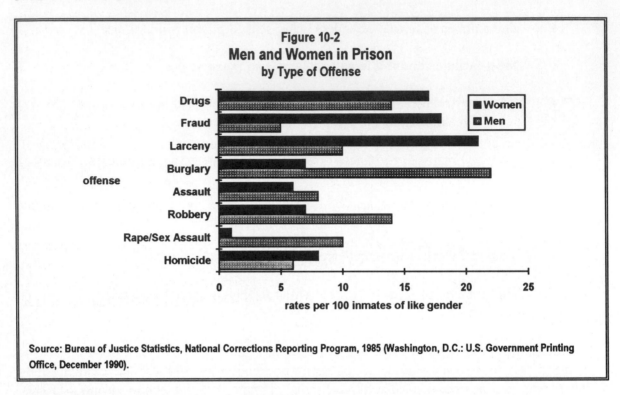

Figure 10-2
Men and Women in Prison
by Type of Offense

rates per 100 inmates of like gender

Source: Bureau of Justice Statistics, National Corrections Reporting Program, 1985 (Washington, D.C.: U.S. Government Printing Office, December 1990).

Other meaningful prison programs for women are often lacking — perhaps because the ones which are in place were originally based upon traditional models of female roles which left little room for substantive employment opportunities. Many trade-training programs still emphasize low-paying jobs such as cook, beautician, or laundry machine operator. Classes in homemaking are not uncommon.

SOCIAL STRUCTURE

Most studies of women's prison have revealed a unique feature of such institutions: the existence of organized families artificially constructed by the inmates. Typical of such studies are Ward and Kassebaum's *Women's Prison: Sex and Social Structure*,[38] E. Heffernan's *Making It in Prison: The Square, the Cool, and the Life*,[39] and Rose Giallombardo's *Society of Women: A Study of Women's Prison.*[40]

Giallombardo, for example, examined the Federal Reformatory for Women at Alderson, West Virginia, spending a year in gathering data (1962–1963). Focusing closely on the formation of families, she entitled one of her chapters "The Homosexual Alliance as a Marriage Unit." In it she describes in great detail the sexual identities assumed by women at Alderson, and the symbols they chose to communicate those roles. Hair style, dress, language, and mannerisms were all used to signify "maleness" or "femaleness." Giallombardo details "the anatomy of the marriage relationship from courtship to 'fall out,' that is, from inception to the parting of the ways, or divorce."[41] Romantic love at Alderson was seen as of central importance to any relationship between inmates, and all homosexual relationships were described as voluntary. Through marriage the "stud broad" became the husband, and the "femme" the wife.

Studies attempting to document the extent of inmate involvement in prison "families" produce varying results. Some have found as many as 71% of women prisoners involved in the phenomenon, while others have found none.[42] The kinship systems described by Giallombardo and others, however, extend beyond simple "family" ties to the formation of large, intricately related, groups. In these groups the roles of "children," "in-laws," "grandparents," and so on may be explicitly recognized. Even "birth order" within a family can become an issue for kinship groups.[43] Kinship groups sometimes occupy a common houschold — usually a prison cottage or dormitory area. The description of women's prisons provided by authors like Giallombardo show a closed society in which social interaction — including expectations, normative forms of behavior, and emotional ties — is regulated by an inventive system of artificial relationships which mirror the outside world.

Some authors have suggested that this emphasis on describing family structures and sexual relationships in women's prisons is unfortunate because it tends to deny other structural features of those institutions.[44] The family emphasis may, in fact, be due to traditional explanations of female criminality which were intertwined with narrow under-standings of the role of women in society.

TYPES OF WOMEN INMATES

As in institutions for men, the subculture of women's prisons is multi-dimensional. Esther Heffernan, for example, found that three terms used by women prisoners she studied — the *square*, the *cool*, and the *life* — were indicative of three styles of adaptation to prison life.[45] Square inmates had few early experiences with criminal lifestyles and tended to sympathize with the values and attitudes of conventional society. Cool prisoners were more likely to be career offenders. They tended to keep to themselves, and were generally supportive of inmate values. Women who participated in the "life" subculture were well familiar with lives of crime. Many had been arrested repeatedly for prostitution, drug use, theft, and so on. "Life" group members were full participants in the economic, social, and familiar arrangements of the prison. Heffernan believed that "the life" offered an alternative life-style to women who had experienced early and constant rejection by conventional society. Within "the life," women could establish relationships, achieve status, and find meaning in their lives. The "square," the "life," and the "cool" represented subcultures to Heffernan, because individuals with similar adaptive choices tended to closely relate to one another and to support the life-style characteristic of that type.

"Square" inmates are definitely in the minority in prisons for both men and women. Perhaps for that reason they have rarely been studied. In an insightful self-examination, however, one such inmate, Jean Harris, published her impressions of prison life after more than seven years in the maximum security Bedford Hills Correctional Facility. Harris was convicted of killing the "Scarsdale Diet Doctor," Herman Tarnower, over a romance gone sour. A successful socialite in her early fifties at the time of the crime, Harris had an eye-opening experience in prison. Her book, *They Always Call Us Ladies*,[46] argues hard for prison reform. Sounding like the "square" she was, Harris says other inmates are: "hard for you and me to relate to,"[47] and describes them as "childlike women without social skills."[48] Speaking to a reporter Harris related, "There's really nobody for me to talk to here."[49]

Recently, the social structure of women's prison has become dichotomized by the advent of "crack kids," as they are called in prison argot. "Crack kids" are streetwise young women with little respect for traditional prison values, for their elders, or even for their own children. Known for frequent fights, and for their lack of even simple domestic skills, these young women quickly estrange many older inmates, some of whom call them "animalescents."

VIOLENCE IN WOMEN'S PRISONS

Some authors have suggested that violence in women's prisons is less frequent than it is in institutions for men. Bowker observes that "[e]xcept for the behavior of a few "guerrillas," it appears that violence is only used in women's prisons to settle questions of dominance and subordination when other manipulative strategies fail to achieve the desired effect."[50] It appears that few homosexual liaisons are forced, perhaps representing a general aversion among women to such victimization in wider society. At least one study, however, has shown the use of sexual violence in women's prisons as a form of revenge against inmates who are overly vocal in their condemnation of such practices among other prisoners.[51]

The Task Force on the Female Offender[52] recommends a number of changes in the administration of prisons for women. Among them are:

- ◆ Substance-abuse programs are absolutely necessary in the treatment of today's female offender.

- ◆ Women inmates need to acquire greater literacy skills, and literacy programs should form the basis upon which other programs are built.

- ◆ "Female offenders should be housed in buildings independent of male inmates."

- ◆ Institutions for women should develop programs for keeping children in the facility in order to "fortify the bond between mother and child."

- ◆ "To ensure equal access to programming, institutions should be built to accommodate programs for female offenders."

❑ ISSUES FACING PRISONS TODAY

Prisons are society's answer to a number of social problems. They house outcasts and misfits. While prisons provide a part of the answer to the question of crime control, they also face problems of their own.   A few of those special problems are the following:

AIDS

An earlier chapter discussed the steps being taken by police agencies to deal with health threats represented by AIDS.   As early as October 1, 1987 the Center for Disease Control reported confirming 1,964 cases of AIDS among inmates of the nation's prisons.[53] Sixty-two percent of reported AIDS cases among correctional inmates were found in the Mid-Atlantic states.

Some prisons covered by the CDC survey counted no cases of AIDS among their inmates.   More than 70% of state and federal systems had fewer than 10 cases.   However, at the other extreme, six state and one city/county system reported over 50 cases each.

Men account for 95% of all inmates affected by AIDS.   Blacks, at 58%, comprise the largest racial/ethnic category; 32% of those infected are white, and 10% are Hispanic.

The incidence of HIV infection among the general population stood at 8.6 cases per 100,000 at the time of the Center for Disease Control's report.   Among inmates, the incidence rate of AIDS was 54 cases per 100,000 — more than six times as great.   The fact that inmates tend to have histories of high-risk behavior, especially intravenous drug use, probably explains the difference.

Contrary to popular opinion, AIDS transmission inside of prisons appears minimal. In a test of inmates at a U.S. Army military prison, 542 prisoners who, upon admission had tested negative for exposure to the AIDS virus, were retested two years later.   None showed any signs of exposure to the virus.[54]   On the other hand, some authorities suggest that it is only a matter of time before intravenous drug abuse and homosexual activity inside of prisons begin to make a visible contribution to the spread of AIDS.[55]   Similarly, prison staffers fear infection from AIDS through routine activities, such as cell searches, responding to fights, performing body searches, administering CPR, and confiscating needles or weapons.

A recent report by the National Institute of Justice[56] suggests that there are two types of strategies available to correctional systems to reduce the transmission of AIDS. One strategy relies upon medical technology to identify seropositive inmates and segregate them from the rest of the prison population.   Mass screening and inmate segregation, however, may be prohibitively expensive. They may also be illegal.   Some states specifically prohibit HIV antibody testing without the informed consent of the person tested.[57]   The related issue of confidentiality may be difficult to manage, especially where the purpose of testing is to segregate infected inmates from others.   In addition, civil liability may result where inmates are falsely labeled as infected, or where inmates known to be infected are not prevented from spreading the disease.

The second strategy is one of prevention through education.   Educational programs teach inmates about the dangers of continued high-risk behavior.   An NIJ model program[58] recommends the use of simple straightforward messages presented by knowledgeable and approachable trainers. Alarmism, says NIJ, is to be avoided.   In anticipation of court rulings which likely prohibit the mass testing of inmates for the AIDS virus, the second strategy seems best.

GERIATRIC OFFENDERS

Some prisoners grow old behind bars. Others are old before they get there. American prisons, serving an aging population, are seeing more geriatric prisoners than ever before. Authorities estimate that while 10% of prisoners in 1990 were over 50 years old, around 40% will fall into that category by the year 2,000.[59]

The "graying" of America's prison population is due to a number of causes: (1) increasing crime among those over 50; (2) the gradual aging of the society from which prisoners come; (3) a trend toward longer sentences, especially for violent offenders; and (4) the gradual accumulation of older habitual offenders in prison.[60]

Crimes of violence are what bring most older inmates into the correctional system. According to one study, 52% of inmates who were over the age of 50 at the time they entered prison had committed violent crimes, compared with 41% of younger inmates.[61] Ronald Wikberg and Burk Foster provide a snapshot of longtermers in their recent study of Angola prison.[62] Wikberg and Foster described 31 inmates at the Louisiana State Penitentiary at Angola who had served a continuous sentence of 25 years or longer, as of early 1988. They found the typical longtermer to be black (27 out of 31), with many of them sentenced for raping or killing a white. Inmate ages ranged from 42 to 71. A common thread linking most of these inmates was that their release was opposed by victim's families and friends. Some had a record as prison troublemakers, but a few had been near-model prisoners.

Longtermers and geriatric inmates have special needs. They tend to suffer from handicaps, physical impairments, and illnesses not generally encountered among their more youthful counterparts. Unfortunately few prisons are equipped to deal adequately with the medical needs of aging offenders. Some large facilities have begun to set aside special sections to care for elderly inmates with "typical" disorders such as Alzheimer's disease, cancer, or heart disease. Unfortunately, such efforts have barely kept pace with problems. The number of inmates requiring round-the-clock care is expected to increase dramatically over the next two decades.[63]

Even the idea of rehabilitation takes on a new meaning where geriatric offenders are concerned. What kinds of programs are most likely to be useful in providing the older inmate with the needed tools for success on the outside? Which counseling strategies hold the greatest promise for introducing socially acceptable behavior patterns into the long-established lifestyles of elderly offenders about to be released? There are few answers to these questions. To date, no federal studies have been done to prepare the nation's prison system for handling the needs of older inmates.[64]

MENTALLY ILL INMATES

The mentally ill are another inmate category with special needs. Some inmates are neurotic or have personality problems which increase tension in prison. Others have serious psychological disorders which may have escaped earlier diagnosis (at trial) or which did not provide a legal basis for the reduction of criminal responsibility. A fair number of offenders develop psychiatric symptoms while in prison. Some news accounts of modern prisons have focused squarely on the problem: "raging mental illness is so common it's ignored," wrote a

Newsweek staffer visiting a women's prison.[65]

Unfortunately, few states have any substantial capacity for the psychiatric treatment of mentally disturbed inmates. In 1982 Hans Toch described the largely ineffective practice of bus therapy, whereby disturbed inmates are shuttled back and forth between mental health centers and correctional facilities.[66] In February 1990, the U.S. Supreme Court, in the case of *Washington State* v. *Harper,* ruled that mentally ill inmates could be required to take antipsychotic drugs, even against their wishes. The ruling stipulated that such a requirement would apply where "the inmate is dangerous to himself or others, and the treatment is in the inmate's medical interest."

Mentally deficient inmates constitute still another group with special needs. Some studies estimate the proportion of mentally deficient inmates at about 10%.[67] Retarded inmates are less likely to complete training and rehabilitative programs successfully than are other inmates. They also evidence difficulty in adjusting to the routines of prison life. As a consequence they are likely to exceed the averages in proportion of sentence served.[68] Only seven states report special facilities or programs for the mentally retarded inmate.[69] Other state systems "mainstream" such inmates, making them participate in regular activities with other inmates.

Texas, one state which does provide special services for retarded inmates, began a Mentally Retarded Offender Program (MROP) in 1984. Inmates in Texas are given a battery of tests that measure intellectual and social adaptability skills Prisoners who are identified as retarded are housed in special satellite correctional units. The Texas MROP program provides individual and group counseling, along with training in adult life skills.

☐ SUMMARY

Prisons are small societies with their own rules, values, norms, and social roles. Complicating life behind bars are the numerous conflicts of interest between inmates and staff. Lawsuits, prisoner unions, and frequent grievances are symptoms of these differences.

The problems which exist in conventional society are mirrored and often magnified inside of prison. Crime does not stop at the prison door, nor does rehabilitation automatically begin. If we are to expect prisons to meet the demands of rehabilitation and reformation, we must be willing to solve the problems of the prison first.

DISCUSSION QUESTIONS

1. Explain the concept of prison subcultures. What purpose do you think such subcultures serve? Why do they develop?

2. What does "prisonization" mean? Describe the U-shaped curve developed by Wheeler as it relates to prisonization. Why do you think the curve is U-shaped?

3. What is prison argot? What purpose does it serve?

4. What are the primary concerns of prison staff? Do you agree that those concerns are important? What other goals might staff focus on?

5. What are some of the special problems facing prisons today which are discussed in this chapter? What new problems do you think the future might bring?

NOTES

1.   Joseph W. Rogers, "Mary Belle Harris: Warden and Rehabilitation Pioneer," *Criminal Justice Research Bulletin,* Vol. 3, no. 9 (Huntsville, TX: Sam Houston State University), (1988), p. 8.

2.   Hans Reimer, "Socialization in the Prison Community," *Proceedings of the American Prison Association, 1937* (New York: American Prison Association, 1937), pp. 151–155.

3.   Donald Clemmer, *The Prison Community* (Boston: Christopher, 1940).

4.   Gresham M. Sykes, *The Society of Captives: A Study of a Maximum Security Prison* (Princeton, NJ: Princeton University Press, 1958).

5.   Donald R. Cressey, ed., *The Prison: Studies in Institutional Organization and Change* (New York: Holt, Rinehart and Winston, 1961).

6.   Lawrence Hazelrigg, ed., *Prison Within Society: A Reader in Penology* (Garden City, NY: Anchor Books, 1969), Preface.

7.   Charles Stastny and Gabrielle Tyrnauer, *Who Rules the Joint?: The Changing Political Culture of Maximum-Security Prisons in America* (Lexington, MA: Lexington Books, 1982), p. 131.

8.   Erving Goffman, *Asylums: Essays on the Social Situation of Mental Patients and Other Inmates* (Garden City, NY: Anchor Books, 1961).

9.   The concept of prisonization is generally attributed to Clemmer, *The Prison Community,* although Quaker penologists of the late 1700s were actively concerned with preventing "contamination" (the spread of criminal values) among prisoners.

10.   Gresham M. Sykes and Sheldon L. Messinger, "The Inmate Social System," in Richard A. Cloward et al., *Theoretical Studies in Social Organization of the Prison* (New York: Social Science Research Council, 1960), pp. 5–19.

11.   Ibid., p. 5.

12.   Sykes, *The Society of Captives*, p. xiii.

13.   Stanton Wheeler, "Socialization in Correctional Communities," *American Sociological Review,* Vol. 26 (October 1961), pp. 697–712.

14.   Ibid., pp. 65–78.

15. Clemmer, *The Prison Community*, pp. 294–296.

16. Stastny and Tyrnauer, *Who Rules the Joint*, p. 135.

17. Ibid.

18. Alan J. Davis, "Sexual Assaults in the Philadelphia Prison System and Sheriff's Vans," *Trans-Action*, Vol. 6 (December, 1968), pp. 8–16.

19. Lee H. Bowker, *Prison Victimization* (New York: Elsevier-North Holland, 1980), p. 8, and Lee H. Bowker, *Prisoner Subcultures* (Lexington, MA: Lexington Books, 1977), p. 42.

20. Bowker, *Prison Victimization*, p. 9.

21. Bowker, *Prisoner Subcultures*, p. 42.

22. Bowker, *Prison Victimization*, p. 1.

23. Hans Toch, *Living in Prison: The Ecology of Survival* (New York: The Free Press, 1977), p. 151.

24. Lucien X. Lombardo, *Guards Imprisoned: Correctional Officers at Work* (New York: Elsevier, 1981), pp. 22–36.

25. Leonard Morgenbesser, "NY State Law Prescribes Psychological Screening for CO Job Applicants," *Correctional Training*, newsletter of the American Association of Correctional Training Personnel (Winter 1983), p. 1.

26. "A Sophisticated Approach to Training Prison Guards," *Newsday*, August 12, 1982.

27. Rosalie Rosetti, "Charting Your Course: Federal Model Encourages Career Choices," *Corrections Today* (August 1988), pp. 34–38.

28. Bureau of Justice Statistics (BJS), *Prisoners in 1991* (Washington, D.C.: The Bureau, 1992).

29. Ibid.

30. This section owes much to the American Correctional Association (ACA), Task Force on the Female Offender, *The Female Offender: What Does the Future Hold?* (Washington, D.C.: St. Mary's Press, 1990), and "The View from Behind Bars," *Time*, Fall 1990 (special issue), pp. 20–22.

31. James C. Fox, "Women's Prison Policy, Prisoner Activism, and the Impact of the Contemporary Feminist Movement: A Case Study" *The Prison Journal*, Vol 64, no. 1 (Spring/Summer 1984), pp. 15–36.

32. ACA, *The Female Offender*.

33. B. Keith Crew, "Sex Differences in Criminal Sentencing: Chivalry or Patriarchy?" *Justice Quarterly*, Vol. 8, no. 1 (March 1991), pp. 59–83.

34. ACA, *The Female Offender*.

35. Ibid.

36.   Mary Jeanette Clement, *National Survey of Programs for Incarcerated Women*, paper presented at the Academy of Criminal Justice Sciences annual meeting, Nashville, TN, March 1991.

37.   Ibid., pp. 8–9.

38.   D. Ward and G. Kannebaum, *Women's Prison: Sex and Social Structure* (London: Weidenfeld and Nicolson, 1966).

39.   E. Heffernan, *Making It in Prison: The Square, the Cool and the Life* (London: Wiley-Interscience, 1972).

40.   Rose Giallombardo, *Society of Women: A Study of Women's Prison* (New York: John Wiley and Sons, 1966).

41.   Ibid., p. 136.

42.   For a summary of such studies (including some previously unpublished) see Bowker, *Prisoner Subcultures*, p. 86.

43.   Giallombardo, Society of Women, p. 162.

44.   Russell P. Dobash, P. Emerson Dobash, and Sue Gutteridge, *The Imprisonment of Women* (Oxford: Basil Blackwell Ltd., 1986), p. 6.

45.   Heffernan, *Making It in Prison*.

46.   Jean Harris, *They Always Call Us Ladies* (New York: Scribners, 1988).

47.   "The Lady on Cell Block 112A," *Newsweek*, September 5, 1988, p. 60.

48.   Ibid.

49.   Ibid.

50.   Bowker, *Prison Victimization*, p. 53.

51.   Giallombardo, *Society of Women*.

52.   ACA. *The Female Offender*, p. 39.

53.   Theodore M. Hammett, *AIDS in Correctional Facilities: Issues and Options*, 3rd ed. (Washington, D.C.: National Institute of Justice, 1988), p. 23.

54.   Ibid., p. 29.

55.   M. A. R. Kleiman and R. W. Mockler, "AIDS, The Criminal Justice System, and Civil Liberties," *Governance: Harvard Journal of Public Policy*, (Summer/Fall, 1987), pp. 48–54.

56.   Hammett, *AIDS in Correctional Facilities*, p. 37.

57.   At the time of writing California, Wisconsin, Massachusetts, New York, and the District of Columbia were among such jurisdictions.

58. Hammett, *AIDS in Correctional Facilities*, pp. 47–49.

59. Sol Chaneles, "Growing Old Behind Bars," *Psychology Today*, October 1987, pp. 47–51.

60. Ronald Wikberg and Burk Foster, "The Longtermers: Louisiana's Longest Serving Inmates and Why They've Stayed So Long," paper presented at the annual meeting of the Academy of Criminal Justice Sciences, Washington, D.C., 1989.

61. Lincoln J. Fry, "The Older Prison Inmate: A Profile," *The Justice Professional*, Vol. 2, no. 1 (Spring 1987), pp. 1–12.

62. Wikberg and Foster, *The Longtermers*.

63. Ibid., p. 51.

64. Chaneles, "Growing Old Behind Bars," p. 51.

65. "The Lady on Cell Block 112A," p. 60.

66. Hans Toch, "The Disturbed Disruptive Inmate: Where Does the Bus Stop?" *The Journal of Psychiatry and Law*, Vol. 10 (1982), pp. 327–349.

67. Robert O. Lampert, "The Mentally Retarded Offender in Prison," *The Justice Professional*, Vol. 2, no. 1 (Spring 1987), p. 61.

68. Ibid., p. 64.

69. George C. Denkowski and Kathryn M. Denkowski, "The Mentally Retarded Offender in the State Prison System: Identification, Prevalence, Adjustment, and Rehabilitation," *Criminal Justice and Behavior*, Vol. 12 (1985), pp. 55–75.

Appendix

THE CONSTITUTION OF
THE UNITED STATES OF AMERICA,
AS AMENDED

PREAMBLE

We the People of the United States, in Order to form a more perfect Union, establish Justice, insure domestic Tranquility, provide for the common defense, promote the general Welfare, and secure the Blessings of Liberty to ourselves and our Posterity, do ordain and establish this Constitution for the United States of America.

ARTICLE I

Section 1. All legislative powers herein granted shall be vested in a Congress of the United States, which shall consist of a Senate and House of Representatives.

Section 2. The House of Representatives shall be composed of Members chosen every second Year by the People of the several States, and the Electors in each State shall have the Qualifications requisite for Electors of the most numerous Branch of the State Legislature.

No Person shall be a Representative who shall not have attained to the Age of twenty five Years, and been seven Years a Citizen of the United States, and who shall not, when elected, be an Inhabitant of that State in which he shall be chosen.

Representatives and direct Taxes shall be apportioned among the several States which may be included within this Union, according to their respective Numbers, which shall be determined by adding to the whole Number of free Persons, including those bound to Service for a Term of Years, and excluding Indians not taxed, three fifths of all other Persons. The actual Enumeration shall be made within three Years after the first Meeting of the Congress of the United States, and within every subsequent Term of ten Years, in such manner as they shall by Law direct. The Number of Representatives shall not exceed one for every thirty Thousand, but each State shall have at Least one Representative; and until such enumeration shall be made, the State of New Hampshire shall be entitled to chuse three, Massachusetts eight, Rhode Island and Providence Plantations one, Connecticut five, New York six, New Jersey four, Pennsylvania eight, Delaware one, Maryland six, Virginia ten, North Carolina five, South Carolina five, and Georgia three.

When vacancies happen in the Representation from any State, the Executive Authority thereof shall issue Writs of Election to fill such Vacancies.

The House of Representatives shall chuse their Speaker and other Officers; and shall have the sole power of Impeachment.

Section 3. The Senate of the United States shall be composed of two Senators from each State, chosen by the Legislature thereof, for six years; and each Senator shall have one Vote.

Immediately after they shall be assembled in consequence of the first Election, they shall be divided as equally as may be into three Classes. The Seats of the Senators of the first Class shall be vacated at the Expiration of the Second Year, of the second Class at the Expiration of the fourth Year, and of the third Class at the Expiration of the Sixth Year, so that one third may be chosen every second Year; and if Vacancies happen by Resignation, or otherwise, during the Recess of the Legislature of any State, the Executive thereof may make temporary Appointments until the next Meeting of the Legislature, which shall then fill such vacancies.

No person shall be a Senator who shall not have attained to the Age of thirty Years, and been nine Years a Citizen of the United States, and who shall not, when elected, be an Inhabitant of that State for which he shall be chosen.

The Vice President of the United States shall be President of the Senate, but shall have no Vote, unless they be equally divided.

The Senate shall chuse their other Officers, and also a President pro tempore, in the absence of the Vice President, or when he shall execute Office of President of the United States.

The Senate shall have the sole power to try all Impeachments. When sitting for that Purpose, they shall be on Oath or Affirmation. When the President of the United States is tried, the Chief Justice shall preside: And no person shall be convicted without the Concurrence of two thirds of the Members present.

Judgment in Cases of Impeachment shall not extend any further than to removal from Office, and disqualification to hold and enjoy any Office of Honor, Trust, or Profit under the United States: but the Party convicted shall nevertheless be liable and subject to Indictment, Trial, Judgment, and Punishment, according to Law.

Section 4. The Times, Places and Manner of holding Elections for Senators and Representatives, shall be prescribed in each State by the Legislature thereof; but the Congress may at any time by Law make or alter such Regulations, except as to the Places of chusing Senators.

The Congress shall assemble at least once in every Year, and such Meeting shall be on the first Monday in December, unless they shall by Law appoint a different Day.

Section 5. Each House shall be the Judge of the Elections, Returns, and Qualifications of its own Members, and a Majority of each shall constitute a Quorum to do business; but a smaller Number may adjourn from day to day, and may be authorized to compel the Attendance of absent Members, in such Manner, and under such penalties as each House may provide.

Each House may determine the Rules of its Proceedings, punish its Members for disorderly Behavior, and, with the Concurrence of two thirds, expel a Member.

Each House shall keep a Journal of its Proceedings, and from time to time publish the same, excepting such parts as may in their judgment require Secrecy, and the Yeas and Nays of the Members of either House on any question shall, at the Desire of one fifth of those Present, be entered on the Journal.

Neither House, during the Session of Congress, shall, without the Consent of the other, adjourn for more than three days, not to any other Place than that in which the two Houses shall be sitting.

Section 6. The Senators and Representatives shall receive a Compensation for their

Services, to be ascertained by Law, and paid out of the Treasury of the United States. They shall in all Cases, except Treason, Felony and Breach of the Peace, be privileged from Arrest during their Attendance at the Session of their respective Houses, and in going to and returning from the same; and for any Speech or Debate in either House, they shall not be questioned in any other Place.

No Senator or Representative shall, during the Time for which he was elected, be appointed to any civil Office under the Authority of the United States, which shall have been created, or the Emoluments whereof shall have been increased during such time; and no Person holding any Office under the United States, shall be a Member of either House during his Continuance in Office.

Section 7. All Bills for raising Revenue shall originate in the House of Representatives, but the Senate may propose or concur with Amendments as on other Bills.

Every Bill which shall have passed the House of Representatives and the Senate, shall, before it become a Law, be presented to the President of the United States; If he approve he shall sign it, but if not he shall return it, with his Objections to the House in which it shall have originated, who shall enter the Objections at large on their Journal, and proceed to reconsider it. If after such Reconsideration two thirds of that House shall agree to pass the Bill, it shall be sent together with the Objections, to the other House, by which it shall likewise be reconsidered, and if approved by two thirds of that House, it shall become a Law. But in all such Cases the Votes of both Houses shall be determined by yeas and Nays, and the Names of the Persons voting for and against the Bill shall be entered on the Journal of each House respectively. If any Bill shall not be returned by the President within ten Days (Sundays excepted) after it shall have been presented to him, the Same shall be a Law, in like Manner as if he had signed it, unless the Congress by their Adjournment prevent its Return in which Case it shall not be Law.

Every Order, Resolution, or Vote, to Which the Concurrence of the Senate and House of Representatives may be necessary (except on a question of Adjournment) shall be presented to the President of the United States; and before the Same shall take Effect, shall be approved by him, or being disapproved by him, shall be repassed by two thirds of the Senate and House of Representatives, according to the Rules and Limitations prescribed in the Case of a Bill.

Section 8. The Congress shall have Power To lay and collect Taxes, Duties, Imposts and Excises, to pay the Debts and provide for the common Defence and general Welfare of the United States; but all Duties, Imposts and Excises shall be uniform throughout the United States;

To borrow money on the credit of the United States; To regulate Commerce with foreign Nations, and among the several States, and with the Indian Tribes; To establish an uniform Rule of Naturalization, and uniform Laws on the subject of Bankruptcies throughout the United States; To coin money, regulate the Value thereof, and of foreign Coin, and fix the Standard of Weights and Measures; To provide for the Punishment of counterfeit the Securities and current Coin of the United States; To Establish Post Offices and Post Roads; To promote the Progress of Science and useful Arts, by securing for limited Times to Authors and Inventors the exclusive Right to their respective Writings and Discoveries; To constitute Tribunals inferior to the supreme Court; To define and punish Piracies and Felonies committed on the high Seas, and Offenses against the Law of Nations;

To declare War, grant letters of Marque and Reprisal, and make Rules concerning Captures on Land and Water; To raise and support Armies, but no Appropriation of Money to that Use shall be for a longer Term than two Years; To provide and maintain a Navy; To make Rules for the Government and Regulation of the land and naval Forces; To provide for calling forth the Militia to execute the Laws of the Union, suppress Insurrections and repel Invasions; To provide for organizing, arming, and disciplining, the Militia, and for governing such Part of them as may be employed in the Service of the United States, reserving to the States respectively, the Appointment of the Officers, and the Authority of training the Militia according to the discipline prescribed by Congress; To exercise exclusive Legislation in all Cases whatsoever, over such District (not exceeding ten Miles square) as may, by Cession of particular States, and the Acceptance of Congress, become the Seat of the Government of the United States, and to exercise Authority over all Places purchased by the Consent of the Legislature of the State in which the Same shall be, for the Erection of Forts, Magazines, Arsenals, dock-Yards, and other needful Buildings and; To make all Laws which shall be necessary and proper for carrying into Execution the foregoing Powers, and all other Powers, and all other Powers vested by this Constitution in the Government of the United States, or in any Department or Officer thereof.

  Section 9. The Migration or Importation of Such Persons as any of the States now existing shall think proper to admit, shall not be prohibited by the Congress prior to the Year one thousand eight hundred and eight, but a Tax or duty may be imposed on such Importation, not exceeding ten dollars for each Person.

  The privilege of the Writ of Habeas Corpus shall not be suspended, unless when in cases of Rebellion or Invasion the public Safety may require it.

  No Bill of Attainder or ex post facto Law shall be passed.

  No Capitation, or other direct, Tax shall be laid, unless in Proportion to the Census or Enumeration herein before directed to be taken.

  No Tax or Duty shall be laid on Articles exported from any State.

  No Preference shall be given by any Regulation of Commerce or Revenue to the Ports of one State over those of another; nor shall Vessels bound to, or from, one State be obliged to enter, clear, or pay Duties in another.

  No money shall be drawn from the Treasury, but in Consequence of Appropriations made by Law; and a regular Statement and Account of the Receipts and Expenditures of all public Money shall be published from time to time.

  No Title of Nobility shall be granted by the United States: And no Person holding any Office of Profit or Trust under them, shall, without the Consent of the Congress, accept of any Present, Emolument, Office, or Title, of any kind whatever, from and King, Prince, or foreign State.

  Section 10. No state shall enter into any Treaty, Alliance, or Confederation; grant letters of Marque and Reprisal; coin money; emit Bills of Credit; make any Thing but gold and silver Coin a Tender in Payment of Debts; pass any Bill of Attainder, ex post facto Law, or Law impairing the Obligation of Contracts, or grant any Title of Nobility.

  No State shall, without the Consent of the Congress, lay any Imposts or Duties on Imports or Exports, except what may be absolutely necessary for executing it's inspection Laws; and the net Produce of all Duties and Imposts, laid by any State on Imports and Exports, shall be for the Use of the Treasury of the United States; and all such Laws shall be subject to the Revision and Control of the Congress.

No State shall, without the Consent of Congress, lay and Duty of Tonnage, keep Troops, or Ships of War in time of Peace, enter into any Agreement or Compact with another State, or with a foreign Power, or engage in War, unless actually invaded, or in such imminent Danger as will not admit of delay.

ARTICLE II

Section 1. The executive Power shall be vested in a President of the United States of America. He shall hold his Office during the Term of four Years, and, together with the Vice President, chosen for the same Term, be elected, as follows:

Each State shall appoint, in such Manner as the Legislature thereof may direct, a Number of Electors, equal to the whole Number of Senators and Representatives to which the State may be entitled in Congress; but no Senator or Representative, or Person holding an Office of Trust or Profit under the United States, shall be appointed an Elector.

The Electors shall meet in their respective States, and vote by Ballot for two Persons, of whom one at least shall not be an Inhabitant of the same State with themselves. And they shall make a List of all the Persons voted for, and of the Number of Votes for each; which list they shall sign and certify, and transmit sealed to the Seat of Government of the United States, directed to the President of the Senate. The President of the Senate shall, in the Presence of the Senate and House of Representatives, open all the Certificates, and the Votes shall then be counted. The Person having the greatest Number of Votes shall be the President, if such Number be a Majority of the whole Number of Electors appointed; and if there be more than one who have such a Majority, and have an equal Number of Votes, then the House of Representatives shall immediately chuse by Ballot one of them for President; and if no Person have a Majority, then from the five highest on the List the said House shall in like Manner chuse the President. But in chusing the President, the Votes shall be taken by States the Representation from each State having one Vote; A quorum for this Purpose shall consist of a Member or Members from two thirds of the States, and a Majority of all the States shall be necessary to a Choice. In every Case, after the Choice of the President, the Person having the greatest Number of Votes of the Electors shall be the Vice President. But if there should remain two or more who have equal Votes, the Senate shall chuse from them by Ballot the Vice President.

The Congress may determine the Time of chusing the Electors, and the Day on which they shall give their Votes; which Day shall be the same throughout the United States.

No person except a natural born Citizen, or a Citizen of the United States, at the time of the Adoption of this Constitution, shall be eligible to the Office of President; neither shall any Person be eligible to that Office who shall not have attained to the Age of thirty five Years, and been fourteen Years a Resident within the United States.

In case of the removal of the President from Office, or of his Death, Resignation or Inability to discharge the Powers and Duties of the said Office, the Same shall devolve on the Vice President, and the Congress may by Law provide for the Case of Removal, Death, Resignation or Inability, both of the President and Vice President, declaring what Officer shall then act as President, and such Officer shall act accordingly, until the Disability be removed, or a President shall be elected.

The President shall, at stated Times, receive for his Services, a Compensation, which shall neither be increased or diminished during the Period for which he shall have been elected, and he shall not receive within that Period any other Emolument from the United States, or any of them.

Before he enter on the Execution of his Office, he shall take the following Oath or Affirmation: "I do solemnly swear (or affirm) that I will faithfully execute the Office of President of the United States, and will to the best of my Ability, preserve, protect and defend the Constitution of the United States."

Section 2. The President shall be Commander in Chief of the Army and Navy of the United States, and of the militia of the several States, when called into the actual Service of the United States; he may be require the Opinion, in writing, of the principal Officer in each of the Executive Departments, upon any Subject relating to the Duties of their respective Offices, and he shall have Power to grant Reprieves and Pardons for Offenses against the United States, except in cases of Impeachment.

He shall have Power, by and with the Advice and Consent of the Senate to make Treaties, provided two thirds of the Senators present concur; and he shall nominate, and by and with the Advice and Consent of the Senate, shall appoint Ambassadors, other public Minister and Consuls, Judges of the supreme Court, and all other Officers of the United States, whose Appointments are not herein otherwise provided for, and which shall be established by Law; but the Congress may by Law vest the Appointment of such inferior Officers, as they think proper, in the President alone, in the Courts of Law, or in the Heads of Departments.

The President shall have power to fill up all Vacancies that may happen during the Recess of the Senate, by granting Commissions which shall expire at the End of their next Session.

Section 3. He shall from time to time give to the Congress Information of the State of the Union, and recommend to their Consideration such Measures as he shall judge necessary and expedient; he may, on extraordinary Occasions, convene both Houses, or either of them, and in Case of Disagreement between them, with Respect to the Time of Adjournment, he may adjourn them to such Time as he shall think proper; he shall receive Ambassadors and other public Ministers; he shall take Care that the Laws shall be faithfully executed, and shall Commission all the Officers of the United States.

Section 4. The President, Vice President and all civil Officers of the United States, shall be removed from Office on Impeachment for, and Conviction of, Treason, Bribery, or other high Crimes and Misdemeanors.

ARTICLE III

Section 1. The judicial Power of the United States, shall be vested in one supreme Court, and in such inferior Courts as the Congress may from time to time ordain and establish. The Judges, both of the supreme and inferior Courts, shall hold their Offices during good Behaviour, and shall, at stated Times, receive for their Services a Compensation, which shall not be diminished during their Continuance in Office.

Section 2. The judicial Power shall extend to all Cases, in Law and Equity, arising under this Constitution, the Laws of the United States, and Treaties made, or which shall be made, under their Authority; to all Cases affecting Ambassadors, other public Ministers and Consuls; to all Cases of admiralty and maritime Jurisdiction; to Controversies to which the United States shall be a Party; to Controversies between two or more States; between a State and Citizens of another State; between Citizens of different States; between Citizens of the same State claiming Lands under the Grants of different States, and between a State, or the Citizens thereof, and foreign States, Citizens or Subjects.

In all Cases affecting Ambassadors, other public Ministers and Consuls, and those in which a State shall be a Party, the supreme Court shall have original Jurisdiction. In all the other Cases before mentioned, the supreme Court shall have appellate Jurisdiction, both as to Law and Fact, with such Exceptions, and under such Regulations as the Congress shall make.

The trial of all Crimes, except in Cases of Impeachment, shall be by Jury; and such Trial shall be held in the State where the said Crimes shall have been committed; but when not committed within any State, the Trial shall be at such Place or Places as the Congress may by Law have directed.

Section 3. Treason against the United States, shall consist only in levying War against them, or in adhering to their Enemies, giving them Aid and Comfort. No Person shall be convicted of Treason unless on the Testimony of two Witnesses to the same overt Act, or on Confession in open Court.

The Congress shall have Power to declare the Punishment of Treason, but no Attainder of Treason shall work Corruption of Blood, or Forfeiture except during the Life of the Person attainted.

ARTICLE IV

Section 1. Full Faith and Credit shall be given in each State to the public Acts, Records, and judicial Proceedings of every other State. And the Congress may by general Laws prescribe the Manner in which such Acts, Records and Proceedings shall be proved, and the Effect thereof.

Section 2. The Citizens of each State shall be entitled to all Privileges and Immunities of Citizens in the several States.

A Person charged in any State with Treason, Felony, or other Crime, who shall flee from Justice, and be found in another State, shall on demand of the executive Authority of the State from which he fled, be delivered up, to be removed to the State having Jurisdiction of the Crime.

No Person held to Service or Labour in one State, under the Laws thereof, escaping into another, shall, in Consequence of any Law or Regulation therein, be discharged from such Service or Labour, but shall be delivered up on Claim of the Party to who such Service or Labour may be due.

Section 3. New States may be admitted by the Congress into this Union; but no new State shall be formed or erected within the Jurisdiction of any other State; nor any State be formed by the Junction of two or more States, or Parts of States, without the Consent of the Legislatures of the States concerned as well as of Congress.

The Congress shall have Power to dispose of and make all needful Rules and Regulations respecting the Territory or other Property belonging to the United States; and nothing in this Constitution shall be so construed as to Prejudice any Claims of the United States, or of any particular State.

Section 4. The United States shall guarantee to every State in this Union a Republican Form of Government, and shall protect each of them against invasion; and on Application of the Legislature, or of the Executive (when the Legislature cannot be convened) against domestic Violence.

ARTICLE V

The Congress, whenever two thirds of both Houses shall deem it necessary, shall propose Amendments to this Constitution, or, on the Application of the Legislatures of two thirds of the several States, shall call a Convention for proposing Amendments, which in either Case, shall be valid to all Intents and Purposes, as part of this Constitution, when ratified by the Legislatures of three fourths of the several States, or by Conventions in three fourths thereof, as the one or other Mode of Ratification may be proposed by the Congress; Provided that no Amendment which may be made prior to the Year One thousand eight hundred and eight shall in any Manner affect the first and fourth Clauses in the Ninth Section of the first Article; and that no State, without its Consent, shall be deprived of its equal Suffrage in the Senate.

ARTICLE VI

All Debts contracted and Engagements entered into, before the Adoption of this Constitution shall be as valid against the United States under this Constitution, as under the Confederation.

This Constitution, and the Laws of the United States which shall be made in Pursuance thereof; and all Treaties made, or which shall be made, under the Authority of the United States, shall be the supreme Law of the Land; and the Judges in every State shall be bound thereby, any Thing in the Constitution or Laws of any State to the Contrary notwithstanding.

The Senators and Representatives before mentioned, and the Members of the several State Legislatures, and all executive and judicial Officers, both of the United States and of the several States, shall be bound by Oath or Affirmation, to support this Constitution; but no religious Test shall ever be required as a Qualification to any Office or public Trust under the United States.

ARTICLE VII

The Ratification of the Conventions of nine States shall be sufficient for the Establishment of this Constitution between the States so ratifying the Same.

AMENDMENT I [1791]

Congress shall make no law respecting an establishment of religion, or prohibiting the free exercise thereof; or abridging the freedom of speech, or of the press; or the right of the people peaceably to assemble, and to petition the Government for a redress of grievances.

AMENDMENT II [1791]

A well regulated Militia, being necessary to the security of a free State, the right of the people to
keep and bear Arms, shall not be infringed.

AMENDMENT III [1791]

No soldier shall, in time of peace be quartered in any house, without the consent of the Owner, nor in time of war, but in a manner to be prescribed by law.

AMENDMENT IV [1791]

The right of the people to be secure in their persons, houses, papers, and effects, against unreasonable searches and seizures, shall not be violated, and no Warrants shall issue, but upon probably cause, supported by Oath or affirmation, and particularly describing the place to be searched, and the persons or things to be seized.

AMENDMENT V [1791]

No person shall be held to answer for a capital, or otherwise infamous crime, unless on a presentment or indictment of a Grand Jury, except in cases arising in the land or naval forces, or in the Militia, when in actual service in time of War or public danger; nor shall any person be subject for the same offence to be twice put in jeopardy of life or limb; nor shall be compelled in any criminal case to be a witness against himself, nor be deprived of life, liberty, or property, without due process of law; nor shall private property be taken for public use, without just compensation.

AMENDMENT VI [1791]

In all criminal prosecutions, the accused shall enjoy the right to a speedy and public trial, by an impartial jury of the State and district wherein the crime shall have been committed, which district shall have been previously ascertained by law, and to be informed of the nature and cause of the accusation; to be confronted with the witnesses against him; to have compulsory process for obtaining witnesses in his favor, and to have the Assistance of Counsel for his defence.

AMENDMENT VII [1791]

In Suits at common law, where the value in controversy shall exceed twenty dollars, the right of trial by jury shall be preserved, and no fact tried by jury, shall be otherwise re-examined in any Court of the United States, than according to the rules of the common law.

AMENDMENT VIII [1791]

Excessive bail shall not be required, nor excessive fines imposed, nor cruel and unusual punishments inflicted.

AMENDMENT IX [1791]

The enumeration in the Constitution, of certain rights, shall not be construed to deny or disparage others retained by the people.

AMENDMENT X [1791]

The powers not delegated to the United States by the Constitution, nor prohibited by it to the States, are reserved to the States respectively, or to the people.

AMENDMENT XI [1798]

The Judicial power of the United States shall not be construed to extend to any suit in law or equity, commenced or prosecuted against one of the United States by Citizens of another States, or by Citizens or Subjects of any Foreign State.

AMENDMENT XII [1804]

The Electors shall meet in their respective states and vote by ballot for President and Vice-President, on of whom, at least, shall not be an inhabitant of the same state with themselves; they shall name in their ballots the person voted for as President, and in distinct ballots the person voted for as Vice-President, and they shall make distinct lists of all persons voted for as President, and of all persons voted for as Vice-President, and of the number of votes for each, which lists they shall sign and certify, and transmit sealed to the seat of the Government of the United States, directed to the President of the Senate; The President of the Senate shall, in the presence of the Senate and the House of Representatives, open all the certificates and all the votes shall then be counted; The person having the greatest number of votes for President shall be the President, if such number be a majority of the whole number of Electors appointed; and if no person have such a majority, then from the persons having the highest numbers not exceeding three on the list of those voted for as President, the House of Representatives shall choose immediately, by ballot, the President. But in choosing the President, the votes shall be taken by states, the representation from each state having one vote; a quorum for this purpose shall consist of a member or members from two-thirds of the states, and a majority of all the states shall be necessary to a choice. And if the House of Representatives shall not choose a President whenever the right of choice shall devolve upon them before the fourth day of March next following, then the Vice-President shall act as President, as in the case of the death or other constitutional disability of the President. The person having the greatest number of votes as Vice-President, shall be the Vice-President, if such number be a majority of the whole number of electors appointed, and if no person have a majority, then from the two highest numbers on the list, the Senate shall choose the Vice-President; a quorum for this purpose shall consist of two-thirds of the whole number of Senators, and a majority of the whole number shall be necessary to a choice. But no person constitutionally ineligible to the office of President shall be eligible to that of Vice-President of the United States.

AMENDMENT XIII [1865]

Section 1. Neither slavery nor involuntary servitude, except as a punishment for crime whereof the party shall have been duly convicted, shall exist within the United States, or any place subject to their jurisdiction.

Section 2. Congress shall have the power to enforce this article by appropriate legislation.

AMENDMENT XIV [1868]

Section 1. All persons born or naturalized in the United States, and subject to the jurisdiction thereof, are citizens of the United States and of the State wherein they reside. No State shall make or enforce any law which shall abridge the privileges or immunities of citizens of the United States; nor shall any State deprive any person of life, liberty, or property, without due process of law; nor deny to any person within its jurisdiction the equal protection of the laws.

Section 2. Representatives shall be apportioned among the several States according to their respective numbers, counting the whole number of persons in each State excluding Indians not taxed. But when the right to vote at any election for the choice of electors for President and Vice President of the United States, Representatives in Congress, the Executive and Judicial Officers of a State, or the members of the Legislatures thereof, is denied to any of the male inhabitants of such State, being twenty-one years of age, and citizens of the United States, or in any way abridged, except for participation in rebellion, or other crime, the basis of representation therein shall be reduced in the proportion which the number of such male citizens shall bear to the whole number of male citizens twenty-one years of age in such State.

Section 3. No person shall be a Senator or Representative in Congress, or elector of President and Vice President, or hold any office, civil or military, under the United States, or under any State, who having previously taken an oath, as a member of Congress, or as a member of any State legislature, or as an executive or judicial officer of any State, to support the Constitution of the United States, shall have engaged in insurrection or rebellion against the same, or given aid or comfort to the enemies thereof. But Congress may by a vote of two-thirds of each House, remove such disability.

Section 4. The validity of the public debt of the United States, authorized by law, including debts incurred for payment of pensions and bounties for services in suppressing insurrection or rebellion, shall not be questioned. But neither the United States nor any State shall assume or pay any debt or obligation incurred in aid of insurrection or rebellion against the United States, or any claim for the loss or emancipation of any slave; but all such debts, obligations and claims shall be held illegal and void.

Section 5. The Congress shall have power to enforce, by appropriate legislation, the provisions of this article.

AMENDMENT XV [1870]

Section 1. The right of citizens of the United States to vote shall not be denied or abridged by the United States or by any State on account of race, color, or previous condition of servitude.

Section 2. The Congress shall have power to enforce this article by appropriate legislation.

AMENDMENT XVI [1913]

The Congress shall have the power to lay and collect taxes on incomes, from whatever source derived, without apportionment among the several States, and without regard to any census or enumeration.

AMENDMENT XVII [1913]

The Senate of the United States shall be composed of two Senators from each State, elected by the people thereof, for six years; and each Senator shall have one vote. The electors in each State shall have the qualifications requisite for electors of the most numerous branch of the State legislatures.

When vacancies happen in the representation of any State in the Senate, the executive authority of such State shall issue writs of election to fill such vacancies: PROVIDED, That the legislature of any State may empower the executive thereof to make temporary appointments until the people fill the vacancies by election as the legislature may direct.

This amendment shall not be so construed as to affect the election or term of any Senator chosen before it becomes valid as part of the Constitution.

AMENDMENT XVIII [1919]

Section 1. After one year from the ratification of this article the manufacture, sale, or transportation of intoxicating liquors within, the importation thereof into, or the exportation thereof from the United States and all territory subject to the jurisdiction thereof for beverage purposes is hereby prohibited.

Section 2. The Congress and the several States shall have concurrent power to enforce this article by appropriate legislation.

Section 3. This article shall be inoperative unless it shall have been ratified as an amendment to the Constitution by the legislatures of the several States, as provided in the Constitution, within seven years from the date of the submission hereof to the States by the Congress.

AMENDMENT XIX [1920]

The right of citizens of the United States to vote shall not be denied or abridged by the United States or by any State on account of sex.

Congress shall have the power to enforce this article by appropriate legislation.

AMENDMENT XX [1933]

Section 1. The terms of the President and the Vice President shall end at noon on the 20th day of January, and the terms of Senators and Representatives an noon on the 3d day of January, of the years in which such terms would have ended if this article had not been ratified; and the terms of their successors shall then begin.

Section 2. The Congress shall assemble at least once in every year, and such meeting shall begin at noon on the third day of January, unless they shall by law appoint a different day.

Section 3. If, at the time fixed for the beginning of the term of the President, the President elect shall have died, the Vice President elect shall become President. If the President shall not have been chosen before the time fixed for the beginning of his term, or if the President elect shall have failed to qualify, then the Vice President elect shall act as President until a President shall have qualified; and the Congress may by law provide for the case wherein neither a President elect nor a Vice President elect shall have qualified, declaring who shall then act as President, or the manner in which one who is to act shall be selected, and such person shall act accordingly until a President or Vice President shall have qualified.

Section 4. The Congress may by law provide for the case of the death of any of the persons from whom the House of Representatives may choose a President whenever the right of choice shall have devolved upon them, and for the case of the death of any of the persons from whom the Senate may choose a Vice President whenever the right of choice shall have devolved upon them.

Section 5. Sections 1 and 2 shall take effect on the 15th day of October following the ratification of this article.

Section 6. This article shall be inoperative unless it shall have been ratified as an amendment to the Constitution by the legislatures of three-fourths of the several States within seven years from the date of its submission.

AMENDMENT XXI [1933]

Section 1. The eighteenth article of amendment to the Constitution of the United States is hereby repealed.

Section 2. The transportation or importation into any State, Territory, or possession of the United States for delivery or use therein of intoxicating liquors, in violation of the laws thereof, is hereby prohibited.

Section 3. This article shall be inoperative unless it shall have been ratified as an amendment to the Constitutions by conventions in the several States, as provided in the Constitution, within seven years from the date of the submission hereof to the States by the

Congress.

AMENDMENT XXII [1951]

Section 1. No person shall be elected to the office of the President more than twice, and no person who has held the office of President, or acted as President, for more than two years of a term to which some other person was elected president shall be elected to the office of President more than once. But this article shall not apply to any person holding the office of President when this article was proposed by the Congress, and shall not prevent any person who may be holding the office of President, or acting as President, during the term within which this article becomes operative from holding the office of President or acting President during the remainder of such term.

Section 2. This article shall be inoperative unless it shall have been ratified as an amendment to the Constitution by the legislatures of three-fourths of the several States within seven years from the date of its submission to the States by Congress.

AMENDMENT XXIII [1961]

Section 1. The District constituting the seat of Government of the United States shall appoint in such manner as the Congress may direct: A number of electors of President and Vice President equal to the whole number of Senators and Representatives equal to the whole number of Senators and Representatives in Congress to which the District would be entitled if it were a State, but in no event more than the least populous state; they shall be in addition to those appointed by the states, but they shall be considered, for the purposes of the election of President and Vice President, to be electors appointed by a state; and they shall meet in the District and perform such duties as provided by the twelfth article of amendment.

Section 2. The Congress shall have power to enforce this article by appropriate legislation.

AMENDMENT XXIV [1964]

Section 1. The right of citizens of the United States to vote in any primary or other election for President or Vice President, or for Senator or Representative in Congress, shall not be denied or abridged by the United States, or any States by reason of failure to pay any poll tax or other tax.

Section 2. The Congress shall have power to enforce this article by appropriate legislation.

AMENDMENT XXV [1967]

Section 1. In case of the removal of the President from office or of his death or resignation, the Vice President shall become President.

Section 2. Whenever there is a vacancy in the office of the Vice President, the President shall nominate a Vice President who shall take office upon confirmation of a majority vote of both Houses of Congress.

Section 3. Whenever the President transmits to the President pro tempore of the Senate and the Speaker of the House of Representative his written declaration that he is unable to discharge the powers and duties of his office, and until he transmits to them a written declaration to the contrary, such powers and duties shall be discharged by the Vice President as Acting President.

Section 4. Whenever the Vice President and a majority of either the principal officers of the executive departments or of such other body as Congress may by law provide, transmit to the President pro tempore of the Senate and the Speaker of the House of Representatives their written declaration that the President is unable to discharge the powers and duties of his office, the Vice President shall immediately assume the powers and duties of the office as Acting President.

Thereafter, when the President transmits to the President pro tempore of the Senate and the Speaker of the House of Representatives his written declaration that no inability exists, he shall resume the powers and duties of his office unless the Vice President and a majority of either the principal officers of the executive department or of such other body as Congress may by law provide, transmit within four days to the President pro tempore of the Senate and the Speaker of the House of Representatives their written declaration that the President is unable to discharge the powers and duties of his office. Thereupon Congress shall decide the issue, assembling within forty-eight hours for that purpose if not in session. If the Congress, within twenty-one days after receipt of the latter written declaration, or, if Congress is not in session, within twenty-one days after Congress is required to assemble, determines by two-thirds vote of both Houses that the President is unable to discharge the powers and duties of his office, the Vice President shall continue to discharge the same as Acting President; otherwise, the President shall resume the powers and duties of his office.

AMENDMENT XXVI [1971]

Section 1. The right of citizens of the United States, who are eighteen years of age or older, to vote shall not be denied or abridged by the United States or by any State on account of age.

Section 2. The Congress shall have the power to enforce this article by appropriate legislation.

Index